# Nine Black Robes

## Also by Joan Biskupic

*The Chief: The Life and Turbulent Times
of Chief Justice John Roberts*

*Breaking In: The Rise of Sonia Sotomayor
and the Politics of Justice*

*American Original: The Life and Constitution
of Supreme Court Justice Antonin Scalia*

*Sandra Day O'Connor: How the First Woman on the
Supreme Court Became Its Most Influential Justice*

# Nine Black Robes

*Inside the Supreme Court's Drive to the Right and*

*Its Historic Consequences*

———

# JOAN BISKUPIC

*wm*

WILLIAM MORROW

*An Imprint of* HarperCollins*Publishers*

HarperCollins books may be purchased for educational, business, or sales promotional use. For information, please email the Special Markets Department at SPsales@harpercollins.com.

FIRST EDITION

Designed by Leah Carlson-Stanisic

Library of Congress Cataloging-in-Publication Data has been applied for.

ISBN 978-0-06-305278-9

23 24 25 26 27 LBC 5 4 3 2 1

*For Clay and Elizabeth*

*No one should be confident that this majority is done with its work.*

DOBBS V. JACKSON WOMEN'S HEALTH ORGANIZATION,
DISSENTING JUSTICES, JUNE 24, 2022

# CONTENTS

# AUTHOR'S NOTE

This book is a group portrait of the Supreme Court during a historic period in American law influenced by the presidency of Donald Trump and its aftermath. The Court overturned nearly a half century of abortion rights, obliterated protections of the 1965 Voting Rights Act (VRA), curtailed government regulatory power, and blurred the separation of church and state. The transformed Court was decades in the making, but its character was solidified by the three appointees of former president Trump. From his campaign of 2016 into the early years of the Joe Biden administration, tensions within the Court spiraled. The justices maneuvered uneasily around each other. Two deaths marked this period—Antonin Scalia's in 2016 and Ruth Bader Ginsburg's in 2020—as did the COVID-19 pandemic.

I have relied on the records of cases, archives, and more than a hundred interviews with people on the Court and in its orbit, including a majority of the justices. This book also builds on my daily journalistic coverage of the Court and my four previous works on individual justices, including a biography of Scalia, the model for the Trump justices, and a biography of Chief Justice John Roberts, who recalibrated his leadership and his approach to the law with each addition to the bench.

Seven men and five women served in the years covered in this book: Roberts, appointed by George W. Bush in 2005; Anthony Kennedy, put on the bench by Ronald Reagan in 1988; Clarence Thomas, by George H. W. Bush in 1991; Ruth Bader Ginsburg, by Bill Clinton in 1993; Stephen Breyer, by Clinton in 1994; Samuel Alito, by George W.

Bush in 2006; Sonia Sotomayor, by Barack Obama in 2009; Elena Kagan, by Obama in 2010; the three Trump appointees, Neil Gorsuch, 2017, Brett Kavanaugh, 2018, Amy Coney Barrett, 2020; and Ketanji Brown Jackson, selected by Biden in 2022 as the first Black woman justice, a groundbreaking appointment to a Court that has been, paradoxically, going backward.

# Nine Black Robes

___

# UNMASKED

The lectern where the lawyers stood to argue their cases had been pushed back twenty feet from the Supreme Court's elevated bench. Dozens of wooden chairs that normally filled the front section of the courtroom were gone. The tableau on this November 1, 2021, morning was spare, as the coronavirus pandemic still raged and extra health precautions were in place. For the few spectators permitted to attend the suspenseful Texas abortion arguments, all wearing high-grade, tight-fitting masks and sitting well spaced on the red upholstered seats, the view of the nine justices was direct and unobstructed.

The Court had scheduled the morning hearing after letting a Texas abortion ban take effect in a midnight order on September 1. For two months, women in America's second-most-populous state had been living without the right to abortion. The Supreme Court had guaranteed that right in its 1973 *Roe v. Wade* milestone and reaffirmed it many times, most definitively in 1992's *Planned Parenthood of Southeastern Pennsylvania v. Casey.* The Texas legislature had flouted those precedents and the Constitution and prohibited abortion after the first sign of fetal cardiac activity, roughly six weeks, a point when many women do not yet know they are pregnant and a point, too, at which fetal heart valves have not developed, making "heartbeat" law a misnomer.[1] So far, the Supreme Court had gone along with Texas and had rejected requests to suspend the ban until its validity could be assessed. The justices' action in the case illuminated how much the Court had changed and no longer could be counted on to protect certain individual rights.[2]

Pregnant women who wanted an abortion were traveling to Oklahoma and other nearby states. Those without the money to leave Texas were panicking, forced to end their pregnancies on their own—many using misoprostol and other oral medications—or to carry an unwanted pregnancy to term.[3] Texas abortion clinics challenged the new law, declaring in a petition for a writ of certiorari, "Texans are in crisis." The clinics implored the Supreme Court to scrutinize the unusual statute, which gave private citizens the right to sue physicians, clinic staff, or any person who helped a woman obtain an abortion.[4] The Texas attorney general argued that the justices lacked jurisdiction even to hear the case because the legislature had written the law, shrewdly, in a way that let private individuals, not state officials, enforce it, thereby shielding officials from lawsuits. The statute granted a minimum of $10,000 in damages for each abortion successfully challenged. The threat of unlimited litigation and ruinous financial liability was forcing clinics to stop most abortions.

When the Supreme Court let the Texas law go forward on September 1, Chief Justice John Roberts dissented, joined by the senior liberal justice, Stephen Breyer, and Justices Sonia Sotomayor and Elena Kagan. The moment revealed a loss of control for the usually persuasive leader of the bench. Surely no proponent of abortion rights, Roberts was nonetheless astonished that a state would attempt to invalidate decisions tracing back nearly fifty years to *Roe v. Wade*. Only the Supreme Court itself had such power. The five conservatives who controlled that September 1 action sided with state officials, saying that the "heartbeat" bill's challengers had failed to show that they were likely to succeed on the merits of the question or be "irreparably" harmed if the ban took effect during litigation. "The applicants now before us have raised serious questions regarding the constitutionality of the Texas law at issue," the majority wrote in the unsigned order. "But their application also presents complex and novel antecedent procedural questions on which they have not carried their burden." The majority brushed aside arguments about women awaiting immediate care, women who lacked the means to travel out of state, and women who, if delayed for even a few more weeks, would be affected by Texas's separate deadlines for obtaining an abortion at all.

After that defeat, abortion clinics persisted with subsequent requests to the Court, and the U.S. Department of Justice entered the fight. Lawyers for President Joe Biden's administration filed a suit asserting that "for half a century, this Court has held that a state may not prohibit any woman from making the ultimate decision to terminate her pregnancy before viability"—with "viability" defined as the ability of the fetus to live outside the womb. The lawyers warned that if Texas was not stopped, any state "could effectively nullify any constitutional decision of this Court," including those favored by conservatives—for example, allowing handguns in the home, or lifting restrictions on corporate spending in political campaigns.[5]

The public commentary on the September 1 late-night opinion had been sufficiently harsh that less than two weeks later, Justice Amy Coney Barrett gave a speech in the Court's defense at the Seelbach Hilton in Louisville, Kentucky, at an event celebrating the University of Louisville's McConnell Center, named for Senate Minority Leader Mitch McConnell, who a year earlier as majority leader had hastened Barrett's confirmation to the Court. He introduced her at the September 13 event. "My goal today is to convince you that this court is not comprised of a bunch of partisan hacks," Barrett told the audience.[6] Her words had the opposite effect; they were widely interpreted as self-regarding at best, and at worst a reflection of the deep partisanship on the modern Court. Samuel Alito, who, like Barrett, had voted to let the ban go forward, leapt to the Court's defense soon afterward. On September 30, in a speech to students at the University of Notre Dame Law School, he said that critics were attempting to intimidate the justices by describing them as "sinister" and "sneaky."[7]

The justices' road show, unprecedented both in the swiftness with which it was carried out and in the degree to which it was roundly judged to have fallen flat, occupied the intervening weeks before oral arguments brought the debate over the Texas ban into the open.[8] Chief Justice Roberts began the special November 1 hearing on a commemorative note, observing that Justice Clarence Thomas's ceremonial investiture had taken place thirty years earlier to the day. What a curve the career of the seventy-three-year-old justice had taken: having joined the bench in 1991 after explosive Senate confirmation hearings, and having been consigned to the ideological fringe for more than twenty-five years, he was in the vanguard now, joined by the conservative appointees of former president Donald Trump.

Roberts also formally welcomed Elizabeth Prelogar, the solicitor general (SG) of the United States. A former assistant SG who had temporarily filled the top job and become familiar to the nine, Prelogar was making her debut argument with the full title after her Senate confirmation. Her filing to the justices, an effort to restore abortion rights in Texas, could not have been more strikingly inconsistent with what the justices had heard from the Trump administration on abortion. Trump had promised during his 2016 campaign to appoint "pro-life" judges to the Supreme Court who would strike down *Roe v. Wade*, leaving the abortion issue to the states.

Trump, in fact, had brought the high court and the country to this moment in late 2021. His legacy was displayed on this bench, its mahogany expanse flanked by two American flags, as much as anywhere. His three appointees—Neil Gorsuch, Brett Kavanaugh, and Amy Coney Barrett—all had voted to let the Texas abortion ban remain in place. Since Barrett's appointment in late 2020, the Court had announced that it would take up an appeal from the state of Mississippi defending a prohibition on abortion after fifteen weeks of pregnancy. Like the Texas law preventing abortion after roughly six weeks, that ban directly clashed with *Roe v. Wade*, which protected a woman's choice of abortion before viability, at about twenty-three weeks. The Court had grounded the right in the Fourteenth Amendment's guarantee of liberty and personal privacy. Unlike in the urgent Texas situation, the Mississippi ban had been suspended by lower-court judges. It also was free of the procedural issues distinct to the Texas dispute. An eventual ruling in the Mississippi case, a direct test of *Roe*, would affect the reproductive rights of women across the country. It would reveal whether the Court had lost its place in the life of the nation.

In the courtroom on November 1 watching this first stage of the abortion controversy were Jane Sullivan Roberts, the chief justice's wife, a legal recruiter for a Washington, D.C., firm and a former pro bono lawyer for Feminists for Life, an antiabortion group; and Justice Breyer's wife, Joanna Breyer (Joanna Freda Hare), a psychologist, writer, and viscount's daughter.[9] Then eighty-three and in his twenty-seventh session, Breyer had been holding on to his seat despite pleas from the Left to step down and give President Biden a chance to replace him with someone younger. Breyer believed he could make a difference on abortion and dissuade his conservative colleagues from rolling back precedent.

Two weeks earlier, as Breyer sat with me for an interview, he minimized public concerns about the Texas case and other moves to the far right. He said that the Court had long engendered controversy and that Americans had accepted decisions even when they believed them wrong. "It's an institution that's fallible, though over time it has served this country pretty well," he said. That was a point increasingly debated. Democrats in Congress and liberal advocates were promoting the addition of more seats on the bench to counteract the conservative dominance. On the Court, the two other remaining liberal justices, Elena Kagan and Sonia Sotomayor, were not as sanguine as Breyer. "Every day the Court fails to grant relief is devastating," wrote Sotomayor when the conservative majority declined a second opportunity to put the Texas law on hold, even as it set the November 1 oral arguments, "both for individual women and for our constitutional system as a whole." A diabetic who took extra steps to preserve her health and the only justice wearing a mask to protect against possible COVID-19 infection during the oral arguments, Sotomayor regularly set herself apart from her colleagues with her consideration of the poor and disadvantaged.[10]

There were some initial signs of collegiality as the justices began the hearing. After Roberts congratulated Thomas on his three decades, they whispered a bit together. Thomas briefly slung his arm over Roberts's shoulder. Soon the conversation and body language turned cold as the reality of the Texas ban's consequences emerged. Lawyer Marc Hearron, representing the clinic consortium Whole Woman's Health, told the justices, "To allow Texas's scheme to stand would provide a roadmap for other states to abrogate any decision of this Court with which they disagree. At issue here is nothing less than the supremacy of federal law."

When Texas solicitor general Judd Stone II stood up to argue, he countered that there were no grounds for blocking the law. "Federal courts don't issue injunctions against laws but against officials enforcing laws," Stone said. "No Texas executive official enforces [the law] . . . so no Texas executive official may be enjoined." On behalf of the Biden administration, Solicitor General Prelogar emphasized the end-run motives behind the law: "States are free to ask this Court to reconsider its constitutional precedents, but they are not free to place themselves above this Court, nullify the Court's decisions in their borders, and block the judicial review necessary to vindicate federal rights." Her warning was clear: if the Texas law stood, other states might try to abolish the Constitution's protections, turning the founding charter on its head by permitting legislative majorities to dictate the breadth of individual rights and liberties.[11]

Kagan was more caustic as she derided the effort to circumvent Supreme Court fundamentals, saying that "after all these many years, some geniuses came up with a way to evade the commands of [precedent] as well as . . . the even broader principle that states are not to nullify federal constitutional rights." Her criticism of her conservative colleagues who had let the law take effect in September was more than implicit: "To say, 'oh, we've never seen this before, so we can't do anything about it,' I guess I just don't understand the argument."[12]

Addressing Texas solicitor general Stone, she said, "The actual provisions in this law have prevented every woman in Texas from exercising a constitutional right as declared by this Court. That's not a hypothetical. That's an actual."[13]

The two justices whose views could have mattered most were Barrett and Kavanaugh. They had cast two of the five votes to let the Texas ban take effect. These newest justices were old friends. Both had been members of the Federalist Society and were committed Catholics who spoke openly of their faith. Barrett sat at the chief justice's far left, erect in her seat, her elbows propped on the bench, hands clasped. Roberts had helped Barrett quickly settle into one of the most desirable chambers in the building by ensuring that the staff of the late justice Ruth Bader Ginsburg packed up the spacious suite with its custom cabinetry immediately after the justice's burial ceremony. Kavanaugh sat in the seat to Roberts's far right, referring to notes as he questioned the lawyers. Roberts and Kavanaugh had known each other for three decades. When Kavanaugh first joined the Court, he aligned closely with Roberts in his votes. Relations strained after just a few years of Kavanaugh's presence, however, as the new justice moved further to the right.

Now Kavanaugh and Barrett both seemed to view the Texas arguments with suspicion. Kavanaugh particularly questioned whether, if states could block abortion rights, they could do the same for firearm rights and free speech. Barrett sounded troubled that the Texas law was written in a way that would deny any challenger a "full constitutional defense." By their remarks, Kavanaugh and Barrett appeared ready to declare for the first time that abortion providers could challenge the law. That conclusion would lead, finally, to a suspension of the law. Many journalists who closely watched the Court thought that the signals from Kavanaugh and Barrett were clear and cast their news stories that way. More important, some of the justices, I later learned, believed that these two crucial justices would side with Whole Woman's Health. Among the justices who had previously dissented—those who believed the "heartbeat" bill blatantly unconstitutional—there was a sense that this would be a turning point in the case. But their optimism was short-lived, and when the votes were cast in private, they realized they had been misled by what they had heard in public. Kavanaugh's and Barrett's comments during oral arguments belied their true sentiment against the abortion clinics.[14]

The parties to the suit, women in Texas, and legions of journalists following the case anticipated that a decision would come quickly. And why not? The justices had set a fast-track briefing schedule for the expedited arguments. And each day added to the denial of rights in Texas. But two weeks passed. Then three weeks. Then four. Meanwhile, the separate Mississippi abortion case was at hand, previously scheduled for oral arguments on December 1. By that point, women in Texas had been without the constitutional right to abortion for three months. Behind the scenes at the Court, the justices were still haggling over their opinions in the Texas case when they took up the Mississippi prohibition on abortion at fifteen weeks of pregnancy. That's when the clarity of the situation emerged for the public. The force of past abortion rights decisions evaporated into the thin courtroom air.

"*Roe v. Wade* and *Planned Parenthood v. Casey* haunt our country," Mississippi solicitor general Scott Stewart told the justices. "They have no basis in the Constitution. They have no home in our history or traditions. They've damaged the democratic process. They've poisoned the law. They've choked off compromise. For 50 years, they've kept this Court at the center of a political battle that it can never resolve. And 50 years on, they stand alone. Nowhere else does this Court recognize a right to end a human life."[15]

He hedged on nothing and had no need to. Stewart had a receptive audience before him. It was evident that the idea of constitutional rights—at least to the conservative majority—was changing. Regard for fetal life appeared to eclipse a woman's right to privacy. Yet after the oral arguments in the Mississippi case, there were months of private negotiations among justices before the public or press knew the resolution and faced the new Court reality.

Meanwhile, the expedited Texas case was nearing a boil. As seen when the justices released their opinions on December 10, the majority again had declined to block the law. It came down to the same 5–4 vote that had been reached September 1 to allow the law to go into effect, with Thomas, Alito, Gorsuch, Kavanaugh, and Barrett in the majority. Roberts was as unconvincing with fellow conservatives on the second round as on the first, despite how Kavanaugh and Barrett had sounded from the bench. The five justices remained united. The Court declared that state officials could not be sued to enjoin the law unless they were part of a narrow category of those who had a role in enforcing it; Thomas broke off from his colleagues on the right to say he would have prohibited lawsuits against all the state officials.[16]

The Court sent the clinics' case back to lower-court judges for further proceedings while the Texas ban stayed in effect. The majority dismissed the Department of Justice lawsuit outright. The dissenting justices were livid, for the abortion rights consequences as well as for the way the decision limited the power of federal court judges to stop unconstitutional laws. "This choice to shrink from Texas' challenge to federal supremacy will have far-reaching repercussions," Sotomayor wrote this time, joined by Breyer and Kagan. "I doubt the Court, let alone the country, is prepared for them."

Her outrage might have been predictable, as Sotomayor had spent years in vigorous dissent against Trump policies and the decisions of his appointees. But that was not the situation for Roberts, who in his tenure since 2005 was accustomed to being in the majority. He despaired at the turn of events, writing, "It is the role of the Supreme Court in our constitutional system that is at stake."[17]

This book explores how the Court and the country, prepared or not, reached this point. The conservative transformation of America's highest court has long been building, accelerated by the efforts in the 1980s of President Ronald Reagan. Roberts, as a young lawyer, participated in that era, and on the contemporary Court has led the right-wing drive to erase voting rights protections and remedies for racial injustices, to forbid federal judges from reviewing extreme gerrymanders, and to lift campaign finance regulations. Relevant to the Texas case, Roberts had also tried to diminish reproductive rights.

But he was now witnessing a Court in overdrive, barreling ahead without him in deciding significant social issues.

The Court was already split along political and ideological lines before Trump. And its makeup already had been heavily influenced by the conservative agenda led by the Federalist Society, founded in the early 1980s. But the Trump presidency and the forceful influence of his three Supreme Court appointees propelled the judiciary into a new period of polarization. It is worth noting, for comparison, that Trump appointed three justices in four years, while the three prior Democratic presidents (Jimmy Carter, Bill Clinton, and Barack Obama) appointed only a combined total of four justices in their total twenty years in office.[18]

The Trump era stoked the justices' ambitions, their political inclinations and defenses, strengths and flaws. Roberts initially was able to seize more control (based on the ideological composition of the nine) in the early Trump years but then found himself dissenting more frequently as the Court began to go off the rails. Gorsuch, Trump's first appointee, stubbornly resisted Court protocols and derided Roberts's reasoning in opinions. Gorsuch was the only justice who refused to wear a mask when the prevalence of COVID was high. Kavanaugh, Trump's second appointee, seemed to struggle with his allegiance to conservative backers and his desire for acceptance among the legal elites who shunned him after his scandalous 2018 Senate hearings.

Justices Kagan and Breyer looked for any avenues for compromise with the conservatives to shield precedents that dated to the 1970s. The first Latina justice, Sotomayor, refused to compromise and regularly called out the destruction of constitutional norms. Conversely, Justices Thomas and Alito, holdovers from the first and second George Bush presidencies, were emboldened by the ascendant conservatism. Joined by the Trump appointees, they echoed the former president's sense of aggrievement on culture war issues, from abortion rights to vaccine mandates. Their time had come.

For nearly all of the Trump presidency Justice Ginsburg was there, clinging to twentieth-century liberalism and trying to ward off the ravages of cancer and outlast the president. The effect of her death within weeks of the 2020 election was felt most deeply on the abortion rights cases.

Supreme Court eras are often identified by their chief justices, as is true of the current period that began with Roberts nearly two decades ago. But the Court can be measured also by presidential influence. Certain presidents, such as Franklin D. Roosevelt, who appointed eight justices in his twelve years in office, had a disproportionate effect on the Court. Ronald Reagan and Richard Nixon also stood out for their imprint. The Trump effect, especially in terms of the individuals chosen and the resulting shift in the balance of power, has been incomparable.[19]

He is gone from office and they are here for life.

## Chapter 1

---

# "INSIDE THE CASTLE"

On the morning of January 20, 2017, the Supreme Court justices gathered for coffee and pastries in an elegant chandeliered room. The light buffet for justices and their staff was an Inauguration Day tradition. So much about their world ran on decorum and adherence to tradition: from the start of their annual session, always on the first Monday in October, to the arrangement of the nine black leather chairs at the mahogany bench, to the marshal's call of "Oyez! Oyez! Oyez!" as the nine entered for oral arguments. When they met in a private conference room to resolve cases, the justices always spoke in order of seniority, and when they marched in any procession, as they would for the inauguration, they lined up in the same rank. Chief Justice John Roberts went first, followed by Anthony Kennedy, Clarence Thomas, Ruth Bader Ginsburg, Stephen Breyer, Samuel Alito, Sonia Sotomayor, and Elena Kagan. On this January day, they were still one justice short. Antonin Scalia had died a year earlier, in February 2016, and the Republican-controlled Senate had prevented any action on President Barack Obama's choice of a successor. The Senate's obstruction of Obama's nominee, then–U.S. appellate judge Merrick Garland, became one of several pivotal moments in the makeover of America's highest court.

The eight justices rode in a gleaming black motorcade for the short trip over to the Capitol. Once there, they donned their black robes in the Old Supreme Court Chamber on the first floor of the north wing. This is where the justices had convened before their own building across the street was completed in 1935. Now, on this January day, the justices sorted through the black wool skullcaps, mittens, and rain ponchos their staff had provided. The sky was overcast, the air blustery, and rain felt imminent. Some justices wanted a poncho at hand.

Once on the West Front platform of the Capitol, the justices squeezed into seats alongside other dignitaries. Nearby were President Obama and Michelle Obama, former president George W. Bush and Laura Bush, and former president Bill Clinton and Hillary Clinton, whom Donald Trump had defeated in the November 2016 presidential election. Just before noon, Roberts, the seventeenth chief justice of the United States, administered the oath of office to Trump, the forty-fifth president. Trump repeated after Roberts: "I, Donald John Trump, do solemnly swear that I will faithfully execute the office of president of the United States, and will to the best of my ability, preserve, protect, and defend the Constitution of the United States."

Up to this point, the morning's traditions held. But then President Trump delivered his inaugural address. In a sixteen-minute diatribe that echoed his campaign rhetoric, he struck antiestablishment themes and blamed his predecessors for economic ruin. "For too long, a small group in our Nation's Capital has reaped the rewards of government, while the people have borne the cost," he declared, implicitly condemning the former presidents on the platform with him. "Washington flourished, but the people did not share in its wealth. . . . That all changes, starting right here and right now, because this moment is your moment—it belongs to you." Invoking urban poverty, rusted-out factories, and failed education systems, Trump declared, "This American carnage stops right here and stops right now." He praised the supporters gathered on the National Mall and said that "the people" were the new "rulers of this Nation." Spectators cheered as they put up umbrellas against the falling rain.[1]

At the Capitol, the Supreme Court justices tried to act as if this president were like any other. Half of the justices were longtime Republicans, and the Republican Party had delivered this New York real estate developer turned reality-TV personality. The justices joined the

Trump entourage, members of Congress, and cabinet designees for the customary luncheon in the Capitol's Statuary Hall. The justices were seated at front-row tables adorned with bouquets of colorful roses. John and Jane Roberts sat alongside the newly nominated secretary of state, Rex Tillerson. Samuel Alito and his wife, Martha-Ann, lunched with the designated attorney general, Jeff Sessions. Justice Anthony Kennedy spent time chatting with Ivanka Trump, the president's daughter.[2]

The luncheon brought together an array of figures who would conspicuously intersect with the Supreme Court over the next four years. Wilbur Ross, the designated secretary of commerce, who generated a pivotal case involving the 2020 decennial census count, entered the hall smiling. Some themes of the day would seem incongruous, however. Senate Chaplain Barry Black delivered a prayer before the lobster-and-beef luncheon that envisioned the new president protecting "those on life's margins, the lost, lonely, last, least, and left out." Another paradox in hindsight: the Capitol building itself seemed so secure and cherished in those hours of ceremony. A military honor guard graced Statuary Hall. Four years later, on January 6, 2021, the building would be ravaged by Trump supporters.

With the Trump presidency began an era for the nation's judiciary that still reverberates. The effect of Trump on judges and American law runs deep. During his presidency, Trump upset virtually every institution in Washington, but his impact on the nation's highest court was profound, and not simply by virtue of his appointment of three new justices in four years. Trump treated the judiciary as if it were his to command, from his early weeks in office to his final weeks after he lost the 2020 election.[3]

When lower-court judges ruled against him or his policies, he suggested he had only to reach the Supreme Court to prevail. He understood that his approach to Supreme Court appointments mattered to the public. "The Supreme Court was one of the main reasons I got elected President," Trump tweeted midway through his term.[4] His actions affected core democratic ideals such as the right to vote. Turmoil marked his tenure, beginning with the Russian interference in the 2016 presidential election and ending with the 2021 insurrection at the Capitol. Along the way, other moments of national drama provoked and revealed the president, such as the 2017 "Unite the Right" rally in Charlottesville, Virginia, during which a self-described neo-Nazi killed a counterprotester, Heather Heyer. That tragedy was one of several episodes in Trump's first year that brought forth his disregard for basic rights and set the tone for what would come.

Trump's challenge to legal norms commenced immediately, when, seven days after his inauguration, he signed an executive order restricting the entry of immigrants from several predominantly Muslim countries. He instituted the travel ban with scant legal vetting by the Department of Justice, spurred on by his advisers Stephen Miller and Steve Bannon. The January 27 order was called "Protecting the Nation from Foreign Terrorist Entry into the United States." It suspended all refugees from entering the United States for 120 days and, separately, barred for 90 days the immigration of any foreign nationals from seven countries—Iran, Iraq, Libya, Somalia, Sudan, Syria, and Yemen. The action followed through on Trump's 2016 campaign pledge to prohibit Muslims from coming into the United States. His vow, first issued in December 2015 and remaining on his campaign website into early May 2017, called "for a total and complete shutdown of Muslims entering the United States until our country's representatives can figure out what is going on."[5]

No matter how expected this order was, given his campaign statements, its immediate impact caused pandemonium. Immigrants, refugees, their families, and lawyers all tried to sort through the new rules, even as some of those affected were already on flights headed toward the United States. Refugees who had for years navigated the system were suddenly blocked from admission. Public-interest lawyers raced to airports to help. So did thousands of protesters, carrying signs that said "This Land Was Made for You and Me," "Refugees Welcome," and "RESIST." Airports turned chaotic, and for several days it was difficult for any travelers at all to get into or out of international hubs in the United States.[6]

Airports such as LAX and JFK, and the streets around the White House in Washington and Trump Tower in New York, attracted thousands of protesters. For days the travel ban, its sweep and inflammatory tone, dominated television and newspapers. U.S. district court judges acted swiftly on lawsuits brought by the American Civil Liberties Union and other advocacy groups to try to ensure that refugees and immigrants would not be immediately returned to their home countries against their will. The challengers alleged that Trump's order violated federal immigration law and unconstitutionally discriminated on the basis of religion. The specific controversy that eventually became the lead case when the U.S. Supreme Court took up the matter—as the ban was in its third iteration—was brought by the state of Hawaii and an imam at a Honolulu mosque, Ismail Elshikh, who said that his Syrian mother-in-law had been prevented from coming to the United States. Hawaiian officials, like state leaders elsewhere, asserted that the order hurt state university recruitment and business hiring.[7]

At the start, the administration had made no threat assessment of foreign nationals; rather, it simply cut off entry to thousands of people. About a week later, on February 3, a U.S. district court judge in Seattle, James Robart, temporarily blocked the Trump ban and imposed a nationwide injunction preventing it from being enforced anywhere in the United States.[8] "Just cannot believe a judge would put our country in such peril," Trump wrote in a Twitter post the same day. "If something happens blame him and court system. People pouring in. Bad!" Trump also referred to Robart as a "so-called judge" who had taken a "ridiculous" action.[9]

A panel of the U.S. Court of Appeals for the Ninth Circuit affirmed Robart's order, again drawing condemnation from Trump. When the full Ninth Circuit then denied a subsequent Trump administration challenge to the injunction, Judge Jay Bybee implicitly criticized Trump for his denigration of judges acting on the travel ban, even though Bybee, an appointee of President George W. Bush, was siding with Trump at this point in the case. Without specifically naming the president, Bybee said attacks on judges were "out of all bounds of civic and persuasive discourse" in a legal case. He continued, "It does no credit to the arguments of the parties to impugn the motives or the competence of the members of this court. . . . Such personal attacks treat the court as though it were merely a political forum in which bargaining, compromise, and even intimidation are acceptable principles." Judge Bybee's warning that the courts could be seen as a political forum for bargaining and intimidation would prove prescient.[10]

Trump continued to vilify judges who did not rule the way he wanted. When he lost back-to-back immigration cases in lower courts around this time, he crowed: "See you in the Supreme Court!"[11] He had a pattern of attributing unfavorable decisions to a judge's political affiliation and, in one high-profile situation, to a judge's race and family background. In 2016, candidate Trump had erupted over U.S. District Court judge Gonzalo Curiel and his actions in a fraud lawsuit brought against the for-profit Trump University, which operated from 2005 to 2010. Students who sued contended that they were lured into real estate classes through false marketing. Judge Curiel, based in San Diego, had rejected a summary judgment request by lawyers for the defunct Trump University.[12] At a campaign rally in San Diego on May 27, Trump declared, "I have a judge who is a hater of Donald Trump, a hater. He's a hater. His name is Gonzalo Curiel." At the same raucous rally, it is worth noting, the fervor of Trump's supporters and their readiness to fight with anyone who showed up to protest the candidate was on display. San Diego police in riot gear arrested thirty-five people that night, prompting Trump to write on Twitter: "Fantastic job on handling the thugs who tried to disrupt our very peaceful and well attended rally." Trump willfully ignored how combative some of his own backers were.[13]

Trump's comments against Curiel were amplified a few days after the San Diego rally when CNN's Jake Tapper asked the candidate why he thought Curiel would not rule fairly on his case. Trump referred to his campaign pledge to build a wall between the United States and Mexico. "This judge is of Mexican heritage," Trump said. "I'm building a wall. . . . He's giving me horrible rulings. . . . I think that's why he's doing it. . . . He's a Mexican."[14]

Calling someone "a Mexican" was, from Trump, an insult. Beyond that racism, Trump utterly disregarded Curiel's contributions in America. The judge's parents had immigrated from Mexico and settled in Indiana, where Curiel was born. He earned his undergraduate and law degrees at Indiana University. He became a federal prosecutor in California, eventually specializing in cases against Mexican drug cartel members. In that work, Curiel was threatened with death and had to travel for a time with federal bodyguards. Republican California governor Arnold Schwarzenegger appointed him to a state court in 2006, and in 2011, President Obama tapped him for the U.S. trial court judgeship in San Diego. When Trump began criticizing Curiel, Schwarzenegger posted on Twitter: "Judge Curiel is an American hero who stood up to the Mexican cartels. I was proud to appoint him when I was Gov."[15] Trump showed no regret. His "Mexican" judge remark revealed his mindset and suggested what would occur during the next four years.

In 2017, after lower-court judges ruled against the first travel ban, administration lawyers scrambled to revise it under established immigration law. President Trump issued a second order in March removing Iraq from the list and dropping restrictions on legal permanent residents returning to the United States. He explained at a rally in Tennessee that the second order was a "watered down version of the first order" to address worries among administration lawyers who had to defend it in court.[16] Judges, however, blocked enforcement of the new measure. A few months later, as the administration tried to generate sufficient justification for yet a third iteration of the order as litigation carried on, Trump tweeted, "People, the lawyers and the courts can call it whatever they want, but I am calling it what we need and what it is, a TRAVEL BAN!"[17]

The Department of Homeland Security eventually finished a review of immigration patterns to provide more plausible grounds for the travel restrictions. Trump announced the third order on September 24. The new restrictions, which were scheduled to take effect in mid-October, included vetting procedures for nationals seeking U.S. entry from particular countries that presented "public safety threats." Civil libertarians and others still found its vague criteria flawed and argued that it remained unconstitutional and a violation of federal immigration law. This third iteration was the basis for the case that eventually reached the Supreme Court, in 2018. In the meantime, the justices decided to let the revised travel ban take full effect, over objections from immigrant rights and civil liberties groups involved in litigation. The justices issued no opinion with their orders, and only Justices Ginsburg and Sotomayor said they would have denied the administration's request to let the disputed policy take effect while it faced a challenge. The action stopped people from eight nations, six of them predominantly Muslim, from entering the United States. The justices' paired orders blocking two lower-court rulings against the ban revealed the high court's openness to the Trump legal agenda. Administration lawyers knew that they were embarking on an untested strategy by seeking emergency intervention from the justices when lower courts had blocked the bold Trump initiatives. But more often than not, they prevailed, winning orders that allowed Trump's policies to be carried out while challenges to them were pending.[18]

At the White House in the early days of Trump's presidency, the new immigration policy targeting Muslims provided just one reason for chaos. The extent of Russia's interference in the 2016 election was becoming clear. As Trump was announcing the first travel ban, the acting attorney general, Sally Yates, an Obama administration holdover, who had indicated that she was not willing to get behind the ban, was warning White House counsel Don McGahn about Michael Flynn, a retired lieutenant general who was Trump's newly named national security adviser. Yates alerted McGahn that the FBI, then led by James Comey, was investigating Flynn for his back-channel contacts with Russian ambassador Sergey Kislyak after Trump's election and while Obama was still president. It turned out that Flynn had urged Kislyak to disregard the sanctions the departing Obama administration had imposed because of Russia's interference in the presidential election. Flynn then apparently lied to Vice President Mike Pence about his contacts with Kislyak. Yates told McGahn that Flynn's lies might compromise him with the Russians and make him vulnerable to blackmail.[19]

When Yates's warnings reached the president, Trump initially tried to protect Flynn and discouraged FBI director Comey from continuing with the investigation. But in mid-February Trump fired Flynn. Meanwhile, Comey's broader investigation into Russia's meddling in the 2016 election was aggravating Trump enough that on May 9, Trump fired Comey. The president's spokeswoman said Trump had acted on the recommendation of Deputy Attorney General Rod Rosenstein. But that was untrue, and Trump himself said the day after the firing in an interview with NBC's Lester Holt: "I was going to fire regardless of recommendation. . . . [Rosenstein] made a recommendation. But regardless of recommendation, I was going to fire Comey, knowing there was no good time to do it." Continuing to explain Comey's dismissal, the president said, "And in fact, when I decided to just do it, I said to myself—I said, you know, this Russia thing with Trump and Russia is a made-up story. It's an excuse by the Democrats for having lost an election that they should've won."[20]

But the Russia probe continued. A week after Comey's firing, Rosenstein, who was serving as acting attorney general at the time, appointed former FBI director Robert Mueller as a Department of Justice special counsel "to investigate Russian interference with the 2016 presidential election and related matters."[21]

Despite all this upheaval that necessarily required internal legal advice, White House counsel McGahn remained laser focused on appointments to the Supreme Court and lower courts. McGahn had first met Trump in 2014 and would prove to be one of the most resistant of his inner circle both to dismissal (he quit in 2018) and to scandal, eventually testifying before the House Judiciary Committee in the Russia investigation.

Connections between the Trump and McGahn families went back to the mid-1980s, when Patrick "Paddy" McGahn, Don's uncle, had represented Trump in casino and other deals.[22] The younger McGahn was an expert in campaign finance who had served on the Federal Election Commission and come into the administration most immediately from private practice. He also was a guitarist in at least two cover bands, "clocking . . . 100 shows a year ('almost kind of a part-time job')." He told *Guitar World* in 2020 that he'd been inspired in the late 1970s by Van Halen.[23] In the midst of the early White House turbulence and with designs both professional and personal, McGahn was helping to choose a successor for the Scalia vacancy, and he was already positioning conservatives for prominent lower-court appointments. On the same day in late January that Trump announced his first travel ban, and the day after McGahn fielded Yates's concerns about Flynn's communications with the Russian ambassador, McGahn telephoned U.S. appeals court judge Neil Gorsuch to let him know that Trump had chosen him to succeed Scalia on the Supreme Court.

Scalia, a combative and eminently quotable hero to conservatives since his 1986 appointment, had died on February 13, 2016, at a resort in West Texas, near Marfa. He was seventy-nine years old and suffered from cardiovascular disease but had appeared vigorous enough that his death came as a surprise. Scalia had just returned from a long trip to Asia that might have strained his health. No autopsy was performed, per the family's wishes; speculation regarding the cause of Scalia's death centered on heart failure or a blood clot. In life, Scalia's contribution to two methods of judicial interpretation could not be overstated: originalism, centered on an understanding of the Constitution at its eighteenth-century adoption; and textualism, focused on the exact words of a statute, without regard to floor statements, committee reports, and other congressional legislative history.[24]

The first Italian American justice—who memorably flicked his chin in a Sicilian gesture to an unwelcome news photographer— Scalia had captivated people on both sides of the ideological divide. When Elena Kagan was dean of Harvard Law School, she called him "the justice who has had the most important impact over the years on how we think and talk about the law."[25] He was a faculty adviser at the founding of the Federalist Society, the once modest debating society that had grown into a monied powerhouse helping Republican presidents screen candidates for the federal bench. Scalia's brand of originalism and textualism nurtured a generation of right-wing adherents. He was more famous for his dissenting opinions than for his views when he wrote for the majority. In 2015, when the Court found a right to same-sex marriage, Scalia declared the outcome unconstitutional and mocked the liberal justices who joined the lofty prose of the centrist conservative justice Anthony Kennedy. "If, even as the price to be paid for a fifth vote, I ever joined an opinion for the Court that began: 'The Constitution promises liberty to all within its reach, a liberty that includes certain specific rights that allow persons, within a lawful realm, to define and express their identity,' I would hide my head in a bag." Scalia's most notable majority opinion was the 2008 decision declaring that the Second Amendment covers an individual right to bear arms for self-defense in the home, in the case of *District of Columbia v. Heller*.[26]

Scalia's death at the start of the 2016 presidential election year shook the country and appeared to usher in a revolution at the highest court—in the opposite direction of what happened. It looked as though President Obama would have an opportunity to replace the conservative stalwart with a liberal and change the 5–4 conservative-liberal balance to a 5–4 liberal-majority bench. Liberal expectations soared. It had been nearly a half century since liberals held a majority. When Chief Justice Earl Warren retired in 1969, President Richard Nixon replaced him with Warren Burger, and set the Court on a new course. Of the total sixteen appointments presidents made since that time, twelve were Republican, four Democrat. Some GOP appointees, such as Harry Blackmun and David Souter, became liberal votes, but, overall, the bench under Chief Justice Burger (1969–1986) and Chief Justice Rehnquist (1986–2005) was conservative. Roberts took the helm of a Court that, with the addition of Samuel Alito for Sandra Day O'Connor, was moving even more to the right.[27]

Now, because of Scalia's sudden death, it seemed that pattern would be reversed, and that John Roberts would become the first chief justice in decades without an ideological majority. This would disrupt the trajectory of Roberts, a first-in-his-class achiever who had enjoyed superb timing as he rose in the legal profession and became the youngest chief justice in two centuries. Ever since he had been a law student in the late 1970s, the Court had been tilting conservative. But liberals appeared on the cusp of a revolution in spring 2016.

Senate Majority Leader Mitch McConnell threw a wrench into all that. McConnell, a Republican, was just beginning a vacation in the U.S. Virgin Islands when he got early word of Scalia's death, through the Federalist Society's Leonard Leo, a personal friend of Scalia's. When Roberts made the news of Scalia's death public, late on February 13, McConnell was ready with his own public statement, issued at an overnight stop on Saint Thomas as he made his way to Saint John. "This vacancy should not be filled until we have a new president," McConnell declared, referring to the upcoming November 2016 election and the January 20, 2017, inauguration.

McConnell's action, taken as the Senate was in recess and without consultation with colleagues, seemed audacious, even in bad taste on the day of Scalia's death. "Later in the week," McConnell recounted, "a couple of my Republican colleagues reached out to me. They were a bit skittish about my unilateral decision. In the end, however, almost all of my colleagues supported the decision I had made in St. Thomas." The ploy worked for McConnell. Senate Republicans blocked all action on Obama's choice of appeals court judge Garland for elevation, and the vacancy was waiting for the new president.[28]

The tall, square-jawed Gorsuch, distinguished by a full head of gray hair and Ivy League credentials, was perfect for a new president drawn to central casting choices. Three days after McGahn's January 27 call alerting him to the president's choice, Gorsuch heard from Trump himself. The president said he intended to make the announcement the very next day, on January 31. The plan had been for a rollout later in the week. But Trump wanted it scheduled immediately. That caused a mad rush to Washington for the nominee, along with quick White House plans for an East Room unveiling. Trump's team managed to prevent any leak to the news media of the president's choice and even encouraged reporters to track other possible nominees, to the point that Gorsuch's own father-in-law, watching television from his home in England, where the nominee's wife of some twenty years, Louise Burleston Gorsuch, had been born, was convinced someone else would be tapped based on news reports that a different U.S. appellate judge was driving toward Washington for the honor. "He had seen all the reporting," Gorsuch later recounted in one of his books, "and he was sure that a friend of mine was about to get the nod. Louise replied that she was *pretty* sure I was the pick. . . . My father-in-law wasn't even convinced when Louise told him that we had slipped through the White House kitchen entrance and were now in the Lincoln Bedroom."[29]

As Trump aides rushed to prepare for the introduction of the Supreme Court nominee, the president had another agenda item on the evening of January 30. He fired Acting Attorney General Sally Yates. He attributed the action to her failure to defend his Muslim-country travel ban. Trump called Yates "weak on borders and very weak on illegal immigration." But he also was aware of her warning to McGahn about Michael Flynn and Flynn's apparent lies about his interactions with the Russian ambassador. After Trump fired Yates, Dana Boente, U.S. attorney for the Eastern District of Virginia, was quickly sworn in as deputy attorney general, and Boente, positioned as the acting attorney general, immediately rescinded a memorandum Yates had issued the same day refusing to defend the travel ban. Boente said that the Justice Department would defend the measure as lawful.[30]

The series of unusual successions flowed from the fact that Trump's designated attorney general, Jeff Sessions, was still awaiting Senate confirmation. Senators were stalled on Sessions, largely because of his dealings with Russian ambassador Kislyak. Sessions, who had been a sitting senator from Alabama and one of Trump's earliest campaign supporters, was eventually confirmed on February 8 by a vote of 52–47.[31]

The morning after Yates's firing, Trump prepared for the Gorsuch ceremony. When he revealed his choice on January 31 to an East Room audience, the president asked, "So was that a surprise? Was it?"[32] He had enjoyed throwing the press off the trail. Among those in attendance for the televised event was Maureen McCarthy Scalia, the wife of the late justice. During the presidential campaign, Maureen, who sometimes described herself as more conservative than her husband, had supported Trump with a large yard sign at her McLean, Virginia, home. (Trump appointed Scalia's eldest son, Eugene, secretary of labor in 2019.)[33]

Gorsuch brought experience, academic credentials, and, being only forty-nine, youth. He had a commanding presence and a broad smile. His self-assurance was manifest. He also had well-connected backers, including the Colorado billionaire Philip Anschutz, whose properties covered the energy industry, telecommunications, real estate, conservative media, and sports and entertainment. The *New York Times* reported that Gorsuch was a "semiregular speaker" at Anschutz's annual dove-hunting excursions "for the wealthy and politically prominent," and that Anschutz in 2006 had lobbied the George W. Bush administration for Gorsuch's first appointment to the bench, on the Denver-based U.S. Court of Appeals for the Tenth Circuit.[34]

Gorsuch, whose mother served in the Reagan administration as head of the Environmental Protection Agency, split his teen years between Colorado and the Maryland suburbs. While in the East, he attended Georgetown Preparatory School, the same Jesuit institution that had drawn his future colleague Brett Kavanaugh. Gorsuch then attended Columbia University and Harvard Law School. At Harvard he became part of a new and powerful cohort, young lawyers who were not just conservative but nurtured by the Federalist Society.

Earlier Supreme Court candidates, including John Roberts, had been vetted by the Federalist Society, but Gorsuch, who entered law school only after the society had penetrated campuses, was the first GOP appointee to have been steeped fully in its culture. By the mid-1990s, the organization had developed an entrenched network, playing a major role in judicial selection and helping to screen candidates for top GOP administration slots. After serving as a law clerk to Justice Byron R. White, a fellow Coloradan, and simultaneously for Justice Anthony Kennedy, Gorsuch worked as a top aide in the Justice Department during the Bush administration, for fourteen months, before his Tenth Circuit appointment in 2006.[35] Over his nearly eleven years on the appellate court, Gorsuch espoused the "originalist" approach, reading the Constitution in terms of its eighteenth-century understanding, a practice widely associated with Scalia and tracing years earlier to Robert Bork, a Yale law professor and U.S. appellate court judge whose own 1987 Supreme Court nomination was defeated in a historic Senate battle. Gorsuch had gone fly-fishing with Scalia in 2014 on the Colorado River and had kept an inscribed photograph from the outing.[36]

Gorsuch's nomination appeared to reinforce Trump's vow to appoint justices who would reverse *Roe v. Wade,* as Gorsuch's record suggested opposition to abortion rights. In his book *The Future of Assisted Suicide and Euthanasia,* published in 2006 by Princeton University Press, Gorsuch argued against such practices and emphasized the "inviolability" of human life.[37]

While Trump was screening candidates for the Scalia vacancy, the Federalist Society's Leonard Leo played a significant role, channeling information between the president's team and various judicial candidates, including Gorsuch. Don McGahn would later observe that critics of the Federalist Society "frequently claim the president has outsourced his selection of judges. That is completely false. I've been a member of the Federalist Society since law school, still am, so frankly it seems like it's been in-sourced." A relentless speaker who rarely paused for breath before an audience, McGahn repeated the "insourcing" quip frequently, at least once adding, "Most of the lawyers in my [White House counsel] office were members. . . . Candidly, we're inside the castle."[38]

In 2013, Federalist Society leaders had chosen Gorsuch to deliver a special lecture at the group's lavish annual dinner. A culminating event at the society's yearly conference, the lecture was named for Barbara Olson, the conservative lawyer and TV commentator killed in the terrorist hijackings on September 11, 2001, when her flight from Dulles was plunged into the Pentagon. The wife of Theodore Olson, U.S. solicitor general in the George W. Bush administration, Barbara had made a frantic final call from the plane to her husband's office that September 11 morning.[39]

Earlier speakers chosen for the Olson lecture included Justice Scalia, in 2004; Chief Justice Roberts, in 2007; Attorney General Michael Mukasey, in 2011; and technology titan Peter Thiel, in 2012. Gorsuch's 2013 speech was standard fare. He took aim at public cynicism, spoke of the success of the rule of law, and presented himself unpretentiously. "Ours is a judiciary of honest black polyester," he said, uttering another line that he would repeat often, including during his confirmation hearings.[40]

Gorsuch's appellate court record of skepticism for federal regulators was an important consideration for some of Trump's vetters. Gorsuch believed that courts had given agencies excessive latitude over such issues as the environment, public health, and safety. Curtailing the "administrative state," as it was sometimes called, was a priority of White House counsel McGahn, who, beginning in May 2016, had a strong hand in creating Trump's list of possible Supreme Court candidates. The presentation of a public Supreme Court list itself was unconventional. Presidential candidates never touted such lists, but for Trump it was a way to try to persuade establishment Republicans that he was not the wild man they observed. Leaders from the Federalist Society and the Heritage Foundation, the latter founded in 1973, helped fill out the list and talked it up among their constituencies. The idea of the list developed in McGahn's D.C. office in March 2016, when the future White House counsel worked at the Jones Day law firm and was Trump's campaign lawyer. McGahn arranged a lunch to bring together such early Trump backers as Senator Jeff Sessions with the Federalist Society's Leonard Leo and other conservative stalwarts. As author David Enrich recounted in his chronicle of the relationship between Jones Day and the Trump administration, a preapproved list of possible judicial nominees went a long way "to assuage conservatives' concerns about a guy who had previously supported abortion rights."[41]

McGahn was aware of Judge Gorsuch's record of rejecting broad regulatory actions over labor and the environment. An August 2016 opinion particularly caught McGahn's attention, one month before Gorsuch was formally added to the Trump Supreme Court list. In the case, *Gutierrez-Brizuela v. Lynch,* Gorsuch argued that judges had run too far with Supreme Court precedent requiring deference to agency interpretations of the statutes that governed them. Past cases, Gorsuch asserted, had allowed "executive bureaucracies to swallow huge amounts of core judicial and legislative power and concentrate federal power in a way that seems more than a little difficult to square with the Constitution of the framers' design. Maybe the time has come to face the behemoth." Gorsuch chastised judges for validating what he believed were excessive agency actions.[42]

McGahn also knew that Gorsuch perhaps had an aversion to big government dating from his mother's role as EPA administrator. A lawyer by the age of twenty-two, Anne Gorsuch Burford wrote about her tumultuous 1981–1983 EPA tenure in *Are You Tough Enough?*, a take-no-prisoners memoir that captures the personal style of its author, who news reporters had characterized as a flamboyant figure clad in a fur coat and waving a cigarette between her fingers.[43] She worked to roll back federal regulations and to cut money for "Superfund" hazardous-waste cleanup, her actions generating a battle with congressional investigators and even fellow Republicans, to whom she became a liability. According to her memoir, which she billed as "an insider's view of Washington's power politics," White House officials failed to back her on their own agenda. She targeted "the unholy trinity of Justice Department lawyers and White House counsel" who set her up for a doomed fight over documents and executive privilege. (Coincidentally, these men were among those who mentored young John Roberts when he was in the Reagan administration, and they included Theodore Olson, who later became U.S. solicitor general and was married to Barbara Olson.)

Congressional committees subpoenaed documents from Anne Gorsuch related to the hazardous-waste cleanup program. Her refusal to release the documents turned into a pivotal fight over the reach of executive privilege. Administration lawyers advised her to withhold the materials. She later wrote that she tried to resist the lawyers' plan and felt she was being used. Eventually she was held in contempt of Congress. She became the first cabinet-level official ever cited for contempt of Congress, as she adhered to Reagan's assertion of executive privilege. Administration lawyers had argued that production of the documents would reveal sensitive information related to the EPA's enforcement strategy. But in dispute was the basic effectiveness of the EPA's enforcement of hazardous-waste law.

This was the kind of interbranch battle that typically was worked out through negotiation, but this time both sides dug in. The *New York Times* quoted Anne Gorsuch from a news conference after the contempt vote in December 1982 as saying, "What happened tonight, if pursued to its conclusion, wouldn't do anything. It would not produce the documents, it would not decide the issue of separation of powers. It would only send me to jail for a much-needed rest."[44] Two months later, the divorced Gorsuch remarried, to Robert Burford, a rancher who was director of the Bureau of Land Management under Reagan. Controversy over her refusal to produce the documents and complaints of mismanagement intensified, and in March 1983, she resigned under pressure from the White House. She believed that she had been betrayed by the administration and wronged by the news media. Her son Neil, then a student at Georgetown Preparatory School, witnessed the personal pressure. "Neil knew from the beginning the seriousness of my problems," she later wrote.[45]

Anne Burford taught her son a lesson about the ways of Washington: you're on your own. As she wrote in her memoir, "When congressional criticism about the EPA began to touch the presidency, Mr. Reagan solved his problem by jettisoning me and my people." She recounted that Neil, who was fifteen when she was pushed out, said, "You should never have resigned. You didn't do anything wrong. You only did what the President ordered. Why are you quitting? You raised me not to be a quitter. Why are you a quitter?" Wrote Burford, "He was really upset."[46]

Neil Gorsuch, in one of his own books, *A Republic, If You Can Keep It*, concerning federal governmental power, referred to his mother's experience at the EPA but said little beyond that she was its first female administrator. He focused instead on her work in Colorado, as the first female lawyer in the Denver district attorney's office and as a state legislator. In the early 1960s, she became the youngest woman admitted to the Colorado bar.[47] "Her idea of daycare often meant me tagging along," Gorsuch wrote. Of his father, David Gorsuch, he wrote that he served in the U.S. Army, became a lawyer, and enjoyed outdoor activities. The young Neil similarly loved to camp and fish and, even after becoming a justice, sometimes rode his bike into work at the Supreme Court from his home in suburban Maryland.[48]

White House counsel McGahn was frank about his attraction to Neil Gorsuch's antiregulation agenda. "Unlike Justice Gorsuch, my mother was not the head of the EPA," he told a law school audience, adding that nonetheless, "I've always had an aversion to concentrated power."[49] The antiregulatory mantra was penetrating the federal judiciary, too. Gorsuch was just one of many Trump appointees ready to reinterpret agency power. And through all the Trump-inspired havoc and distractions, the machinery of judicial selection never stopped churning.

Trump's glee over the Gorsuch nomination was temporarily deflated a few days after the announcement when Gorsuch, as was the custom for nominees, walked the Senate corridors for preliminary "courtesy visits." Connecticut Democratic senator Richard Blumenthal, who met with the nominee, told reporters that Gorsuch had expressed dismay at Trump's attacks on federal judges, particularly related to the Muslim-country travel ban. The Blumenthal-Gorsuch meeting occurred around the time of Trump's tirade against Seattle judge Robart's nationwide injunction against the first travel ban. Blumenthal told reporters that Judge Gorsuch described Trump's comments as "demoralizing" and "disheartening." Trump immediately lashed out at Blumenthal, calling the senator a liar. But a White House aide who had accompanied Judge Gorsuch to the meetings confirmed the comments.[50]

Trump threatened to pull the nomination, according to a story in the *Washington Post* months later. He believed that Gorsuch had failed to show him sufficient gratitude. The *Post* reported that Trump criticized Gorsuch in a meeting with Senate Majority Leader Mitch McConnell and then–House Speaker Paul Ryan and had declared: "He's probably going to end up being a liberal like the rest of them. You never know with these guys." The *Post* revealed that Gorsuch had written a note to Trump on March 2, about three weeks after his remarks to Blumenthal, thanking the president for the nomination. Referring to Trump's speech at a joint session of Congress, Gorsuch wrote, "Your address to Congress was magnificent. And you were so kind to recognize Mrs. Scalia, remember the justice, and mention me. My teenage daughters were cheering the TV!" He added, "The team you have assembled to assist me in the Senate is remarkable and inspiring. I see daily their love of country and our Constitution, and know it is a tribute to you and your leadership for policy is always about personnel. Congratulations again on such a great start."[51]

I learned later that Trump never contacted Gorsuch directly, although the nominee of course heard through intermediaries about the criticism. Gorsuch was not going to walk back remarks that he believed reflected judicial independence. Trump wanted constant loyalty and genuflection. It was a rare Trump appointee or executive branch associate who managed to enter his world and avoid some personal compromise. Trump could test even the most hard-bitten veterans of politics and destroy reputations.

For his Senate Judiciary Committee hearings, Gorsuch told Senate advisers that he preferred a plain wooden desk over the customary cloth-draped table that nominees before him had used. He wanted to project a humble image. "Putting on a robe reminds us judges that it's time to lose our egos and open our minds," he said as he testified, referring again to "honest black polyester."[52]

Held in late March, the hearings overall were uneventful. Gorsuch said he would rule based on law and Supreme Court precedent. When the subject of *Roe v. Wade* came up, Senator Lindsey Graham asked Gorsuch if Trump had asked him in his interview to "overrule" the decision. "No, Senator," Gorsuch said. Graham followed up, "What would you have done if he had asked?" Responded Gorsuch: "Senator, I would have walked out the door. It is not what judges do. They do not do it at that end of Pennsylvania Avenue, and they should not do it at this end either, respectfully."

No doubt Trump would never have asked that directly. Trump had already made clear where he stood on the topic.

As Gorsuch was testifying, the Supreme Court across the street handed down a ruling that put him on the spot. *Endrew F. v. Douglas County School District* centered on public school services for children with disabilities. The dispute had been brought by parents of an autistic child who believed that their Colorado school district had failed to sufficiently provide educational services for their son under a law that dictated that schools receiving federal funds provide "free, appropriate education." In *Thompson R2-J School District v. Luke P.*, a similar Tenth Circuit case from Colorado involving an autistic boy, Gorsuch had narrowly interpreted what was required under the Individuals with Disabilities Education Act (IDEA). Rejecting arguments from the boy's family, he wrote that the law protecting disabled students compelled schools to provide benefits "merely . . . 'more than *de minimis*'"—that is, minimally. "The Act does not require that States do whatever is necessary to ensure that all students achieve a particular standardized level of ability and knowledge," he wrote. "Rather, it much more modestly calls for the creation of individualized programs reasonably calculated to enable the student to make some progress towards the goals within that program."[53]

The Supreme Court determined in its case that the IDEA standard was "markedly more demanding," and that the law dictated greater benefits for students. "When all is said and done," Chief Justice Roberts wrote in the decision, issued as Gorsuch appeared before senators, "a student offered an educational program providing 'merely more than *de minimis*' progress from year to year can hardly be said to have been offered an education at all."[54]

Illinois Democratic senator Dick Durbin pounded Gorsuch on his record related to education issues, particularly in the context of the new Supreme Court case. He cited a National Education Association report that detailed the nominee's decisions against students with disabilities and went on to observe that the high court had just rejected Gorsuch's view of the Individuals with Disabilities Education Act. "It is a powerful decision," Durbin declared of the new ruling in *Endrew F. v. Douglas County School District*. "It is a unanimous decision. It was written by the Chief Justice of the Court. It is an issue which we need to face in America with the incidence of autism and children with severe disabilities. Why, why . . . did you want to lower the bar so low to 'merely more than *de minimis*' as a standard for public education to meet this Federal requirement under the law?"[55]

"Senator, I really appreciate the opportunity to respond to that," Gorsuch said, "because I just saw the opinion. It was handed to me as I was headed to the bathroom a moment ago." Referring to his opinion in *Thompson R2-J School District v. Luke P.*, he said, "*Luke P.* was a unanimous decision by my court. . . . We were bound by Circuit precedent. . . . If anyone is suggesting that I like a result where an autistic child happens to lose, it is a heartbreaking accusation to me, heartbreaking."[56]

A separate Gorsuch decision from the Tenth Circuit drew the harshest scrutiny and lived on, even in Gorsuch's retelling. A truck driver whose trailer broke down in subzero temperatures had unhitched the rig and temporarily left it behind as he became numb in the cold. His employer fired him for leaving the trailer. The Tenth Circuit majority found that the driver should have been protected by federal worker-safety law. Judge Gorsuch dissented, emphasizing that the employer had told the driver to wait for help and finding that his claim fell outside the worker-safety law's plain meaning. Minnesota Democratic senator Al Franken mocked the result as "absurd" and pressed Gorsuch about what he would have done under the circumstances. "Senator, I don't know, I wasn't in the man's shoes," Gorsuch said.[57]

The nomination was then put before the full Senate. Democrats threatened a filibuster, leading the Republican Senate majority to change Senate filibuster rules by lowering the 60-vote threshold for cutting off debate of Supreme Court nominees to 51. Afterward, some on the left second-guessed the strategy and its application to Gorsuch, who was, after all, succeeding a fellow conservative. The filibuster might have been preserved as a tool for subsequent and more consequential nominations, as when Trump chose Brett Kavanaugh to succeed moderate justice Anthony Kennedy or Amy Coney Barrett to succeed liberal Ruth Bader Ginsburg.

Once the filibuster possibility was eliminated, Gorsuch was approved on a 54–45 Senate tally. He took his seat in April and his formal investiture at the Supreme Court was June 15. Trump attended, as did the

Republican old guard, including Fred Fielding, Ken Starr, and Alberto Gonzales, men who had had a hand in Supreme Court appointments from the Reagan to George W. Bush administrations.

Two days later, Don McGahn was still savoring the Gorsuch celebration when President Trump called him. McGahn thought that he might want to talk about the Supreme Court investiture. Instead, Trump pressed McGahn to figure out a way to fire Special Counsel Robert Mueller, calling the investigation into his possible ties to Russia's 2016 election interference "a witch hunt."

"It was a conversation we'd had many times before," McGahn recalled later in an interview with the House Judiciary Committee. "I thought I had been clear on my views and my advice, but we were having the same conversation again and again and again, coupled with the fact that it was a Saturday. . . . You know, after the investiture of Neil Gorsuch, I thought we were going to take a little pause over the weekend and smile for once. But we did not smile; we continued wanting to talk about conflicts of interest and Bob Mueller." Trump remained preoccupied by the Russia investigation. McGahn had a different focus, one centered on the federal judiciary, which would turn out to be far more consequential.[58]

Like his mother, Gorsuch lived by his own rules and interests. Once on the bench, he resisted any freshman role and refused to bend to certain Court formalities. He tussled with Chief Justice Roberts on matters of protocol, skipping the justices' first private session after his Senate confirmation and pressing for some time to speak at the investiture ceremony, which was attended by President Trump. The private meetings for the nine, known as "the conference" and held in a near-sacred space off the chambers of the chief justice without staff in attendance, were important substantively for action on cases but also for the collective harmony fostered. After more than a year with just eight justices, Roberts wanted a full showing of the nine. But Gorsuch had previously scheduled an out-of-town trip and simply did not want to postpone it to conform to Roberts's interests. Gorsuch could catch up on the case discussions and, as he would continue to demonstrate, felt no compunction to bend to the will of the group. As for the public courtroom investiture, these were traditionally brief, tightly scripted affairs, highlighted by use of a black horsehair chair that had belonged to the great chief justice John Marshall and which was positioned at the front of the courtroom. After a new justice was escorted from the Marshall chair to the bench, the chief justice administered the oath, the new justice took his seat, and the ceremony ended. But Gorsuch wanted to offer formal remarks, words of appreciation, to the spectators, and as the event was being planned made his desire known. Roberts, who would preside, refused to entertain any break in the tradition, and the courtroom event remained brief, about five minutes.[59]

Gorsuch had plenty of supporters outside the Court ready to fete him. Senate Republican leader McConnell, who had kept the Scalia seat open, invited him for an event at the McConnell Center at the University of Louisville in the fall of 2017. Gorsuch was later the keynote speaker at the conservative Fund for American Studies at the Trump International Hotel in Washington at a time when the hotel was already caught up in litigation over possible conflicts of interest.[60]

Then in November 2017, Gorsuch headlined the annual Federalist Society dinner. He was met with rousing standing ovations. Before an audience of two thousand at the black-tie gala, he expressed pride in his legal approach. "Originalism has regained its place at the table of constitutional interpretation, and textualism in the reading of statutes has triumphed. And neither one is going anywhere on my watch," Gorsuch said, as the crowd roared. The new justice also used the Federalist Society occasion to defend his decision in the case of the trucker whose rig broke down in the cold. Gorsuch derided his critics, saying they implied that he was forced to rule in a "really, really stupid" manner, or perhaps worse, that "I just hate truckers."[61]

Gorsuch had won a lifetime appointment. He shrugged off the kind of concerns about appearances that preoccupied Chief Justice Roberts. On the bench, he followed his conservative instincts, and when he voted with the Left in the rare but attention-getting case, he did not wring his hands about what Trump or any of his benefactors would say.

That was not the situation for lower-court judges who began jock-eying for attention and possible placement on the Trump Supreme Court list. "They are trying to peacock for an appointment," one appellate judge told me, reinforcing the obvious: if the president starts a list, certain judges are going to want to be on it, in anticipation of a vacancy up the line. The judicial nomination process established by McGahn and McConnell for lower courts was turning out candidates at a rapid pace. Among those pushed through were Amul Thapar, a former U.S. attorney and protégé of McConnell, for the U.S. Court of Appeals for the Cincinnati-based Sixth Circuit; and University of Notre Dame law professor Amy Coney Barrett, championed by Mc-Gahn, a Notre Dame graduate himself, for the U.S. Court of Appeals for the Chicago-based Seventh Circuit.[62]

Barrett, a former law clerk to Justice Scalia, had developed a following among conservatives through her writings on faith and the law. In the late 1990s, she coauthored a law review essay that contended that Catholic judges who were opposed to capital punishment should recuse themselves rather than impose a death sentence. In that piece, she also referred to Catholic opposition to abortion and euthanasia, writing, "The prohibitions against abortion and euthanasia (properly defined) are absolute; those against war and capital punishment are not. There are two evident differences between the cases. First, abortion and euthanasia take away innocent life. This is not always so with war and punishment." Later, as a professor, Barrett, the mother of seven children, signed public statements opposing *Roe v. Wade* and abortion rights.[63]

Her Senate hearing for the Seventh Circuit position came just eight months into the Trump presidency, and McGahn made a point of sitting behind Barrett as she testified. The September session was punctuated by a tense exchange with senior Democratic senator Dianne Feinstein over Barrett's writings about her Roman Catholic faith and the law. "Why is it that so many of us on this side have this very uncomfortable feeling that, you know, dogma and law are two different things. . . . In your case, Professor, when you read your speeches, the conclusion one draws is that the dogma lives loudly within you. And that's of concern when you come to big issues that large numbers of people have fought for, for years in this country."[64]

Barrett and her supporters viewed the question as presenting an impermissible "religious test." Even Democrats thought that Feinstein had handled the matter awkwardly. The incident thrust Barrett to greater prominence, especially among evangelicals. The Senate approved Barrett for the U.S. appellate court post by a 55–43 vote. When she referred to the Feinstein query later in a speech she said, "It seems to me that the premise of the question is that people of faith would have a uniquely difficult time separating out their moral commitments from their obligation to apply the law. And I think people of faith should reject that premise."[65] Many judges well before Barrett had rejected that premise, including notable liberals such as Supreme Court justice William Brennan, a Roman Catholic.

Barrett's hearing that September was consolidated with two other nominees, including a lawyer headed to the Department of Justice's division for civil rights.[66] So the session provoked comments that reflected Democrats' broader concerns about Trump's indifference to civil rights and implicit regard for white nationalist groups. In her opening remarks, Senator Feinstein referred to the deadly Charlottesville rally of a few weeks earlier, which had brought into stark relief Trump's attitudes, a set of attitudes foreshadowing the line that would extend to the violence at the Capitol on January 6, 2021. "Most public officials condemned this violence and condemned the hateful ideology that motivated it," Feinstein said, adding, "the president did not, initially."

What happened in Charlottesville rattled notions of American progress on civil rights, and Trump's refusal to voice any real objection to the racial violence offered another early instance of the president's chilling mindset. Trump had responded briefly to the killing of counterprotester Heather Heyer: "We condemn in the strongest possible terms this egregious display of hatred, bigotry, and violence on many sides, on many sides."[67] Pressed to speak more forcefully, he said two days later that racism was "evil," and that "those who cause violence in its name are criminals and thugs, including the KKK, neo-Nazis, white supremacists and other hate groups that are repugnant to everything we hold dear as Americans."[68]

The next day, however, Trump intensified his comments in the opposite direction, declaring, "You had a group on one side that was bad. You had a group on the other side that was also very violent. . . . nobody wants to say that, but I'll say it right now." Trump, throwing more fuel on the fire, added that there were "very fine people on both sides."[69]

Among those troubled by the comparison was former vice president Joe Biden, who believed that Trump ceded moral authority to white supremacists: "The president of the United States assigns moral equivalence to these dark forces," Biden said at a Democratic campaign event in Youngstown, Ohio.[70] Biden later said that it was Trump's response to Charlottesville that impelled his entry into the 2020 campaign for president. His announcement came in a video released twenty months after Heyer's death: "The first words Joe Biden spoke," noted two reporters, "were 'Charlottesville, Virginia.'"[71]

Trump's public callousness was on full display around the events in Charlottesville and other incidents in the summer of 2017. Speaking before a gathering of law enforcement officers at Suffolk County Community College on Long Island that same summer, Trump appeared to encourage police cruelty. "When you guys put somebody in the car and you're protecting their head, you know, the way you put their hand over?" Trump said, miming the physical motion of an officer covering a suspect's head to keep it from bumping against the squad car. "Like, don't hit their head, and they just killed somebody—don't hit their head," Trump continued. "I said, You can take the hand away, okay?" Trump's comments were met with applause in the room that day. But law enforcement officials across the country later criticized him.[72]

A couple of weeks later, Trump took advantage of the power of his office as he chose to grant his first presidential pardon to former Arizona sheriff Joe Arpaio, who epitomized racial profiling in law enforcement. At a rally in Phoenix before he made the pardon public, Trump asked the crowd, "Do the people in this room like Sheriff Joe?" To applause, Trump said, "So was Sheriff Joe convicted for doing his job? . . . I'll make a prediction: I think he's going to be just fine."[73] American Bar Association president Hilarie Bass said in a statement, "The crime that Arpaio was convicted of committing—criminal contempt of court for ignoring a judge's order—showed a blatant disregard for the authority of the judiciary. . . . Granting Arpaio an expedited pardon sends the wrong message to the public."[74]

At the time, and throughout his first full year, Trump was unconcerned with sending the "wrong message." He mocked norms. Unlike some leaders in the legal arena, and many law professors, none of the Supreme Court justices referred in public to Trump's provocations. They said nothing when Trump attacked Judge Curiel as "a Mexican" who could not be fair, or when he denounced Judge Robart and others who ruled in the travel ban cases. Perhaps it was difficult then to imagine how Trump's words and deeds would affect public regard for the rule of law. He was so unlike any other American president. He was never chastened, never regretful. And in his first year, there seemed no penalty for what he said or did.

---

## Chapter 2

# "NOBODY ON THAT COURT IS LIKE ANYBODY ELSE ON THAT COURT"

Even before Donald Trump entered the White House, the Roberts Court naturally had its internal tensions. As the nine worked to forge majority decisions on cases, they brought their own notions of justice and their own quirks of personality. Chief Justice John Roberts, who presided over the public and private sessions, exerted a strong hand on cases and in the Court's operations. Samuel Alito, a fellow appointee of President George W. Bush, bristled at Roberts's control, especially the chief's institutionalist moves that diluted conservative outcomes on cases. Through the years, Alito appeared to grow angrier, even as his positions prevailed with the addition of more rigid conservatives. His attitude emerged in his written opinions and in public speeches, as he railed against members of Congress (particularly Democrats), the news media, and progressive causes, such as LGBTQ rights. Alito wore a heavy cloak of grievance, as if he were perpetually wronged and destined to be misunderstood. Clarence Thomas shrugged off most of the friction among his colleagues and the outside criticism. He, too, picked up more votes with the Trump appointees. Ruth Bader Ginsburg and Sonia Sotomayor staked out the far left, with Sotomayor often dissenting in intensely personal terms about the cost to America of the Court's direction. Stephen Breyer and Elena Kagan worked the middle to try to broker ideological compromise. Their personalities were suited to it, and as part of a liberal minority, the two justices were often in the position of trying to coax colleagues to the middle.

The Trump years intensified these patterns. All administrations influence which cases the justices hear and how they decide those cases, primarily through arguments made by the U.S. solicitor general, the administration's top lawyer before the Court, often dubbed the "tenth justice." In this the Trump administration was no different. But through some combination of his sheer presence and brazen arguments, as well as the particular character of his judicial appointees, Trump had an outsize impact on the Court. His effect on the justices' relationships with each other was even at times pernicious as he sowed distrust. They had their individual attitudes toward Trump— from Thomas's implicit approval of his agenda and willingness to participate in White House events, to Sotomayor's willingness to call out his racist and destructive ways. Collectively, the Court wanted to keep its distance. Just three months into his presidency, in April 2017, the White House said Trump was scheduled to dine with all the justices. Court officials were surprised by the announcement. No dinner invitation had been accepted, and there was even some question about whether an invitation had been extended. After a furor on social media about the propriety of the event, White House officials said it was being postponed. No such dinner ever happened. During all four years, however, Trump constantly tweeted about the justices, keeping an unwanted spotlight on them.

Under the U.S. Constitution, the president appoints each justice for life. The number of Supreme Court seats is set by Congress and has varied over the centuries, from a low of five to a high of ten. Since 1869, the number of seats has remained set at nine. Various elected officials have at times advocated expanding the number of seats, and that idea was in the air after Trump secured three appointments. Liberals wanted to counteract Trump's dominance. But proposals failed to gather any momentum in Congress.[1]

The Supreme Court building, dubbed the "Marble Palace," brims with allegories of justice and motifs of ancient lawgivers. Bronze gates separate the public spaces from the justices' private corridors and oak-paneled chambers. Many of the justices have embellished their walls with paintings on loan from the National Gallery of Art. The chambers ooze tradition, solemnity, and mystery. For all their majesty, it must be observed that during the Trump period the Court battled a serious mouse infestation. The mice were not new and certainly were common to the White House and other grand old government buildings. But in these years, complaints about mice in chambers escalated.

The courtroom is distinguished by its symmetry, from the evenly spaced marble pillars to the floral coffered ceiling, its pattern replicated in the crimson carpeting. The velvet drapes and upholstered seats are also crimson, contrasting elegantly with the mahogany and white marble throughout. The courtroom is a quiet place, the air still. No cell phones or other electronics are allowed.

Designed by architect Cass Gilbert in the neoclassical tradition, the columned marble structure was completed in 1935 and stood in harmony with the Capitol across the street and other existing federal buildings. From the beginning, in that New Deal era, people regularly lined up outside on the plaza to attend arguments and glimpse the justices. In more recent years, public access to the building diminished. Because of the COVID pandemic, it was closed to the public for more than two years. But quite apart from those extraordinary circumstances, the Court was walled off from the people in other ways.

In 2010, the majority voted to close the iconic bronze doors at the top of the exterior marble steps, under the portico inscribed with "Equal Justice Under Law." Roberts had pushed for closure for security reasons. Four justices thought the move went further than necessary. Justices Breyer and Ginsburg publicly dissented. At the time, Justices Stevens and Scalia were also opposed to the closure. But they declined to sign on to Breyer and Ginsburg's statement. Stevens and Scalia told me later that they were persuaded that it was best to avoid airing the 5–4 internal division. Breyer, joined only by Ginsburg, wrote,

The significance of the Court's front entrance extends beyond its design and function. Writers and artists regularly use the steps to represent the ideal that anyone in this country may obtain meaningful Justice through application to this Court. And the steps appear in countless photographs commemorating famous arguments or other moments of historical importance. In short, time has proven the success of Gilbert's vision: To many members of the public, this Court's main entrance and front steps are not only a means to, but also a metaphor for, access to the Court itself.

Breyer said he understood the security concerns but wrote, "Potential security threats will exist regardless of which entrance we use. And, in making this decision, it is important not to undervalue the symbolic and historic importance of allowing visitors to enter the Court after walking up Gilbert's famed front steps."[2]

Inside the Court, each justice was part of the whole but independent of it, too. The late justice Lewis F. Powell Jr. referred to the Court operation as "nine separate law firms."[3] The justices had colleagues they were drawn to, or avoided. William Rehnquist, John Roberts's predecessor as chief justice, used to quip that a justice spent his early years wondering how he got there and the rest of the time wondering how the *others* got there. The nine had their inherent rivalries but were also brought together by a common bond: only they understood what they were up against, the frustrations and rewards of serving on the country's highest court, the shared pressure of being in the public eye.

For Chief Justice Roberts, the impulsive, vulgar Trump represented everything he tried to avoid. Still, Roberts was a lifelong Republican and could appreciate President Trump's views on executive power and social policy. The liberalism of Hillary Clinton, Trump's 2016 election opponent, no doubt turned off Roberts. He had been a GOP loyalist in two administrations. Clinton, as a senator, had voted against Roberts's confirmation for chief justice in 2005. Roberts had managed, nevertheless, to win over half the Democratic senators at the time, with his final 78–22 confirmation vote. That tally could not match the robust Senate support in 1993 and 1994 for Ginsburg and Breyer, who had been the most recently confirmed justices. But it was a strong showing given the developing polarization of the Senate. No Supreme Court nominee of either party has come close to Roberts's 78-vote majority since 2005.[4]

Roberts seemed bound for success at a young age, an inevitable "first among equals," as the chief justice role has been called. He grew up in northern Indiana, where his father was an executive at a Bethlehem Steel plant on Lake Michigan. An only son with three sisters and the pride of his family, Roberts was educated at an all-male Roman Catholic boarding school not far from his home. To gain entry to the La Lumiere School, he wrote a letter that administrators years later placed under glass in the school library. It said, in part: "I've always wanted to stay ahead of the crowd, and I feel that the competition at La Lumiere will force me to work as hard as I can. At an ordinary high school it would probably be easy to stay ahead. I realize that going to La Lumiere will be a lot of study and hard work, but I feel confident that these labors will pay off in large amounts when it comes time to apply for admission to college. I'm sure that by attending and doing my best at La Lumiere I will assure myself a fine future. I won't be content to get a good job by getting a good education, I want to get the best job by getting the best education."[5]

Roberts was admitted, finished first in his class, and went on to Harvard. He graduated in three years and stayed for law school, leaving with his J.D. in 1979, just as a new conservatism was emerging in America. After prestigious appellate and Supreme Court clerkships (the latter for then–associate justice Rehnquist), he joined the Ronald Reagan administration. He said he heard the president's inauguration speech in January 1981 and felt the "call" to join his revolution. Roberts later became a deputy solicitor general in the George H. W. Bush administration. In that post and then in private practice, he was regarded as a star appellate advocate, arguing thirty-nine cases before the justices. President George W. Bush appointed Roberts to the U.S. Court of Appeals for the District of Columbia Circuit in 2003 and then elevated him to the Supreme Court in 2005.[6]

Well into his sixties, Roberts retained a clean-cut boyishness and the tight discipline of the high school wrestling star he once was. If one were to draw an invisible square around Roberts, close in at his shoulders and arms, as he sat in an upholstered chair for an interview or as he stood at a public lectern, rarely would a single gesture of his break out of that square. On a stage in front of a law school audience in Boston in 2016, answering familiar questions about how the Court works, Roberts kept his hands folded, occasionally tapping his index fingers together. When he was asked what it was like to become chief justice at the age of fifty and begin serving with eight older, more experienced associate justices, he said, "It's a real honor and pleasure to be able to work with them." He paused for effect, then added, "Most of the time." Only then did he reach outside the imaginary box for a glass of water on the table next to him.

The chief justice tried to stay in most of his colleagues' good favor and to remain flexible enough to take into account their different personalities. "Nobody on that Court is like anybody else on that Court," he said at the 2016 Boston appearance. The range of personalities, the wild and woolly display of human nature among the Roberts Court justices, was indeed vast.[7]

Roberts himself was the picture of caution and reserve. Behind his controlled presentations was exhaustive preparation, and nervousness. When he was a lawyer arguing in regional appeals courts, he made a practice of flying in early to see the courtroom and talk to the bailiff. He wanted to know how the judges wished to be addressed and if there were special procedures to be followed. Roberts's delivery was smooth and his arguments clear. But for many of his years of advocacy, he feared speaking in public and would sometimes feel sick to his stomach on the day of arguments. Colleagues noticed his hands shaking. He was so determined and disciplined that he could keep the nervousness at bay as he presented his case. On the way up to the courtroom, he tapped a foot of the large bronze statue of a seated John Marshall, situated on the ground floor of the building, in the Lower Great Hall. When he became chief justice, he continued his take-no-chances approach. Colleagues said he practiced a kind of three-dimensional chess in the ways he laid out cases, anticipated the votes of fellow justices, and kept an eye on related disputes headed toward the Court.[8]

The chief justice worked out of a large suite of offices that included the justices' private conference room, where they decided cases. He decked his walls with landscape paintings of Indiana, where he was reared, and of Maine, where he owned a vacation home. Roberts also had a small historic sofa in his office that was brought over from the Capitol. John Quincy Adams, the sixth president of the United States, had died on the sofa during his return service in the U.S. House of Representatives, and Roberts frequently regaled visitors with the settee's past.[9]

Perhaps Roberts's most difficult period before the Trump era arose from deliberations over the Affordable Care Act in 2012, when he switched votes to uphold the heath care overhaul legislation. Fellow conservatives felt betrayed because Roberts originally voted with them to sink the law known for its presidential sponsor as "Obamacare." Roberts agreed with his colleagues on the right that the sweeping act of Congress could not be sustained under Congress's power to regulate interstate commerce. But he declared, based on his own distinct rationale, that the law could nonetheless be upheld under Congress's power to tax.[10]

The act, providing health care coverage to an estimated forty-five million Americans who were then without insurance, created new marketplaces to buy insurance and prohibited providers from excluding people based on preexisting conditions such as cancer and diabetes. At the center of the system intended to encompass young, healthy people, as well as older subscribers, was an individual insurance mandate requiring most uninsured people to sign up with some provider or pay a penalty. Although the Obama administration had defended the legislation based largely on Congress's power to regulate interstate commerce, it had alternatively argued that if the justices found that authority insufficient to support the individual insurance mandate, Congress's taxing power covered it. Roberts agreed, singlehandedly saving the law. The four liberals to his left found the traditional commerce-power rationale valid. The four justices on Roberts's right believed nothing justified the sweeping legislation, which also expanded Medicaid benefits for lower-income people and allowed children to stay on their parents' policies until age twenty-six.[11]

Roberts faced a torrent of criticism for his decision. The *Wall Street Journal* editorial page, which had argued against the legislation, wrote, "The remarkable decision upholding the Affordable Care Act is shot through with confusion—the mandate that's really a tax, except when it isn't, and the government whose powers are limited and enumerated, except when they aren't. One thing is clear. This was a one-man show, and that man is John Roberts." Donald Trump, then known mainly for his New York real estate ventures and reality TV shows, took to Twitter: "Wow, the Supreme Court passed @ObamaCare. I guess Justice Roberts wanted to be part of Georgetown society more than anyone knew."[12]

One year later, in contrast, Roberts produced a 5–4 opinion in a voting rights case, *Shelby County v. Holder,* that demonstrated his true conservatism and where he shunned compromise. As a young lawyer, he had advocated narrow readings of the federal Voting Rights Act and brought that emphasis to the bench. Now he wrote the Court's opinion striking down a section of the Voting Rights Act that required states with a history of discrimination to obtain advance approval ("preclearance") for any electoral change. The provision of the 1965 law covered mainly southern jurisdictions. Roberts wrote that things had changed in the South and all of America and that the preclearance requirement was no longer needed: "In 1965, the States could be divided into two groups: those with a recent history of voting tests and low voter registration and turnout, and those without those characteristics. Today, the Nation is no longer divided along those lines, yet the Voting Rights Act continues to treat it as if it were." He grounded his legal rationale in the novel principle that "equal sovereignty" demanded that Congress treat all states the same way. Ginsburg, who wrote the dissent, countered that throwing out the requirement, which had been working, was "like throwing away your umbrella in a rainstorm because you are not getting wet." And indeed, *Shelby County v. Holder* had immediate consequences, as southern states that had previously had to clear their rules with the Justice Department began enforcing voter identification requirements that civil rights advocates claimed fell heaviest on Blacks and Hispanics.[13]

The tensions Roberts experienced with his colleagues in his first decade as chief paled, however, compared with those in the next half decade, when Trump was center stage. The Court found itself in the vortex of rampant conspiracy theories, a politics of personal destruction, and challenges to the rule of law. QAnon and other conspiracy theorists, for example, circulated blatantly false stories in early 2019 that Ginsburg, then recovering from lung cancer, was actually dead, and in late 2020 that Chief Justice Roberts had visited the private island of Jeffrey Epstein, accused of trafficking underaged girls for sex. The purported photo of Roberts on the island was beyond belief and widely discredited. Several high-profile Trump supporters were associated with QAnon, spreading false claims about Ginsburg even as she was actively participating in cases. Trump, who was not involved in those instances, was nonetheless always ready to engage in personal attacks, as in 2018 when he publicly mocked the woman who claimed Brett Kavanaugh had sexually assaulted her when they were young.[14]

In addition, the coronavirus pandemic deprived the justices of their usual routines throughout most of 2020 and 2021, including in-person oral arguments and face-to-face contact in their private sessions. (They returned to the bench in late 2021 but kept their building closed to the public through most of 2022.) The trappings of their imposing, columned building reinforced the justices' sense of their institutional authority and separation from the other governmental branches.

After Roberts, the two most senior justices during Trump's first year were Anthony Kennedy, confirmed in 1988 after the failed nomination of U.S. appellate judge Robert Bork, and Clarence Thomas, confirmed in 1991. Kennedy, a Sacramento native, was the last of the Ronald Reagan appointees. He was old school, favoring matching ties and pocket squares. In Sacramento, his father was a lawyer and lobbyist at the statehouse, his mother a homemaker. Among the varied figures in the young Kennedy's life were Earl Warren, the Republican governor and future chief justice, who lived nearby, and the writer Joan Didion, a close friend of Kennedy's sister.

Kennedy returned to Sacramento after Harvard Law School. He became a law professor and worked as a lawyer, sometimes with then-governor Reagan. At Reagan's urging, President Gerald Ford in 1975 appointed Kennedy to the U.S. appellate court for the Ninth Circuit. In late 1987, Reagan decided to elevate Kennedy after the Senate rejected Bork, and Reagan's second choice, Judge Douglas Ginsburg, withdrew after news broke about occasional past marijuana use.

Like the jurist he succeeded, Lewis Powell, Kennedy often controlled the Court with his moderate conservative vote, particularly on such social policy issues as gay marriage and abortion rights. In the 1992 case of *Planned Parenthood v. Casey,* his vote saved *Roe v. Wade.* He also cast a crucial vote to preserve university affirmative action, yet he was reliably conservative on many other controversies. Kennedy controlled decisions especially after January 2006, when centrist justice Sandra Day O'Connor retired. His swing vote at the ideological center set much of the law in the country. Spectators hung on his questions at oral arguments, knowing that the outcome of cases sometimes hinged on whether he was satisfied with the answers he heard.

Kennedy was the voice of the Court on gay legal rights and cast the decisive vote in *Obergefell v. Hodges* (2015), making same-sex marriage a constitutional right. "Since the dawn of history, marriage has transformed strangers into relatives," Kennedy said solemnly when he announced that decision from the bench. "This binds families and societies together, and it must be acknowledged that the opposite sex character of marriage, one man, one woman, has long been viewed as essential to its very nature and purpose. And the Court's analysis and the opinion today begins with these millennia of human experience, but it does not end there." He said that attitudes toward gay rights had changed, and that "under the Due Process and Equal Protection Clauses of the Fourteenth Amendment couples of the same sex may not be deprived" of the right to marry. "The nature of injustice," he said, "is that we do not always see it in our own times."[15]

When I asked him during one interview about his pivotal role across the board, Kennedy brushed it off as exaggerated. His colleagues, however, believed that he savored his middle position and the difference his single vote could make. They were aware that Roberts kept Kennedy's interests at the forefront, and after the nine met privately and voted on cases, the chief justice conferred, first, with Kennedy as he decided who would get to write the various decisions for the Court. Kennedy's clerks also tended to be in the center of the informal staff network that quietly relayed information among justices' chambers over the shape of negotiations, when five votes were holding and when they might be slipping. Some of the other justices admitted to frustration with how much they had to persuade Kennedy at times, but they also recognized that he was inclined to compromise and defused some conflicts among the nine. When Roberts became the justice at the ideological center vote after Kennedy's retirement, his attitude about being the crucial fifth vote differed. He had an institutional interest against divisive 5–4 rulings, and colleagues said he preferred to bring along another justice for a 6–3 decision when possible.[16]

From his chambers, Kennedy had a spectacular view of the Capitol grounds. He adorned his office with a California grapes painting by the artist Edwin Deakin and had a Thomas Holland bronze horse sculpture. Kennedy kept his desktop cleared. He spoke of a desire for long service because of his generation's place in history. "My generation didn't have a president," he told me in 2014, then nearing eighty and rejecting any suggestions of retirement. At the time, he had seen a succession of Baby Boom–era presidencies, those of Bill Clinton, George W. Bush, and Barack Obama. In 2021 and after Kennedy had retired, Joe Biden, like Kennedy a member of the so-called Silent Generation, entered the White House at age seventy-eight, six years younger than Kennedy.[17]

Justice Thomas was next in seniority and in place throughout the Trump presidency. As a candidate, Trump had held up Thomas, along with Scalia, as models of the kind of justice he would seek. Once in office, Trump's administration hired many of Thomas's former law clerks. Virginia (Ginni) Lamp Thomas, Clarence Thomas's wife, also became a loyalist and inside adviser. Thomas kept a bust of the grandfather who had raised him in his chambers, and the justice often recounted his Pin Point, Georgia, roots in poverty. His mother had picked crabs to support her family of two sons and a daughter. Thomas's father had left the home, and after a fire destroyed their house, Clarence and his younger brother were sent to live with their grandparents in Savannah. Lessons of hard work were seared into him, through his grandfather and the nuns at the parochial school he attended in Savannah. After a brief period in a Missouri seminary, Thomas transferred to College of the Holy Cross in Worcester, Massachusetts, and then attended Yale Law School.

Like Roberts, Clarence Thomas joined the Reagan administration in the 1980s. Thomas served first in the Department of Education and then in the Equal Employment Opportunity Commission (EEOC). President George H. W. Bush appointed Thomas to the D.C. Circuit in 1989 and then in 1991 to the Supreme Court. The African American jurist succeeded civil rights legend Thurgood Marshall, the court's first Black justice. They were opposites on the law. Marshall's life's work was greater constitutional protections for racial minorities, the poor, and the disenfranchised. Thomas wanted such protections left to elected lawmakers and consistently ruled against expansive views of constitutional rights and liberties. Thomas, like John Roberts, narrowly construed antibias law. Thomas believed that affirmative action was stigmatizing. A product of affirmative action himself, he said he regarded his Yale Law degree as practically worthless because, he believed, it was clouded by perceptions that he had benefitted from racial preferences. In his memoir, he described taking a "fifteen-cent price sticker off a package of cigars" and affixing it to his framed degree, a reminder of "the mistake I'd made by going to Yale." He added, "I never did change my mind." And he never displayed the degree. "Instead of hanging it on the wall of my Supreme Court office, I stored it in the basement of my Virginia home—with the sticker still on the frame." Above his office desk is a portrait of the abolitionist Frederick Douglass.[18]

Senate Democrats' quarrels with Thomas's positions on the substance of the law during his 1991 confirmation hearings were largely set aside once Anita Hill, a former employee of Thomas's, came forward with claims of sexual harassment against him. A University of Oklahoma law professor at the time, Hill accused Thomas of sexually harassing her when she worked for him at the EEOC and earlier at the

Department of Education. She recounted details of his pornography-laced conversations.

When senators questioned him about her claims, Thomas categorically denied them and declared: "From my standpoint as a Black American, as far as I'm concerned, it is a high-tech lynching for uppity Blacks who in any way deign to think for themselves, to do for themselves, to have different ideas, and it is a message that unless you kowtow to an old order, this is what will happen to you. You will be lynched, destroyed, caricatured by a committee of the US Senate, rather than hung from a tree."[19] The Senate narrowly voted for confirmation, 52–48.

Through the years he chalked up the accusations to his nontraditional views. "Come on, we know what this is all about: this is the wrong Black guy. He has to be destroyed," he said in a 2020 documentary.[20] Thomas had addressed the criticism he experienced from traditional civil rights groups early in his tenure. "It pains me deeply, more deeply than any of you can imagine, to be perceived by so many members of my race as doing them harm," he told the National Bar Association, a predominantly Black organization, in 1998. "All the sacrifice, all the long hours of preparation, were to help, not to hurt. . . . Isn't it time to move on? Isn't it time to realize that being angry with me solves no problems? Isn't it time to acknowledge that the problem of race has defied simple solutions, and that not one of us, not a single one of us, can lay claim to the solution?"[21]

Thomas was at odds with civil rights advocates, but the justice who grew up in the segregated Jim Crow South exhibited a visceral reaction to cross burning cases and any subject that touched on the national experience with lynching. For years, he rarely spoke at oral arguments, and when he did, it was often to address a subject that had a racial dimension. In a 2002 case from Virginia over whether states could ban cross burning, he invoked the Ku Klux Klan era of lynching. "This was a reign of terror, and the cross was a symbol of that reign of terror. It is unlike any symbol in our society." A year later, in 2003, when the court narrowly allowed the continuation of racial affirmative action on college campuses, Thomas demonstrated yet again the differences between himself and his predecessor Justice Marshall and the civil rights community. "I believe blacks can achieve in every avenue of American life without the meddling of university administrators," he wrote in *Grutter v. Bollinger*.[22]

By the time Trump won office, Thomas was long past being stung by the public slights he had endured. He knew precisely what he believed about the law. He was a committed practitioner of the originalism approach also favored by Scalia. Thomas was not buffeted by the winds of the day or colleagues' persuasion. Thomas and his wife spent summers traveling the country in a large RV. "One of the great things about motor homing is that you don't fly over great swaths of the country," he told me as he pointed up his desire to connect with people outside his East Coast socioeconomic world. He was a NASCAR fan, rooted for University of Nebraska teams in the home state of his wife, Ginni, and was, among the justices, known for the warmth he displayed to the staff who maintained the Court building.[23] He learned their first names and knew what was going on with their families.

Many of Thomas's former law clerks shot to prominence when Trump was elected, landing top Executive Office jobs and life-tenured seats on federal appellate courts.[24] President Trump liked Thomas's middle-America associations and unyielding conservatism: against abortion, against press rights, against gun control, against many federal regulations. Thomas advocated reversing *Roe v. Wade*'s abortion rights and the press freedom embodied in *New York Times v. Sullivan*. On the whole, he criticized the Supreme Court's reliance on stare decisis, a principle that values stability in the law and usually prevents reversal of precedent, and he took to saying, "We use stare decisis as a mantra when we don't want to think."[25]

Through most of Thomas's first three decades on the bench, he rarely asked questions during oral arguments. He would go for more than five years at a stretch without a single query. He offered multiple reasons for keeping quiet, saying, for instance, that he believed his colleagues interrupted the lawyer at the lectern too much. In 2000, he told a school group that he had grown up self-conscious about speaking in public because he and most people in his native Pin

Point, Georgia, spoke Geechee (Gullah), a creole language. When the justices were relegated to teleconference questioning through the COVID pandemic, however, and speaking in a more regimented order of seniority, Thomas and his robust baritone suddenly became part of the give-and-take. As the justices returned to the bench after the pandemic eased, Thomas continued to be a vocal participant, with the assistance of the other justices, who agreed in advance to give him a chance to ask the first question.

Ginni Thomas became nearly as prominent as her husband, because of her Trump connection. She had become an ardent Trump ally after first supporting Texas senator Ted Cruz in his 2016 presidential bid. She worked the trenches, carrying Trump signs and rising early to stand outside the polls on Election Day. She appeared at the National Press Club for a news conference the day after the November 8 election with a group of conservative activists led by Richard Viguerie, whose work dated to Barry Goldwater's presidential campaign in 1964 and who declared, on November 9, "Yesterday's election results were the opening battle of an American political revolution from the Presidency to the Congress to the federal courts." A former Tea Party leader, then the president of Liberty Consulting, Ginni Thomas opened her own remarks on November 9 by giving "credit and honor and glory to God first of all for answered prayers." She predicted a new era for American conservatives.[26]

Ginni Thomas's unyielding activism on behalf of Trump, even after he was voted out of office, and her communications with the legal team that tried to overturn the 2020 election, raised ethics questions regarding Justice Thomas's decisions on related issues. Thomas declined to recuse himself from cases related to the presidential election or the January 6 inquiry, or even to address ethics queries from news reporters. Investigative journalists began to examine Ginni's life as much as Thomas's. In a piece in *The New Yorker* entitled "Is Ginni Thomas a Threat to the Supreme Court?" Jane Mayer outlined her subject's numerous "leadership positions at conservative pressure groups that have either been involved in cases before the Court or have had members engaged in such cases." Mayer observed that Ginni's parents, Donald and Marjorie Lamp, had campaigned for Goldwater, Viguerie's first presidential candidate.[27]

Like Thomas, Chief Justice Roberts declined to respond to journalist queries about the situation. Roberts touted the integrity of the judiciary but had no real control over Thomas. Each justice decided when to recuse himself or herself from a case, and there was no process for other justices to review the decision. In one of his rare comments on recusals, Roberts had said in 2011 that he had "complete confidence in the capability of my colleagues to determine when recusal is warranted." Adding to whatever dilemma Roberts felt in the 2020s, Thomas enjoyed a personal loyalty among his colleagues. Even privately, as they criticized Ginni Thomas's various political schemes, including those tied to Trump's effort to reverse the 2020 election results, most justices did not judge Thomas harshly.[28]

Samuel Alito, next in seniority on the right wing, was one of the most formidable interlocutors from the bench, asking questions that often stumped lawyers. But his tone could turn sour and even uncivil, in marked contrast to those of his fellow conservatives. He sounded perpetually aggrieved and protested that he was continually taken the wrong way. During a controversy over the administration's response to the coronavirus pandemic, Alito said, "I don't want to be misunderstood in making this point because I'm not saying the vaccines are unsafe. The FDA has approved them. It's found that they're safe. It's said that the benefits greatly outweigh the risks. I'm not contesting that in any way. I don't want to be misunderstood. I'm sure I will be misunderstood."[29]

Alito came from a modest household in Trenton, New Jersey. During his confirmation hearing, he spoke of the poverty his father had known, coming to America as an infant, losing his mother as a teenager, and being unable to obtain a job after college. "He found that teaching jobs for Italian-Americans were not easy to come by, and he had to find other work for a while," Alito told senators. "But eventually he became a teacher, and he served in the Pacific during World War II, and he worked . . . for many years in a nonpartisan position for the

New Jersey Legislature, which was an institution that he revered." Alito's mother became a teacher. He had one sister. Alito was a serious student and, after attending public high school, earned admission to Princeton, where his page in the yearbook said, "Sam intends . . . eventually to warm a seat on the Supreme Court." Alito graduated from Yale Law School. He married Martha-Ann Bomgardner, a law librarian, in 1985, and they had two children.[30]

Alito worked in the U.S. solicitor general's office during the Reagan administration and then was appointed U.S. attorney in New Jersey. President George H. W. Bush named him to the U.S. Court of Appeals for the Third Circuit in 1990. When President George W. Bush in 2005 interviewed Alito for possible appointment to the high court, the president said he had trouble loosening up the judge. Bush, a former owner of the Texas Rangers, turned the conversation to baseball and the Philadelphia Phillies, a known passion of Alito's. "Sam is as reserved as they come," Bush wrote about Alito's seeming so ill at ease. "As we talked about the game, his body language changed." Once on the Court, Alito brought his collection of baseballs to his chambers to display.[31]

The former prosecutor was an enduring law-and-order man who could be counted on to vote against criminal defendants. Succeeding centrist-conservative O'Connor, Alito thrust the Court further right on issues such as religion and abortion. When he drew public attention, it was often inadvertent, and almost inevitably the matter would cast him in an unfavorable light. In 2010, television cameras captured him mouthing "not true" to President Barack Obama's criticism, in his State of the Union address, of the Court's momentous *Citizens United v. Federal Election Commission* campaign finance decision, particularly that it would open the floodgates to special interests and foreign money. The Alito moment went viral on social media. Roberts implicitly expressed some sympathy for his colleague a few weeks later when the chief justice spoke at the University of Alabama and complained about the "political pep rally" atmosphere of the State of the Union. "The image of having the members of one branch of government standing up," Roberts said, "literally surrounding the Supreme

Court, cheering and hollering, while the Court, according to the requirements of protocol, has to sit there expressionless, I think is very troubling." Three years later, in an episode not caught on film but repeated on social media through reporting by journalists' accounts from the courtroom, Alito rolled his eyes and grimaced as Justice Ginsburg read a dissenting opinion to his majority view in a dispute over workplace discrimination. When I spoke to Ginsburg a few weeks later, she said she was not distracted by his expressions, and she remarked lightly, "I'm in such good company. I'm in the company of the president." There seemed to be a "that's just Sam" acceptance of Alito. They were all there for life, and nobody thought they could change the unconventional or difficult characters among them.[32]

Alito was irritated with justices on his left and on his own right flank, especially as Roberts shifted toward the center of the bench. Alito cared little for consensus-building, and he resisted the consideration of factors beyond the law of a case. He chafed at talk of institutional interests and public perceptions of the Court. As more justices whose views were closer to his joined the bench, his conservatism gained greater support. But he increasingly showed frustration, especially on gay marriage and LGBTQ disputes. In a November 2020 speech to the Federalist Society, he argued that the 2015 *Obergefell v. Hodges* decision, which declared a right to same-sex marriage, was infringing the free-speech rights of anti-LGBTQ advocates. "You can't say that marriage is the union between one man and one woman. Until very recently that's what the vast majority of Americans thought. Now, it's considered bigotry," he declared. A few weeks earlier, Alito had joined Thomas in a statement in the case of a Kentucky county clerk who refused to give marriage licenses to gay couples. Clerk Kim Davis had declined the licenses based on her Christian religious objections. She was held in contempt of court and briefly jailed. Alito and Thomas agreed with the majority of justices that Davis's appeal should not be taken up, but they insisted in a statement that Davis had become "one of the first victims of this Court's cavalier treatment of religion in its Obergefell decision, but she will not be the last."[33]

Alito believed that religious freedom was under siege. In the address to the Federalist Society in late 2020 during the COVID-19 lockdowns, he asserted, "The pandemic has resulted in previously unimaginable restrictions on individual liberty," and he highlighted the consequences for "churches closed on Easter Sunday, synagogues closed for Passover and Yom Kippur." Alito protested that he was not minimizing the death toll of the coronavirus or commenting on "the legality" of pandemic-era rules, but he nonetheless emphasized, "We have never before seen restrictions as severe, extensive and prolonged as those experienced for most of 2020." He brought up his prior concerns about agency regulation, which he called "lawmaking by executive fiat rather than legislation," and declared: "The Covid crisis has served as a sort of constitutional stress test and in doing so, it has highlighted disturbing trends that were already present before the virus struck." Alito spent much of the early months of the pandemic away from the Court building, working remotely from his second home on the New Jersey shore.[34]

Through virtually all of the Trump presidency, the senior liberal was Ruth Bader Ginsburg. Born in 1933, a generation before Roberts, she was reared in Brooklyn, where her father was a furrier and then a haberdasher and her mother a homemaker. Her older sister died of meningitis before Ruth was two years old. Her mother died of cervical cancer just before her surviving daughter's high school graduation. An academic standout, Ginsburg attended Cornell and then Harvard Law School, one of only nine women in a class of five hundred, completing her degree at Columbia Law School. Her decision to leave Harvard was provoked by a desire to be in New York City with her husband, Martin, who had finished Harvard Law a year ahead of her. Her first teaching position was at Rutgers; eventually she returned to Columbia. She helped establish the American Civil Liberties Union Women's Rights Project and developed a signature strategy of using male plaintiffs to challenge sex discrimination and sex-based policies. She won, for example, invalidation of a federal Social Security rule that allowed benefits for children who had lost a father but not a mother, using the widowed Stephen Wiesenfeld.[35]

President Jimmy Carter named Ginsburg to the U.S. Court of

Appeals for the District of Columbia Circuit in 1979. As a New Yorker, she would have preferred an appointment to the New York–based U.S. appellate court, but Carter's staff never seriously considered her for the Second Circuit. A D.C. Circuit opportunity arose when Judge Harold Leventhal, sixty-four, suffered a fatal heart attack. Carter had just enough time left in office to push through Ginsburg's nomination. "He was playing tennis," Ginsburg recalled years later of Leventhal's untimely death and the sudden judicial opportunity. "Who could have predicted that?"[36]

On the D.C. Circuit, Ginsburg befriended Scalia, who served on that bench from 1982 to 1986. Both former law professors with an exacting sense of language, they exchanged drafts of each other's opinions for editing. They delighted in each other's company on theater outings and trips abroad. Ginsburg differed from Scalia in personality and on the law. She had a modest demeanor. She kept her hair pulled back in a small ponytail and wore large-rimmed glasses. She was diminutive and delicate-looking even on her strongest days at a courtroom lectern. In 1993, President Bill Clinton chose Ginsburg for elevation to the high court. She became the second woman justice, following Reagan's appointment of Sandra Day O'Connor in 1981.

By the Trump years, Ginsburg had gained improbable pop culture status as the "Notorious RBG," a twist on the name of the late rapper Notorious B.I.G. Shy and reserved, Ginsburg nonetheless relished her newfound fame, generated by her attention-grabbing dissent in *Shelby County v. Holder*. "A second-year student at NYU Law School [Shana Knizhnik] started the Notorious RBG as a Tumblr," Ginsburg told NBC in a televised interview in 2017. "This young woman was, to put it mildly, disappointed by the Supreme Court's decision in the Shelby County case, the decision that held a key part of the Voting Rights Act of 1965 no longer constitutional." *Saturday Night Live* featured actress Kate McKinnon as the black-robed justice in what became a long-running "Ginsburn" parody, torching her male colleagues, who, Ginsburg quipped, "are judiciously silent about the Notorious RBG." At the Court, she was known for her intense work habits, which included showing up on the bench the day after the

June 2020 death of her husband, Martin, to announce one of the final decisions of the annual session.[37]

Ginsburg had not fathomed Donald Trump winning the presidency. "He's a faker," she told me in an interview in her chambers during the summer of 2016. "He has no consistency about him. He says whatever comes into his head at the moment. He really has an ego." After Ginsburg's comments were published, candidate Trump declared on Twitter: "Her mind is shot." He said she should step down. Some of Ginsburg's usual supporters briefly turned against her. "Washington is more than partisan enough without the spectacle of a Supreme Court justice flinging herself into the mosh pit," the *New York Times* said in an editorial. Ginsburg soon issued a statement: "On reflection, my recent remarks in response to press inquiries were ill-advised and I regret making them. Judges should avoid commenting on a candidate for public office. In the future I will be more circumspect."[38]

On the morning after Trump's November 8 election, when the eight Supreme Court justices gathered in a private robing room before they ascended the bench for oral arguments, Ginsburg wore a collar that she usually reserved for days when she took the rare step of reading excerpts of her dissenting opinion from the bench. The collar was black with small silver crystal accents. A few weeks later, she did not hesitate to mock President-Elect Trump and other conservatives in a personalized role with the Washington National Opera. She appeared in Gaetano Donizetti's *The Daughter of the Regiment,* as the Duchess of Krakenthorp. (Ginsburg, an opera buff, had on a few earlier occasions dressed in costume and appeared briefly onstage in Kennedy Center productions.)[39] She amended her part in the Krakenthorp script to include a reference to a fruitless quest for a birth certificate, ridiculing Trump's groundless claim about Barack Obama lacking a U.S. birth certificate. Appearing in the nonsinging role for one night only, Ginsburg declared that the best leaders have "open but not empty minds" and are "willing to listen and learn." She said it was no surprise, then, that "the most valorous Krakenthorpians have been women." The audience ate it up. Ginsburg also managed to squeeze in a variation on a line from her *Shelby County v. Holder* dissent: "Dropping traditions that have worked and continue to work is like throwing away your umbrella in a rainstorm because you are not getting wet," she said. There was nothing subtle about her frustration with the turn of events.[40]

With Trump's election, Ginsburg, who turned eighty-three in 2016 and had survived two serious cancer ordeals, had a new trial. She wanted to stay on the bench at least four more years, through Trump's presidency. Ginsburg had resisted pressure from fellow liberals to leave office earlier in Obama's tenure when he had a Democratic Senate and might have easily gotten a successor through. Even under better political circumstances, she believed Obama could not have won confirmation of a liberal in her mold. "So tell me who the president could have nominated this spring that you would rather see on the Court than me?" she asked me rhetorically during a 2014 interview.[41]

Stephen Breyer, Bill Clinton's second appointee, joined the bench in 1994. Raised in San Francisco, he was the son of a lawyer who served as counsel to the San Francisco school district. As a justice, Breyer wore the Omega Seamaster wristwatch the school board had given his father upon retirement. He had one sibling, a brother, Charles, who became a U.S. district court judge in San Francisco. Breyer attended Stanford University and Harvard Law School, earning a Supreme Court clerkship with Justice Arthur Goldberg.

Breyer exuded the air of the preoccupied professor he once was. He had taught full time at Harvard Law School before becoming a U.S. appellate judge and then a Supreme Court justice. He filled the shelves of his chambers with antique books on philosophy that he had inherited from an uncle. In contrast to his colleagues' tidy offices, Breyer's was piled with books and papers. It was not unusual to see his suit jacket and open books on the couch. Chairs were filled, too. An assistant bringing in tea for the justice and a guest would sometimes have to teeter it atop books stacked on the coffee table.

Breyer's general air of seeming obliviousness masked a strategic interest in compromise to keep the Court from pulling too far to the right. A Senate Judiciary Committee staffer after he clerked for Justice Goldberg and taught full time at Harvard, he had witnessed the art of negotiation. He constantly repeated a mantra of Massachusetts senator Ted Kennedy, whom he had worked alongside in the late 1970s and early 1980s as counsel to the U.S. Senate Committee on the Judiciary, about sharing credit to achieve goals. Breyer made it a practice to drop in on colleagues at the Court to talk out differences. "That is why I don't like dissents," he said. "A dissent is a failure."[42]

One of Breyer's most notable opinions, however, was a 2007 dissent in a Seattle school district dispute. Roberts had declared in the case that schools could not consider a student's race in the effort to integrate districts, and that "the way to stop discrimination on the basis of race is to stop discriminating on the basis of race." Breyer was concerned that prohibiting such racial policies could lead to resegregation, compromising the promise of 1954's *Brown v. Board of Education:* "This is a decision that the Court and the Nation will come to regret," he wrote in *Parents Involved in Community Schools v. Seattle School District No. 1.*[43]

On the left with Ginsburg and Breyer were the Obama appointees Sonia Sotomayor and Elena Kagan. Sotomayor was the justice most willing to directly challenge the Trump administration. In the courtroom, where Trump's positions were formally presented and rinsed of their incendiary tone, she refused to look past the president's denigration of racial minorities and immigrants. She also questioned Trump's policy switches, which the conservative justices disregarded, in contrast to their approach with the Obama administration. The U.S. solicitor general is in the position to defend such about-faces. During the early months of the tenure of Solicitor General Noel Francisco—whom one writer described as "one of the lesser-known figures in the slow shaping, or reshaping, of the rule of law to the whims of a president who never cared much for it"—Justice Sotomayor asked, "Mr. General, by the way, how many times this term already have you flipped positions from prior administrations?"[44]

Sotomayor grew up in a Bronx housing project, the daughter of parents from Puerto Rico. She won scholarships to Princeton University and Yale Law School. Sotomayor often spoke of the beautiful white coat her mother bought her as she left for college. It inspired her to feel that she could fit in and succeed, and she wore it until it was practically in tatters. After law school, she worked as a prosecutor in Manhattan and eventually earned appointment to a federal district court (nominated by President George H. W. Bush) and U.S. appellate court (by President Clinton). She came to the bench more experienced than most appointees because of that combined trial judge (1992–1998) and appellate judge (1998–2009) experience.

Soon after she became a justice, Sotomayor wrote a bestselling memoir focused on her family's roots, *My Beloved World,* for which her advance exceeded $3 million. The Trump era caused her to amplify her voice and call attention to racial prejudice. She spoke, often alone among the justices, on behalf of criminal defendants, those facing execution, and undocumented immigrants. The way the Court was headed, this uncompromising liberal could have been penning dissents every week, but Sotomayor picked her battles.[45]

For her chambers, Sotomayor settled into an airy suite one floor up from the other justices, who occupied the main floor of the Court building. (Ginsburg had previously held the chambers, which were more spacious than the other suites and offered a prime setting for contemporary decor and more room for law clerks. Ginsburg had moved down to chambers that had been vacated by David Souter in 2009 and newly renovated.) Sotomayor filled her space with modern Latino art, along with photos taken in September 2009, when she threw out the first pitch for the Yankees, and from multiple appearances on *Sesame Street.* On the popular PBS children's show, she modeled how to solve disputes, demonstrated the virtues of helping others, and talked about her Puerto Rican identity.

Sotomayor's fellow justices sometimes brushed off her racial emphasis, and Roberts was explicit about it. In 2014, Sotomayor put her personal sentiments on the line in a Michigan dispute testing a state ban on racial affirmative action at public universities and other programs, writing, "Race matters because of the slights, the snickers, the silent judgments that reinforce that most crippling of thoughts: 'I do not belong here.'" Turning what had become one of Roberts's perhaps best-known adages about race against him, she wrote, "The way to stop discrimination on the basis of race is to speak openly and candidly on the subject of race." Roberts responded by criticizing her for "expounding . . . policy preferences," saying that it "does more harm than good to question the openness and candor of those on either side of the debate." Sotomayor refused to stop questioning the candor of her colleagues.[46]

Appointed the year after Sotomayor, Justice Kagan, a former Harvard Law School dean and U.S. solicitor general, was uniquely prepared to navigate the Trump era. She was the junior justice when Trump took office but had already begun exerting outsize influence. She was receptive to negotiations with Roberts and compromises that would blunt the force of the conservative majority. Kagan understood how weak the liberals' hand was but felt they had some bargaining power given Roberts's effort to avoid as many 5–4, ideologically divided rulings as possible. She believed it important to close the divide when possible, saying, "I definitely do not think compromise is a dirty word."[47]

The only daughter (with two brothers) of a schoolteacher mother and lawyer father, Kagan attended Hunter College High School in Manhattan. In one yearbook photo, she wore a black robe and carried a gavel, demonstrating her judicial aspirations. She went to Princeton, then Harvard Law, and served as a clerk to Justice Thurgood Marshall, returning to Harvard Law School as its dean. A New York intellectual with a down-to-earth manner, she played poker and followed the latest in movies, comics, and all manner of pop culture.

Like Roberts, Kagan had extensive executive branch experience, hers dating to the Clinton administration. President Obama appointed her U.S. solicitor general when he took office in 2009. Kagan was the first woman ever to hold the post. She came with no appellate background, scant experience as a litigator, even, but with sufficient political skills to land the post. The first case she argued in any court was *Citizens United,* the decision that gave rise to Alito's viral "not true" at the State of the Union. The government was bound to lose, given the justices' decision to aggressively broaden the scope of the case and reexamine campaign-regulation precedent after an initial hearing. The government did lose, although Kagan earned favorable reviews for her arguments and ability to spar with justices. ("Kagan is so loose and relaxed, you'd think this was her 100th argument," Dahlia Lithwick wrote on Slate.)[48]

Kagan developed a natural kinship with Ginsburg. She also befriended Scalia, her opposite in the law but a self-assured New York soulmate. (Scalia grew up in Queens.) Kagan began hunting with him. "I shot myself a deer," she said in a 2013 onstage interview at the Aspen Ideas Festival. Kagan explained why she and Scalia became hunting partners. "You know the NRA [National Rifle Association] has become quite a presence in judicial confirmations, and that means . . . both Republicans and Democrats ask you about your views on the Second Amendment." She said senators wanted to know whether she had ever gone hunting, held a gun, or known anyone who had gone hunting. Kagan, who grew up on Manhattan's Upper West Side, acknowledged she was in unfamiliar territory and said she told one senator that if he invited her hunting, she would go. She immediately thought the better of it: "This look of total horror passed over his face. You know, 'Has this woman just invited herself hunting with me?' And I thought, I've gone too far . . . I said, 'I didn't really mean to invite myself, but I'll tell you what, if I'm lucky enough to be confirmed, I will ask Justice Scalia to take me hunting.'"[49]

Kagan showed more of her humor at her confirmation hearing, in a memorable exchange with Senator Lindsey Graham, who tried to draw her out on a suspect charged in an al-Qaeda bomb plot. The bomber had attempted to set off explosives concealed within his underwear on a Northwest Airlines flight from Amsterdam to Detroit on Christmas Day 2009. When Graham, a Republican from South Carolina, raised the incident, Kagan declined to comment on the pending case. Graham said all he wanted to know was "where you were at on Christmas." Kagan shot back, "Like all Jews, I was probably at a Chinese restaurant."[50]

At the Supreme Court, Kagan worked in an airy office with floor-to-ceiling bookcases, a standing desk, and little clutter. A case during her first session showed that she was ready to joust with Roberts. The chief justice had gained a narrow majority to strike down an Arizona law that provided public financing to candidates who agreed to limit their private spending in a campaign. He rejected the state's arguments that it was trying to fight political corruption. He pointed to evidence that he said revealed the state's true intentions, what Kagan termed in her dissent to be his purported "smoking guns." Added Kagan, "The only smoke here is the majority's, and it is the kind that goes with mirrors."[51]

But Kagan also collaborated with Roberts where possible to mute the force of the right wing. Perhaps because she and Sotomayor joined the Court within a year of each other and were both Obama appointees, their respective approaches were often debated by law professors and other outside legal observers: Sotomayor's go-it-alone style with emphatic dissents versus Kagan's collaborative, transactional mindset.

An example of their differences and the broader divisions surfaced in a religious rights case, *Trinity Lutheran Church of Columbia v. Comer*, argued shortly after Justice Gorsuch's appointment in the spring of 2017. It emerged as the administration's new secretary of education, Betsy DeVos, wanted to funnel more public funding to religious schools. Part of an affluent, politically powerful Michigan family that promoted conservative Christian causes, DeVos was a supporter of school choice and voucher programs. She became one of Trump's most controversial cabinet choices and had won confirmation only after Vice President Pence took the chair in the Senate and cast the tie-breaking vote.

This major test of First Amendment religious free exercise arose from an otherwise unremarkable Missouri Scrap Tire Program. It was set up to reduce the number of tires in landfills and simultaneously to improve playground surfaces and prevent injuries to children by replacing gravel with material from recycled tires. At the time of the controversy, Missouri and more than thirty other states prohibited the public funding of churches, synagogues, and other places of worship. State officials had rejected Trinity Lutheran Church's application for a grant to replace its pea gravel.

Trinity Lutheran sued, contending that its exclusion from the scrap-tire program violated its First Amendment free exercise rights.

The Missouri supreme court ruled against the church, which appealed to the U.S. Supreme Court. Roberts had a majority among the conservatives to reverse the state court, but he wanted to avoid a 5–4 opinion split along predictable ideological lines.[52]

Kagan was open to compromise and during internal negotiations let Roberts know she would sign a narrow decision. It was a way to slow the conservatives' interest in allowing—even compelling—public funding for religious schools. Roberts limited his legal rationale and added a footnote that suggested the ruling applied only to school playgrounds. The chief drew a line between the church's religious status and possible religious use, declaring that the state had excluded Trinity Lutheran from its program based purely on religious status. Kagan joined Roberts's opinion and wrote no separate statement to put a different gloss on the matter. The only other justices who agreed unreservedly with the Roberts approach were Kennedy and Alito. Breyer concurred in the judgment and wrote that he regarded the Missouri state grant as "a general program designed to secure or to improve the health and safety of children."[53]

Justices Gorsuch and Thomas, alternatively, wanted to go further. To them, Roberts's distinction between religious status and religious use made no sense. "Respectfully, I harbor doubts about the stability of such a line," Gorsuch wrote in a concurrence, joined by Thomas. "Does a religious man say grace before dinner? Or does a man begin his meal in a religious manner? Is it a religious group that built the playground? Or did a group build the playground so it might be used to advance a religious mission?"

Justices Sotomayor and Ginsburg would have none of any middle ground and emphasized that past cases had allowed states to withhold public money from houses of worship. Sotomayor predicted that the decision would likely lead to greater public funding of religion. Education Secretary DeVos declared that the *Trinity Lutheran* ruling "marks a great day for the Constitution."[54] There was little to stop the Trump administration from expanding the reach of the decision. And the Roberts Court itself continued to rule for religious adherents, especially favoring Christians.[55]

The high court majority had already been headed in this direction, but the Trump administration hastened the pattern. And it was not without some cost: mixing church and state, siphoning funds from public education, undermining LGBTQ rights, and reducing access to health care. The Supreme Court had already exempted certain corporate employers from the Affordable Care Act's requirement of birth control coverage for employees, based on corporate owners' religious objections. The Trump administration expanded the exemptions.[56]

*Trinity Lutheran* also offered a glimpse into the trade-offs the justices undertook behind closed doors, even as they abhorred suggestions that they engaged in deals or horse-trading. Sometimes such arrangements made a difference at the margins; sometimes they changed the outcome, as documented in the 2012 *National Federation of Independent Business v. Sebelius* (Affordable Care Act) and the 2013 *Fisher v. University of Texas at Austin* (racial affirmative action) cases. The latter twice came to the Supreme Court on appeal.[57]

The justices necessarily collaborate to produce a decision, and negotiations have many dimensions, from minor concessions over points of legal reasoning or language to more significant pacts. They were all lawyers, accustomed to working with pen and paper, and most of the negotiations occurred through memos. But on occasion, they would pick up the phone to talk out an idea, or cross the halls to buttonhole a colleague in chambers. Generally, all justices were to receive copies of memos between individuals bargaining over the language of an opinion, so that all nine could keep track of the state of play. But sometimes pairs broke off with private discussions, before looping in the group.

I learned of a subtle understanding between Roberts and Kennedy in June 2017, when the Court handled two gay rights cases in tandem. *Masterpiece Cakeshop v. Colorado Civil Rights Commission* was brought by a baker, Jack Phillips, who had been sanctioned for refusing to create a cake for two gay men celebrating their marriage. *Pavan v. Smith* involved an Arkansas Department of Health policy dictating that a birth certificate be issued only with the birth mother's name if there was no male partner. That meant that in situations involving lesbian couples, a second woman would not be listed. The lead couple in the case, Terrah and Marisa Pavan, had married in New Hampshire in 2011 and four years later had a child in Arkansas through a sperm donation. The two disputes presented the first major gay rights controversies after 2015's *Obergefell v. Hodges*, in which a five-justice majority had declared a fundamental right to same-sex marriage. Kennedy had written that decision. Roberts had dissented and was so opposed to the majority's ruling that he took the occasion to deliver his first and only dissenting statement from the bench.

Kennedy and the four liberal justices who had composed the majority in *Obergefell*—Ginsburg, Breyer, Sotomayor, and Kagan—wanted to reverse the Arkansas state court, based on *Obergefell*'s protections for same-sex couples, and they believed the matter straightforward enough to be done through a summary reversal opinion. Under a private court rule, however, such action required six votes, not the usual majority of five. (Thomas and Alito, who had dissented in *Obergefell*, would not agree to an out-and-out reversal of the Arkansas court decision, and Gorsuch, who had just joined the bench, felt the same way.) Separately, Kennedy was reluctant to take up the baker's case. I learned that he'd previously told colleagues he was skeptical of religious exemptions for retailers who would deny services to gay people. So the baker's petition languished, as Alito worked on a testy dissenting opinion from the justices' initial vote to deny it. Yet, Alito's dissent, circulated to his colleagues and described to me by Court sources, never saw the light of day, because the justices eventually decided to hear the baker's claim of religious discrimination.

Roberts had not wanted to take up the case without some confidence that Kennedy was receptive to the religious discrimination claim, and in time they reached a mutual understanding for both cases. Roberts quietly, with no public record, provided the requisite sixth vote in *Pavan*, ensuring that lesbian parents in Arkansas could be jointly named on their children's birth certificates, and Kennedy dropped his resistance to the *Masterpiece Cakeshop* petition.

The justices' public action in both cases was deliberately announced on the same day, June 26, 2017. That reflected a pattern of Roberts's.

The acceptance of an appeal from a baker who had refused to create a cake for a gay couple could easily have led to a perception of new Supreme Court hostility toward gay rights. The action in the *Pavan* case, reversing the Arkansas supreme court's birth-certificate ruling, at least in the moment, countered that perception.[58]

The *Masterpiece Cakeshop* appeal was scheduled for full review later in 2017. During those oral arguments, Kennedy continued to be torn, and the Supreme Court in the end declined to decide whether a business has a First Amendment free exercise right to discriminate against LGBTQ customers. Kennedy wrote the opinion, which reflected the tentativeness he'd had in the first place: "The outcome of cases like this in other circumstances," he said, "must await further elaboration in the courts, all in the context of recognizing that these disputes must be resolved with tolerance, without undue disrespect to sincere religious beliefs, and without subjecting gay persons to indignities when they seek goods and services in an open market." Ginsburg and Sotomayor were the only dissenters, homing in on the bias the gay men faced: "What matters," Ginsburg wrote regarding the baker, "is that Phillips would not provide a good or service to a same-sex couple that he would provide to a heterosexual couple."[59]

Justices are loath to discuss what happens behind closed doors. In a few rare situations, however, a justice who suddenly finds himself or herself on the losing side cannot help but hint publicly at the convoluted negotiations. The dispute over racial affirmative action from the University of Texas at Austin took several turns over two separate rounds of consideration lasting four years. I learned that Sotomayor had written a blistering draft dissent that—after privately circulated to her colleagues—forced the majority to hold off on reconsidering and rejecting race-based admissions at the University of Texas. When the Court eventually resolved the case three years later, in June 2016, the majority upheld the affirmative action program and dissenting Justice Alito wrote, "Something strange has happened since our prior decision in this case." But neither he nor any other justice publicly referred to Sotomayor's actions behind the scenes.[60]

I have discovered over the decades that in many instances, law clerks know about a pact struck between justices. In other situations, only the two justices involved truly know. Sometimes, various chambers have dueling accounts of what happened. And here is the most consistent obstacle to ferreting out a questionable vote or a switch at a place of such secrecy: even individual justices are not quite sure why a colleague voted the way he or she did. When I learned that Roberts had switched two different votes in the 2012 controversy over the Affordable Care Act (on the individual mandate and on the Medicaid expansion), there were almost as many inside explanations as justices.

Internal dealmaking can usually be documented only years later, after the archives of deceased justices become public. (Not all justices release their Court files; among the most illuminating since the 1990s have been the archives of William Brennan, Thurgood Marshall, Harry Blackmun, and Lewis Powell.) In Brennan's files at the Library of Congress are his personal case histories, essentially a narrated window into negotiations. In one set he recounts internal debate leading up to the Court's landmark opinion in the 1978 *Regents of the University of California v. Bakke* case, particularly how he tried to lay the groundwork for a decision favoring race-based admissions policies and a concession he made to woo Blackmun. Other justices' papers, including those of Marshall, the first Black justice, reveal the passions the case inspired among the nine. The *Bakke* decision became the touchstone for diversity in higher education and survived numerous challenges over the decades. Its fate was newly in doubt as conservatives in late 2022 revisited the 1978 precedent in two cases, involving Harvard and the University of North Carolina.[61]

The negotiations in the original dispute shed light on the stakes and the inner workings of the Court. As the liberal Brennan began preparing for the dispute initiated by Allan Bakke, a white student rejected from the UC Davis medical school who argued that racial quotas had kept him out of the program, he wrote, "I soon discovered that several of my Brethren were already deeply immersed in Bakke and that at least one was already involved in preliminary maneuvering." Marshall was trying to figure out a way "to get rid of the case," fearing adverse votes among their four Nixon-appointed colleagues, Chief Justice

Burger and Justices Blackmun, Powell, and Rehnquist. "I told TM . . . I simply could not be a party to any such action [to dismiss the case] and that I would prefer losing on the merits to seeing the Court once again avoid decision of this issue after having granted cert. In any case, I did not then share TM's pessimism."[62]

Brennan recounted that as he tried to persuade the wavering Blackmun to favor the use of race in admissions, Blackmun wanted something from him in an unrelated case that was yet to be assigned. When the chief justice is in the majority, he has the power to decide who will write the opinion for the court. But when he is in dissent, the senior justice in the majority has the assignment power. That would often fall to senior liberal Brennan, and he sometimes used it for leverage. "During the week prior to the special conference" for the *Bakke* case, Brennan wrote, referring to Blackmun by his initials,

> I found myself in a position to assign the Court opinion in Franks v. Delaware, in which the Court had voted to overrule the longstanding rule that a court cannot look beyond the 'four corners' of a search warrant in determining whether a search satisfied the Fourth Amendment. HAB approached me immediately after Conference and . . . ask[ed] me for the assignment. His request caused me great difficulty. Thus far this term, HAB had, in my view, mishandled the court opinions in [two separate cases]. . . . But, on the other hand, I recognized that, if I irritated him on the eve of the Bakke conference, I risked losing his vote. So in the end I relented, to the consternation of my clerks. HAB, however, was delighted.

Resolution of *Bakke* eventually came down to a splintered 5–4 decision, with Powell casting the crucial vote and writing the main opinion to allow the use of race in admissions (with other criteria) for campus diversity but to forbid quotas. Blackmun joined Brennan's separate opinion seeking to go further to endorse the UC Davis medical school program.[63]

It is unlikely Brennan would have acknowledged the inside tactics at the time. He was outraged a year later when the authors of the 1979 book *The Brethren,* Bob Woodward and Scott Armstrong, portrayed him as trading a vote to the detriment of a criminal defendant. Woodward and Armstrong wrote that Brennan cast a vote that compromised his true position in a case to attract Blackmun on separate pending abortion and free speech cases. The *New York Times* columnist Anthony Lewis, a friend of Brennan's, set out to disprove the account.[64]

Publication of *The Brethren* had rattled the high court world with its tales of how the nine operated. Chief Justice Burger was portrayed as overbearing, surrounded by eight associate justices who operated based on their own egos and interests. The book became a reference point for anyone delving into the world of the Burger Court (1969–1986), including a young John Roberts. After graduating from Harvard Law School and serving as a law clerk to U.S. appellate judge Henry Friendly in New York, Roberts was working for then–associate justice Rehnquist and wrote to Judge Friendly, "Nothing that I have witnessed suggests that there will be any lessening of the divisions on the Court this term. But I was pleased to see that the rumors of personal animosity and pettiness circulating in the wake of *The Brethren* do not seem to have any substance."[65]

Rehnquist, it turned out, was one of the justices who had privately assisted Woodward and Armstrong. Brennan had declined to meet with the authors. Much of their information, however, came from law clerks, and Woodward and Armstrong said clerks had related the story that involved Brennan's supposed vote-trading. The *New York Times'* Anthony Lewis was convinced that Woodward and Armstrong had contrived the episode about a 1972 Illinois murder case, *Moore v. Illinois.* In that case, Lyman "Slick" Moore contended that he had been wrongly convicted in the murder of a bartender in Lansing, Illinois. He said the prosecutors had failed to disclose evidence that would have helped his defense and that the case had been mishandled in other ways. The Illinois Supreme Court had rejected Moore's claims. A Supreme Court majority in June 1972 affirmed the state court ruling and spurned Moore's request for a new trial.[66]

According to Woodward and Armstrong, the initial vote among

the justices in their private conference was 7–2 to uphold Moore's conviction; but once Marshall sent around a draft of his dissent, he convinced two other justices to switch to his side. That meant that Marshall needed only one more vote to gain a majority and rule for Moore. This is when the action of Brennan, a close ally of Marshall, became important. "One of Brennan's clerks thought that if Brennan had seen the facts as Marshall presented them, he would not have voted the other way," Woodward and Armstrong wrote. They said that the law clerk talked to Brennan and returned to his fellow clerks looking "shaken." The clerk said, according to *The Brethren*'s account, that Brennan understood that Marshall's position was correct, but he was not going to switch sides. "Brennan felt that if he voted against Blackmun now," the authors wrote, "it might make it more difficult to reach him in the abortion cases or even the obscenity cases."[67]

Lewis wrote a disparaging review of *The Brethren* for the *New York Review of Books*, questioning the truth of the *Moore v. Illinois* scenario.[68] Woodward and Armstrong stood by their narrative. For his part, Justice Brennan privately expressed dismay to Lewis regarding his portrayal in the book. "Cases have never been fungible goods for me," Brennan wrote in a January 14, 1980, letter to Lewis. "The vote in each has been considered in good faith on its own merits. I have been a judge for thirty-one years and have cast votes in over 100,000 cases. I find it unreal that I should have to affirm that I have never cast a vote against my conscience."[69]

The episode faded. The authors moved on. But the accounts revealed the fraught context for anyone trying to figure out what happened behind closed doors. Beginning in 2017, the pressure of Trump added another dimension, and a paradox, to justices who shuddered at the suggestion of dealmaking: some internal pacts were made precisely to avoid a look of politics. Justices declined cases, delayed cases, or made compromises to avoid 5–4 conservative-liberal, Republican-Democratic splits. To some justices, that breached the integrity of the bench. To others, it was the only way to avoid the partisan abyss.

## Chapter 3

---

## "JOINING US FOR TONIGHT'S CEREMONY IS EVERY SITTING SUPREME COURT JUSTICE"

The young woman known to the courts only as Jane Doe ran away from her Central American home in 2017. She traveled up through Mexico and across the southern U.S. border into Texas. When U.S. border agents captured her, she was seventeen years old and eight weeks pregnant. They brought her to a federal shelter in Brownsville. Alone, without family support, she wanted to end her pregnancy, but the new Trump administration had just changed policies to try to prevent refugees from obtaining abortions. The shelter staff brought Jane Doe to a religious, antiabortion pregnancy crisis center and forced her to cancel appointments related to an abortion. Jane Doe's legal odyssey to exercise her rights soon reached the Supreme Court, in October 2017. First, however, her case was handled by lower-court judges, including Brett Kavanaugh, then sitting on the U.S. Court of Appeals for the District of Columbia Circuit. He wrote an opinion siding with the Trump administration and disregarding precedent. Democratic critics said it also showed him to be "auditioning" for Supreme Court selection. During Trump's presidential run, Trump had proclaimed his opposition to *Roe v. Wade*, the 1973 decision that made abortion legal nationwide. "I am putting pro-life justices on the Court," the candidate said in an October 2016 debate, suggesting that reversal of *Roe* was the goal. "That'll happen automatically, in my opinion," when appointees took their seats, he said. "It will go back to the states, and the states will then make a determination."[1]

In Texas, as in many states, minors needed the permission of a parent or guardian to obtain an abortion. Jane Doe was alone, so Rochelle Garza, a lawyer who specialized in cases involving children and immigrants, was designated to represent her in a state court proceeding. "I will never forget meeting Jane for the first time," Garza later testified. "She was a petite seventeen-year-old. But as I quickly learned, no one should underestimate her. Her resolve was strong, and she was very certain about her decision to terminate her pregnancy." Garza said that Doe had fled physical abuse by her parents. She said that when an older sister became pregnant, their parents beat her until she miscarried.[2] A Texas state court judge hearing the case said that Doe should be allowed to obtain an abortion. But the Office of Refugee Resettlement (ORR) staff at the Brownsville shelter refused to let her follow through with the medical appointment she and Garza had arranged. The ORR was part of the Department of Health and Human Services, and the staff was abiding by a new prohibition against any action, taken without the approval of the ORR director, "that facilitates an abortion." At the crisis pregnancy center, she was discouraged from ending her pregnancy. The center staff performed an ultrasound so she could see the fetus. "People I do not even know are trying to make me change my mind," Doe said later. "I made my decision, and that is between me and God." She wanted an abortion.[3]

Lawyers from the American Civil Liberties Union took the case to a federal court judge, saying that Doe's situation was not an isolated one and noting that many minors who crossed the border alone were pregnant, sometimes victims of rape.[4] Doe would become part of an ACLU class action lawsuit certified the following year, brought on behalf of young pregnant women held in federal shelters, but in fall 2017, her case constituted the first major test of the Trump anti-abortion agenda. The administration was also trying to end a federal requirement that employers provide birth-control coverage under the Affordable Care Act and was separately taking steps to withdraw federal funding of Planned Parenthood. These actions, like those by the Trump team against gay rights, were made in the name of religion. As the ORR was preventing Jane Doe from obtaining an abortion, Trump told a Values Voter Summit in Washington, "I pledged that, in a Trump administration, our nation's religious heritage would be cherished, protected, and defended like you have never seen. . . . We are stopping cold the attacks on Judeo-Christian values." Religious conservatives were heartened by Trump's declaration, but there was no evidence that Judeo-Christian values were broadly under attack in government programs.[5]

The Supreme Court had in earlier cases considered how judges should respond when a minor wanted to make an abortion decision on her own, without a parent who might try to prevent her from ending the pregnancy.[6] The justices had ruled that the government must provide a way for the minor to avoid asking permission but ensure that she was mature enough to make the decision on her own. Under what became known as a "judicial bypass" alternative, minors could turn to a judge and offer reasons for seeking an abortion. Jane Doe had received the requisite permission from the Texas state court judge.

In response to the ACLU filing, Justice Department lawyers representing the ORR countered that the federal government had its own set of interests that would be undermined if a federal judge intervened: "The government has strong and constitutionally legitimate interests in promoting childbirth, in refusing to facilitate abortion, and in not providing incentives for pregnant minors to illegally cross the border to obtain elective abortions while in federal custody." Because the administration could not outright prevent the young woman from exercising her right to abortion, it was arguing that it could force her, under refugee-resettlement policy, to first find a sponsor to guide her decisions related to the pregnancy.[7]

U.S. district court judge Tanya Chutkan, hearing the first round of the case in Washington, D.C., rejected the Trump administration's position—which essentially came down to "return home to Central America or carry the pregnancy to term"—and ordered the government to permit an abortion. She forbade the government from revealing Jane Doe's desire for an abortion to her mother. But that prohibition came too late, because the shelter staff had already passed word to her mother.[8]

Unlike Judge Chutkan, several men and women on the bench viewed President Trump with an approving eye. They believed his initiatives constitutional and even laudable, and in reinforcing Trump administration policy they were able to lend their own voices to the debate. For Judge Kavanaugh, then on the U.S. appeals court in Washington, D.C., the Jane Doe case offered a chance to assert his narrow interpretation of reproductive rights under the Constitution. When he cast a vote in the controversy over the pregnant minor, he was part of a 2–1 majority that reversed Judge Chutkan's decision to allow Jane Doe an abortion. His panel endorsed the government's view that she first needed to secure a sponsor. Kavanaugh was joined in the order by Judge Karen LeCraft Henderson, an appointee of George H. W. Bush. Henderson wrote a separate concurring statement going further. She said that Jane Doe's migrant status denied her a right to an abortion, a contention that lacked a basis in Supreme Court precedent. But even requiring a sponsor for Doe, as Kavanaugh wanted, would take time, because of the requisite sponsor vetting. The refugee office had already tried without success to find Doe a suitable sponsor. Brigitte Amiri, deputy director of the ACLU's Reproductive Freedom Project, later characterized Kavanaugh's move as "a dishonest punt," forcing a delay that could risk Jane Doe's chance for any abortion in Texas.[9]

Judge Patricia Millett, an appointee of Barack Obama, dissented from the panel's decision, emphasizing the vulnerability of young migrants exposed to abuse, rape, and sexual exploitation. She noted that Jane Doe had fulfilled the Texas requirements of a court determination that she was mature enough to decide for herself whether to continue the pregnancy.[10]

The ACLU, on behalf of Jane Doe, immediately asked for reconsideration by the full D.C. Circuit, sitting "en banc," that is, with all judges, rather than only the usual three-judge panel. Four days later, the court reversed the Kavanaugh panel decision and declared that Jane Doe had the right to an abortion. Kavanaugh's dissent in that second stage of the case was notable for its tone. He declared that the en banc majority's decision had established "a new right for unlawful immigrant minors in U.S. Government detention to obtain immediate abortion on demand."[11]

Jane Doe, in fact, had not asked for "abortion on demand" and was abiding by Texas's restrictions for obtaining the procedure. Nor had the D.C. Circuit majority created any new right. It had not waived the judicial bypass process and other requirements of Texas state law. But Kavanaugh persisted, writing, "The majority's decision represents a radical extension of the Supreme Court's abortion jurisprudence. It is in line with dissents over the years by Justices [William] Brennan, [Thurgood] Marshall, and [Harry] Blackmun, not with the many majority opinions of the Supreme Court that have repeatedly upheld reasonable regulations that do not impose an undue burden on the abortion right recognized by the Supreme Court in *Roe v. Wade*." Kavanaugh noticeably invoked the names of three of the most liberal justices of the late twentieth century, and the reference to a "radical extension of the Supreme Court's abortion jurisprudence" was equally startling. The case came down to whether the Trump administration could force Jane Doe to wait several more weeks for a sponsor (after she had already been cleared by a Texas state judge). Doe was seeking an abortion in a previability period of time. The Kavanaugh panel's position would have pushed her nearer to a point of possible conflict with Texas law, which restricted abortions after twenty weeks of pregnancy.

Judge Millett, in the majority for the full D.C. Circuit decision, wrote of the full court's reversal of the Kavanaugh panel's majority, "Today's decision rights a great constitutional wrong by the government." She observed that the government had put the burden on Jane Doe to extract herself from government custody to exercise her right to abortion, "like some kind of legal Houdini."

The Trump administration began preparing to appeal to the Supreme Court. But an abrupt development changed its course. Before the administration could file its appeal, Jane Doe obtained the abortion, on October 25, the day after the full D.C. Circuit decision. The ACLU announced the action in a news release that day.[12] Justice Department lawyers said they were blindsided. They told the Supreme Court they had not expected Doe to seek the procedure until the next day, October 26, and that they were moving quickly to get the Supreme Court to intervene and block the full D.C. Circuit's ruling.

Administration lawyers asked the Court to discipline the lawyers who had ensured that Jane Doe got the abortion and to wipe the D.C. Circuit decision off the books so it would have no precedential value for other cases. Solicitor General Noel Francisco wrote that the ACLU had engaged in "a deliberate effort to prevent" review. The ACLU called the government's position "extraordinary and baseless."

The nine justices tangled for months over how to resolve the motions. Conservative justices had been outraged by the ACLU's quick action to procure an abortion for Jane Doe, but liberal justices believed that the Trump administration had interfered so significantly in her personal choice that her lawyers would have disserved her if they had waited for the administration's next move. Finally, by June, the justices' tempers had cooled. The Court vacated the D.C. Circuit decision that had favored Garza, saying the case was moot, and the justices declined to impose any sanctions. In the unsigned opinion, the Court said it took the administration's allegations seriously but had to balance several factors: "On the one hand, all attorneys must remain aware of the principle that zealous advocacy does not displace their obligations as officers of the court. . . . [I]t is critical that lawyers and courts alike be able to rely on one another's representations. On the other hand, lawyers also have ethical obligations to their clients and not all communication breakdowns constitute misconduct." The Court said it did not need to resolve the dueling assertions as it addressed whether to vacate the D.C. Circuit decision. The justices agreed to drop their differences, or at least keep them from public view.[13]

A few weeks after the Jane Doe case first went to the Supreme Court, White House counsel McGahn appeared at the Federalist Society's 2017 conference and announced that five names had been added to Trump's list of potential candidates for the Supreme Court. Kavanaugh was one of them, as was Amy Coney Barrett, who had been confirmed for a U.S. appellate court a month earlier. The *New York Times* reported that when McGahn read the names aloud, Kavanaugh's drew the loudest applause. The White House said in a statement, "These additions, like those on the original list released more than a year ago, were selected with input from respected conservative leaders." There was no vacancy. But there was anticipation around what Anthony Kennedy, a Republican appointee, might do, or how long eighty-four-year-old Ruth Bader Ginsburg, a Democratic appointee, might be able to hang on.[14]

Meanwhile, Trump's first choice, Neil Gorsuch, was becoming one of the most prolific and visible new justices, writing separate opinions laying out his views and often chastising his colleagues for what he believed were misguided constitutional interpretations. Gorsuch's rhetorical style drew nearly as much commentary as his opinions. He was fond of suggesting that his colleagues failed to respect the Constitution as he did. "I start with the text of the Constitution," he said during one set of oral arguments, "always a good place to start." A week later, he said, "Maybe we can just for a second talk about the arcane matter, the Constitution."[15] The *New York Times* columnist Linda Greenhouse likened him to "the boy on the playground who snatches the ball out of turn"—"in his colleagues' faces pointing out the error of their ways, his snarky tone oozing disrespect toward those who might, just might, know what they are talking about." Slate's Mark Joseph Stern declared Gorsuch's writing clunky, self-conscious, and downright "terrible." Gorsuch had not always been viewed that way. Adam Liptak, the *Times*' Supreme Court reporter, wrote that Gorsuch "arrived at the Supreme Court last year with a reputation as a fine writer. He promptly lost it."[16]

Gorsuch ignored the criticism and began negotiating a book contract to bring his ideas to a wider audience. Penguin Random House paid him an advance of $225,000 for the book to be entitled *A Republic, If You Can Keep It*. He had taken over Scalia's chambers and, conferring with the late justice's family, decided to keep a large six-point elk head on the wall. Scalia had bagged the elk on one of his hunting trips. Gorsuch moved the head out of his main chambers and into his clerks' office. In his own office, he displayed a bust of his first judicial mentor from Colorado, Justice Byron White, and a portrait of Justice John Marshall Harlan, who had served from 1877 to 1911 and was known as a "great dissenter." Most notably, he dissented when the Court in *Plessy v. Ferguson* (1896) upheld the "separate but equal" doctrine.

On the law, Gorsuch landed securely on the right wing. In one of his most important opinions in his first full year, he wrote the Court's ruling that businesses could prevent workers from banding together in a class action lawsuit for overtime pay and other conditions of employment that were subject to mandatory arbitration agreements. The controversy involved overlapping provisions of the National Labor Relations Act (1935) and the Federal Arbitration Act, from ten years earlier. The former gave workers a right to engage in "concerted activity" and to join unions for their mutual protection; the latter was intended to free businesses of the pressure and cost of court proceedings. Gorsuch wrote that arbitration agreements must be enforced as written, even if they were a condition of employment and undermined the usual labor protections.[17] He emphasized that the disputed arbitration contracts that prohibited collective proceedings had been signed in good faith and voluntarily. The four liberal justices, who believed employees had little choice but to sign if they wanted to secure a job, asserted that the majority had wrongly diminished workers' rights in favor of management. Ginsburg declared that the Court had retrenched on eighty years of federal labor law. "Nothing compels the destructive result the court reaches today," she said, adding that the case could take the country back to the early–twentieth century era of "yellow dog" contracts that prevented workers from joining labor unions.

As the justices were getting accustomed to Gorsuch, Justice Kennedy, who had joined the Court in 1988, was moving to the periphery. As Kennedy finished his thirtieth year, he was growing weary. He was speaking less at oral arguments, and when he did, he sometimes became irritable. He barely hid his impatience with the lawyers in *Janus v. American Federation of State, County, and Municipal Employees,* an important labor union case concerning the constitutionality of "fair-share" fees that allowed public-sector unions to obtain fees from nonunion members for collective bargaining. He derided such union-state partnerships, which he said created "a greater size workforce, against privatization, against merit promotion, for teacher tenure, for higher wages, for massive government, for increasing bonded indebtedness, for increasing taxes . . . Doesn't it blink reality to deny that that is what's happening here?"[18]

In private Court sessions, Kennedy went off on tangents, fellow justices said later, seeming less engaged in the business of the Court and ready to move into a new phase of life. He also relinquished his usual centrist role, and in the 2017–2018 session consistently provided a fifth vote for his fellow justices on the right. Some colleagues said Roberts had greater influence on Kennedy as he neared the end of his service. Kennedy also had a relatively good relationship with Trump, which was on display during the president's first speech to a joint session of Congress in February 2017. As Trump worked his way through the crowded floor of the House of Representatives, he stopped when he reached the Supreme Court justices and said to Kennedy, "Say hello to your boy. Special guy." Kennedy responded, "Your kids have been very nice to him." Trump returned, "Well, they love him, and they love him in New York." Kennedy's son Justin socialized with Trump's adult children. Justin had previously worked at Deutsche Bank, which loaned money to Trump's businesses.[19]

A few weeks later, Trump's daughter, Ivanka, brought her own daughter, five-year-old Arabella, to the Supreme Court for oral arguments as guests of Justice Kennedy. They sat in the special red-cushioned seats at the front of the courtroom. Ivanka Trump posted on Instagram afterward: "Arabella and I visited the Supreme Court this morning and attended a hearing. I'm grateful for the opportunity to teach her about the judiciary system in our country firsthand. #SCOTUS #SupremeCourt #ImportantLessons #Mother-Daughter."[20] The case they watched involved the terms of arbitration agreements under Kentucky law, providing exposure to a topic that may have been challenging for even some of the adult spectators. There was something wholesome about the episode, a parent bringing her child to see American civics in action. Ivanka Trump put a positive, pleasing face on her father's presidency—and now added her young daughter's appearance. Perhaps it was merely ironic that her choreographed field trip to the Supreme Court came at a time when Trump was executing a plan that would transform the institution and the nation's law, especially in regard to women's rights.[21]

White House counsel Don McGahn was at the same time fostering a relationship with Justice Kennedy. "I'd always been a fan," McGahn said of Kennedy. Referring to conservative complaints regarding the justice's liberal votes on social issues, McGahn said, "Some folks that I hang out with were not as big of fans. But being more of a First Amendment kind of guy, more of a kind of libertarian streak in me, I really appreciated a lot of Kennedy's jurisprudence." Kennedy consistently opposed campaign finance regulations, based on First Amendment grounds, and wrote the landmark 2010 *Citizens United v. Federal Election Commission* decision that lifted expenditure limits for corporations and labor unions. In their private sessions, McGahn said, Kennedy regaled him with tales from his Sacramento days.[22]

In Kennedy's final term, which coincided with Trump's first year, he was one of the five solid conservatives (with Gorsuch in place) who voted for the new Trump positions favoring employers over workers in a series of disputes that followed the arbitration case. *Janus*, the most consequential ruling in the labor series, rolled back a four-decade-old decision, *Abood v. Detroit Board of Education*, which had allowed public-sector unions to obtain "fair share" fees from nonunion members for collective bargaining.

*Janus* began in Illinois when Republican governor Bruce Rauner tried to end the agency-fee requirement in state law. Mark Janus, a child support specialist, was one of the public employees who joined the lawsuit against the American Federation of State, County and Municipal Employees. Janus contended that requiring public employees to pay toward the union's advocacy infringed on his free speech rights. Trump's legal team had joined the case against the labor union practice. Alito wrote for the majority, which included Roberts, Kennedy, Thomas, and Gorsuch. He said that the 1977 case of *Abood* had been inconsistent with other First Amendment cases and essentially forced nonunion members to endorse ideas they found objectionable. In dissent, Kagan said that the majority's legal reasoning reflected nothing more than their sheer dislike of the *Abood* decision and desire to overrule it. She noted that twenty-two states had authorized fair-share provisions. "The majority overthrows a decision entrenched in this Nation's law—and its economic life—for over 40 years," she wrote, "weaponizing the First Amendment" and "unleash[ing] judges, now and in the future, to intervene in economic and regulatory policy."[23]

Reversal of the 1977 precedent was years in the making, and even without support from the Trump administration, the Roberts majority had appeared ready to strike down such state laws.[24] But just minutes after the ruling in *Janus,* Trump celebrated the decision, tweeting: "Big loss for the coffers of the Democrats!"[25]

A crucial early test of the relationship between the Roberts Court and the Trump administration centered on the Muslim-country travel ban, the first iteration of which Trump had tried to enforce just seven days into his presidency. It confirmed the harmony between the Court majority and the administration. In contrast, the Roberts majority had been antagonistic to the Obama administration, suggesting at the time that the president's team was pushing the bounds of the law. Justice Department lawyers at the courtroom lectern in the Obama years had faced stern criticism for refusing to adopt positions held by the predecessor Republican administration.

As a general matter, consistency in administrations' arguments at the Court furthers stability in the law, but any new administration can be expected to abandon some ideologically incompatible positions. Nonetheless, Justice Antonin Scalia had asked U.S. solicitor general Donald Verrilli at one point: "Why should we listen to you rather than the solicitors general who took the opposite position? Why should we defer to the views of the current administration?" When Verrilli responded that the new Obama administration position was "persuasive," Chief Justice Roberts interjected, "Your successors may adopt a different view. . . . Whatever deference you are entitled to is compromised by the fact that your predecessors took a different view."[26] It was an unforgiving stance for someone who as a deputy U.S. solicitor general in the 1990s had himself orchestrated changes in the government's legal positions. One of Roberts's first actions back then reversed the government's position defending Federal Communications Commission "set-asides," special allocations for minority-owned broadcast licenses.[27]

The Court gave Trump a clear victory when in 2018 it upheld the travel ban. In *Trump v. Hawaii,* Roberts wrote for the majority that federal immigration law provides presidents the authority to bar certain people from entering the United States. The majority rejected arguments that Trump's prelude to the executive order revealed religious bias. Roberts highlighted the administration's broad discretion to suspend the entry of immigrants and refugees "detrimental to the interests" of the country. He dismissed Trump's derogatory statements about Muslims as largely irrelevant to the Court's interpretation of the president's action. Referring to the proclamation, Roberts observed, "The text says nothing about religion."

Roberts cast Trump as just another president, handling difficult dilemmas but staying within the guardrails of office. He compared Trump with Presidents Ronald Reagan, Bill Clinton, and George W. Bush, writing, "The 12-page Proclamation [travel ban]—which thoroughly describes the process, agency evaluations, and recommendations underlying the President's chosen restrictions—is more detailed than any prior order a President has issued under" relevant immigration law. The chief justice observed that different presidents have responded differently to perceived threats by Muslims. He referred to President Dwight D. Eisenhower at the 1957 opening of the Islamic Center of Washington, D.C. "Just days after the attacks of September 11, 2001, President George W. Bush returned to the same Islamic Center to implore his fellow Americans—Muslims and non-Muslims alike—to remember during their time of grief that '[t]he face of terror is not the true faith of Islam,' and that America is 'a great country because we share the same values of respect and dignity and human worth.'" Roberts, an appointee of Bush, might not have had equal regard for Trump, but he was determined to afford him wide latitude as president.[28]

Justice Kennedy wrote a separate concurring statement of caution. "There are numerous instances in which the statements and actions of Government officials are not subject to judicial scrutiny or intervention," he said. "That does not mean those officials are free to disregard the Constitution and the rights it proclaims and protects. . . . An anxious world must know that our Government remains committed always to the liberties the Constitution seeks to preserve and protect." The anxious world—as Kennedy put it—failed to be reassured by Trump as time wore on.[29]

The four liberal justices dissented, Sotomayor most passionately. Reading excerpts of her opinion from the bench after Roberts delivered the majority's opinion, Sotomayor recounted that Trump had said, "Islam hates us" and "We're having problems with Muslims coming into the country," and that he blamed "terrorist attacks on Muslims' lack of 'assimilation' and their commitment to 'Sharia law.' . . . He opined that Muslims 'do not respect us at all.'"

Speaking for more than fifteen minutes, she said, "Take a brief moment and let the gravity of those statements sink in. . . . Then remember that most of these words were spoken or written by the current president of the United States, the man who issued the three executive orders at the center of this case." In her written dissenting opinion, Sotomayor, joined only by Ginsburg, said, "Our Founders . . . embed[ed] the principle of religious neutrality in the First Amendment. The Court's decision today fails to safeguard that fundamental principle. It leaves undisturbed a policy first advertised openly and unequivocally as a 'total and complete shutdown of Muslims entering the United States' because the policy now masquerades behind a façade of national-security concerns." Looking back at Trump's statements, Sotomayor said that people could have concluded that the travel ban arose from anti-Muslim animus, in violation of the First Amendment's establishment clause. She said that the Roberts majority ignored the facts and misconstrued precedent, and declared that the Court was "turning a blind eye to the pain and suffering the Proclamation inflicts upon countless families and individuals, many of whom are United States citizens." *Turning a blind eye.* Sotomayor would level that charge repeatedly at her colleagues.[30]

The next day, June 27, the last day of the 2017–2018 sitting, Justice Kennedy's wife, Mary, was in the courtroom with some of the Kennedy grandchildren. They listened to the final case announcements and heard Roberts express gratitude to the court staff for their service over the past year. When the justices left the bench, they retreated to their private conference room to settle lingering business for the term. That's when Kennedy told his colleagues that he was retiring.

He had arranged to issue a statement. "It has been the greatest honor and privilege to serve . . . in the federal judiciary for 43 years, 30 of those years on the Supreme Court," he wrote, adding that his decision to retire arose from a desire to spend more time with his family. Kennedy then cut short his lunch with his colleagues and, as prearranged with McGahn and Jeffrey Minear, counselor to the chief justice, was driven to the White House to tell President Trump.[31]

Kennedy was feeling the effects of his age and that of his wife, Mary. But it was simultaneously true that the Trump administration craved a Court opening, and McGahn and others in the Trump world were in regular contact with Kennedy. The justice, who was about to turn eighty-two that summer, could easily have been led to believe his protégé Kavanaugh was on deck for his seat. Yet it also seemed likely that he would have stepped down regardless.

Once Justice Kennedy had personally relayed his retirement news to the president, McGahn called his friend Kavanaugh, who was at the D.C. Circuit courthouse just finishing up lunch. McGahn later said his private meetings with Kennedy were not intended to push retirement or promise that a Kennedy protégé, particularly Kavanaugh, would be chosen. McGahn said that Kennedy did not press him to focus on any possible successor: "He never did," McGahn insisted. "The guy is a master of protocol, etiquette, and judicial ethics."[32]

Kennedy would not have had to convince McGahn of a Kavanaugh choice. McGahn and Kavanaugh were old friends. A decade earlier, McGahn, newly a member of the Federal Election Commission, an appointment urged by Senator Mitch McConnell, had asked Kavanaugh to swear him in. At the time, McGahn told Shannon Flaherty, a Capitol Hill staffer whom he would marry two years later, that he believed Kavanaugh would someday become a Supreme Court justice.[33] In 2018, the White House counsel indeed ensured that Kavanaugh stayed at the top of the heap. McGahn did so by going head-to-head with insiders who backed other candidates, including U.S. appeals court judges Amy Coney Barrett, Raymond Kethledge, and Thomas Hardiman, who had lost out to Gorsuch a year earlier. Barrett was the choice of many on the religious right, some of whom faulted Kavanaugh for not joining Judge Henderson's opinion discounting any right to abortion for the young migrant Jane Doe. But there was a feeling among some on Trump's legal team that she would be a more natural choice for a possible Ginsburg successor.[34]

Kavanaugh, fifty-three at the time Trump chose him, had grown up in suburban Washington. His father had been a lobbyist for the cosmetics industry, his mother a homemaker who went to law school when Kavanaugh was young. She became a judge on the Montgomery County Circuit Court. Kavanaugh earned his undergraduate and law degrees at Yale. He served as a law clerk for U.S. court of appeals judge Alex Kozinski, a well-connected Ronald Reagan appointee based in Pasadena, California, who had a reputation for brilliance as well as bullying. (Kozinski resigned under a cloud of sexual harassment accusations in 2017.)[35] Kavanaugh became a law clerk to Supreme Court justice Anthony Kennedy after a short stint in the Department of Justice working for then–U.S. solicitor general Ken Starr.

When Kavanaugh's one-year clerkship at the Supreme Court ended, he went briefly into private practice at Kirkland & Ellis, a large national firm where Starr had become a partner. After Starr took over the independent counsel investigation of President Bill Clinton in 1994, Kavanaugh joined the Starr team. Kavanaugh built a network of influential men he continued to cultivate over the years, from Kozinski to Starr but also including John Roberts, with whom he first worked in the solicitor general's office under Starr. As a lawyer in private practice, Roberts had represented Kavanaugh's father, Ed, and cosmetics-industry interests.[36]

Kavanaugh had an affable personality and regularly socialized with a wide range of lawyers, law professors, and journalists. Yet he inevitably turned up at the scene of highly charged GOP efforts, such as the Starr investigation of former President Clinton and *Bush v. Gore,* in the latter appearing on TV to support then–Texas governor George W. Bush's drive to claim Florida's crucial electors in the disputed 2000 election case. Then as he served in the Bush administration, Kavanaugh helped shepherd court nominees, before becoming a judge himself, and accumulated institutional knowledge for this moment in 2018. He knew how the gears of a confirmation turn or become jammed. He was also ready to offer the kind of flattery Trump craved. "No president has ever consulted more widely or talked with more people from more backgrounds to seek input about a Supreme Court nomination," Kavanaugh declared the night Trump announced his nomination to a televised audience.[37]

Once Trump settled on Kavanaugh, controversy erupted over access to his records from the George W. Bush White House, which included his work on the selection of judges and on detainee policy after the September 11, 2001, attacks. Kavanaugh, who served first in the White House counsel's office and then as Bush's staff secretary, had been at the center of some the Republicans' most contentious battles over lower-court judges and had an inside view as the Bush-Cheney team developed antiterrorism practices and interrogation methods for the men picked up after September 11, which killed nearly three thousand people.

The National Archives, which in the past had screened and compiled materials for Senate confirmations, needed months to process Kavanaugh's records for public release. As an alternative—one certainly favoring Kavanaugh—McGahn and former president Bush arranged for documents to be screened by a team assembled by a private lawyer, William Burck, who had worked in the Bush administration and was a friend of Kavanaugh and McGahn. Burck often served as a fixer for the Republican establishment. McGahn had already hired him to be his personal lawyer as the White House counsel cooperated with Robert Mueller's Russia investigation. Burck was also representing Steve Bannon.[38]

Like Kavanaugh, Burck had graduated from Yale Law School and served as a law clerk to Judge Kozinski and to Justice Kennedy. Their parallel tracks continued as Burck became a counsel in the Bush administration. In the end, despite protests from Senate Democrats (outnumbered by Republican senators, who controlled the Senate Judiciary Committee and confirmation process), Kavanaugh's records from his staff secretary days were kept secret and his White House counsel materials heavily culled before public release by Burck's team.[39]

Other controversy turned on Kavanaugh's activities with Ken Starr in the 1990s investigation of the Clintons, which began with the Whitewater land deals in Arkansas and evolved into a probe of President Clinton's sexual involvement with former White House intern Monica Lewinsky. Kavanaugh, then thirty-three, worked on the team's effort to obtain documents from the attorney of Vince Foster, a deputy White House counsel who had come to Washington with his old friends from Arkansas and became the subject of anti-Clinton conspiracy theories following his suicide. The Starr team wanted notes from conversations between Foster and his lawyer and argued that attorney-client privilege expired with his death. Starr tapped Kavanaugh to argue the case at the Supreme Court. It was a plum opportunity for Kavanaugh, although he ended up with a losing argument. The justices ruled 6–3 for Foster's lawyer in a 1998 decision.[40]

Kavanaugh's censorious memos reflected the almost gleefully prurient tone of the independent counsel's investigation of the Clinton-Lewinsky relationship. "The President has disgraced his Office, the legal system, and the American people by having sex with a 22-year-old intern and turning her life into shambles—callous and disgusting behavior that somehow has gotten lost in the shuffle," Kavanaugh wrote in an August 15, 1998, memo that urged Starr to take a hard-hitting approach. "He should be forced to account for all of that and to defend his actions. It may not be our job to impose sanctions on him, but it is our job to make his pattern of revolting behavior clear—piece by painful piece." In an interview with me at the time of Kavanaugh's nomination, Starr justified Kavanaugh's emphasis, saying, "Brett was a superb lawyer who was part of an office-wide effort to deal with the unfortunate fact that the President was aggressively and adamantly denying the nature of the [Lewinsky] relationship. We had to determine where he lied under oath, and that required specificity."[41]

Clinton was impeached by the House and then acquitted by the Senate, and finished out his presidency. Kavanaugh, after returning briefly to private practice, joined the new Bush administration in 2001. He had long aspired to become a judge, and in 2003, President Bush nominated him to the U.S. Court of Appeals for the District of Columbia Circuit, a proven stepping stone to the Supreme Court. The nomination stalled, as Senate Democrats considered him too partisan for the bench. "You have been the 'go to' guy among young Republican lawyers appearing at the epicenter of so many high-profile controversial issues in your short career," Senator Chuck Schumer of New York told him during one confirmation hearing, referring to the Starr investigation of the Clintons and Kavanaugh's advocacy during the 2000 Florida recount dispute and *Bush v. Gore* legal battle.

President Bush held firm on his drive to seat Kavanaugh, although he did retreat on other nominees as deals were reached with senators. Kavanaugh was confirmed for the D.C. Circuit in May 2006, and President Bush presided over a Rose Garden investiture ceremony for him, a rarity for any lower-court appointee. Justice Kennedy administered the oath. Kavanaugh's wife, Ashley Estes Kavanaugh, who had been President Bush's personal secretary, held the Bible. Their marriage, President Bush quipped, "was the first lifetime appointment" he had arranged for Kavanaugh.[42]

During his years on the appellate court, Kavanaugh stayed in close contact with Judge Kozinski and Justice Kennedy, continuing to help select clerks for Kennedy's chambers. Former clerks joked that Kavanaugh often knew more about what was going on behind the scenes at the high court than the current clerks serving there.

Kavanaugh's Senate confirmation hearings seemed rather predictable in the beginning. Abortion was a flash point, as it had been for decades. Senators asked Kavanaugh to explain his position in the Jane Doe migrant case, including his claim that the D.C. Circuit majority's view would lead to a new right for "immediate abortion on demand."

Senator Richard Blumenthal observed that Kavanaugh had not been on Trump's list of Supreme Court candidates until a month after his opinion in the Jane Doe case. The Connecticut Democrat said it looked as if Kavanaugh had landed on the list because of his false assertion of a new right to abortion on demand. Kavanaugh said he believed Trump added him to the list because "a lot of judges and lawyers I know" urged the consideration, "based on my record from the past 12 years." Senators also questioned a 2003 memo Kavanaugh wrote while in the Bush White House in which he appeared to question the value of *Roe* as precedent. Kavanaugh told senators he was merely introducing the view that some scholars failed to consider *Roe* settled. By 2003, however, *Roe v. Wade* had been the law of the land for thirty years, and the exchange suggested Kavanaugh's lack of true regard for *Roe*.[43]

Despite some bumps during the hearing, it appeared that Kavanaugh would be confirmed in the Republican-controlled Senate. But that air of inevitability was shaken when Christine Blasey Ford, a Palo Alto University professor, came forward with allegations of sexual assault from an incident when they were both teenagers in the Washington, D.C., area. As she related first to a California member of Congress and to the *Washington Post*, Ford said that one night in the early 1980s, Kavanaugh and another boy trapped her in the bedroom at the house of a mutual friend. Kavanaugh jumped on her and tried to pull off the bathing suit she was wearing under her clothes, all the while keeping his hand over her mouth. She feared that Kavanaugh would inadvertently suffocate her before she managed to flee.

Kavanaugh denied the accusations and his GOP supporters immediately went on the defensive. A confirmation vote was postponed and a second set of hearings scheduled, all of which recalled the similar late-breaking Clarence Thomas ordeal of 1991. Suddenly rumors of new claims from women were in the air, along with various theories to defend Kavanaugh.[44]

When Ford appeared in front of the committee, she recounted the scene for senators, before a televised audience, and said that the episode had traumatized her: "indelible in the hippocampus is the laughter" of Kavanaugh and the other boy, she recalled. Hearing her testimony, Trump grew worried. "Immediately after Dr. Ford had completed her testimony that morning, the phone rang," Senate Majority Leader McConnell later recounted in his memoir. "It was a familiar voice: the president. . . . he wanted to get my views. He and I both agreed that Dr. Ford had been a compelling witness. I expressed to the president that it was only 'halftime,' however, and that he should wait until completion of the second half before making any decisions."[45] Trump also called McGahn, but the counsel, fearing he wanted to pull the nomination, refused to take the call. McGahn was talking to Kavanaugh at the time and pressing him to show his anger and fight for the nomination, *New York Times* reporter Michael Schmidt wrote in his book *Donald Trump v. The United States*. McGahn told his top aide, according to Schmidt's account, to put off Trump: "Tell him I don't talk to quitters." When McGahn returned Trump's call a few minutes later, as Kavanaugh was about to testify, Trump apparently said he was sticking with Kavanaugh.[46]

When it came time for Kavanaugh to be in the witness chair, he denied Ford's claims. In tearful testimony, he declared that Ford's accusations arose from critics' revenge. "This whole two-week effort has been a calculated and orchestrated political hit, fueled with apparent pent-up anger about President Trump and the 2016 election, fear that has been unfairly stoked by my judicial record, revenge on behalf of the Clintons, and millions of dollars in money from outside left-wing opposition groups. . . . And as we all know, in the United States political system of the early 2000s, what goes around comes around."

Democratic senators pressed the nominee on past behavior, including his reputation for heavy drinking. At one point, he engaged in a combative exchange with Democratic Minnesota senator Amy Klobuchar. The senator, referring to the fact that her father had struggled with alcoholism, asked Kavanaugh if he ever drank so much that he "didn't remember what happened the night before or part of what happened."

"You're asking about blackout, I don't know, have you?" Kavanaugh shot back.

"Could you answer the question, judge?" she said, adding, "So, you have, that's not happened? Is that your answer?"

"Yeah, and I'm curious if you have," Kavanaugh said.

"I have no drinking problem, judge," Klobuchar said.

The committee took a break, and when Kavanaugh returned, he apologized for his remarks: "Sorry I did that. This is a tough process. I'm sorry about that." Klobuchar responded, "I appreciate that. I'd like to add when you have a parent that is an alcoholic, you are pretty careful about drinking."

McConnell said that after the hearing was over, Trump called and apparently felt better about the matter. "We both thought that Kavanaugh had done well," McConnell wrote.

Separate to Ford's claims, former Yale classmates had passed on to senators allegations of sexual misconduct and excessive drinking. Those claims appeared in news stories but were never publicly aired or investigated. The FBI conducted a limited, six-day review of various allegations. It separately set up a tip line, the first time ever for a nominee undergoing Senate confirmation, "to centralize and manage incoming information related to the nomination." The FBI later acknowledged receiving more than 4,900 tips but also said, following instructions from the White House counsel, the so-called requesting entity, that it had turned over all "relevant" tips to that office.[47]

Kavanaugh's performance, particularly the assertion that he was the victim of Democratic revenge, so troubled the retired justice John Paul Stevens that he told a Florida audience that there was "merit" to the criticism that the nominee had "demonstrated a potential bias involving enough potential litigants before the Court that he would not be able to perform his full responsibilities." Never before had a justice, sitting or retired, so publicly criticized a nominee. Stevens had been a justice from 1975 to 2010, and he differentiated Kavanaugh's statements from those of Clarence Thomas in 1991 during the Anita Hill ordeal. Stevens said, "There's nothing Clarence did in the hearings

that disqualified him from sitting in cases after he came on the Court."
Stevens was not alone in his criticism. More than 2,400 law professors
from more than 190 schools sent a letter to the Senate questioning
Kavanaugh's judicial temperament.[48]

Some justices told me later that they found the Kavanaugh hearings too painful to watch. The sessions stirred their own anxieties from
their time in the witness chair, and even those who found Ford credible shuddered at the public thrashing of Kavanaugh. They knew that
he was destined to join their ranks and already felt some institutional
allegiance.

Ford's confusion on some facts from the decades-old incident led
to a public mocking by Trump. At a rally in Mississippi, he tried to
imitate her testimony to the Senate Judiciary Committee. "I had one
beer. Well, do you think it was—nope, it was one beer. . . . How did you
get home? I don't remember. How'd you get there? I don't remember.
Where is the place? I don't remember. How many years ago was it? I
don't know." The crowd laughed at Trump's rendition and applauded.
"Think of your son. Think of your husband," he said, adding that he
himself had faced "false allegations." (Since Trump began his 2016
campaign for president, more than a dozen women had accused him
of sexual misconduct and assault. He had bragged about some of his
exploits, most memorably in the *Access Hollywood* tape made public
in October 2016, just a few weeks before the November presidential
election. On it, he could be heard saying, "And when you're a star, they
let you do it. You can do anything. Grab 'em by the pussy. You can do
anything.")[49]

Senator Susan Collins, a moderate Maine Republican, cast a crucial vote to confirm Kavanaugh, telling fellow senators she believed
he would vote to uphold abortion rights and that Ford's claims
against the nominee failed to meet a "more likely than not" standard
that Collins said she believed was necessary under the circumstances.
"The facts presented do not mean Professor Ford was not sexually
assaulted that night or at some other time, but they do lead me to
conclude that the allegations fail to meet the 'more likely than not'
standard," Collins said.[50]

McConnell, who'd had lunch with Collins earlier in the day, described her floor remarks as one of the "great speeches in the annals of the Senate." Recounting their time together at lunch, he said, "During our meal, she seemed relaxed and fully at ease. As we ate, I did not ask for her vote, and she did not volunteer it. But, given her demeanor, I intuited that she was going to vote for Kavanaugh." The Senate approved Kavanaugh for the Supreme Court on October 6, 2018, by a vote of 50–48, largely along party lines.[51]

Immediately after that vote, Kavanaugh was driven over to the Supreme Court, entering through the basement garage, so that Chief Justice Roberts could swear him in. Crowds of protesters swarmed the exterior of the building, pounding on the doors. No one breached the building, which was closed to the public at the time.

Two days later, Trump arranged a celebratory televised investiture in the East Room of the White House. The president invited all the justices, and Don McGahn worked to win their attendance. Some thought that the president was setting them up and about to use them in some way. In the past, justices had normally declined to attend White House investitures, resisting the optics that would conflict with the separation of powers.[52]

The Kavanaugh celebration would be more fraught than any contemporary succession. An appearance by the full contingent of sitting justices could look like an endorsement of the president, and news networks still buzzed with coverage of the Senate hearings, especially Ford's statement and Kavanaugh's denial. Roberts moved cautiously. Other justices said he sought reassurance from the White House counsel's office that the event would not be overtly political. Their fears calmed, the chief justice and eight other associate justices went to the White House. With cameras flashing, they took their front-row seats in the East Room. Jane Roberts sat behind her husband. At her side were Ginni Thomas, Joanna Breyer, Martha-Ann Alito, and Louise Gorsuch.

When President Trump opened the festivities, he immediately highlighted the rare attendance of the full Supreme Court at a White House investiture: "Joining us for tonight's ceremony is every sitting

Supreme Court justice." He announced their names, individually, like blue ribbons he had just won: "Chief Justice Roberts. Thank you. Justice Thomas. Thank you. Justice Ginsburg. Thank you. Justice Breyer. Thank you, justice. Justice Alito. Thank you. Justice Sotomayor. Thank you. Justice Kagan. Thank you. And Justice Gorsuch."[53]

The audience applauded. What came next shattered the decorum of a judicial investiture. "I would like to begin tonight's proceeding differently than perhaps any other event of such magnitude," President Trump said. "On behalf of our nation, I want to apologize to Brett and the entire Kavanaugh family for the terrible pain and suffering you have been forced to endure. Those who step forward to serve our country deserve a fair and dignified evaluation, not a campaign of political and personal destruction based on lies and deception.

"What happened to the Kavanaugh family violates every notion of fairness, decency, and due process," the president continued. "[In] our country, a man or woman must always be presumed innocent unless and until proven guilty. And with that, I must state that you, sir, under historic scrutiny, were proven innocent."

There had been no trial, not even much of an investigation of Ford's accusations. But as with so many of Trump's assertions, the truth did not matter to him or to a certain number of his supporters. When Kavanaugh stepped to the lectern and began his remarks, he singled out Roberts. "I'm honored to serve on a Supreme Court headed by Chief Justice John Roberts," Kavanaugh said. "Chief Justice Roberts is a principled, independent, and inspiring leader for the American judiciary. As a country, we are fortunate to have John Roberts as Chief Justice of the United States."

Most of the justices sat stone faced. Some justices told me later that they were sorry they had gone. Justice Thomas, conspicuously enthusiastic, alone applauded heartily after Kavanaugh spoke. A Department of Justice spokeswoman, Kerri Kupec, later described Thomas as "the life of the party" at the event.[54]

To varying degrees, the justices felt tricked, made to participate in a political exercise at a time when they were trying to prove themselves impartial guardians of justice, rather than tools of Republican interests. Overall, the moment exacerbated this uneasy chapter of the Roberts Court. Ideologically divided, with five conservatives and four liberals, the justices were already in the middle of an epic struggle over the country's constitutional guarantees. The East Room affair, with Trump trying to keep the justices in his clutches, widened the fissures.

## Chapter 4

---

# THE TRIUMVIRATE

If anyone understood President Trump and his ability to exploit others, as when he turned the justices into props for Justice Kavanaugh's investiture, it was Don McGahn. "He is a different kind of cat," McGahn said of his boss. "What you see is what you get. It works out for him. It's an unorthodox style. He ran as a disrupter. He is actually doing what he said he would do." McGahn was a different kind of cat, too. He fashioned himself as an outsider but possessed sharp instincts about insiders and what motivated them. Watching him navigate Trump world, as he dodged the president's loyalty tests, shepherded controversial judicial nominees, and parried difficult questions in an array of settings, one could not help but be struck by McGahn's bare-knuckle success in Washington politics. He had his own code of loyalty. In encouraging the justices to attend the Brett Kavanaugh investiture, he may have been less interested in offering Trump a televised victory lap than in providing his friend Kavanaugh a show of Supreme Court solidarity.[1]

McGahn returned to private practice halfway through the Trump presidency but remained in demand for his election-law expertise. He stayed close with Senator Mitch McConnell, with whom he shared a disdain for campaign finance regulations and with whom he partnered to choose the president's judicial nominees.[2] The third important player in the Trump judicial-selection apparatus was Leonard Leo, the Federalist Society leader and personal friend to several justices. Leo scouted new judicial candidates and raised millions for advertising campaigns related to their confirmation.[3] The three men understood the importance of the federal courts to a long-term policy agenda, from business interests to individual rights. How much can government control labor practices, regulate the environment, and protect consumers? Can states limit access to birth control or outright ban abortion? Can government channel money to religious schools? These questions came down to jurists appointed ostensibly as neutral arbiters but who in reality held to their own ideologies and were subject to varying degrees of political pressure.

McGahn, McConnell, and Leo tapped Federalist Society loyalists and other close associates for coveted judgeships, among them Justin Walker, who had tight ties to McConnell: by the end of the Trump tenure, he had won two federal spots, one on the Washington, D.C.–based federal appellate court—known, as we have seen, as a springboard to the Supreme Court. For another loyalist, Matthew Petersen, who had served with McGahn on the Federal Election Commission, the alliance proved less than fortuitous. Nominated for a U.S. district court post, he ended up withdrawing after a blowup over his qualifications brought about by a conservative Republican senator irked at the power McGahn wielded.

That kind of setback was rare, and, based on the number of appointments that White House counsel McGahn oversaw, his role in transforming the federal bench cannot be overstated. Harvard University law professor Jack Goldsmith, a Federalist Society stalwart, declared on Twitter in August 2018, in the midst of multiple Trump legal scandals, "McGahn will forever be a (deserved) hero to the conservative establishment for his role in helping select and confirm great conservative judges and justices. Everything else, it increasingly appears, is a cost of doing business." To the Left, McGahn's success on judges warranted derision rather than praise. Liberals saw him as a Trump enabler who helped ram extreme candidates with bare majorities through the Senate confirmation process, fueling public cynicism about the independence of the judiciary.[4]

Politics ran in McGahn's blood. His own New Jersey relatives experienced the consequences of down-to-the wire elections, political grudge matches, and even the retribution of Donald Trump. Mc-Gahn was born in 1968 in Atlantic City, the grandson of a local saloonkeeper whose sons became civic leaders and spurred development of the Atlantic City gambling industry. One of Don McGahn's uncles, Joseph, was an obstetrician who became a New Jersey state senator (running at various times as a Democrat, an independent, and a Republican). Joseph cosponsored the law that opened the city to casino gaming in 1979. Don's uncle Paddy, according to a *New York Times* obituary, was known for his "outsize personality and his devotion to the United States Marine Corps." Local news reports chronicled his dueling lawsuits with Trump over legal work for his casino when Trump sued him for allegedly overbilling. Don Mc-Gahn's father, Donald Sr., became a lower-profile government lawyer, serving as a special agent at the Treasury Department. Don Jr.'s mother, Noreen, was a school nurse.[5]

Don McGahn graduated from parochial schools and briefly attended the U.S. Naval Academy—his father and uncles had served in the military—but left in his first year and earned his bachelor's degree at the University of Notre Dame. When he was nineteen, he watched the Senate hearings for Robert Bork. "My father taped them and made me watch them, and I'm glad he made me watch them," McGahn later told a law school audience of the 1987 hearings. Bork's limited views of individual rights and candid conservatism led to his 58–42 Senate defeat, and the loss ignited a desire for GOP payback that would become a catalyst for confirmation fights to come. One of the conventional lessons taken from the Bork battle was that a deep record could be a liability. But McGahn said that he and Trump looked for precisely that. "He wanted people with paper trails," McGahn said. "He wanted to know what he was buying."[6]

After Notre Dame, McGahn attended Widener University in Pennsylvania for law school, becoming president of its chapter of the Federalist Society. While there, he was captivated by another set of Supreme Court confirmation hearings, those for Clarence Thomas, in 1991. Unlike Bork, Thomas was able to clear the hurdles of the

Democratic-majority Senate, but just barely, his vote then the closest in more than a century.[7]

McGahn interviewed for a law firm job with Patton Boggs in Washington, D.C. It was 1994, a turning point in the national elections, and he said that he asked the firm's Democrat-connected partners about their strategy for when, as McGahn anticipated, the Republicans suddenly took over Congress. McGahn was seeing the signs of what would eventually be a Republican revolution as he watched the Pennsylvania U.S. Senate campaign between Republican Rick Santorum and Democrat Harris Wofford. He sensed that Santorum's rise would be a harbinger of a national trend. As McGahn later told it to audiences, Washington power lawyers who invested in the lobbying of Democrats failed to see the GOP takeover coming. Whatever Patton Boggs may have forecast that year, it had already begun hiring a few prominent GOP lawyers, including Republican National Committee (RNC) attorney Ben Ginsberg in 1993. But McGahn's instincts, as he later described them, were right. The 1994 elections added fifty-four new Republican members to the U.S. House of Representatives and eight to the Senate. Newt Gingrich became the House majority leader, setting a new tone for combative politics in the nation's capital. Patton Boggs hired McGahn.[8]

From 1999 to 2008, McGahn was also counsel to the National Republican Congressional Committee (NRCC). And he represented Tom DeLay, a U.S. House member from Texas who became Republican House majority leader in 2003 and was criminally indicted two years later for having violated Texas election law in 2002. He resigned the House leadership in 2005. (He was convicted in 2010 and the conviction was reversed on appeal in 2013.) McGahn's mastery of the intricacies of campaign finance law helped keep many politicians out of trouble. Critics said he was skilled at operating right up to the line of what was legal.[9]

Following his appointment by President George W. Bush to the Federal Election Commission, he became known for corralling fellow GOP commissioners to vote the way he did. "From the moment he walked in the door in 2008, McGahn made no secret of his disdain for the agency, its mission and commission staff," wrote FEC commissioner Ellen Weintraub when Trump chose McGahn in late 2016 to be White House counsel. "I have served on the FEC for 14 years with 14 commissioners. . . . No other commissioner has been as intransigent, as hostile to other points of view and as determined to undermine the law and the commission as McGahn was." Weintraub was not alone in her criticism, as various government watchdogs and news reporters likened McGahn to the fox guarding the henhouse. The *New York Times*' Eric Lichtblau related a tale of McGahn ripping the pages out of an FEC regulation manual at a commission meeting during a case against American Crossroads, a political action committee founded by Karl Rove to support Republican candidates. "McGahn was not just an ideologue," Meredith McGehee, a lobbyist for campaign reform, later told Charles Homans for a *New York Times Magazine* story. "He was a skilled knife-fighter."[10]

One of his clients at Jones Day, where he landed in 2014, was David Bossie, the president of the conservative advocacy group Citizens United, whose documentary *Hillary: The Movie* and attendant lawsuit had led to the 2010 landmark Supreme Court ruling against campaign finance regulation. Bossie was also an early supporter of Trump for president, so in 2015, when McGahn was considering which candidate to support in the 2016 contest, Bossie asked him, "What about Trump?" Recalled McGahn, "I said, 'What about Trump?'" McGahn's feeling was that Trump was perpetually claiming he was going to run for president.[11]

But McGahn was intrigued enough to travel up to New York to meet with the candidate at Trump Tower. "He signed a book for me," McGahn said later. "He actually signed it to my son." Don and Shannon McGahn had two sons, and Don was persuaded that Trump had "a pretty good instinct about how to handle people." Such instincts were part of McGahn's own repertoire. He regularly joked about attending schools outside the Ivy League, unlike his law firm colleagues and the judicial candidates he screened. But he was schooled in the corridors of Congress. Or, or as he put it regarding judicial nominations, he could "speak Senate."[12]

When McGahn signed on to the Trump campaign, the presidential field for 2016 was still sprawling, and former Florida governor Jeb Bush and Texas senator Ted Cruz appeared to be better bets. McGahn was at the scene for the first real sign of Trump's potential success, the New Hampshire primary, on February 9. Trump won more of the popular vote and more delegates than any of the other candidates, coming in first, with former Ohio governor John Kasich second and Cruz third. When Trump and his family took the stage in Manchester, to the blaring strains of the Beatles' "Revolution," the six-foot-two McGahn was right behind the candidate, with Trump's wife, Melania, standing with them. Forty-seven, his face not yet creased by time in the administration, McGahn could have passed for much younger. The long hair he had favored in years past was gone, and he was all formality in a dark suit, white shirt, and blue tie. His early bet on Trump had paid off in the nation's first primary. He smiled broadly and clapped enthusiastically as the candidate told his cheering audience, "We are going to make America great again." McGahn was now among such figures as Corey Lewandowski, Trump's first campaign manager, serving in what started out as a ragtag operation and uniquely positioned to obtain the job he wanted, White House counsel.

McGahn's allegiance to Trump surprised his conventional Jones Day colleagues. But in time many came along for Trump, and Jones Day lawyers benefitted as they secured spots in the Trump administration. Recruits included Noel Francisco, tapped for solicitor general, and Gregory Katsas, Trump's first appointee to the powerful federal appeals court for the District of Columbia Circuit. Jones Day lawyers secured jobs across the upper echelons of the Trump administration, particularly in the White House counsel's office and the Department of Justice. Author David Enrich, who chronicled the relationship between the law firm and Trump in his 2022 *Servants of the Damned*, observed, "Any new administration draws heavily from the partnerships of major corporate law firms, and Jones Day attorneys had previously served under Obama and other presidents. But what transpired at the dawn of the Trump era was an extraordinary transfer of talent from a single law firm to a new administration." It was a mutually beneficial relationship that especially affected the federal judiciary.[13]

In the West Wing, McGahn became a study in self-preservation, and he successfully used the post for his priorities for the federal bench. But as counsel to the president, he was also trapped in Robert Mueller's investigation of Russian election interference. From the start of his May 2017 appointment as Department of Justice special counsel, Mueller began exploring whether U.S. campaign finance laws had been broken, whether Americans acted as foreign agents for the Russian government, and whether President Trump had then tried to obstruct the investigation. Trump's characterization of the investigation as "a witch hunt" and the pressure he exerted on McGahn to figure out a way to get rid of Mueller was seen in their June 17, 2017, phone call, a month after the appointment of the special counsel. McGahn got the call at home. Trump told him to contact Deputy Attorney General Rod Rosenstein and have him remove Mueller from his post. McGahn refused and decided that he would rather resign than deal with constant pressure from the president. Colleagues talked McGahn out of leaving, and Trump, in his erratic way, backed off for a time. McGahn stayed on for sixteen more months.[14]

Addressing the Mueller-related pressure, McGahn later likened his dilemma to that of Robert Bork, solicitor general (at the time the number three official at the Department of Justice) before he became a federal judge. It was Bork who, in October 1973, fired Watergate prosecutor Archibald Cox, on orders from President Richard Nixon. The task fell to Bork after the attorney general and his deputy at the time resigned rather than follow Nixon's order. Bork defended his firing of Cox, saying that the episode had caught him off guard and that he had simply wanted to restore order to the Justice Department. But the so-called Saturday Night Massacre left a lasting taint on Bork's reputation. Nearly fifty years later, McGahn told Mueller's team that he "wanted to be more like Judge Robert Bork and not 'Saturday Night Massacre' Bork."[15]

Mueller's report concluded that Trump's attempts to fire him failed largely because McGahn and others refused to carry out the president's orders. Mueller separately documented multiple instances of possible obstruction of justice by Trump, even though he presented no evidence that Trump conspired with the Russians as they systematically tried to disrupt U.S. elections. Mueller said that his team never reached any conclusion on whether Trump should be charged because Department of Justice guidelines dictated that a sitting president could not be indicted.[16]

McGahn resigned before that spring 2019 report was issued. He left the White House counsel post just after Brett Kavanaugh was confirmed, in October 2018. Trump had unceremoniously announced on Twitter two months earlier that McGahn would soon be leaving. By the time it was official, McGahn had helped place Gorsuch and Kavanaugh on the Supreme Court and positioned Amy Coney Barrett on the Chicago-based Seventh Circuit U.S. appeals court, a spot that would eventually launch her to the high court.[17]

When McGahn first established his judicial selection machine for Trump and turned to McConnell for advice, the latter warned against sharing power with other executive branch lawyers. Keep the selection power close, he advised. "His view was 'Don't have a committee. Just take it and run,'" McGahn recalled. "He was a great ally and invaluable partner to the president on this. He really is a master of the inside game of the Senate. . . . We ended up being quite the team early on."[18]

In McConnell's telling, he decided to feel out McGahn's approach. McConnell wrote in his memoir, *The Long Game*, that he called McGahn a week after the November 2016 election. "I wanted to see if this was someone I could do business with. The answer proved to be yes. During our phone call, I strongly urged Don to take personal control over the judicial nominations process. As I explained, I had seen numerous instances of the White House Counsel's Office and the Department of Justice struggling for control over judicial nomination, the result being delay, delay, and still more delay." McConnell also said he would work with then–Senate Judiciary Committee chairman Chuck Grassley to end a tradition by which senators could essentially block lower-court nominees from their home states by refusing to return the traditional "blue slip" piece of paper that the Judiciary Committee used to solicit views of senators regarding a nominee from their state.[19]

McConnell, born in 1942 in Alabama, was twenty-six years older than McGahn but had been similarly fascinated by judicial politics in his younger years. He survived polio as a child, and the family moved to Louisville for his father's managerial job at DuPont. In junior high, Mitch became student council vice president, and at duPont Manual High School, he was president of student government and set his sights on politics as he went to the University of Louisville and then the University of Kentucky College of Law. He interned with Kentucky Republican U.S. senator John Sherman Cooper. Later, as an aide to Kentucky Republican senator Marlow Cook, McConnell had a close-up view of the Senate rejection of two Supreme Court nominees of President Richard Nixon: Clement Haynsworth Jr. in 1969 and G. Harrold Carswell in 1970. McConnell included the experience in a law review piece he wrote exploring the Senate's advice-and-consent power. During the Gerald Ford administration, McConnell worked in the Department of Justice and got to know Bork, still serving as the solicitor general, and Scalia, who was an assistant attorney general for the Office of Legal Counsel.[20]

In 1984, McConnell ran a long-shot campaign for the Senate against the Democratic incumbent, Dee Huddleston. He said he knew at the time that to win the statewide election, "it helped to be three things: rich, well connected, and a Democrat. Because there was nothing I could do about that last one, I had to assemble the best team I could to help with the others." McConnell hired Roger Ailes, the GOP strategist who later became CEO of Fox News. McConnell picked up momentum, began drawing checks from the National Republican Senatorial Committee, and beat Huddleston by about 5,100 votes, less than half of 1 percent.[21]

Once in the Senate, McConnell helped the banking industry, fought campaign finance regulations, and became partial to pinstripe suits. He was known for his ability to raise money. In 1997, the *Washington Post* writer George Lardner captured the McConnell lifestyle, writing that he appeared to live modestly, preparing meals for himself and his second wife, Elaine Chao, and picking up their dry cleaning. "But he loves money," Lardner wrote, "perhaps more than any other politician on Capitol Hill. He likes to raise it and he likes to spend it. It's what made him the father of the modern-day Republican Party in Kentucky, and it's what he sees as the key to expanding influence for the GOP in Washington." McConnell became chairman of the National Republican Senatorial Committee for the 1998 and 2000 election cycles.[22] He had married Chao in 1993, when she was president and CEO of United Way; she had served as secretary of labor for George W. Bush and became secretary of transportation under Trump.[23] When McConnell made that fateful decision to block any Obama nominee for the Scalia vacancy, Chao was with him in the Virgin Islands.

McConnell understood the power of the judiciary in campaign finance cases, taking the lead in *McConnell v. Federal Election Commission* (2003), the first challenge to the previous year's McCain-Feingold law, which regulated financing for federal political candidates and campaigns. Sandra Day O'Connor had not yet retired her seat to Samuel Alito, and McConnell lost, with the Court upholding most of the law. That included the regulation of "issue ads" and the ban on national party committees and candidates from raising "soft money" outside existing prohibitions. Once Alito was in place, however, regulations on campaign money began evaporating, paving the way to the ruling in *Citizens United v. Federal Election Commission.*

Every defeat in the Senate, most strikingly the Bork nomination, seemed etched in McConnell's mind. In October 1987, as President Reagan's choice of Bork was failing, McConnell stood on the floor and recalled his work as a legislative aide during the failed Haynsworth and Carswell nominations. He said that he was abandoning his once idealistic notions about the Senate's advice-and-consent power. "Advice and consent in 1987, as a result of the imminent defeat of Judge Robert Bork, means this: We in the Senate are going to make our decision on any basis we darn well please, and if we object as a matter of philosophical persuasion to the direction the President is trying to move the Court, whether to the right or to the left, we can just stand up and say that and vote accordingly." Looking ahead, McConnell said, "This new standard is, after all, a bit of freedom for each of us to do our thing. We may not be able to pick the nominee, but we can sure shoot him down—we can shoot them all down."[24]

McConnell had a way of carrying out his threats. In 2013, he warned of the consequences when then–majority leader Harry Reid persuaded his Democratic majority to amend the filibuster rules for lower-court nominees. McConnell was taking advantage of the sixty-vote threshold to end debate and was blocking several of Obama's judicial nominees from any floor consideration. Reid and fellow Democrats changed the rules to allow lower-court judicial nominees to win approval with a simple fifty-vote majority. McConnell said Democrats would rue the day they changed those rules. "You'll regret this, and you may regret it a lot sooner than you think," McConnell warned in 2013. By 2017, McConnell was majority leader and needed to extend that new simple-majority rule to Supreme Court nominees to win approval of Trump's first justice, Neil Gorsuch. McConnell had the majority to ditch the filibuster, and he justified it based on the Democrats' action in 2013.[25]

By 2018, McConnell had become the longest-serving GOP Senate leader in U.S. history.[26] He never flinched as he blocked legislation or stalled a judicial nominee, most spectacularly Merrick Garland. Alternately, McConnell could speed through favored initiatives and nominees. All three eventual Trump justices—Gorsuch, Kavanaugh, and Barrett—made sure that one of their first public appearances after joining the bench was at a McConnell-related occasion.

The makeup of the contemporary federal bench represented a powerful legacy for McConnell, who described his blocking of Merrick Garland for the Scalia seat in 2016 as "the most consequential decision of my career." That decision sealed the fate of the Supreme Court for decades. It also arguably led to the election of Trump, as conservatives became motivated in part based on the Court vacancy. McConnell later acknowledged that he might not have been able to act peremptorily if the Senate had not been in recess and his Republican colleagues similarly vacationing, or back in their home states, or overseas on official travel. "Had Scalia passed away while the Senate was in session,"

McConnell wrote, "I might have delayed announcing my position until I had had a chance to try and persuade my membership of this course of action at one of our thrice-weekly lunches. However, under the circumstances, consultation with fifty-some senators spread across innumerable time zones was simply not realistic."[27]

That resolve against Garland crowned years of impeding Obama's choices for the federal bench. McConnell had issued a warning to Obama soon after his inauguration. In March 2009, McConnell, then leading a Republican minority, joined other GOP senators in a letter to the new president declaring that they would be ready to block any nominee whose name was put forward without consultation with GOP home-state senators.[28] McConnell's tactics on judges were effective across the board. His stalling of Obama's nominees was so persistent that when Trump and McGahn came into office, there were one hundred lower-court seats waiting to be filled.[29]

The filling of those vacancies often began with Leonard Leo. In fact, before Neil Gorsuch met with Trump in 2017, he had to run a gauntlet of lieutenants, and tellingly, it started with Leo, who was on leave from the Federalist Society and working with the presidential transition team. Gorsuch met with Leo on December 2, 2016, and had additional follow-up conversations with him as he met in January with McGahn; vice president elect Mike Pence; Steve Bannon, who became a senior adviser to Trump; Mark Paoletta, counsel to Vice President Pence; and Reince Priebus, who became Trump's first chief of staff. Before Gorsuch met with Trump in person, he had yet another telephone conversation with Leo. It was McGahn, of course, who let Gorsuch know Trump had settled on him. But throughout, Leo was helping to steer the screening and advising Gorsuch.[30]

Such involvement attested to Leo's power and the Federalist Society's as well. The law-and-public-policy group had been founded in the early 1980s by Steven Calabresi, then at Yale Law School, and two University of Chicago Law students, Lee Liberman and David McIntosh—the three had met as Yale undergraduates and were part of a debating society. Their aim was to buck prevailing liberalism, which dominated campuses nationwide. With the election of Ronald Reagan in 1981, the three sensed that there might be an appetite for such an organization. The founders chose the name the Federalist Society after the Federalist Papers and used a silhouette of James Madison as their logo.[31]

Scalia was teaching at the University of Chicago at the time, and Liberman and McIntosh enlisted him to be one of the faculty advisers. Scalia immediately recognized the value of conservatives banding together with a common mission. Being a conservative on campus, Scalia told me when I was interviewing him for a 2009 biography, was a lonely endeavor, and he wanted the shared intellectual fellowship. At the University of Chicago chapter's first meeting, he read from Federalist Number 49: "The reason of man, like man himself, is timid and cautious when left alone, and acquires firmness and confidence in proportion to the number with which it is associated." He told me he wanted a passage that reflected the benefits of organizing for "physical and intellectual courage." Rereading that Scalia comment more than a decade and a half later, in 2022, I am struck by how much it speaks to the potency of a six-justice majority over that of a five-justice bloc. The numbers have given the right wing a new confidence, beyond a single extra vote, to reconsider and overturn a half century of rights and regulations.

Scalia's presence helped with early fundraising from such conservative charities as the former New York–based John M. Olin Foundation, the Milwaukee-based Lynde and Harry Bradley Foundation, and the Pittsburgh-based Scaife Foundations. Within a few years, the Federalist Society had a national office in Washington, dozens of student chapters, and a budget in the millions. "We thought we were just planting a flower among the weeds of academic liberalism," Scalia said. "It turned out to be an oak."[32]

Joining about a decade later after its founding, Leo became as much of a force in Federalist Society history as Liberman, McIntosh, and Calabresi, who themselves became part of various GOP administrations' judicial selection processes. But Leo almost took a different career turn at the start, as Clarence Thomas, a longtime friend of his, liked to tell it. In 1991, he was finishing a clerkship with Judge Raymond Randolph (then sitting on the D.C. Circuit with Thomas) and felt torn between two offers, one at a law firm in New Jersey, the other from the Federalist Society, based in Washington. Thomas recalled years later in a public appearance with Judge Gregory Katsas at a Federalist Society event that he asked Leo where his heart was. Leo said it was with the Federalist Society, which he then helped grow to the point that Justice Thomas declared in the 2020 appearance with Katsas, "Look at the difference he has made!"[33] By then Leo had transformed an organization that began as a debating society for law students into a national networking and judge-producing machine.

He was born on Long Island in 1965 but spent most of his childhood in New Jersey, where the family moved after Leonard's father died and his mother remarried. (He died when Leonard was about four.) Leonard's maternal grandfather was a tailor who became an executive in the Brooks Brothers manufacturing department. The roots of the bespoke attire of Leo's adulthood traced to those years.

As a child, Leonard wore a navy blue blazer with a silk lining and gold buttons, later passing the jacket down to his sons. He attended public school in Monroe Township, where his nickname, in a nod to his fundraising ability as class president, was "Moneybags Kid." At Cornell, he wore jackets, trousers, and coats that Brooks Brothers produced as samples. "It was a pretty ridiculous wardrobe during my college years," he allowed, and it carried over to Cornell Law.[34]

In Washington, as he helped steer the Federalist Society, Leo became the consummate networker and money-raiser, regularly joining power brokers over breakfast at the Mayflower or the Hay-Adams. He deepened the Federalist Society's money channels to the Koch brothers, Richard Scaife, and other leading right-wing donors. His crusades led George Mason University to rename its law school to honor Justice Scalia immediately after his death. The justice and Leo were committed conservatives and shared a deep Roman Catholic faith, Scalia and his wife producing nine children and Leo and his wife, Sally, seven. The eldest, Margaret, died at age fourteen of complications related to spina bifida. Leo said he tried to attend daily Mass, encouraged, he said, by Margaret's "zeal" for the daily ritual.[35]

Even before it looked like Trump's campaign would succeed, Mc-

Gahn and Leo discussed candidates for his potential Supreme Court and lower-court nominations. Their work, along with that of the Heritage Foundation, manifested itself in Trump's May 2016 list of eleven candidates for the Supreme Court. No presidential candidate had ever promoted a field of Supreme Court possibilities the way Trump did. The list started to take shape on February 13, 2016, the evening of Scalia's death, when Trump and other GOP primary candidates gathered in South Carolina for a televised debate. In a phone call that evening, McGahn advised Trump to offer during the debate possible candidates for the Scalia vacancy. He gave him some names of U.S. appeals court judges that would help Trump suggest he was serious about appointing conservatives, and Trump went ahead and offered the audience two possibilities: Diane Sykes, of Wisconsin, and Bill Pryor, of Arkansas, who had had long been on right-wing lists of possible Court nominees. McGahn thought that mentioning them would appeal to traditional Republicans who were skeptical of a candidate who cut an imprudent profile with his red "Make America Great Again" cap and anti-immigrant rhetoric. Onstage and under the lights, Trump also told the moderator, John Dickerson of CBS News, that Republicans should prevent Obama from making an appointment: "I think it's up to Mitch McConnell and everybody else to stop it," Trump said. "It's called delay, delay, delay."[36]

When Trump then released the May 2016 list, it somehow seemed fitting that the characteristic "disrupter," as McGahn called him, put it out on a day that coincided with a highly choreographed annual spring musicale at the Supreme Court. The musicale was a formal affair for the justices and their invited guests, part of a tradition dating from the 1980s, when the British Institute donated a piano to the Court. That first piano had been chosen and was signed by Leonard Bernstein, "with Justice for all." News of the Trump list broke just before the event was to be held, and the document, audacious in the sheer message it conveyed, seized the attention of news reporters at the Court building and beyond. Not one of the names on the original list of eleven was ever selected by Trump, but it mattered not. The list represented an important development in Trump's use of the judiciary as a tool, as if he were putting the judiciary on the ballot with him.[37]

After he won, Leo visited the president-elect at Trump Tower in Manhattan in November 2016 to talk about judges. Trump was especially captivated by Justice Scalia, his reputation and take-no-prisoners opinions. He had heard that the justice's widow, Maureen Scalia, had been a Trump campaign supporter, and he pressed Leo for more details about the Scalia family. Leo suggested he call Maureen and gave him her phone number. "I didn't think he would call her," Leo said later, "but he did." I learned from a source close to Maureen Scalia that Trump asked her if it was true that she had one of his signs in her yard. She answered, "And a bumper sticker, too." Trump followed up a few weeks later to make sure she had received her tickets to inaugural events. He then invited Maureen Scalia to the unveiling of the Gorsuch nomination and to subsequent judicial investitures at the White House.[38]

Justice Scalia had personified the GOP judicial effort dating to the early 1980s. President Ronald Reagan's legal team systematically sought out young conservatives for powerful U.S. court seats across the country.[39] Reagan wanted judges who would narrowly construe their roles in societal dilemmas and stay away from such liberal-era interventions as those on school desegregation, prison conditions, and environmental cleanup. Reagan's vetting teams looked for law professors and other prominent thinkers who would generate a following of like-minded lawyers and jurists. Scalia was selected for the prominent U.S. Court of Appeals for the District of Columbia Circuit in 1982 and then elevated to the Supreme Court in 1986.

Thus, a blueprint for the conservative takeover of the U.S. judiciary had existed long before Trump's election. The new president embraced it. As Leo and Trump talked at Trump Tower about the Scalia vacancy and other openings, Leo asked him, "What do you care about? What do you want? You now have twenty names on your list, and the list has to be winnowed." Leo recalled that Trump wanted impressive credentials from the nominees, and that he wanted to avoid anyone who would turn out to be other than as advertised, such as Justice David

Souter. "He talked about Souter," Leo said of Trump. "That was of his generation. He knew the Souter problem."[40]

An appointee of President George H. W. Bush in 1990, Souter had been heavily promoted by Senator Warren Rudman and White House chief of staff John Sununu, both from New Hampshire, with the latter calling the nominee a "home run" for conservatives.[41] But Souter ended up ensconced in the liberal wing during his 1990–2009 tenure. It was not as if he changed all that much. The successor to Justice William Brennan, he had voiced an expansive view of due process rights during his confirmation hearings and voted center-left nearly from the start of his tenure. But the administration's vetting team had been swayed by friends who had vouched for his conservatism. Souter also had a scant federal court record. He had been on New Hampshire state courts from 1976 until early 1990 and then a judge for a few months on the Boston-based U.S. Court of Appeals for the First Circuit.

McGahn and his allies were determined to keep the screening tight and to avoid ideological missteps. They also were undeterred by "Not Qualified" ratings from the American Bar Association. In the end, Trump's appointees constituted one-third of the Supreme Court and nearly that much of the lower courts. Trump filled 54 of the 179 appeals court judgeships, or 30 percent, and 177 of 682 district court judgeships (26 percent). The appeals court numbers were significant because the Supreme Court took up so few cases, and appellate judges generally were the last stop for a dispute. Before Trump's tenure, four of the thirteen U.S. appeals courts had Republican majorities. When Trump was finished, seven of the thirteen were dominated by Republican appointees. Joe Biden came to office intent on counteracting the Trump judicial juggernaut through his own appointment machinery, with the Senate controlled by the Democrats, and succeeded in matching the Trump numbers on the lower courts in the first two years.

Trump's judges were younger on average than Obama's and Biden's appointees, meaning that they would likely serve longer than their counterparts. They were also far less diverse. In terms of race and sex, 84 percent of Trump's appointees were white and 76 percent were male. For comparison, 64 percent of Obama's appointees were white and 58 percent were men. Biden's appointees were even more diverse. Russell Wheeler of the Brookings Institution's Governance Studies Program, who had collected such data for decades, found that only 37 percent of Biden's appointees as of September 2022 were white, and of that total, 30 percent were white women. Biden focused on elevating Black women, who constituted slightly more than 20 percent of his total appointments.[42]

Through Trump's four years, Senate Republican leaders and the White House were almost always on the same page to fill vacancies as soon as they arose. Key senators including then–Senate Judiciary Committee chairman Grassley urged older judges to retire, so more seats could be Trump's. The president's team filled openings through his final days. He appointed fourteen judges after the November 3 election, about 6 percent of his total of 234.[43]

McGahn, McConnell, and Leo had their favorites along the way. McGahn, however, stumbled with two people close to him: his former FEC colleague Matthew Petersen, and Brett Talley, the husband of McGahn's then–chief of staff, Annie Donaldson. Talley was thirty-six at the time, had served as a deputy solicitor general in Alabama, and had then joined the Department of Justice Office of Legal Policy. The American Bar Association rated Talley "Not Qualified" based on his lack of trial experience or the requisite equivalence. Equally significant, Talley failed to reveal his wife's connection to the White House counsel on his Senate questionnaire, which angered senators of both parties. He withdrew in December 2017.[44]

Petersen's nomination around the same time to a U.S. district court in Washington, D.C., led to a much more public retreat. Petersen lacked trial experience but had years of experience on regulatory matters and was deemed "Qualified" by the ABA. He might have gotten through the confirmation process if Louisiana Republican senator John Kennedy had not targeted the former McGahn colleague as a proxy for his dissatisfaction with McGahn's screening process. Senator Kennedy thought that the White House counsel was pushing nominees through the Senate too quickly and showing disrespect to Kennedy by forgoing consultation on Louisiana judicial choices.

Kennedy put Petersen through a series of basic trial questions, catching the nominee off guard and humiliating him at the public hearing. "Mr. Petersen, have you ever tried a jury trial?" "I have not." "Civil?" "No." "Criminal?" "No." "Bench?" "No." "State or federal court?" "I have not." "Have you ever taken a deposition?" "I was involved in taking depositions when I was an associate at Wiley Rein when I first came out of law school. But that was . . ." "How many depositions?" "I'd be struggling to remember."

"When's the last time you read the Rules of Civil Procedure?" "In my current position, I obviously don't need to stay as invested in those on a day-to-day basis." "Can you tell me what the Daubert standard is?" "Senator Kennedy, I don't have that readily at my disposal but I would be happy to take a closer look at that." "Do you know what a motion in limine is?" "I would probably not be able to give you a good definition right here at the table."[45]

And on it went. Typical of the news coverage was a *New York Times* story headlined "Trump Judicial Nominee Attracts Scorn after Flopping in Hearing." Petersen and his White House handlers had anticipated tough questions from Democrats about Petersen's Federal Election Commission votes diminishing the force of regulations on campaign money. But they failed to foresee the consequences of the feud between McGahn and Kennedy and the scrutiny the Louisiana Republican was giving Petersen's record. A video of the painful exchange between the senator and the nominee was widely circulated on social media by Senator Sheldon Whitehouse, a Rhode Island Democrat critical of Petersen's FEC policies. He tweeted: "MUST WATCH: Republican @SenJohnKennedy asks one of @realDonaldTrump's US District Judge nominees basic questions of law and he can't answer a single one. Hoo-boy." The clip gained Whitehouse millions of viewers.[46]

Petersen pulled out three days later. In his December 16, 2017, letter to President Trump, he said that he had believed that his twenty years in regulatory law might have prepared him for the U.S. district court in Washington, D.C. "I had hoped my nearly two decades of public service might carry more weight than my worst two minutes on television," Petersen wrote. "However, I am no stranger to political realities, and I do not wish to be a continued distraction from the important work of your administration and the Senate."[47]

Petersen was unprepared for Kennedy's questions, but he also was the victim of a rivalry between the senator and the White House counsel. Kennedy had earlier been pressured to accept a choice of McGahn's for the New Orleans–based U.S. Court of Appeals for the Fifth Circuit: Kyle Duncan, lead attorney for the conservative Christian Becket Fund for Religious Liberty. Duncan was the kind of lightning rod the Trump administration sought. He had helped lead the litigation against the Affordable Care Act's requirement that employers provide contraceptive insurance coverage to their workers and had actively fought gay rights legal protections. "I first learned about Mr. Duncan's nomination when I received a phone call, actually a series of phone calls, from Mr. Don McGahn," Kennedy recalled, "and Mr. McGahn was very firm that Mr. Duncan would be the nominee, to the point that he was on the scarce side, in one conversation, of being polite."[48]

Kennedy said that he, too, wanted a committed conservative, and that Trump could have tapped a local candidate rather than one tied to Washington. "Mr. Duncan is staunchly and vociferously pro-life. So am I," began Kennedy. "Mr. Duncan is staunchly and vociferously pro-religious liberty. So am I. . . . I have received scores of phone calls from experienced, accomplished, whip-smart, pro-life, pro-religious liberty . . . lawyers and judges, who have asked me why I would support a Washington lawyer over them, and not the second cousin of someone who is connected in the Washington swamp."[49] Kennedy said that McGahn later apologized to him. And McConnell held a private breakfast in his office with Kennedy, McGahn, and Leo to try to smooth over relations and ensure that the judicial-confirmation machinery kept moving. "It was Mitch's idea," Leo told me, "to deflect" some of the ill feelings.[50]

Predictably, McConnell's own choices moved through the process quickly. Amul Thapar, a former U.S. attorney in Kentucky, became the first Trump nominee confirmed for a U.S. appellate court seat, in the spring of 2017. And Justin Walker offered the best illustration of how the clubby system for judicial selection could benefit one of its own.

Walker's maternal grandfather, Frank Metts, a real estate developer and Kentucky state transportation secretary, was a close friend of Mc-Connell's. When McConnell was running for Senate reelection in the early 1990s and Walker was just about eight years old, his mother put a McConnell sign in their front yard. "I've got to hand it to you, Mom," Walker said later, recalling the episode publicly. "It has been extremely important to me that Kentucky's senior senator is Mitch McConnell."[51] Walker attended Duke University and became a summer intern for McConnell. He then went to Harvard Law School, where he got to know Elena Kagan, then dean, who would later recommend him for a Supreme Court clerkship. But first, Brett Kavanaugh hired Walker to be a judicial clerk to him on the D.C. Circuit. Walker subsequently became a clerk to Justice Anthony Kennedy. Along the way, he also helped on the George W. Bush reelection campaign, worked at the Pentagon under Donald Rumsfeld, and worked at the law firm of Gibson Dunn. After the Supreme Court clerkship, he returned to Kentucky to teach at the University of Louisville law school.

He aspired to a judgeship, and in June 2018, when it looked like Kavanaugh might have a shot at elevation to the Supreme Court, Walker approached McConnell about the seat on the D.C. Circuit. He was then just thirty-five, and his conversation with McConnell about the possible vacancy occurred a few days before Justice Kennedy even announced his retirement. (Most people did not know a vacancy was on the near horizon, although McGahn and Kavanaugh were clued in.) Once Trump selected Kavanaugh as the successor a few weeks later, Walker publicly praised his former boss in every way he could, writing op-eds and blog posts on his behalf and engaging in more than one hundred interviews with news outlets.[52]

Walker's support of Kavanaugh actually began immediately after Kennedy announced his retirement, when various judicial candidates and their benefactors were jockeying for attention at the White House. Walker emphasized Kavanaugh's right-wing record, saying that he would be "no David Souter." Conservative critics were speculating that Kavanaugh was not fully committed to their cause, because of his inside-the-Beltway alliances and his 2011 punt in a dispute over the Affordable Care Act. Opposition to "Obamacare" had become a litmus test for conservatives. Trump ran against it in 2016, vowing to repeal the sweeping law if he became president. Republicans had opposed the legislation throughout congressional negotiations, and once the law intended to cover millions of previously uninsured Americans passed, they immediately challenged it in court, mainly targeting the individual mandate.

Kavanaugh had handled an early Obamacare case on the D.C. Circuit, sidestepping a decision on the merits of the mandate. He said he could not resolve the core question of its constitutionality because of a procedural flaw in the timing of the case. Yet he criticized the Affordable Care Act extensively, asserting that if the mandate were upheld, Congress might similarly be able to force other purchases, such as college savings accounts.[53] As Walker sought to counteract right-wing suspicion of Kavanaugh because he had failed to vote to strike down the ACA, he described his mentor's opinion as a "thorough and principled takedown of the mandate." He also insisted that Kavanaugh's opinion on the D.C. Circuit had guided the Supreme Court justices who had dissented in the Supreme Court's 2012 landmark ruling upholding the law. It was while that case came before the Court that Walker had clerked for Kennedy, one of the four dissenting justices in *National Federation of Independent Business v. Sebelius.*

Chief Justice Roberts, of course, had cast the decisive vote with the four liberal justices to uphold the law, tying the penalty for people who refused to obtain insurance to Congress's taxing power rather than Congress's traditional power over interstate commerce. Having first voted to strike down the law, Roberts had angered fellow conservatives with his move, and Kennedy had joined his right-wing colleagues in protest: "The Court today decides to save a statute Congress did not write. It rules that what the statute declares to be a requirement with a penalty is instead an option subject to a tax. . . . The Court regards its strained statutory interpretation as judicial modesty. It is not. It amounts instead to a vast judicial overreaching."[54]

As Walker tried to vouch for Kavanaugh's conservatism during the selection phase, he pointed to his own insider credentials from 2018, saying that he was "very familiar with" *National Federation of Independent Business v. Sebelius* because of his Kennedy clerkship. "I can tell you with certainty that the only justices following a roadmap from Brett Kavanaugh were the ones who said Obamacare was unconstitutional," Walker wrote. Two years later, Walker went further to condemn the Roberts opinion, saying in a public speech, "The greatest words you can hear from Justice Kennedy are: 'You're hired.' And the worst words are: 'The chief justice thinks this might be a tax.'"[55]

Kavanaugh indeed became Trump's choice. But then, despite all of Walker's promotional efforts, the White House decided against selecting him immediately for the new D.C. Circuit vacancy. Instead, Trump chose Neomi Rao, a former law clerk to Justice Clarence Thomas who was nearly ten years older than Walker and far more experienced, particularly in efforts against government regulation. Trump had earlier appointed Rao to run the Office of Information and Regulatory Affairs at the Office of Management and Budget. Seven months after the Rao court announcement, Trump selected Walker for a federal trial court in Louisville, putting him on deck for eventual elevation to the D.C. Circuit.

The American Bar Association rated Walker "Not Qualified" in 2018 for the U.S. district court seat because he lacked trial experience. But that assessment did not hurt him. McConnell easily had the votes. After he was confirmed, 50–41, McConnell issued a statement praising his protégé, adding, "His thoughtful and deliberate approach fit the mold of a federal judge who—imagine this—will uphold the laws and the Constitution as they are actually written, not as he might wish them to be."[56]

Walker was not about to forget the American Bar Association and his other critics. "Thank you for serving as an enduring reminder that although my legal principles are prevalent, they have not yet prevailed," he said at his district-court investiture, "and although we are winning, we have not won, and although we celebrate today, we cannot take for granted tomorrow or we will lose our courts and our country to critics who call us terrifying and describe us as deplorable."[57]

McConnell, Kavanaugh, and McGahn all flew down for the March

2020 investiture. The coronavirus pandemic was gripping the country. The trip was risky. But they attended, in service to each other. Walker paid homage to his benefactors during his investiture speech. Addressing Kavanaugh, who wore his black robe for the special swearing-in, Walker said, "What can I say that I haven't already said on Fox News?" It was a reference to all the media interviews he had conducted on Kavanaugh's behalf, especially with conservative media. He brought up Kavanaugh's 2018 confirmation battle: "You are like St. Paul, hard pressed on every side but not crushed. Perplexed but not in despair. Persecuted but not abandoned, struck down but not destroyed. Because in Brett Kavanaugh's America, we will not surrender while you wage war on our work, or our cause, or our hope, or our dream."[58]

Such battle-cry language breached the usual decorum. But it was becoming standard fare in some GOP circles, reinforcing the dissolution of judicial norms. A similar culture-war bluster rang through Walker's decisions as a district court judge. In April 2020, a few weeks after his investiture and as government officials were forbidding large gatherings to prevent the spread of the coronavirus, Judge Walker issued an order that ensured that drive-in religious services could continue on Easter Sunday. He blocked a proposed mandate from Louisville mayor Greg Fischer that disallowed any church gatherings, in person or drive-in. It happened that Walker intervened in the dispute before Fischer had tried to enforce any limits on drive-in services and the facts of the situation were still emerging. As Walker issued a temporary restraining order, he wrote, "On Holy Thursday, an American mayor criminalized the communal celebration of Easter. That sentence is one that this Court never expected to see outside the pages of a dystopian novel, or perhaps the pages of The Onion." Walker's rhetoric seemed designed to draw attention and was likely to reinforce his standing with conservatives.[59]

And, in fact, the same month, President Trump announced that he would be elevating Walker to the U.S. appeals court for the D.C. Circuit. Veteran appellate judge Thomas Griffith, who knew McConnell from his time as Senate legal counsel, had just made public his retirement. The connections among Griffith and McConnell and Walker seemed all too coincidental, and a liberal advocacy group, Demand Justice, filed a complaint seeking an investigation into whether McConnell had pressured Griffith to step down or promised him anything in exchange for the resignation. In a report on that filing, the *New York Times* noted that the D.C. Circuit chief judge, Sri Srinivasan, had asked Chief Justice Roberts to assign the inquiry to another circuit to avoid a conflict of interest. National Public Radio followed up with a story, for which Judge Griffith gave the network a statement: "My decision was driven entirely by personal concerns and involved no discussions with the White House or the Senate." He told NPR that his "sole reason" for retirement was that his wife was dealing with a "debilitating chronic illness" that had been diagnosed eleven years earlier. (Griffith separately told me that he had not discussed his retirement timing with McConnell.)[60]

At the time, Chief Justice Roberts decided against transferring the inquiry that had been forwarded by Judge Srinivasan to another circuit and instead returned it to the D.C. Circuit. A letter from his top aide, counselor Jeffrey Minear, noted that the complaint had not undergone any D.C. Circuit inquiry or verification. Soon after, D.C. Circuit judge Karen LeCraft Henderson took control of the matter and dismissed the Demand Justice complaint involving Griffith. "The subject judge has publicly stated that his decision to retire was motived entirely by personal considerations. Complainant has provided nothing that calls into doubt the judge's explanation of his decision," Henderson wrote in a memorandum attached to her May 15, 2020, order.[61]

Overall, the federal courts' system for resolving misconduct and other ethics complaints was marked by a lack of transparency. It fell especially short when it came to Supreme Court justices, as was seen after dozens of ethics complaints were filed against Kavanaugh. Eighty-three people, many of them lawyers, had lodged the complaints around the time of his confirmation hearings, largely centered on his heated response to the Christine Blasey Ford testimony. Kavanaugh had asserted that her assault claims traced to his political enemies. Some of those who filed said Kavanaugh's response was inappropriately partisan, demonstrated bias, and showed a lack of judicial temperament. All eighty-three complaints were dismissed by a federal panel of judges, who said that "while the complaints 'are serious,' there is no existing authority that allows lower court judges to investigate or discipline Supreme Court justices." Supreme Court justices were not covered by the judiciary's code of conduct, which dated to 1973, as lower courts were.[62]

In the end, no one was positioned to conduct a serious investigation: not the Trump White House, not the FBI, and not the judiciary.

Roberts understood that the Kavanaugh confirmation had bruised the institution and complicated his desire to disentangle the Court from politics. But he liked Kavanaugh, and one of the unshakable principles of Court life was that the justices closed ranks against outside critics. Soon after the confirmation, Roberts used a long-scheduled appearance at the University of Minnesota in Minneapolis to defend Kavanaugh and the impartiality of the judiciary. Referring to the "contentious events in Washington of recent weeks," Roberts said, "I will not criticize the political branches. We do that often enough in our opinions. But what I would like to do, briefly, is emphasize how the judicial branch is—how it must be—very different. . . . We do not sit on opposite sides of an aisle, we do not caucus in separate rooms, we do not serve one party or one interest. We serve one nation. And I want to assure all of you that we will continue to do that to the best of our abilities, whether times are calm or contentious."[63]

Other justices eased the way for Kavanaugh, too. Thomas, who had confronted his own accusations of sexual harassment from Anita Hill in 1991, tried to buck up his new colleague. Alito, who had complained about his 2006 confirmation for years afterward, was chastened by what Kavanaugh had experienced. No longer would he joke that when he walked around the Capitol Hill area, he crossed the street to avoid passing in front of the Hart Senate Office Building, where his hearings had been held. Alito liked Kavanaugh personally, and his son, Philip, had been a law clerk for Kavanaugh on the D.C. Circuit.

Justice Sotomayor put the institution's reputation first and made sure her regard for Kavanaugh was evident. Sotomayor said that she had welcomed him with a story she had learned from Thomas about his transition onto the Court after the Anita Hill hearings. In an interview with David Axelrod for CNN, she recounted, "It was Justice Thomas who tells me that when he first came to the Court, another justice approached him and said, 'I judge you by what you do here. Welcome.' And I repeated that story to Justice Kavanaugh when I first greeted him." Sotomayor described Kavanaugh as part of their "family" now. "When you're charged with working together for most of the remainder of your life, you have to create a relationship," she said. Ginsburg praised Kavanaugh for hiring all female law clerks his first term. In the courtroom, where Kagan sat next to Kavanaugh for oral arguments, she whispered and joked lightly with him. All three women justices wanted to move beyond the confirmation hearing spectacle, and they made their gestures of support public.[64]

The following year, *Time* magazine named both Kavanaugh and Ford among the "100 Most Influential Americans," which set off a new round of controversy. "You put her on the same list as the man she said assaulted her. So disappointing @TIME," the actress Jessica Chastain wrote on Twitter. Fittingly, the *Time* essay saluting Kavanaugh was written by Senator McConnell. The Ford tribute was written by Senator Kamala Harris, a California Democrat who was among the many candidates then launching a 2020 presidential bid.[65]

Soon after, when George Mason University's Antonin Scalia Law School hired Kavanaugh to teach a course on the origins of the U.S. Constitution in Runnymede, England, students protested at the suburban Virginia campus and demanded that the university cancel Kavanaugh's teaching arrangement. In response, George Mason University's president, Ángel Cabrera, said in a statement, "The law school has determined that the involvement of a U.S. Supreme Court Justice contributes to making our law program uniquely valuable for our students. And I accept their judgment. This decision, controversial as it may be, in no way affects the university's ongoing efforts to eradicate sexual violence from our campuses." Kavanaugh's course stayed on the schedule.

Justice Kavanaugh's first appearance outside of Washington occurred in May 2019, in Milwaukee, Wisconsin, with virtually no advance publicity. Justice Kennedy accompanied Kavanaugh and appeared with him onstage in the Pfister Hotel ballroom as they spoke of Court traditions and the rule of law. During Kavanaugh's brief remarks at that Seventh Circuit conference, he rejected the suggestion that judges automatically side with the interests of the president who appointed them—an idea that Trump himself had advanced. "We owe our allegiance to the Constitution," Kavanaugh said, pulling a small booklet copy of the U.S. Constitution from his jacket pocket. He told the audience that it was the copy he first had as a law clerk to Justice Kennedy in the early 1990s.[66]

Kavanaugh and the men who enabled his rise wanted to put the confirmation hearings behind them. When McGahn spoke in 2020 at a Princeton University forum entitled "The Politics of Judicial Nominations in an Age of Mistrust," several questions were posed to him about the Kavanaugh confirmation. Rutgers history professor David Greenberg asked if Trump would have named Kavanaugh if he had known about the Ford allegations before making the choice. Greenberg told me he asked the question because he believed that if the allegations had been examined before the nomination was made, the high-voltage confirmation politics might have been avoided.

McGahn swatted back Greenberg's question, rejecting the premise that any of Kavanaugh's behavior would have warranted early investigation and suggesting that Ford's claim was fictional. That's "not reality," McGahn said. "The guy's on the Supreme Court. Reality is reality. Facts are facts. . . . No. . . . It didn't happen. The guy is on the Supreme Court."[67]

## Chapter 5

# A MOMENT OF TRUTH

When Elena Kagan was young, she wanted to keep up with a brother who was a comic book aficionado, so she devoured tales of Spider-Man. As a justice, Kagan similarly tried to understand colleagues' interests and meet them where they lived, as when she took up hunting with Justice Antonin Scalia. The two justices became friends, and in 2015, their jurisprudence united in a case that, it just so happens, involved Spider-Man.[1]

The Spider-Man dispute showcased Kagan's legal approach, her arguments for stare decisis, and the notion that the Court should stick even to misguided decisions to promote stability in the law. "An argument that we got something wrong—even a good argument to that effect—cannot by itself justify scrapping settled precedent," Kagan wrote in *Kimble v. Marvel Entertainment*. She would invoke this principle even when it did not necessarily serve her progressive purposes, conceivably to shore up credibility for when significant precedents were on the line. Conservatives continued their ascendancy after Scalia's death, and by 2019, Kagan's colleagues had their eye on a range of precedents, including the 1973 *Roe v. Wade*.

The Spider-Man case started with Stephen Kimble, a lawyer turned inventor who obtained a patent in 1990 on a toy that shot pressurized foam string into what looked like a web. Marvel Entertainment, which marketed products featuring Spider-Man, rejected a deal with Kimble and soon after began marketing its own "Web Blaster." Kimble sued

Marvel for patent infringement. The two sides eventually agreed that Marvel would purchase Kimble's patent for a set sum and then pay a royalty on their future sales of the toy. There was no end date for the royalties. Marvel lawyers later discovered, however, that a 1964 Supreme Court case, *Brulotte v. Thys Co.*, dictated that once a patent expired, a patentee could not receive royalties for sales. Marvel asked a U.S. district court judge for a declaratory judgment so it could stop royalty payments in 2010, the end of Kimble's patent term. Lower-court judges sided with Marvel, though they had some misgivings about the wisdom of the 1964 case.[2]

Kimble appealed, and the justices voted 6–3 to uphold *Brulotte v. Thys Co.* and the proposition that a patent holder lost any royalties when the patent term expired. Scalia, the most senior justice in the majority, assigned the Court's opinion to Kagan. She was the junior justice at the time, but she ran with it, not so much for patent law principles as for the value of stare decisis. She quoted Stan Lee and Steve Ditko's hero—"In this world, with great power there must also come—great responsibility"—and went on to write: "What we can decide, we can undecide. But *stare decisis* teaches that we should exercise that authority sparingly. Finding many reasons for staying the *stare decisis* course and no 'special justification' for departing from it, we decline Kimble's invitation to overrule *Brulotte*."[3]

After the addition of the first two Trump appointees, Kagan stepped up the theme during oral arguments in a December 2018 case. "You know, part of what *stare decisis* is, is a kind of doctrine of humility, where we say we are really uncomfortable throwing over 170-year-old rules that 30 justices have approved just because we think we can kind of do it better." In March 2019 arguments, she said of the conditions for reversal of precedent, "Usually we look to something terrible that's happening: This is unworkable. This is an anomaly in the doctrine. It no longer has any support in the surrounding legal landscape, something like that. This is so grievously wrong that we can't stand to live with it anymore."[4]

More than many of her colleagues, Kagan looked to cases on the horizon, matching the strategic approach of Roberts in that regard.

She also appreciated Roberts's desire to protect the institution in the public eye. The two, along with Stephen Breyer, had worked together on the Obamacare compromise in 2012. After Justice Kennedy's retirement, Kagan recognized that Roberts was open to a middle ground. The presence of Kennedy, a Reagan appointee who sometimes voted with the Left, had provided Roberts with some cover against accusations of a politicized bench. Now any variation on a politicized lineup was in his hands: without Kennedy, he marked the ideological center.

Roberts liked and respected Kagan. But their relationship had not always been smooth, as when Roberts had chastised Kagan, then solicitor general, for responding to a question from the bench with a question of her own. "Usually, we have the questions the other way," Roberts said. The pattern was pronounced enough that *Newsweek* ran a story under the headline "Does the Chief Justice Hate Elena Kagan?" Their respective backgrounds at the center of Republican or, alternatively, Democratic, administrations, and their similar tactical instincts, suggested that they would be natural rivals. But once Kagan was on the Court, their sparring became mutually respectful and Roberts publicly praised her questions as "incisive," her opinions as "clear, careful," and her mode in deliberations as "collegial." For good measure, in an early interview at a judicial conference, Roberts mentioned that she had shone as a new member of the Court's cafeteria committee by getting a frozen yogurt machine installed, apparently a popular move with the staff.[5]

Kagan returned the favor, speaking publicly of how Roberts had welcomed her, giving her a personal tour of the Court's conference room and robing area and the justices' dining room. In the robing room, each justice has a tall wooden locker identified by a little brass nameplate. Justice Stevens's name was still on his locker when they started the tour. When they finished and Roberts brought Kagan back to the robing room, Stevens's nameplate had been removed and Kagan's name—per Roberts's request—had been affixed to her new locker at the end of the row of nine.

Kagan's professional path appeared seamless, but she told audiences that her career looked that way only in hindsight. She hinted at setbacks, although typically without elaboration. A decade before her Supreme Court appointment, Kagan suddenly seemed to have few prospects. President Clinton had nominated her to the U.S. Court of Appeals for the District of Columbia Circuit in 1999, but the Republican-controlled Senate declined to give her a hearing. The University of Chicago Law School did not welcome her back to her tenured position. She tried, unsuccessfully, for the deanship at the University of Texas. She obtained a visiting professorship at Harvard, a temporary refuge. But it was there, at her alma mater, that she quickly rose again, becoming dean. She won over students and faculty, engaging in gestures small (free coffee) and large (bringing in ideologically diverse faculty). When Barack Obama won the presidency in 2008, she headed back to Washington to work in the Justice Department as solicitor general.[6]

By early 2019, senior liberal Ruth Bader Ginsburg was moving into a new phase of health difficulties, and turning more to Kagan. The two women had developed a deep bond, in spite of some differences. Kagan, twenty-seven years younger than Ginsburg, was more moderate than her colleague. In classic blazer and slacks, Kagan exuded a no-frills sensibility that differed from the designer-clad, opera-loving Ginsburg. Ginsburg appreciated that Kagan understood Roberts and negotiated with the chief in a way that she could not. While Ginsburg did not refer to Roberts with the warmth that she had showed his predecessor William Rehnquist (whom she called "my chief"), she seemed to hold no general animosity toward him. Ginsburg left internal dealings to Kagan, and to Breyer, simply because they were naturally suited toward such give-and-take. Law clerks said Kagan always had a plan.

About a month after Brett Kavanaugh had been seated and the new nine were still finding their bearings, Ginsburg discovered that she had lung cancer. This was especially upsetting news for a justice trying to outlive the Trump presidency. The diagnosis followed a freak mishap on November 7, 2018. Then eighty-five, Ginsburg had been working late in her office. Her chambers were spacious and among the most desirable in the building. She had spent years getting the interior decor and customized cabinetry to suit her, including a special cupboard for her dozens of collars and jabots. Ginsburg kept her fireplace lit most months of the year. As she sat reading, she often draped herself in a shawl. A couple of times a week, she took a break at around seven P.M. for a session with her personal trainer downstairs in a justices-only workout room.

On this November evening, she slipped to the floor in her office. The sharp pain in her left side left no doubt as to what had just happened. In 2012, when the justices were deliberating over the Affordable Care Act case, she had fallen and broken her ribs at her Watergate apartment. She had worked through the pain as her ribs slowly healed. The following year, in 2013, she again fell in her apartment. "It was almost identical," she told me, saying that she had refused to go to the hospital. "There's nothing you could do. You just live on painkillers for a while."[7]

But now, in late 2018, the pain felt overwhelming. The next morning, a Supreme Court police officer drove her to George Washington University Hospital to be examined. Three ribs were fractured. But that was not the end of it. Physicians found something more serious. The justice who had survived colorectal cancer in 1999 and pancreatic cancer in 2009 now had two cancerous nodules on her left lung. They would have to be removed. Ginsburg released a public statement referring only to the fractured ribs. She was then back on the bench in early December for two weeks of oral arguments. It was not until the afternoon of December 21, 2018, that the Court's public information office revealed that Ginsburg had cancer and had undergone surgery to remove the cancerous growths from her lung.[8]

As Ginsburg began a protracted recovery in early 2019, the justices prepared to take up two major cases with consequences for equal representation in apportionment and voting districts. The disputes typified the new dilemmas of the day. One was distinct to the Trump administration and its attempt to manipulate the 2020 census. The other arose from conservative efforts to keep federal judges out of state gerrymandering and voting rights disputes. The stakes were enormous, because so many rights and liberties traced to the ability to vote and choose representatives for Congress, state capitals, and other corridors of power.

The gulf between Republicans and Democrats was growing, and with five Republican-appointed justices on one side and four Democratic-appointed justices on the other, the nation's divisions were reflected in the Court's handling of cases. The 2020 presidential election was still a year off, yet already Democrats worried about Trump-inspired Republican efforts to interfere with the vote and crush the voices of opponents.

In the weighty 2020 census dispute, the question was whether Commerce Secretary Wilbur Ross had offered valid, lawful grounds for adding a citizenship query to the long-form questionnaire that would be sent to all U.S. households in the decennial count. The Constitution requires an "actual enumeration" of all people living in the United States. Article 1, Section 2, states in part that "Representatives . . . shall be apportioned among the several States . . . according to their respective Numbers" and that an "Enumeration" shall occur every ten years. The count provides numbers for the distribution of power and resources, most importantly for the reapportionment of seats in the U.S. House of Representatives and the allocation of federal dollars. A citizenship question had not appeared on the census form since 1950. Some targeted forms asked the question, and other surveys by the Census Bureau and various agencies provided an estimate of the number of citizens in states and localities.

Census Bureau officials warned that adding the question for every household would discourage recent citizens and Hispanics from completing the decennial questionnaire. The bureau wanted to obtain the fullest count possible. In the political, practical world, any deflation of immigrant numbers would affect the distribution of congressional seats and federal funding in places where immigrants were concentrated, largely urban areas.

Ross, a bespectacled, balding private equity investor, had been approved in the Senate to serve as commerce secretary by an easy majority of 72–27, over objections from consumer advocates such as Massachusetts senator Elizabeth Warren, who wrote on Twitter, "Wilber Ross is practically a cartoon stereotype of a Wall Street fat cat with no interest in anyone but himself."[9] Soon after taking office in spring 2017, Ross conferred with Steve Bannon and other Trump allies who had made stopping immigration, especially among Latinos, a core tenet. Among them was Kansas secretary of state Kris Kobach, a well-known anti-immigrant activist who was also vice chair of a commission Trump established to find out whether election fraud had prevented him from winning the popular vote in 2016. Ross and Kobach discussed the effect a citizenship question would have on congressional apportionment—that is, plainly to increase Republican seats.[10]

Ross had earlier turned to the Department of Justice for a rationalization that he could use to justify his demand to the Census Bureau. He suggested that department officials say that the question was necessary to enforce the Voting Rights Act. Ross's whole scheme was suspicious, but invoking the Voting Rights Act was especially dubious. The landmark 1965 act, arising out of a bloody chapter of American civil rights struggle and intended to protect Blacks and Hispanics at the polls, was constantly under threat by right-wing Republicans who sought to leave voter protections to the individual states. It seemed implausible that the Trump administration would seek better enforcement of the Voting Rights Act by asking a citizenship question on the decennial form, because the question would certainly reduce the representation of people of color.

The Justice Department moved slowly on the Ross request, and the commerce secretary grew impatient. He decided to go directly to Attorney General Jeff Sessions and ask him to speed up the formal request. Sessions turned to John Gore, acting assistant attorney general for civil rights, to provide grounds for the citizenship query. Gore, who like Don McGahn and many other lawyers had come into the administration from Jones Day, obliged, according to the record in the case.[11] At the bidding of Sessions, doing the bidding of Ross, doing the bidding of Trump advisers (some outside the government), DOJ lawyers crafted a letter saying that the citizenship question was needed to enforce the Voting Rights Act. The letter was dated December 12, 2017, and signed by a DOJ general counsel, Arthur Gary.[12]

Three months later, Ross announced the plan through a public memo to the Census Bureau that opened with the DOJ request as justification and referred to valuable "block-level" data within voting precincts. He specifically stated that he began considering the issue *after* the DOJ request, which completely obscured his role in prompting the DOJ bid.[13] New York State and other largely Democratic states and cities that would be hurt by a skewed count immediately sued the Department of Commerce. Separate but similar claims were filed by civil liberties groups and immigration organizations.[14]

The one that reached the Supreme Court originated in New York City, where U.S. district court judge Jesse Furman was assigned the case and began moving quickly on the matter, as was his reputation. The 2012 Obama appointee had grown up in New York, the son of a real estate developer father and psychologist mother. His mentors and former bosses ranged across the political spectrum. Furman had been a law clerk to U.S. district court judge Michael Mukasey, a Republican appointee; later, when President George W. Bush tapped Mukasey as an attorney general, Furman, who was then working as a federal prosecutor for the Southern District of New York, became a counselor to Mukasey. In between his service to Mukasey, Furman was a law clerk to U.S. appellate judge José Cabranes, a Democratic appointee with moderate instincts, and U.S. Supreme Court justice David Souter, a Republican with liberal tendencies. As Furman began trial proceedings in 2018, he ordered Ross and John Gore to provide depositions to the states and groups that had sued over the questionnaire controversy. Furman also ordered the Commerce Department to turn over additional relevant files, because the administrative record the department had submitted appeared incomplete.

Department of Justice lawyers objected and quickly sought Supreme Court intervention to block the depositions of Secretary Ross and Acting Assistant Attorney General Gore. The justices privately wrangled for days over the politically charged dispute, as Roberts tried to craft some compromise. They met late into October 22, 2018, issuing an evening order. The justices completely blocked the deposition of Secretary Ross. The Court, however, allowed Furman to take testimony from Gore and obtain additional information beyond the original record. The Court's summary action offered a prime example of a pattern by which the Trump administration went to the justices for extraordinary intervention, and the majority largely obliged. This began to occur routinely, often late at night, on the Court's so-called shadow docket, where cases were handled in an emergency fashion without a hearing or full briefing on the merits.[15]

Indicative of how the census controversy even at this early stage roiled the justices, Neil Gorsuch, joined by Clarence Thomas, expressed exasperation at Furman's methods. Seeking the extra-record materials, Gorsuch wrote, was "highly unusual, to say the least." Gorsuch also targeted Furman's order for the new documents and the suggestion that the commerce secretary was withholding pertinent information. "Leveling an extraordinary claim of bad faith against a coordinate branch of government requires an extraordinary justification," Gorsuch wrote. Gorsuch and Thomas obviously thought Furman lacked grounds to try to understand the motives of Trump administration officials. But in time, evidence emerged that the officials indeed were not operating on the level.[16]

When Furman ruled in January 2019, he concluded that the Department of Commerce had breached Administrative Procedure Act protections against arbitrary government actions. He said that because the Supreme Court had shielded Ross from testifying, it was impossible to assess the challengers' additional claims that the department had violated the Constitution's guarantee of equal protection of the law. "Secretary Ross's intent—as the official decision-maker—was crucial to the equal protection claim," Furman wrote. "Secretary Ross's testimony could have revealed the nature of his conversations with Kobach, Bannon, and Attorney General Sessions, and whether President Trump directed the addition of the citizenship question. But Plaintiffs were denied the opportunity to depose Secretary Ross because the Supreme Court stayed this Court's order authorizing such a deposition."[17]

Furman went on to document that Ross had discussed the addition of the citizenship question with Bannon and solicited the DOJ request tied to the Voting Rights Act to back up his plan. "Perhaps most egregiously," Furman wrote in his 277-page opinion, "the evidence is clear that Secretary Ross's rationale was pretextual—that is, that the real reason for his decision was something other than the sole reason he put forward in his Memorandum, namely enhancement of DOJ's VRA enforcement efforts." He ruled that Ross had violated the Administrative Procedure Act's prohibition on "arbitrary and capricious" agency choices.

Furman homed in on Ross's apparent disregard for the public trust.[18] Yet as distressed as Furman was regarding the Trump administration's moves, he didn't know the half of it. He was unaware of a key element in the origins of the citizenship question. That additional piece would emerge later, when the Supreme Court was considering the Trump administration's appeal.

Normally, a party that has lost a case at the trial stage goes next to a regional appellate court. So the Trump administration would have appealed to the New York–based U.S. Court of Appeals for the Second Circuit. But Solicitor General Noel Francisco asked the nine justices to review Furman's ruling without any appellate court hearing. Francisco told the justices that the administration was up against a tight June 30 deadline to begin printing the 2020 census forms for distribution. He wanted the Court to hear the case, reverse Furman, and make clear that the trial judge wrongly allowed the submission of evidence at trial that had not been in the administrative record. Francisco argued that there were no grounds to the claim that the citizenship question had been devised for other than objective reasons.

As the justices considered whether to hear the case before an intermediate court acted, Ginsburg was recovering from the difficult lung surgery. She continued to work as much as possible, in the privacy of her apartment, with her aides traveling back and forth with briefs and other Court materials. But there were times she could hardly pull herself up from bed or out of a chair. In the past, she had been able to overcome whatever pain she had endured. During her recovery from pancreatic cancer surgery, she had made sure to attend President Barack Obama's first joint session of Congress in 2009. "I wanted people to see that the Supreme Court isn't all male," Ginsburg told me at the time. "I also wanted them to see I was alive and well, contrary to that senator who said I'd be dead within nine months." That was Jim Bunning, a Kentucky Republican who had predicted that her cancer would kill her. Bunning, who soon after apologized, died in 2017, and Ginsburg outlived him.[19]

But now Ginsburg's health was the shakiest it had been since she had become a justice. She could work at home out of the public eye on emergency cases and orders. She cast a dissenting vote with her three liberal colleagues when the Court's five-justice conservative majority revived President Trump's policy of preventing transgender people from serving in the military, at a preliminary stage of the case. Lower-court judges had put the policy on hold while lawsuits challenging it worked their way through the judicial system. Ginsburg did not have to reveal her weak voice or frail body for that action.[20] Oral arguments were a separate matter. She was in no condition to appear on the bench. She missed the entire two-week session of oral arguments in mid-January 2019. Before then, she had never skipped even a day of arguments.

In late February, just as she was well enough to return to work at the Court building, the majority voted on Francisco's request for an expedited hearing and agreed to set the census-questionnaire case for oral arguments. When the justices heard the case, Francisco sought to counteract the chronology laid out by Furman and to justify Ross's request by arguing the connection to the Voting Rights Act. Chief Justice Roberts was sympathetic to that assertion, and when New York solicitor general Barbara Underwood tried to dispute it, Roberts suggested that the citizenship question was like prior demographic queries. "We've had demographic questions on the census—I don't know how far back, but, certainly, it's quite common. . . . Sex, age, things like that. . . . Do you own your house? Do you own a radio? I mean, the questions go quite beyond how many people there are," Roberts said. The chief justice also showed an interest in the Voting Rights Act rationale, saying that knowing the citizen voting-age population was a "critical element in voting rights enforcement."[21]

Underwood said that questions about home ownership, radios, and other such domestic matters were wholly different and unlikely to skew population counts: "We have no comparable evidence about any of those other questions that they depress the count in this substantial a way and in this disproportionate a way." She said that Commerce Department evidence indicated that the citizenship question would actually compromise, not improve, voter information: "The Secretary decided to add this question about citizenship to the 2020 census although the record before him contained uncontradicted and strong evidence that it will cause a decline in the response rate of non-citizens and Hispanics, to the detriment of the states and localities where they live." Underwood said that Ross's justification for the question failed to meet the requirements of the Administrative Procedure Act (APA), and she added that Ross's assertion of insufficient evidence related to the citizenship question's effect was "flatly contrary to the record."[22]

ACLU lawyer Dale Ho separately appeared at the lectern to challenge the Department of Commerce. He said that Ross had "misstated the evidence in the record" regarding the citizenship question. "The secretary's decision rested primarily on one assertion, that it would improve the accuracy of citizenship data provided to the Department of Justice. But the administrative record revealed precisely the opposite, that it would make that data less accurate and thus harm the secretary's stated purpose of Voting Rights Act enforcement." Evidence showed that a citizenship query would skew the census data because noncitizens would be reluctant to complete the form or to answer the question truthfully. Ho avoided impugning Ross's motives during the argument. Lawyers involved in practice sessions with him known as "moot courts" had offered conflicting advice over how hard to hit Ross's pretextual rationale. Just two years earlier, Roberts had brushed aside arguments regarding Trump's anti-Muslim motivations in the travel ban case. So some lawyers thought it best not to assail the character of Trump officials. One lawyer advising the advocates countered (presciently) at a moot court, "The only way to get the chief on board is to make him think the decision was dirty, top to bottom."[23]

It was Kagan who homed in during oral arguments on the possibility that Ross had cooked up his rationale. "So you can't read this record without sensing that this need is a contrived one," she told Francisco, observing that former DOJ officials had never made such pleas connected to the Voting Rights Act. Francisco responded that it was "quite common for cabinet secretaries to come into office" with their own policy ideas, and he declared, "There's no evidence in this record that the Secretary would have asked this question had the Department of Justice not requested it. And there's no evidence in this record that the Secretary didn't believe that the Department of Justice actually wanted this information to improve Voting Rights Act enforcement."[24]

That was an overconfident assertion, but overconfidence was Francisco's signature. At the lectern, his claims on behalf of the government were sweeping. He believed in the Trump administration's positions heart and soul. He exuded more bravado than most appellate advocates beyond the courtroom, too, driving around town in a red Ford Mustang convertible, sometimes puffing on a cigar. Forty-seven when he became the government's top lawyer before the Court, he had risen quickly in GOP legal circles. He grew up in Oswego, New York, where his father, Nemesio, had immigrated from the Philippines and was a physician. Francisco's Pacific Islander roots were central to his identity, and in an address at the Department of Justice marking Asian American and Pacific Islander Heritage Month in May 2018, he recalled how his father was able to come to the United States from a country under siege soon after the Japanese attack on Pearl Harbor. "As a very young boy, my father was driven from his home by invading soldiers. He once told me how, for days, he was forced in live in the remnants of a bombed-out tank. My father's family pooled all of their resources to send him—the youngest son—to medical school and, eventually, to the United States, where he met my mother." Her name was Therese, and she had been reared in Oswego. Francisco described the similar-looking sons of other Filipino physicians in the area who visited his family when his father was dying of lung cancer in 1989. "The other

Filipino doctors and their families—known to me as my 'aunties, un-cles, and cousins'—came to say goodbye. And what struck me was how all of my 'cousins' and I looked alike. And it wasn't our jet black hair and brown skin. Rather, in the fashion of the time, all of us boys had pony tails and earrings. . . . [W]hat was clear was how thoroughly American all of us were, just one generation later."[25]

Francisco earned a law degree at the University of Chicago and be-came a law clerk to Justice Scalia. During the 2000 *Bush v. Gore* fight in Florida, he worked on the legal team defending Bush; afterward, he joined the administration. In the Obama years, he was a partner at Jones Day, the home of Don McGahn. He represented the Cath-olic bishops in challenges to the Affordable Care Act's birth control insurance coverage. Now he was aggressively pressing Trump's legal positions and at times had to send the Court a letter after arguments backtracking from what he said at the lectern.[26]

In the census case, Roberts had been persuaded by Francisco's pre-sentation of the administration's position, and when the justices met in their private session two days after the arguments, the chief justice was ready to rule for Ross. He believed that the administration mer-ited deference, and he disliked that Furman had looked to materials outside the record. Justice Thomas, who was next in seniority at the conference table, agreed with Roberts on the bottom line. He believed that Furman had set out to find fault with the Trump administra-tion's process. Next to vote was Justice Ginsburg, who wanted to affirm the Furman decision that Ross had violated federal procedural stan-dards when he devised the plan to add the citizenship question. Justice Breyer, voting next, agreed with Ginsburg. And so it went: a 5–4 tally along ideological lines. Roberts said he would write the opinion for the majority to reverse Furman, and Ginsburg, senior among the liberal dissenters, asked Breyer to write for their foursome on the left. But positions would shift, influenced especially by Kagan, as the weeks un-folded. She believed the evidence collected by Furman flatly belied the claim related to voting rights enforcement. Even though Roberts was siding with Secretary Ross, I learned that Kagan sensed an opening to try to convince the chief justice of the risk to the Court's integrity if it accepted the obviously contrived grounds for the census question. Roberts had not blanched at the Trump legal positions during the administration's first two years, but he was beginning to show concern that the administration was falling short and the Court's reputation was increasingly on the line in how it ruled in Trump cases.[27]

During these same spring weeks in 2019, a separate controversy crucial to American democracy and political representation was underway. This one found Kagan at odds with Roberts to the very end. The dispute centered on extreme partisan gerrymandering—the practice of legislators drawing voting districts along political lines to preserve their own interests, entrenching themselves in power and making it nearly impossible for the rival party to overcome, even with support among the electorate. Such detailed outcome-driven maps were made possible through the use of voter data collected from past elections and sophisticated computer methods. Modern technology allowed statehouse officials essentially to pick their voters, rather than ensuring that voters chose their candidates.

The watchdog group Common Cause, along with the North Carolina Democratic Party and a group of state voters, had sued to block a North Carolina legislative map drawn to ensure that the state's Republicans could maintain a 10–3 seat dominance. Such partisan gerrymandering was not unique to Republican officials. Democratic leaders did it when they controlled a statehouse, too. But at the time of the Supreme Court challenge, the practice was largely benefitting Republicans, because the GOP dominated the nation's state legislatures. Irrespective of party, the practice could demoralize voters because it gave inordinate authority to those drawing the maps and diminished real power at the polls. Results on Election Day often seemed preordained.

A special U.S. district court had heard the North Carolina case and ruled that Common Cause and state Democrats could sue in federal court over the manipulated districts, based on violations of the Fourteenth Amendment's equal protection guarantee and First Amendment protection of free speech and free association, the latter of which protects the activities of people who gather together for political or governmental purposes. The Republican defenders argued that legislative redistricting was a matter for politicians, not judges. The Supreme Court had been wrestling with that jurisdictional question for decades, never outright forbidding judges to become involved in gerrymandering disputes, but never striking down a political gerrymander or setting standards for when legislators had gone too far, either.

The Court had laid down a marker in the 1962 case of *Baker v. Carr,* when it ruled for the first time that the drawing of legislative districts could be challenged in the federal courts. (The Court rejected the notion that such apportionment challenges were "political questions" that judges could not resolve.) In *Davis v. Bandemer* (1986), the justices said that challenges to partisan gerrymandering were justiciable under the equal-protection clause. In the early 2000s, the possibility of judicial review had seemed in the hands of Justice Anthony Kennedy—the key fifth vote in a 2004 Pennsylvania case, *Vieth v. Jubelirer*—to leave open the possibility that courts could intervene in extreme gerrymanders. In *Vieth,* four justices had said that claims of partisan gerrymandering were off limits for judges as a political question. Four other justices had said just the opposite. Kennedy cast the deciding vote, finding that the claims in the particular Pennsylvania case could not be resolved but saying he "would not foreclose all possibility of judicial relief if some limited and precise rationale were found to correct an established violation of the Constitution in some redistricting cases."[28]

Yet Kennedy never went further and, at any rate, had since retired. No longer would there be a possible fifth vote to find an extreme partisan gerrymander unconstitutional. Roberts, now center of the Court, opposed the judicial review of such cases. He had asserted in a 2018 dispute that if judges began umpiring such cases, they would necessarily side with one political party over the other and be viewed as politically motivated themselves. "We will have to decide in every case whether the Democrats win or the Republicans win," he said during the 2018 case. "So it's going to be a problem here across the board. And if you're the intelligent man on the street and the Court issues a decision, and let's say the Democrats win, and that person will say: Well, why did the Democrats win? . . . It must be because the Supreme

Court preferred the Democrats over the Republicans. . . . And that is going to cause very serious harm to the status and integrity of the decisions of this Court in the eyes of the country." Roberts seemed less concerned that gerrymanders would cause people to believe their votes were meaningless and lead to a loss of faith in democracy.

Republicans, who controlled the majority of the state legislatures since the 2010 reapportionment and redistricting cycle, had perfected the gerrymandering practice. That was in no small measure because of the man at the center of the North Carolina case, Thomas Hofeller. Coincidentally, Hofeller's handiwork was in the background of both the census and gerrymandering cases. Hofeller, who had carefully remained obscure in life, found new notoriety in death in a way that would tie the census and gerrymandering cases together. A redistricting guru with a Ph.D. and decades of statehouse experience, Hofeller, who died in August 2018, had used data from precinct-level election results over a series of years to produce maps that maximized Republican voting strength.[29]

In the larger picture involving extreme gerrymanders, the justices were picking up where they had left off in 2018, just a year earlier, with a Wisconsin controversy over Republican manipulation of voting districts. That dispute had illuminated the practices known as "packing and cracking," by which voters of the opposing political party were consolidated ("packed") into a district where they could prevail by a great majority but essentially waste votes, and divided ("cracked") among multiple districts so they failed to gain a majority in any of them. A federal district court panel had ruled that the GOP-crafted state legislative map in the 2018 Wisconsin case was drawn for the purpose of entrenching the GOP. By impeding the effectiveness of citizens' votes, the court panel said, the map violated the equal protection clause and guarantees of free speech and association.

After hearing an appeal in the Wisconsin case, the Supreme Court had thrown out the lower-court decision. The opinion in that case, *Gill v. Whitford*, was written by Roberts, who had rejected the Democratic challengers on procedural grounds. (They had failed to demonstrate sufficient harm for legal standing.) Although the

Supreme Court declined to rule on the substance of the case and the constitutionality of the legislative map, Roberts made plain that when the time came, he would conclude that no matter the peril to democracy, gerrymanders were not a subject for judges. "This Court is not responsible for vindicating generalized partisan preferences," he wrote in *Gill*. "The Court's constitutionally prescribed role is to vindicate the individual rights of the people appearing before it."[30]

Justice Kagan concurred in the bottom-line judgment against the voters challenging the Wisconsin map, but she wrote a separate opinion, joined by the three other liberals, offering a blueprint for future cases against extreme gerrymanders. She said that challengers might be able to show that their votes were unconstitutionally diluted in individual districts or, alternatively, mount a statewide case based on the First Amendment right of free association. More fundamentally, Kagan contended that gerrymanders degraded democracy. She warned that state legislators who benefitted from gerrymanders would not change their ways. This point was critical to those on the left who believed federal judges should be able to review extreme gerrymanders: given the state of modern politics, elected officials would never stop the practice; only judges were situated to effectively intervene. Roberts deemed Kagan's point in the Wisconsin dispute constitutionally irrelevant and took the unusual step of writing in his opinion for the Court that her concurring opinion should not be a basis for future cases. He said that the Court's view was set forth in his opinion "and none other."[31]

Now, a year later, the justices were hearing the North Carolina dispute, in which a lower court had ruled for challengers in part by relying on Kagan's opinion in the Wisconsin case. North Carolina legislators knew that they would have a receptive audience, yet they left nothing to chance, enlisting former U.S. solicitor general Paul Clement, who had represented the federal government during the George W. Bush administration and become one of the smoothest, most respected advocates before the justices. He was the go-to lawyer for countless conservative causes, from opposition to Obamacare, to gun rights, to voting district issues. The Wisconsin native and former Scalia clerk argued without notes and displayed an ease and familiarity with most of the justices. Responding to Breyer at one point during the gerrymandering arguments, he said, "In all candor, there's so much in that that I disagree with that it's a little hard to know where to start." His main point, however, was one Chief Justice Roberts and fellow conservatives wanted to hear: "This Court has repeatedly failed to identify a justiciable standard for partisan gerrymandering claims. . . . [T]he root cause of this failure is the basic decision of the framers to give responsibility for congressional districting to political actors. The framers consciously chose to give the primary authority to state legislatures."[32]

Roberts was ready to accept those arguments. He remained skeptical that judges could set any standards for when map-drawers went too far, and he was dubious of assertions from the voting rights groups that had challenged North Carolina that Republicans were micromanaging voting maps to guarantee the desired results. Roberts asked Emmet Bondurant, the lawyer for Common Cause, "What do you do with the fact that partisan identification is not the only basis on which people vote? Do you see electoral results change dramatically depending, for example, on the particular appeal of individual candidates?" Bondurant pointed to social science experts, including Hofeller, who he said had designed the North Carolina plan by using comprehensive voter data from past elections. Bondurant characterized the tabulated data as "the best predictor" of how people will vote and told the Court that "all partisan gerrymandering in the modern era is based on that kind of social science."[33]

Roberts sounded unconvinced, and implicitly raised Trump's surprise victory from November 2016: "But it turns out that a lot of the predictions in this area—and I don't know if this applies to North Carolina or not—prove to be very, very wrong very often," the chief justice said. "Even as in the more recent cycle, I understand that a lot of things that were never supposed to happen happened." Bondurant countered by bringing Roberts back to the North Carolina situation: "In this case, on this undisputed record, the way this was done was that Dr. Hofeller used a composite of seven statewide elections over four election cycles to come up with a calculation of partisan advantage and predictability. And it predicted ten Republican districts, and the Republicans won all ten."

When the justices voted in their private conference later that week, Roberts had a majority to declare once and for all that judges could not review partisan gerrymanders. The vote was 5–4, with the liberals dissenting. Roberts kept this opinion for himself, too. Knowing Kagan's interest in the controversy related to voting power, Ginsburg asked her to write the dissent. Kagan began gathering materials, including on Hofeller's work to help create the North Carolina map that maintained the composition desired by the state's congressional delegation: ten Republicans and three Democrats. The record showed that when he turned it over, one of the satisfied cochairs of the redistricting committee that adopted his handiwork announced, "I think electing Republicans is better than electing Democrats. So I drew this map to help foster what I think is better for the country."[34]

With the April arguments over, the justices focused on opinion-writing and, without the yoke of the in-courtroom schedule, were able to travel. Ginsburg felt healthy enough to carry through with a commitment to fly to Sweden to receive the Gilel Storch Award from the Judisk Kultur i Sverige (Jewish Culture in Sweden) organization. The award recognized commitment to gender equality and civil rights. Early in her legal career, Ginsburg had written a comparative study of U.S.-Swedish civil procedure, and she remained enthusiastic as a justice about procedural rules that provide guardrails for any substantive changes in the law. Breyer separately flew to Paris as part of his role as juror for the Pritzker Prize for architecture.

At the same time, the justices were putting the finishing touches on two cases that were not as closely watched as the census and redistricting controversies but tested when the five-justice right-wing bloc would discard precedent. A case brought by a microchip inventor named Gilbert Hyatt took several turns before landing at the Supreme Court on the question of whether a state could be sued in another state's court. (A Nevada jury had awarded Hyatt about $400 million in damages for a claim against the Franchise Tax Board of California.) When his case reached the Supreme Court in 2019, Hyatt would have won, based on the precedent of *Nevada v. Hall* (1979), when the Court said that a state could be sued in another state's court. But the majority reversed course and declared that states should be shielded from such lawsuits. That position relied on state sovereign immunity. Justice Clarence Thomas, writing for the 5–4 conservative majority, concluded that the 1979 case "misreads the historical record" and "misapprehends the implicit ordering of relationships within the federal system." Breyer, in his dissent, contended that the 1979 case had been well reasoned and caused no serious practical problems to warrant reversal. He said that there must be a better reason to overrule precedent than that the current majority would have decided the case differently. "Today's decision can only cause one to wonder which cases the Court will overrule next," Breyer declared. To emphasize his defense of precedent, Breyer referred to Kagan's "Spider-Man" opinion, requiring "special justification" for reversal, and in an attention-getting move, cited the Supreme Court's 1992 *Planned Parenthood v. Casey*, which stood for adherence in precedent even in the controversial case of *Roe v. Wade*.[35]

A second case soon after answered Breyer's "what next?" question. A June property rights controversy from North Carolina was breaking along the same 5–4 lines, with the conservative majority again discarding a decades-old ruling, the 1985 *Williamson County v. Hamilton Bank*, which confined such property cases to state courts. "Its reasoning was exceptionally ill-founded," Roberts wrote of the precedent. In her dissent, Kagan contended that "Under cover of overruling 'only' a single decision, today's opinion smashes a hundred-plus years of legal rulings to smithereens." Referring to Breyer's question about what precedent would next be overruled, she wrote, "Well, that didn't take long. Now one may wonder yet again."[36]

The pointed remarks of Breyer and Kagan revealed the frustration and fear among liberal justices of where the majority was headed. They had to weigh how loudly to denounce the majority's reversal of precedent when they were simultaneously at the table bargaining for compromise in other important cases. In the Wilbur Ross case, for example, liberals had been unable to persuade Roberts that the commerce secretary had acted arbitrarily and abused his discretion. But they had made headway in showing Ross's phony justification for the census questionnaire, and the chief justice was rewriting his opinion.

That May, there was a wholly coincidental public revelation in the case, arising from a separate North Carolina redistricting dispute. It just so happened that a team of lawyers assisting the ACLU in the census case (from the private firm of Arnold & Porter) were also representing Common Cause in North Carolina and conducting discovery in a challenge to state-district maps (as distinct from the congressional-district challenge underway at the Supreme Court). The lawyers received evidence from Stephanie Hofeller, Thomas Hofeller's estranged daughter, who had found a hard drive containing hundreds of documents arising from his work with Republican legislators, some of which related to GOP efforts to put a citizenship question on the census. According to the documents obtained from Hofeller's computer and subsequently laid out in a letter from the ACLU to the Supreme Court, Hofeller had concluded that adding a citizenship question to the 2020 Census "would clearly be a disadvantage to the Democrats" and be "advantageous to Republicans and Non-Hispanic Whites" in apportionment and subsequent redistricting.[37] No one in the Trump administration, and certainly not Commerce Secretary Ross, had revealed Hofeller's role. The ACLU told the Supreme Court that the evidence underscored the Commerce Department's fabrication. Lawyers involved also alerted the *New York Times* to the documents, and the paper ran a front-page story that explored how Hofeller had developed the rationale for the Trump administration's citizenship query.[38]

U.S. solicitor general Francisco dismissed the evidence in a letter to the Court, calling it a "last ditch effort to derail the census case." Columnists seized on the new information. The *New York Times* editorialized about the doubts sown regarding Ross's motives and separately published a guest opinion piece by Joshua Geltzer, a visiting Georgetown law professor who had previously been critical of Francisco's assertions to justices, entitled "Will the Legitimacy of the Supreme Court Survive the Census Case?" The *Wall Street Journal* ran an op-ed, "Census Target: John Roberts," declaring, "Whenever you read 'legitimacy' in a sentence about the Court, you know it's a political missile aimed directly at Chief Justice John Roberts."[39]

But by this point, however, I learned that Roberts even without the new Hofeller materials had in fact come to believe that Ross's rationale for the citizenship question had been contrived, and that if the justices accepted it, they would appear to have been duped. His opinion, scheduled to be distributed to fellow justices by the first week in June, had already made a sharp turn from where he had begun immediately after oral arguments. He was still ready to give the administration officials great latitude for policy choices, but he had been persuaded to draw a line at a falsehood. "Several points, considered together," Roberts wrote, "reveal a significant mismatch between the decision the Secretary made and the rationale he provided.... And unlike a typical case in which an agency may have both stated and unstated reasons for a decision, here the VRA enforcement rationale—the sole stated reason—seems to have been contrived."

Roberts remained conflicted until the end, however. And his opinion showed it. Spectators in the courtroom on the June day that Roberts announced the opinion in *Department of Commerce v. New York*, as well as the lawyers reading the digital version online from offices outside Washington, could initially have believed that he was endorsing Ross's moves. The first twenty-four pages of his twenty-nine-page decision favored Ross. And the chief justice stressed in his opinion excerpt from the bench that judges should defer to the administration's development of census form questions—that is, provided the justification for its choices was true.

This is where Roberts shifted. To accept Ross's explanation grounded in the Voting Rights Act, the chief justice said in the final pages of his opinion, would essentially allow administration officials to deceive judges. Quoting the late U.S. appeals court judge Henry Friendly, for whom he once served as a law clerk, Roberts wrote, "Our review is deferential, but we are 'not required to exhibit a naivete from which ordinary citizens are free.'" Roberts's decision was finely tuned to nonetheless give the executive branch something for later cases. His rationale expansively interpreted an administration's right to customize the census and enforce policy-related administrative orders. But the bottom line was that once contrary evidence was produced, it could not be ignored.

Roberts's eleventh-hour switch recalled his changed positions in the 2012 dispute over the Affordable Care Act, when he ultimately sided with the four liberals to uphold the Obama-sponsored law and outraged his conservative colleagues. In the ACA case, four justices (Scalia, Kennedy, Thomas, and Alito) banded together for a rare joint dissent to Roberts's rationale saving Obamacare based on Congress's taxing power. They described his arguments as "feeble" and declared that instead of interpreting a statute, he had rewritten it. In the Department of Commerce case, Thomas, in the lead dissent, suggested that Roberts was hypocritical to find that trial judge Furman abused his discretion in ordering the extra-record discovery, but then relied on it for a decision against the administration.

"The Court engages in an unauthorized inquiry into evidence not properly before us to reach an unsupported conclusion," Thomas wrote. "Moreover, each step of the inquiry offends the presumption of regularity we owe the Executive." And of Furman himself, Thomas, joined by Justices Gorsuch and Kavanaugh, wrote, "I do not deny that a judge predisposed to distrust the Secretary or the administration could arrange those facts on a corkboard and—with a jar of pins and a spool of string—create an eye-catching conspiracy web." That was a bold complaint against a fellow federal judge, that Furman had somehow crossed the line. Kavanaugh had signed on to Thomas's dissent, but indicative of how he was always conscious of how he might be perceived, Kavanaugh sent Furman a private note saying he did not intend to personally disrespect him. The correspondence—revealed to me by a Supreme Court source—suggested some duplicity and showed the lengths to which Kavanaugh would go to appear conciliatory. He joined an opinion challenging Furman's integrity but then wrote the judge a note that pled the opposite. The episode certainly added to an understanding of how Kavanaugh operated. But it may also have demonstrated something of the larger personal and political balancing justices undertake.

In a separate dissent, Alito criticized the majority's focus on Ross's motivations. "If this case is taken as a model," he wrote, "then any one of the approximately 1,000 district court judges in this country . . . may order the questioning of Cabinet officers and other high-ranking Executive Branch officials, and the judge may then pass judgment on whether the decision was pretextual. What Bismarck is reputed to have said about laws and sausages comes to mind. And that goes for decisionmaking by all three branches."

The tone of the public writings in the case overall reinforced an us-versus-them mentality that was emerging among justices and judges. Courts were also becoming more ideologically polarized. Roberts might have been further persuaded to rule against Ross to avoid a partisan look. Kagan similarly tried to resist ideological and political inclinations in judicial outcomes. "The last thing that the Court should do is to look as polarized as every other institution in America," she told an audience at the University of Colorado Law School a few months after the census decision. "The only way to be seen as not that—is not to be that."[40]

After the justices had ruled against Ross, it seemed as if the census case was over. But it wasn't for Trump and his new attorney general, William Barr. They would not relinquish the fight, even though Ross had announced that he was moving on and that census forms would be printed without the citizenship question. Immediately after the decision, Trump posted on Twitter: "I have asked the lawyers if they can delay the Census." The following week, in the face of reports that indeed the printing of forms would soon begin, he fired off another tweet: "The News Reports about the Department of Commerce dropping its quest to put the Citizenship Question on the Census is [*sic*] incorrect. . . . We are absolutely moving forward, as we must, because of the importance of the answer to this question."[41]

Attorney General Barr was publicly backing Trump, telling the *New York Times* in an interview that the administration was developing strategy for the inclusion of the citizenship question. Behind the scenes, Barr was navigating differently, between a demanding president and a legal reality.[42]

Trump had chosen Barr after firing his first attorney general, Jeff Sessions. In February 2019, at the White House, Barr had taken the constitutional oath of office, administered by his old friend John Roberts. They had worked together in the George H. W. Bush administration, and this was the second time around for Barr as attorney general, the nation's chief law enforcement official.[43]

In a 2001 interview for the Miller Center presidential oral history project, Barr addressed his first turn as attorney general and lamented that the Bush administration had not moved faster on judicial appointments. He referred in the interview to a quest for a kind of ideological perfection:

> It's like when you have a baby. Your first baby drops the pacifier, and you boil it in water. By the time you have your third kid, you pick up the pacifier and plug it right back in the kid's mouth. It was the same as selecting judges. . . . My attitude was, "Look, okay, circuit court judges, let's be a little bit more attentive to who we put on there and make sure they've got their philosophy straight and we're happy with it, okay?" But we can't do that for every district court judge. . . . I'm anti-abortion myself, but I can live with a few district court judges who are not "right" on right to life.[44]

Trump was drawn to Barr because of a memo Barr wrote and passed on to Justice Department officials in summer 2017 criticizing the investigation of Special Counsel Robert Mueller. Barr called the efforts to determine whether Trump had obstructed justice related to the Russia election-interference probe "grossly irresponsible" and "fatally misconceived." Such arguments played directly to Trump's sentiment that he had been subject to a Mueller "witch hunt." Barr believed that the president's executive power was absolute, even on matters that concerned his own conduct.[45]

The new attorney general demonstrated his loyalty to Trump immediately, in March 2019, by skewing the results of the Mueller report.[46] Now, four months later, in July, Barr was ready to publicly defend the administration's census questionnaire effort, telling the *New York Times*, "The president is right on the legal grounds. . . . It makes a lot of sense for the president to see if it's possible that we could clarify the record in time to add the question."[47] Barr then wrote in his memoir that Trump was pounding on Wilbur Ross "to come up with a way to include the question in the 2020 census by pushing back the printing date. He was implacable. The lawyers in the Solicitor General's office and the Civil Division were dismayed, and understandably so. Their credibility with the courts would be shot if, after invoking the June 30 deadline, we now tried to embark on a new decision and new set of expedited judicial proceedings that would take us far beyond that date." When the Justice Department tried to switch out its legal team on the case, without providing sufficient explanation, Judge Furman refused to allow the change, prompting Trump to write on July 9 on Twitter, "So now the Obama appointed judge on the Census case (Are you a Citizen of the United States?) won't let the Justice Department use the lawyers that it wants to use. Could this be a first?"[48]

Barr met with Trump in the Oval Office the next day, on July 10, planning to tell him that the effort to get the question included was being dropped. "The meeting promised to be the tensest of any I'd had so far with the President," Barr said, recounting that "the President, as usual, sitting behind his desk, looked miffed as I walked into the room. . . . He started performing one of his nervous tics: when he expects controversy, he absentmindedly moves things on this desk, as if to clear a path down the center for the coming fusillade. Repeating the substance of his tweets, he started off blasting the court's decision as ridiculous."

Trump eventually had to retreat. There was no time to write a new justification for the citizenship question and defend it in court. The president announced that he would issue an executive order regarding the collection of citizenship information from the usual agencies charged with that responsibility. Barr put a positive, if misleading, spin on it during a Rose Garden appearance with Trump and Ross. "Thank you, Mr. President, and congratulations on today's Executive Order," Barr declared, "which will ensure that we finally have an accurate understanding of how many citizens and non-citizens live in our country."[49]

On the same June day that the Supreme Court issued the census decision, it handed down the consequential *Rucho v. Common Cause* decision, forbidding federal judges from reviewing extreme partisan gerrymandering. The decision would affect all states and reverberate as the country headed into the 2020 census and a new round of redistricting.

In his opinion for the Court, Roberts stuck with his long-held views that federal judges should be prevented from hearing such claims. He had a ready majority—with Kavanaugh as successor to Kennedy—to prevent federal courts from ever resolving such disputes. Roberts said that concerns about fairness in state legislative redistricting should be addressed by elected officials, not judges. "Federal judges have no license to reallocate political power between the two majority political parties, with no plausible grant of authority in the Constitution, and no legal standards to limit and direct their decisions," he wrote. The chief justice swept aside efforts by lower-court judges to develop standards for assessing when a partisan gerrymander went too far and compromised voting rights. He acknowledged the objectionable elements of gerrymanders but clearly viewed them as no serious threat to America's representative form of government.[50]

Roberts's opinion was a model of indirection masquerading as directness. He insisted partisan gerrymanders were "nothing new," disputed the notion that expert mapmakers could even predict electoral outcomes, and concluded, regardless, that judges lacked the constitutional authority to address a problem that could subvert democracy.

Justice Kagan read part of her dissent from the bench: "Of all the times to abandon the Court's duty to declare the law, this was not the one," she said. "The practices challenged in these cases imperil our system of government. Part of the Court's role in that system is to defend its foundations. None is more important than free and fair elections."

She said that the redistricting practices by Republicans in North Carolina, and in a companion case involving Democratic gerrymandering in Maryland, amounted to rigging elections. "Is this how

American democracy is supposed to work?" she asked. She detailed in her opinion Hofeller's work behind the scenes for GOP gerrymanders in North Carolina. She referred to the redistricting chairman's comment that "electing Republicans is better than electing Democrats. So I drew this map to help foster what I think is better for the country." Her rejoinder: "You might think that judgment best left to the American people. But give [the chairman] . . . credit for this much: The map has worked just as . . . planned and predicted." More broadly, Kagan reminded the courtroom audience of the Supreme Court's special responsibility to safeguard "one person, one vote," a principle jeopardized when state mapmakers could essentially cherry-pick voters.[51]

Charles Fried, who had been a U.S. solicitor general under Reagan, wrote that *Rucho* provided "an occasion of deep sorrow—for the Court and its chief, for the rational development of doctrine, but most of all for American democracy. Read it and weep." Kagan herself had sounded mournful when she read aloud portions of her dissent. She later told a university audience that she was indeed sad but had to get over it, adding that she clung to old advice from Scalia: "If you take this personally, you're in the wrong business."[52]

The question, however, when it came to voting and equal representation, was whether the erosion of democratic principles would no longer be an issue only of personal defeat but would become one of larger societal destruction.

## Chapter 6

---

# "JUSTICE IS NOT INEVITABLE"

Chief Justice Roberts spoke out against President Trump just once during his four years in office. Roberts's comments came at about the midpoint of Trump's tenure, in November 2018. It was a remarkable public clash between a chief justice and a president. Yet as striking as it was, the incident turned out to be mere prelude to greater friction across the judicial and executive branches. The atmosphere of public recrimination, amplified in the Trump years, turned justices and lower-court judges on each other, too.

Roberts faced tensions within the Court, but the challenges provoked by Trump and the polarization in Washington during his presidency were of another order of magnitude. Some of Roberts's colleagues were suspicious of his maneuverings on cases and what they saw as an exalted sense of his authority as chief justice. He exerted a strong hand on internal operations at the Court building, and in various public communications separated himself from the eight associate justices. His team wanted public information materials, printed and on the Court's website, to separately enumerate chief justices (Roberts was only the seventeenth in U.S. history) and the scores of associate justices. When Brett Kavanaugh was confirmed, Roberts noted he was the "102nd associate justice," as opposed to the 114th justice. Roberts's predecessor as chief justice, William Rehnquist, had not insisted on such separation, welcoming Ruth Bader Ginsburg in 1993, for example, as the 107th justice.

Such internal matters were secondary, however, to Roberts's insistence that the Court be regarded as a neutral, nonpartisan institution. Two months after Justice Kavanaugh's confirmation hearings, Roberts tried to dispel partisan tensions by stressing the judiciary's independence from the legislative and executive branches. "The judicial branch is and must be very different," he said. "We do not speak for the people, but we speak for the Constitution. Our role is very clear."[1]

Trump continued to undercut the notion of judicial independence and thus brought about the only real public clash between himself and Roberts. The men presented a study in contrasts. Both had been prep school boys from privileged homes, but only one, Roberts, had been known for earning awards by studying late at night and early in the morning. Trump bragged about trying to beat the system. He craved attention and rarely prepared or read up on a subject. Roberts was naturally reserved and prepared extensively for public appearances. The two men had few face-to-face encounters, most in formal settings like the State of the Union speech. Yet their spheres kept colliding, and Trump's pressure on the judiciary was constant.

The most public conflict began when a San Francisco–based U.S. district court judge issued a preliminary decision on Trump's asylum policy and the president attacked him as an "Obama judge." On November 9, as Trump warned of "caravans" of migrants from Central America coming north into the United States, the administration had imposed restrictions on where migrants at the southern border could seek asylum, limiting entry points to legal border crossings. East Bay Sanctuary Covenant, represented by the American Civil Liberties Union, sued the administration and sought an order blocking the restrictions. Previously, applicants could present themselves to immigration officers outside designated entry points. Granting a temporary order favoring the challengers on November 19, U.S. district court judge Jon Tigar wrote, "Whatever the scope of the president's authority, he may not rewrite the immigration laws to impose a condition that Congress has expressly forbidden. . . . Asylum seekers will be put at increased risk of violence and other harms at the border, and many will be deprived of meritorious asylum claims." Judge Tigar ordered the administration to accept asylum applications irrespective of where a person crossed the border to enter the United States.[2]

Tigar had been appointed by President Barack Obama in 2012, after a decade as a superior court judge in Alameda County, California, and work in private practice in San Francisco. Two decades earlier, serving as a law clerk to U.S. appeals court judge Robert Vance in Alabama, he had been exposed, by association, to the greatest risk any judge could face. Just before Christmas in 1989, Judge Vance opened a package mailed to his home and was instantly killed by a shrapnel-wrapped pipe bomb. It turned out to be the work of Walter Leroy Moody, a man seeking revenge on the courts. Moody was eventually executed for the murder.[3]

Tigar's childhood had connected in a brief and unusual way with the inner world of the Supreme Court. His father, Michael, who became a premier criminal defense lawyer, civil rights advocate, and law professor, had begun his legal career with an offer, in 1965, to clerk for Justice William Brennan. But Brennan—pressured to examine the young man's history of protest activity at the University of California, Berkeley, including opposition to the House Un-American Activities Committee—rescinded the offer just as Michael moved to Washington to begin the job. The rescission captured national news headlines, in part because of Brennan's reputation as a free-speech advocate and a liberal.[4]

What most struck Trump when Judge Tigar ruled on the administration's asylum policy, however, was the connection to Obama. Responding to reporters' questions after Tigar's asylum order, Trump said, "This was an Obama judge, and I'll tell you what, it's not going to happen like this anymore. . . . We will win that case in the Supreme Court of the United States."[5]

The remark, coming less than two months after the Kavanaugh appointment, gave Chief Justice Roberts reason to decide against silence this time. He had kept quiet after other instances of Trump's blustering, such as when Trump criticized Judge Gonzalo Curiel, who was then hearing the Trump University fraud case, as a "Mexican" judge. But this new declaration directly contradicted the chief justice's assertions that judges are loyal to the Constitution, not to any president. Just before Thanksgiving, as he was heading out of town to join relatives for the holiday, Roberts wrote up a statement that he provided first to the Associated Press: "We do not have Obama judges or Trump judges, Bush judges or Clinton judges. What we have is an extraordinary group of dedicated judges doing their level best to do equal right to those appearing before them. That independent judiciary is something we should all be thankful for."[6]

Trump fired back on Twitter immediately: "Sorry Chief Justice John Roberts, but you do indeed have 'Obama judges,' and they have a much different point of view than the people who are charged with the safety of our country." The dueling statements were extraordinary. But Roberts, having earlier abandoned his usual reticence, stopped it there. He issued no further statement regarding Trump. The president kept going, claiming without real grounds that California-based federal judges were favoring immigrants and making the country unsafe.[7]

Roberts's no "Obama judges or Trump judges" line was quoted ceaselessly and with considerable reverence. Any extracurricular statement from Roberts was rare, and Trump no doubt deserved criticism for how much he was politicizing the judiciary. The statement constituted an assertion of judicial integrity, a reflection of Roberts's regard for the Supreme Court as an institution. Yet Roberts himself may not have subscribed to the notion that judges could be separated from presidential administrations.

In his younger years, during the Reagan and first Bush administrations, he was part of a selection machine that looked for candidates with conservative ideologies. Law clerks and fellow justices said Roberts kept his eye on the affiliations of lower-court judges whose rulings came up to the Court. He had high regard for the institution but was not without his own interests, shaded by politics. His response to Trump's "Obama judge" remark was as memorable as his 2005 confirmation hearings mantra, that judges are like umpires purely calling balls and strikes. But that, too, came with an unstated caveat: that there was plenty of discretion in the work of a judge. Rarely were things black-and-white, as judges interpreted ambiguous statutes and the open-ended framework of the U.S. Constitution. Supreme Court justices often divided based on ideologies, if not their politics. While the imperative to keep the judiciary independent only increased under Trump, it simply remained an open question how faithfully Roberts could follow his own maxims.[8]

For the first two years of Trump's presidency, the Justice Department's investigation into Russia's intrusion in the 2016 election and the relationship between the Trump campaign and Russia dominated the news. It looked like that controversy might be Trump's undoing. But the greater threat to him in 2019, at least at the hands of Congress, came from his dealings with Ukraine. On the Russia probe, Robert Mueller brought charges against several of Trump's associates but never reached a determination about whether Trump conspired with the Russians as they tried to disrupt the U.S. presidential election. In congressional testimony on July 24, 2019, Mueller emphasized that Department of Justice guidelines prohibited the indictment of a sitting president, and that while his report did not address whether Trump committed a crime, it did not exonerate him.[9]

The July hearing marked the first time that much of the public had laid eyes on the special counsel or heard an account of his investigation. Mueller appeared weary and fumbled at times. Earlier public depictions of an all-powerful counsel investigating an out-of-control president did not hold up. Mueller's halting testimony spurred criticism from Trump and members of Congress, Republicans and Democrats alike. Democrats had hoped that the longtime prosecutor and decorated Vietnam veteran would ferret out criminal activity and charge Trump, or, at least before Congress, present a more vigorous case. Instead, Mueller answered questions monosyllabically, and Trump, who focused on whatever theater derived from the nation's business, was gleeful, tweeting, "This has been a disaster for the Democrats and a disaster for the reputation of Robert Mueller," citing an analysis by Chris Wallace, a *Fox News Sunday* host at the time. Todd Purdum, writing in *The Atlantic*, condemned the attention on optics. "If Mueller's testimony frustrated Democrats—and delighted the Trump White

House—it's because he repeatedly refused to be drawn into either partisan talking points or legal and constitutional hypotheticals," Purdum wrote.[10]

As Congress and the public had awaited Mueller's final report, Attorney General William Barr had preempted and misrepresented its findings, continuing a pattern that had started with the memo on presidential authority that had gotten him hired by Trump in the first place.[11] After receiving an advance briefing by Mueller, Barr put an early public slant on the report, writing to Congress on March 24, 2019, that "the investigation did not establish that members of the Trump Campaign conspired or coordinated with the Russian government in its election interference activities." Barr omitted that, as the report documented, "the investigation established that the Russian government perceived it would benefit from a Trump presidency and worked to secure that outcome," and he minimized the findings related to obstruction. Later that day, Trump wrote on Twitter, "No Collusion, No Obstruction, Complete and Total EXONERATION. Keep America Great!"[12]

Incensed, Mueller wrote to Barr that his summary failed to "fully capture the context, nature, and substance of this Office's work and conclusions. . . . There is now public confusion about critical aspects of the results of our investigation. This threatens to undermine a central purpose for which the Department appointed the Special Counsel: to assure full public confidence in the outcome of the investigations."[13]

On July 25, the day after Mueller's testimony, President Trump, perhaps further emboldened to breach the norms of office, engaged in a phone call with Volodymyr Zelensky, the president of Ukraine, that occasioned even greater congressional scrutiny. It was this latter episode, rather than the Mueller report, that spurred the late 2019 House of Representatives impeachment and the intersection of President Trump and Chief Justice Roberts at a historic early 2020 Senate trial.

In the call, Trump asked Zelensky to investigate the Ukrainian activities of former vice president Joe Biden, who was positioning himself to challenge Trump's reelection in 2020. Trump and Zelensky were discussing U.S. military aid to Ukraine to counteract Russian aggression. Having stalled on the military assistance, Trump now told Zelensky, "I would like you to do us a favor, though." He said he wanted an investigation of Biden and his son Hunter, who had been a member of the board of a Ukrainian natural gas company, Burisma Holdings, when his father was vice president. It sounded as if President Trump was conditioning the $400 million in military aid Congress had already directed to help Ukraine against Russia on a Ukrainian investigation of a political rival. But he was not explicit. He told Zelensky that his personal attorney Rudy Giuliani and Attorney General Barr would follow up on his behalf. Continuing his fixation on the 2016 election, Trump also urged Zelensky to advance the widely discredited theory that Ukraine, not Russia, had interfered in the 2016 U.S. presidential contest.[14]

Trump's request concerning the Bidens appeared to represent a new effort to influence the 2020 presidential race, even as he still faced questions over possible wrongdoing related to his 2016 election. Mueller had finished his work, but congressional and state probes of Trump were still underway. Listening in on the call, Lieutenant Colonel Alexander Vindman of the National Security Council became concerned about the deal Trump appeared to be proposing, and Vindman later testified that he thought it improper for the president to demand that a foreign government investigate a U.S. citizen. President Trump described the Zelensky call as appropriate, even "perfect." [15] Two and a half years later, of course, with the Russian invasion of Ukraine, Zelensky's name would become a household word.

When a partial transcript of the call became public, Trump's acting chief of staff, Mick Mulvaney, confirmed that the administration in fact held up the funds for Ukraine: "We do that all the time with foreign policy." Mulvaney later clarified what had been taken as an admission of a quid pro quo: "The only reasons we were holding the money was because of concern about lack of support from other nations and concerns over corruption."[16]

That was not the end of the matter but the beginning.

In September, while the justices were finishing their summer travels and their new law clerks were working to master the intricacies of the certiorari process, the Democrat-led U.S. House of Representatives, already following up on leads from the Mueller report, began considering a different investigation into President Trump, related to Ukraine. But, like earlier probes, it faced several obstacles. Committees of the House of Representatives had been unable to obtain documents and witness testimony from the administration on earlier concerns of possible misconduct. The president had blocked former White House counsel Don McGahn from testifying before Congress regarding whether Trump had obstructed the Mueller probe, and House committees were trying to enforce subpoenas for financial documents. House members and the Manhattan district attorney in a separate investigation had turned to federal judges for orders that would enforce the subpoenas, and the courts were, as expected, moving slowly.[17]

House Speaker Nancy Pelosi had resisted an impeachment inquiry into President Trump's possible obstruction of the Mueller investigation. But once Trump's apparent bargaining on the Ukrainian military aid became public and it seemed he was trying to manipulate the 2020 presidential contest, the California Democrat changed her mind.

Trump declared that he would not answer questions and that his aides would refuse to participate. "The whole thing is a scam. It's a fix," he said. White House counsel Pat Cipollone wrote a letter to Speaker Pelosi and other House leaders declaring the impeachment investigation unconstitutional and repeating that staff would not cooperate. The Cipollone letter reinforced the administration's pattern of resistance and added to House leaders' skepticism that they would gather sufficient information. Trump's directive to McGahn that he not testify in the Mueller probe dated from spring 2019, and now he forbade Mulvaney, Secretary of State Mike Pompeo, and others with knowledge of the Ukrainian situation to answer questions.[18]

When the House impeachment committee finished its report, it concluded that Trump had used the power of his office to solicit foreign interference on his behalf for the 2020 election and had subverted U.S. policy toward Ukraine and America's broader national security. The full House voted along party lines to impeach Trump on two counts, abuse of power and obstruction of Congress, setting up a Senate impeachment trial for the president, over which, according to the Constitution, the chief justice would preside.[19]

The Supreme Court was simultaneously preparing to handle separate controversies over President Trump's desire to keep his tax returns and other personal business records private. In some respects, the timing was coincidental. But there was an inevitability, too, because Trump had been in office long enough that the consequences of his transgressions on many fronts were catching up to him. Lower-court judges had ruled that Trump had to produce the personal financial documents for investigations underway by Manhattan District Attorney Cyrus Vance Jr. and by U.S. House committees working on matters unrelated to the Ukrainian-inspired impeachment.

From the start of his run for president in 2016, Trump had declined to make his tax returns public, setting himself apart from past candidates. Public interest in his tax returns only intensified after the Manhattan grand jury coordinating with Vance issued a subpoena for the returns and other records from Trump's longtime accounting firm, Mazars USA. Vance was looking into possible fraud committed by the Trump Organization and the president himself, including whether Trump had, when a candidate, directed "hush money" to women who claimed to have affairs with him. Trump denied the affairs. Michael Cohen, Trump's lawyer, had said that during the campaign, his client authorized payments to two women, Stormy Daniels and Karen McDougal, buying their silence. As a result, the payments could have been campaign expenditures required to be part of federal financial disclosures. Trump's lawyers were fighting the New York grand jury subpoena, contending that a sitting president was fully immune from any criminal proceeding while in office.

During an appellate court hearing on the case that became known as *Trump v. Vance*, Second Circuit judge Denny Chin asked Trump's lawyer William Consovoy how far the immunity would stretch and if it would reach his client's own well-known hypothetical scenario about committing murder in Manhattan. (During the presidential campaign, in January 2016 before the Iowa caucuses, Trump had boasted,

"I could stand in the middle of Fifth Avenue and shoot somebody and I wouldn't lose voters.") Judge Chin asked, "Local authorities couldn't investigate? They couldn't do anything about it?" And Consovoy answered, "That is correct. That is correct."[20]

When the Second Circuit panel ruled, it said in a unanimous opinion written by Judge Robert Katzmann that "presidential immunity does not bar the enforcement of a state grand jury subpoena directing a third party to produce non-privileged material, even when the subject matter under investigation pertains to the President." The Justice Department had entered the case on the side of Trump, as an amicus curiae, and argued that the grand jury had to meet a heightened standard of need for the financial materials. The Second Circuit rejected that argument, saying that such a high standard didn't apply because the information sought related to the president's personal business rather than official duties.

The separate case, *Trump v. Mazars,* arose from a subpoena the House Committee on Oversight and Reform issued to Mazars USA for information related to Trump and his family businesses. The House argued that it needed the information to execute legislative work, specifically, to write new ethics regulations covering money laundering and foreign interference in U.S. elections. Trump's lawyers countered that the House was simply harassing the president and lacked a legislative purpose. The D.C. Circuit sided with the House, finding that the subpoena served "a valid legislative purpose" and fell within Congress's broad constitutional authority.

The D.C. Circuit decision against Trump was 2–1, with the two Democratic appointees in the majority, a Republican appointee in dissent. After a comprehensive review of past disputes between the legislative and executive branches, the panel majority concluded that the challenged subpoena arose from a "legitimate legislative investigation" and validly sought information on a subject on which legislation could be developed. The dissenter was Judge Neomi Rao, whom Trump had put on the bench in 2018 after Kavanaugh was elevated. She emphasized that if Congress wanted to pursue any wrongdoing of Trump's, it had the option of impeachment, and she rejected the asserted

"legislative purpose" of the subpoenas, writing that the majority's opinion "would turn Congress into a roving inquisition over a co-equal
branch of government." Judge David Tatel, who wrote the D.C. Circuit's majority opinion, discounted Rao's criticism, saying that her approach "would reorder the very structure of the Constitution" and leave
Congress to "the Hobson's Choice of impeachment or nothing."[21]

The limited effectiveness of impeachment itself would soon be seen.
But that process was just beginning. As the Supreme Court announced
it would hear Trump's appeals from the Second Circuit and D.C. Circuit rulings in the financial records cases in late 2019, the full House of
Representatives was preparing to vote to impeach the president.

As the year ended, Chief Justice Roberts again tried to counteract the
public perceptions of a politicized judiciary, which the Trump documents cases appeared to reinforce because the judges involved had
divided along partisan lines. "I ask my judicial colleagues to continue their efforts to promote public confidence in the judiciary, both
through their rulings and through civic outreach," Roberts wrote in
his annual report at the close of 2019. "We should celebrate our strong
and independent judiciary, a key source of national unity and stability.
But we should also remember that justice is not inevitable."[22]

That last note rang especially true. These were difficult times for
the rule of law. The justices, in personal terms, too, were in a difficult
stretch. Roberts's ninety-year-old mother, his lifelong booster, died on
December 28. A few months earlier, the Court community had lost a
beloved figure, the third-longest-serving justice in history, John Paul
Stevens, who had retired in 2010. Stevens had just traveled to Lisbon
with Justices Ginsburg and Sotomayor. Within days of their return, he
suffered a stroke and died.

"Perhaps he knew that at age ninety-nine, distant travel was a risk,"
Ginsburg said at his memorial service, "but he wanted to experience
fully the joys of being alive, and he did just that almost to the end."
Ginsburg recalled riding with him to museums, a vineyard, and castles
on the Lisbon trip. "His mind remained vibrant," she said. "En route,
he spoke of court cases, even footnotes in opinions, his military ser-

vice, ball games he attended. His conversation was engaging, his memory, amazing."[23] Stevens had led a singular life. The scion of a wealthy family that operated a luxurious hotel on Michigan Avenue in Chicago, he had met Amelia Earhart and Charles Lindbergh as a child. Stevens joined the navy to serve in World War II and was awarded a Bronze Star for his intelligence work on a code-breaking team. He earned his pilot's license. The University of Chicago and Northwestern University School of Law graduate found success as a lawyer and jurist, first on the U.S. Court of Appeals for the Seventh Circuit and then for thirty-five years on the Supreme Court.[24]

Stevens had just finished his third book, a memoir. Appointed to the appellate court by President Richard Nixon and then elevated to the Supreme Court by President Gerald Ford, he exemplified the ideal that jurists do not necessarily adhere to the interests of the presidents who appoint them. The Republican appointee moved left as the Court moved right. By the late 1990s, Stevens was the leader of the liberal wing. He and a handful of other justices with whom he served similarly resisted easy ideological labels: Byron White, an appointee of president John F. Kennedy, who ended up voting most often with conservatives; Lewis Powell, a Nixon appointee who was a centrist; and David Souter, named by President George H. W. Bush and more liberal like Stevens. Justices of that unpredictable, less ideological stripe were long gone by 2019.[25]

From outward appearances that summer, Justice Ginsburg seemed healthy, having fully recovered from the lung cancer first diagnosed in late 2018. But she had discovered a recurrence of her pancreatic cancer. She kept it quiet until late August, when she finished radiation treatment. Only then did she publicly reveal that doctors had detected the tumor on her pancreas in early July after a routine blood test. A biopsy showed that the tumor was malignant. She then began three weeks of outpatient radiation at Memorial Sloan Kettering in New York City. A court spokeswoman said that the tumor was treated "definitively" and that no evidence of disease was found elsewhere in her body. Ginsburg canceled her annual summer visit to Santa Fe for the opera but insisted she would maintain her public commitments. She began by fulfilling a multistop speaking tour beginning in Buffalo a few days after the cancer announcement.[26]

Ginsburg continued to believe that it was important to be seen. At stake was far more than her own appearances and perseverance. If the senior liberal who had just experienced her fourth bout with cancer felt the need to retire, President Trump would be able to appoint a third conservative jurist. This would not be the swap of one conservative for another, as had happened in 2017 and 2018, but a new conservative replacing a liberal icon. Ginsburg was doing everything she could in 2019 to stave off a serious cancer recurrence.

After the House of Representatives impeachment vote, President Trump's fate was in the Senate's hands, with Roberts set to oversee the trial. The U.S. Constitution dictates that "when the President of the United States is tried, the Chief Justice shall preside." It is the only duty of the chief justice delineated in the Constitution. Only twice before in American history had a president been impeached by the House and tried in the Senate: Bill Clinton in 1999 and Andrew Johnson in 1868. Both times the president was acquitted. A vote of two-thirds of the Senate was needed for conviction. In the House, only a simple majority was needed to impeach. So the hurdle for conviction was high.

Roberts had watched his mentor, William Rehnquist, preside over the Clinton proceedings, initiated after the president lied under oath to a federal grand jury when asked about his sexual relationship with former White House intern Monica Lewinsky. When the Senate trial was over, Rehnquist said of his time presiding, "I underwent the sort of culture shock that naturally occurs when one moves from the very structured environment of the Supreme Court to what I shall call, for want of a better phrase, the more free-form environment of the Senate." And, referencing Gilbert and Sullivan's *Iolanthe,* the chief justice said, "I did nothing in particular, and did it very well." (He was such a fan of the light opera that he affixed to his robes the four stripes worn by one of its generals in a local production that he attended.)[27]

Roberts found the Senate to be free-form and then some. On a practical level, he was trading the routinized world of the Court, with its traditional morning hearings, for the chaotic, late-night atmosphere of the Senate. On a more substantive level, the trial that began on January 21 added to the burdened relationship between the seventeenth chief justice of the United States and the forty-fifth president, whom House prosecutors portrayed during the trial as someone who constantly put his own interests above those of the country.

As Rehnquist had, Roberts set up a temporary office at the Capitol in the ceremonial President's Room, rich in Italian frescoes and vibrant floor tiles. He sat on an elevated dais, above the one hundred senators at their small wooden desks, hearing hour after hour of allegations about a corrupt, scheming Trump and the diminishment of America's global stature, typified by the Ukrainian bargaining. Trump's lawyers countered that whatever conduct their client had undertaken, it did not rise to the requisite "high crimes and misdemeanors" for conviction. Based on the Constitution and Senate practice, Roberts was not there to decide Trump's fate. His role was largely ministerial. He kept the clock and maintained order with a small nub ivory gavel.

The chief justice briefly stopped the proceedings one night after midnight because of an argument between House Judiciary Committee chairman Jerry Nadler and White House counsel Cipollone over the possibility of a Senate subpoena to obtain the testimony of former national security adviser John Bolton. Bolton, who had monitored Trump's dealings related to Ukraine security assistance and was later fired, had reportedly tried to prevent the president's allies from pressuring Ukraine for political help. He said that he had not wanted to be "part of whatever drug deal" the president and his cronies were "cooking up." Bolton would not testify without a court order.[28]

Republican senators who held the majority were not about to call witnesses or order subpoenas, which prompted Nadler to declare, "So far, I'm sad to say, I see a lot of senators voting for a coverup. A vote against honest consideration of the evidence against the President. A vote against an honest trial. A vote against the United States." Cipollone responded by saying that Nadler was making "false allegations" against senators and President Trump. "The only one who should be embarrassed, Mr. Nadler, is you, for the way you addressed this body. This is the United States Senate. You're not in charge here."

Chief Justice Roberts broke in. "I think it is appropriate at this point for me to admonish both the House managers and the president's counsel, in equal terms, to remember that they are addressing the world's greatest deliberative body." He pulled out a citation dating from the century-old Senate impeachment trial of Judge Charles Swayne of Florida. "In the 1905 Swayne trial, a senator objected when one of the managers used the word 'pettifogging,' and the presiding officer said the word ought not to have been used. I don't think we need to aspire to that high of a standard, but I do think those addressing the Senate should remember where they are."[29] It was a rare interruption by Roberts, who generally tried to stay offstage.

Watching from the other end of Pennsylvania Avenue, Trump denigrated the proceedings, pointed to his popularity among Republicans, and highlighted his judicial appointments. "Now up to 187 Federal Judges," he tweeted, "and two great new Supreme Court Justices. We are in major record territory. Hope EVERYONE is happy!" On January 24, midway through the trial, he tweeted, "More than anything else, the Radical Left, Do Nothing Democrats . . . are angry & 'deranged' over the fact that Republicans are up to 191 Federal Judges & Two Great New Supreme Court Justices. Don't blame me, blame Obama!"[30]

The chief justice concealed his own views throughout, maintaining his flat Indiana-bred tone as he referred to Trump's various misdeeds in questions he read aloud, submitted on cards by senators during the proceedings. Roberts had little control in the setting, unlike across the street at the Supreme Court. He also suddenly faced intense media attention, compared with the camera-free Court. In a piece headlined "John Roberts Comes Face to Face with the Mess He's Made," *Washington Post* columnist Dana Milbank dissected his every move, as the chief justice fiddled with his pen, took his glasses off, and put them back on during the hours of arguments on the floor. But the most disparaging aspect of Milbank's piece was substantive rather than stylistic. "There is justice in John Roberts being forced to preside silently over the impeachment trial of President Trump, hour after hour, day after tedious day," Milbank asserted. "He is forced to witness, with his own eyes, the mess he and his colleagues on the Supreme Court have made of the U.S. political system." Milbank referred to Supreme Court rulings that undercut campaign finance rules and voting rights.[31]

The public scrutiny was intense, as were Democrats' attempts to pull Roberts into the Trump controversy. The chief justice wanted no leading role in this legislative-executive drama and made clear he would not cast any vote on any procedure of significance. Senate Minority Leader Chuck Schumer, a New York Democrat, challenged Roberts at one point. "Is the chief justice aware that in the impeachment trial of President Johnson, Chief Justice Chase, as presiding officer, cast tie-breaking votes on both March 31 and April 2, 1868?" Roberts responded: "I am, Mr. Leader. The one concerned a motion to adjourn; the other concerned a motion to close deliberations. I do not regard those isolated episodes 150 years ago as sufficient to support a general authority to break ties. If the members of this body elected by the people and accountable to them divide equally on a motion, the normal rule is that the motion fails." And then Roberts got to his main point: "I think it would be inappropriate for me, as an unelected official from a different branch of government, to assert the power to change that result so that the motion would succeed."[32]

There was no tie vote in the Senate on any of the trial motions, so Roberts's assertion was never tested. He refused to offer any substantive guidance and pulled back as much as he could. By taking no action to ensure the presentation of witnesses and documentary evidence, he implicitly threw his weight to the Republicans in their quest for a swift, superficial trial. Like Rehnquist two decades earlier, Roberts suggested throughout that his role was meant to be a modest one.

The night before the 2020 Senate trial ended, Trump delivered his previously scheduled State of the Union address to a joint session of Congress. Chief Justice Roberts and Justices Elena Kagan, Neil Gorsuch, and Brett Kavanaugh, all wearing their robes, attended. When President Trump made his way past their seats, he shook hands with Roberts. The chief's jaw was clenched, his mouth set. Kagan, standing next to Roberts, her brow furrowed, appeared apprehensive as Trump in turn shook her hand and moved on to the other two justices. During the speech, all of the justices sat with their hands clasped on their laps, mostly staring straight ahead, expressionless. The cameras did not capture their expressions when, as the president ended, Nancy Pelosi ripped up the text of the speech. Trump again shook the four justices' hands as he made his way out of the House chamber.[33]

The next day, February 5, the Senate voted 48–52, rejecting the House's charge of abuse of power, and 47–53, rejecting its charge of obstruction of Congress—both votes thus failing to win even a simple majority, let alone the requisite two-thirds (67 votes) for conviction. The only senator to break the partisan pattern was Utah Republican Mitt Romney, who voted to convict on abuse of power and to remove Trump from office. "The grave question the Constitution tasks senators to answer is whether the president committed an act so extreme and egregious that it rises to the level of a 'high crime and misdemeanor,'" Romney said in his floor speech. "Yes, he did. The president asked a foreign government to investigate his political rival. The president delayed funds for an American ally at war with Russian invaders. The president's purpose was personal and political. Accordingly, the president is guilty of an appalling abuse of the public trust."[34]

No other senator's mind was changed to alter the party line. Nothing anyone said about Trump in the thirteen-day trial struck any other senator as sufficiently revelatory. After the second article was defeated, Roberts declared, "It is therefore ordered and adjudged that the said Donald John Trump be, and he is, hereby acquitted of the charges in said articles." On a personal note, Roberts later told senators that he looked forward to seeing them again "under happier circumstances." He had nearly lost his voice, and it appeared that the long days and nights had taken a toll on his health.[35]

The Senate had voted against any fresh witness testimony, and the House declined to seek any court action for subpoenas against Bolton and others. Even if the House had gone to court to try to enforce a subpoena, it appeared that no timely resolution was possible. By this point, U.S. district court judge Ketanji Brown Jackson had ruled in the Mc-

Gahn testimony lawsuit from spring 2019. But her district court was only the first of three federal levels to be scaled. Judge Jackson opened the door to McGahn's testifying before House investigators. "However busy or essential a presidential aide might be," she wrote, "and whatever their proximity to sensitive domestic and national-security projects, the President does not have the power to excuse him or her from taking an action that the law requires." She said that "the primary takeaway from the past 250 years of recorded American history is that Presidents are not kings." Further, she called the White House's immunity defense "a fiction that has been fastidiously maintained over time through the force of sheer repetition," adding that it "simply has no basis in the law."[36] The White House had appealed the ruling, and any McGahn testimony was still on the far horizon. (In June 2022, Jackson would become a Supreme Court justice.)

Trump seemed untouchable. And he used his impeachment acquittal as a badge of honor. The day after the verdict, he threw a victory party in the White House East Room and waved a copy of the *Washington Post* with the banner headline "Trump Acquitted." "We went through Russia, Russia, Russia . . . and it was all bullshit," he said. In attendance, along with the many Republican senators, cabinet officials, and members of his legal team, was Ginni Thomas, the wife of Justice Thomas, who cheered with others in the audience as Trump heaped scorn on the House investigation ("it was evil, it was corrupt"). Attorney General Barr clapped heartily with everyone else. The celebration had the look and sound of a campaign rally, only in swankier, upholstered East Room seats.

Trump singled out freshman Missouri senator Josh Hawley and veteran chamber leader Mitch McConnell as favorites and, in typical fashion, derided those who had taken any actions against him, including Senator Romney. "There were some that used religion as a crutch," Trump said, referring to Romney's membership in the Church of Jesus Christ of Latter-Day Saints. Romney had prefaced his vote by saying that he was "a profoundly religious person." He referred to the trial oath of "impartial justice" all senators took. "I take an oath before God as enormously consequential," he added. "I knew from the outset that being tasked with judging the president, the leader of my own party, would be the most difficult decision I have ever faced."[37]

With his audience still applauding, Trump called Romney "a failed presidential candidate . . . a guy who can't stand the fact that he ran one of the worst campaigns in the history of the country." (Romney was the GOP nominee in 2012.) Trump then saluted Senator Mike Lee, also a Utah Republican, seated before him: "Tell them I'm sorry about Mitt Romney. . . . We can say Mike Lee is by far the most popular senator from the state."[38] It was an act directly from Trump's playbook—he relished turning against each other any two individuals who might otherwise be working in common cause.

As Trump's corrosive effect spread to the judicial branches and stirred judges' distrust of him and, in some cases, of each other, U.S. district court judge Carlton Reeves of Mississippi was among the few unwilling to remain silent. In a speech at the University of Virginia in April 2019, he spoke expansively against Trump. An African American appointed by President Obama in 2010, Reeves publicly cataloged Trump's efforts to undermine the judiciary and highlighted the president's racist comments, reminding his audience of the candidate's 2016 attacks on "Mexican" judge Gonzalo Curiel.[39]

Without uttering Trump's name, Reeves said, "I know what I heard when a federal judge was called very biased and unfair because he is of Mexican heritage. When that judge's ethnicity was said to prevent his ability to issue fair rulings, when the judge was called a hater simply because he is Latino, I heard the words of James Eastland, a race baiting politician, empowered by the falsehood of white supremacy questioning the judicial temperament of a man solely because of the color of his skin." That reference was to Mississippi senator Eastland, who taunted Thurgood Marshall during his Supreme Court confirmation hearings in 1967. Judge Reeves also invoked Alabama's segregationist governor George Wallace, saying, "When the executive branch calls our courts and their work 'stupid,' 'horrible,' 'ridiculous,' 'incompetent,' 'a laughingstock,' and a 'complete and total disgrace,' you can hear the slurs and threats of executives like George Wallace echoing into the present."

Reeves spoke of his experiences as a Black judge: "The proof is in my mailbox, in countless letters of hatred," he said. He urged his fellow judges to do more to enhance and defend the judiciary. With an obvious reference to Supreme Court justices Neil Gorsuch and Brett Kavanaugh, Reeves said, "We have as many justices who have graduated from Georgetown Prep as we have justices who have lived as a non-white person." The only justices of color at the time were Thomas and Sotomayor.[40]

Although Reeves stood alone among judges in expressing such views and in pointing up broader failings of the judiciary, internal cleavages were evident elsewhere. When the Richmond-based U.S. Court of Appeals for the Fourth Circuit revived a conflict-of-interest case involving Trump, the judges berated each other, raising Trump-related biases. The case had begun when officials in Maryland and the District of Columbia claimed that diplomats and others who rented rooms at Washington's Trump International Hotel were essentially compensating Trump—prohibited under the Constitution's emoluments clause, which requires a president to obtain the consent of Congress to receive gifts from foreign dignitaries or state officials.

Trump's lawyers countered that the federal courts lacked jurisdiction to resolve the case. U.S. Fourth Circuit judge Diana Gribbon Motz disagreed and wrote for the majority at a preliminary stage of the Maryland case, "We recognize that the president is no ordinary petitioner, and we accord him great deference as head of the executive branch. But Congress and the Supreme Court have severely limited our ability to grant the extraordinary relief the president seeks." Motz addressed "the dramatics" of dissenting judges who refused to take the majority decision against Trump's legal position at face value.

Judge James Wynn, in the majority with Motz, separately asserted that the dissenters were undermining the integrity of the judiciary in defending Trump. "Editorial writers, political speechwriters, and others are free, of course, to make a career out of accusing judges who make decisions that they dislike of bias and bad faith," Wynn wrote. "But the public's confidence and trust in the integrity of the judiciary suffer greatly when judges who disagree with their colleagues' view of the law accuse those colleagues of abandoning their constitutional oath of office."

Judge J. Harvie Wilkinson, writing the lead dissent, had declared,

> Can we not see the political cloak we are asked to don? No federal court has ever allowed a party to sue the President under the Domestic Emoluments Clause. Until this President. No federal court has ever permitted the same with respect to the Foreign Emoluments Clause. Until this President. . . . And no federal court has ever entertained the prospect of an injunction against a President in connection with the performance of his official duties. Until this President. Following this barrage of doctrinal firsts, would it not be fair for our fellow Americans to suspect that something other than law was afoot?

That was strident language from Wilkinson, a 1984 Reagan appointee who usually held himself to a rigorous code of southern courtesy. (Wilkinson had a personal connection to the Trump administration. His son-in-law was Jeffrey Wall, a deputy solicitor general who then became the acting solicitor general when Noel Francisco stepped down.)

The tone of the opinions was self-conscious, as the judges referred to increased public scrutiny of their own motives in the era of Trump. Some conservative judges believed that Trump was being hounded, and they regarded colleagues on the left as part of a broader political and ideological resistance. Few liberal judges actually spoke out. To do anything other than remain silent put them at risk of being targeted by Trump's wrath or of violating judicial codes of conduct.

U.S. district court judge Lynn Adelman of Wisconsin fell into that trap. In thirty-five partisan-inflected pages of a law review piece entitled "The Roberts Court's Assault on Democracy," Adelman took aim at Chief Justice Roberts, Trump, and Republicans: "By now, it is a truism that Chief Justice John Roberts' statement to the Senate Judiciary Committee that a Supreme Court justice's role is the passive one of a neutral baseball 'umpire who [merely] calls the balls and strikes' was a masterpiece of disingenuousness. Roberts' misleading testimony inevitably comes to mind when one considers the course of decision-making by the Court over which he presides."

Adelman, a former Wisconsin state senator appointed to the bench by President Clinton, criticized Court decisions limiting the reach of the 1965 Voting Rights Act and lifting campaign finance regulations. "The Roberts Court has been anything but passive," he wrote. "Rather, the Court's hard right majority is actively participating in undermining American democracy." Adelman called Trump "an autocrat . . . disinclined to buck the wealthy individuals and corporations who control his party." [41]

Soon after Adelman's piece was published by the American Constitution Society–affiliated *Harvard Law & Policy Review*, three complaints against Adelman were filed under the Judicial Conduct and Disability Act. (The American Constitution Society is often regarded as the liberal counterpart to the Federalist Society.) Taking up the complaints, the judicial council of the Seventh Judicial Circuit admonished Adelman, saying that his criticisms "could reasonably be understood by the public as an attack on the integrity of the Chief Justice rather than disagreement with his votes and opinions in controversial cases." The council added that Adelman's complaints about the Republican Party raised questions about his impartiality. "The opening two sentences regarding the Chief Justice and the very pointed criticisms of Republican Party policy positions could be seen as inconsistent with a judge's duty to promote public confidence in the integrity and impartiality of the judiciary and as reflecting adversely on the judge's impartiality," the council wrote.[42] In a letter to Seventh Circuit chief judge Diane Wood, Adelman expressed regret for his essay's "inappropriately worded" criticism.[43]

In 2022, Mark Walker, another U.S. district court judge, took a subtler but still noteworthy shot at Roberts—in particular, his decision in *Shelby County v. Holder*—and at the Supreme Court's entire approach to voter rights. In a ruling that invalidated newly imposed restrictions on Florida voters, Walker wrote flatly, "This Court recognizes that the right to vote [is] under siege." He cited *Shelby County* and several other contemporary decisions by the high court. Then, after detailing what he described as Florida's "grotesque history of racial discrimination" at the polls, he added, "What is this Court to make of this history? To be sure, there are those who suggest that we live in a post-racial society. But that is simply not so." He referred to the page of the *Shelby County* decision on which Roberts had asserted, "Our country has changed, and while any racial discrimination in voting is too much, Congress must ensure that the legislation it passes to remedy that problem speaks to current conditions."[44]

As Walker, an Obama appointee, dove into the evidence leading up to the Florida legislature's passage of new voter restrictions known as Senate Bill 90, or SB 90, he wrote, "Florida's painful history remains relevant; it echoes into the present and sets the stage for SB 90." Even without racial animus, he said, some Republican legislators had secured their incumbency through legislation that targeted Blacks, who generally voted Democratic. "Sadly, the record before this Court suggests that, in the past 20 years, Florida's legislators and cabinet officials have given into that temptation several times—targeting Black voters because of their affiliation with the Democratic party." And he returned once more to the Supreme Court's handiwork in this area of the law, complaining that the justices had ruled inconsistently and referring to decisions that disfavored minority rights. He pointed to the Court's shifting interpretations of a 2006 case, *Purcell v. Gonzalez* (which dictates that judges not alter election rules on the eve of an election), and cited the justices' conflicting definitions of "eve," typically issued in summary orders. "In short," Walker wrote, "without explaining itself, the Court has allowed its wholly judge-made prudential rule to trump some of our most precious constitutional rights."[45]

Confidence in the Supreme Court was slipping, among judges and with the public at large. Over time, the public has expressed more trust in the judicial branch than in the executive and legislative branches, according to the Gallup polling agency. But between 2020 and 2021, public trust dropped precipitously. Gallup reported that the approval rating for the Supreme Court was just 40 percent in September 2021, the lowest percentage recorded since 2000, when the polling group began tracking public opinion of the high court. Such polls may be seen to have limited value, but their results continued to worsen, and the underlying view of citizens questioned about the judiciary was not unlike Roberts's own: "Justice is not inevitable."[46]

That adage would only take on more weight and for the Roberts Court seem grimly truer as the months wore on.

*Chapter 7*

---

# CULTURE WARS IN A TIME OF COVID

Stanford University law professor Pamela Karlan came to the Supreme Court in October 2019 with a forceful argument about why a landmark 1964 law prohibiting race and sex discrimination on the job covered gay and transgender employees. The advocate also brought her effortless wit and put it to the test when her arguments momentarily silenced the justices.[1]

Karlan, in dark-rimmed glasses and leaning forward over the lectern in the well of the courtroom, was representing two gay men, one fired from his job as a skydiving instructor in New York and the other who lost his position as a county child-services coordinator in Georgia. She told the nine justices that Title VII of the 1964 Civil Rights Act prevented employers from treating a man who is attracted to men differently from a woman who is attracted to men. Karlan believed that this approach offered the best chance of winning a cross-ideological victory from a Court deeply conflicted over such social issues as abortion and gay rights.

"When an employer fires a male employee for dating men but does not fire female employees who date men, he violates Title VII," Karlan said. "The employer has . . . discriminated against the man, because he treats that man worse than women who want to do the same thing." She added that such discrimination could not be differentiated from forms of discrimination already recognized by courts, such as that "against men who are effeminate rather than macho."[2]

After some initial questioning, Karlan further elaborated with a scenario that momentarily quieted the justices. It involved two employees who tell their boss that they have just married a man named Bill. "When you fire the male employee who married Bill, and you give the female employee who married Bill a couple of days off so she can celebrate the joyous event, that's discrimination because of sex."

The justices just looked at her, digesting the scenario, suddenly at a loss for words at the start of what was supposed to be a half hour of give-and-take.

"Well," Karlan said, "if no one has any further questions, I'll reserve the remainder of my time for rebuttal." Laughter erupted from the justices and some spectators in the crowded courtroom.

"I think we'll have further questions," Chief Justice John Roberts said, with enough levity to prompt more laughter. Soon enough, the justices had plenty of questions and all humor dissolved.

The sharpest conflicts between conservative justices and liberal justices usually revolved around decades-old precedent: Would the majority retrench on abortion rights, or the separation of church and state, or the reach of regulatory power? In some rare times, however, the justices confronted cases that tested whether they would go the opposite way and break ground in the progressive direction. That was the situation as they explored whether Title VII covered claims of discrimination based on sexual orientation and gender identity. The text of Title VII prohibited employers from denying anyone a job or promotion "because of such individual's race, color, religion, sex, or national origin." The precise question in the LGBTQ dispute centered on the "because of . . . sex" phrase. Advocates like Karlan, as well as liberal justices on the bench, believed that their best route to a ruling in favor of LGBTQ interests rested with a "textualist" reading, focused tightly on the words of that phrase.

The legal issue would have broad societal consequences, as millions of Americans identified as gay, and lower-court judges were divided on how to interpret Title VII. The Trump administration was arguing that it should be construed narrowly, as if "because of sex" meant "because of being a woman." It had sided with employers who, in three separate cases, had fired two gay men and a transgender woman. The employers contended that Title VII did not cover such dismissals.

Congress passed the sweeping Civil Rights Act of 1964 to prevent and remedy discrimination across the country, including on the job. The act had originally been proposed by President John F. Kennedy. After Kennedy's assassination in 1963, President Lyndon B. Johnson urged Congress to honor his memory by passing the stalled law, declaring, "We have talked long enough in this country about equal rights." Johnson, with a bipartisan alliance in Congress, then overcame the longest continuous Senate filibuster in history, sixty days.[3]

There was a directness to the test advanced by Karlan, a former Supreme Court law clerk (to Harry Blackmun) who argued often before the justices and had worked in the Obama Department of Justice. Her argument, as straightforward and bold as it was, contained an echo of something Chief Justice Roberts himself had said nearly five years earlier in *Obergefell v. Hodges*, the case establishing a constitutional right to same-sex marriage.

During oral arguments in *Obergefell*, Roberts had asked the lawyer arguing against same-sex marriage, "Counsel, I'm not sure it's necessary to get into sexual orientation to resolve this case. I mean, if Sue loves Joe and Tom loves Joe, Sue can marry him and Tom can't. And the difference is based upon their different sex. Why isn't that a straightforward question of sexual discrimination?"

At the time, in 2015, Roberts's question had been tangential to the constitutional inquiry regarding same-sex marriage; but nearly five years later, it got to the core of the Title VII dispute. And while it was not known outside the private Court chambers as the justices heard the new case, I learned that Roberts had hinted that he was open to a broader interpretation of Title VII—a piece of information that would have been picked up by the law clerks' subtle network and discreetly passed on to their respective justices. He might vote to extend protections based on sex to gay and transgender workers.[4]

There was reason to suspect the reverse—that Roberts would be unsympathetic to Karlan's arguments. After all, he had dissented in *Obergefell*, writing, "The majority's decision is an act of will, not legal judgment. The right it announced has no basis in the Constitution or this Court's precedent. . . . As a result, the Court invalidates the marriage laws of more than half the States and orders the transformation of a social institution that has formed the basis of human society for millennia, for the Kalahari Bushmen and the Han Chinese, the Carthaginians and the Aztecs. Just who do we think we are?"[5]

The trajectory of the new LGBTQ case defied easy forecast. During internal debate, in fact, there were surprising votes and concessions, yet some bitter recriminations, too. In some ways that was not surprising, given the nature of the dispute. While Justice Thomas often told his audiences that he had never heard a voice raised in anger at the private conferences, these sessions could become heated and unnerving. Inside the Court, it was known that the 2015 session that produced the 5–4 vote for a right to same-sex marriage was marked by loud voices and ire, on the part of Scalia and Roberts, who later channeled their wrath in separate memorable dissents. The new case—with Scalia gone and Roberts unexpectedly with the majority—most obviously enraged Alito. He spent months penning his dissent, first in his oak-paneled chambers, then at a home on the Jersey shore.

The sudden emergence of COVID-19 upended everything. The cases were argued in late 2019 but then drafted and negotiated throughout spring 2020, when the Court and the country went into lockdown to fight the coronavirus pandemic.

The nine justices were protected from the virus more than most people, in terms of financial security and personal safety. Some of them, like Alito, owned second homes and had options for getting away from crowded urban areas. Yet the pandemic could not help but affect their dealings with each other. They were creatures of ritual. They were accustomed to the trappings of their building, the courtroom with the thirty-foot-high Ionic columns on four sides, as well as the intimacy of the small conference room where they met to vote privately on cases. No longer could they just drop in on each other to talk about thorny points in a case or engage in one-on-one persuasion.

Their last face-to-face encounter as they navigated this annual session occurred during the first week of March 2020.

The justices were already on shifting ground with the LGBTQ job-discrimination case. It was the first such controversy since the retirement of Justice Anthony Kennedy, who had steered gay rights decisions since 1996, when he crafted a majority opinion in a Colorado gay-bias dispute. Kennedy went on to author decisions that invalidated state laws criminalizing intimate gay relations (in 2003) and that struck down U.S. policy denying same-sex couples the tax breaks, Society Security, and other federal benefits given opposite-sex couples (in 2013). The capstone of that aspect of his career was *Obergefell*. Kennedy's successor, Brett Kavanaugh, had not shown any inclination to vote as Kennedy had on LGBTQ issues and other matters concerning individual rights. So the parties on both sides of the Title VII case went into the dispute with a high degree of uncertainty.

The national momentum beyond the judicial sphere favored the acceptance and legalization of gay rights. Some eleven million adults in the U.S. identified in 2020 as LGBTQ—lesbian, gay, bisexual, transgender, or queer. (The number in 2022 was closer to eighteen million.)[6] Major companies had policies protecting workers from discrimination based on their sexual orientation or gender identity. But legal protections depended on where a person lived and worked. That was evident in the way lower courts had ruled in the cases the justices heard.[7]

Gerald Bostock worked as a child welfare services coordinator for Clayton County, Georgia, advocating for children who had suffered from abuse and neglect. After a decade in the job and having helped the county win awards for its welfare program, Bostock joined a gay recreational softball league. He soon began to hear disparaging comments at work about his sexual orientation and then was fired for conduct "unbecoming" a county employee. He sued under Title VII, contending that the county had unlawfully fired him because of his sexual orientation. A regional U.S. appellate court, the Eleventh Circuit, rejected the claim, based on circuit precedent that precluded sexual orientation complaints under Title VII.

In New York, however, when Donald Zarda, a gay man employed by Altitude Express as a skydiving instructor, was fired, the Second U.S. Circuit Court of Appeals allowed his case to proceed. Zarda, who had been with Altitude Express for several seasons, was fired after revealing to a female skydiving student that he was gay. (Zarda died while the litigation was ongoing, after a skydiving accident in Switzerland, and a sister and his partner continued his case.)

The third lawsuit before the justices was brought by Aimee Stephens, who had presented as male when she first went to work at R. G. & G. R. Harris Funeral Homes in Garden City, Michigan. After a few years on the job, she began treatment for despair and loneliness. She was diagnosed with gender dysphoria and began living as a woman. When she was in her sixth year with Harris Funeral Homes, she wrote the company a letter explaining that she planned to "live and work full-time as a woman." She was fired. "This is not going to work out," the employer said. After she sued, the Sixth Circuit sided with Stephens and declared that discrimination based on transgender identity is inherently sex discrimination under Title VII.

During two hours of oral arguments at the Supreme Court, the justices heard from five different lawyers: Karlan for Bostock and Zarda; David Cole for Aimee Stephens; Jeffrey Harris for the Clayton County and Altitude Express employers; John Bursch for Harris Funeral Homes; and Solicitor General Noel Francisco for the Trump administration, backing both sets of employers.

The justices zeroed in on the text and history of the 1964 law. Some voiced religious liberty concerns and worries about shared bathrooms and dress codes. Roberts asked about employers setting policies to cover bathrooms for "a transgender man transitioning to [a] woman." The chief justice speculated that it would be easier to consider discrimination based on sex when it came to hiring and firing than on specific work requirements, for example, related to sex-segregated bathrooms and locker rooms.[8]

"So if the objection of the transgender individual is that I want to use a bathroom consistent with my gender identity, rather than biological sex," Roberts asked Cole, who was director of litigation at the

American Civil Liberties Union, "do you analyze it . . . [as discrimination] based on the transgender status or do you analyze it on the basis of biological sex?"

"I think our argument rests on biological sex or what we think is more accurately referred to as sex assigned at birth," Cole responded, adding, "Here's the thing: this case asks whether when someone fires someone because they're transgender or because they fail to conform to sex-based stereotypes, is that because of sex? That's what this case asks."[9]

Justice Elena Kagan, for her part, reinforced Karlan's line of argument in the Bostock and Zarda cases, that a man fired because he loved other men rather than women necessarily fell under Title VII's "because of . . . sex" coverage. "If he were a woman, he wouldn't have been fired," Kagan said. "This is the usual way in which we interpret statutes now. We don't look to predictions. We don't look to desires. We don't look to wishes. We look to laws." Such an assertion here bolstered the employees' side and also conformed to the "textualist" approach of Justice Neil Gorsuch, tied to the plain words of a statute without regard to legislative floor statements and other contextual materials at the time of passage.

If Kagan and the other liberals had a chance of prevailing with their interpretation of Title VII, they needed the vote of either Roberts or Gorsuch. At the time, Gorsuch seemed the best bet. During the arguments, he focused on Title VII's text even as he voiced hesitancy regarding the wider implications of the case. "I'm with you on the textual evidence," Gorsuch told Cole. "It's close, okay? . . . We're not talking about extra-textual stuff. We're talking about the text. It's close. The judge finds it very close. At the end of the day, should he or she take into consideration the massive social upheaval that would be entailed in such a decision, and the possibility that Congress didn't think about it?"

Cole challenged Gorsuch's premise of potential social disruption: "So, first of all, federal courts of appeals have been recognizing that discrimination against transgender people is sex discrimination for 20 years," Cole said. "There's been no upheaval. As I was saying, there are transgender male lawyers in this courtroom following the male dress code and going to the men's room, and the Court's dress code and sex-segregated restrooms have not fallen. So the notion that somehow this is going to be a huge upheaval, we haven't seen that upheaval for 20 years, there's no reason you would see that upheaval."

Neither Roberts nor Gorsuch seemed convinced in the moment. Both appeared more open to arguments from Francisco, representing the Trump administration, who argued that a broader interpretation of Title VII should fall to Congress, not the Court. With an eye to Roberts and his brethren on the right, Francisco argued, "In *Obergefell*, this Court made very clear that there were good and decent people who had different views with respect to gay marriage and they should be respected. The legislative process is the process that allows those views to . . . be respected."

Justice Sotomayor interjected, "At what point does a Court continue to permit invidious discrimination? . . . At what point does a court say, Congress spoke about this, the original Congress who wrote this statute told us what they meant? They used clear words. And regardless of what others may have thought over time, it's very clear that what's happening fits those words." Francisco rejoined sharply, "I guess my answer, Your Honor, would be at the point when Congress actually addresses the issue."

Remarks from the justices suggested that the employees could lose. But things were not always what they seemed, and justices' views could be fluid. The many months between an oral argument and the eventual decision in a difficult case could mean multiple twists and turns. Roberts still controlled much of the action because of his authority as chief to steer internal debate and assign opinions, and also because he was at the ideological center of the bench, holding a fifth vote in close cases for the four conservatives to his right or, alternatively, the four liberals to his left.

When the nine retreated to a private session in the small conference room within the chief justice's suite, there was some agreement. At this point in their 2019–2020 term, they were still able to meet together, face-to-face. Shed of their black robes and seated in their usual chairs in a morning session behind closed doors, the discussion followed the pattern of seniority. They all had notes on paper in front of them. On the substance of the cases, a straightforward reading of the word "sex" in the Title VII law would lead a majority to side with gay men and lesbians. Some justices wavered, however, on whether Title VII's plain-language protections would cover transgender claims of discrimination, as brought by Aimee Stephens. The Court had resolved several gay rights cases before. This was its first transgender dispute. A majority was prepared to reverse the decision against Bostock and affirm the ruling for Zarda. But should they uphold or vacate the lower-court decision that favored Stephens? That is, should they outright declare Title VII coverage for transgender employees or return the case to lower courts for further proceedings? That latter move could have offered a tempting incremental step for Roberts, often looking for ways to thinly slice cases and offer something to each side.

Religious liberty consequences preoccupied Roberts and Gorsuch. Religion had been in the backdrop of *Obergefell* and in the foreground of the 2018 Masterpiece Cakeshop controversy. The justices had ruled in the latter that a Colorado commission had wrongly sanctioned baker Jack Phillips, demonstrating religious bias against him. The Michigan-based Harris Funeral Homes had originally argued that its Christian owner had a religious right to fire Stephens as she began presenting herself as a woman. But Harris Funeral Homes had lost that claim tied to religion in lower court and had not appealed to the justices on that ground. So there was no live controversy to resolve on religious rights. That helped the momentum for consensus on the three cases.

Gorsuch and Roberts were also aware of evolving attitudes on gay rights. Both men had known gay and lesbian employees and, at the time of the case, had college-age children. Although both had suggested, in oral arguments, that they anticipated societal "upheaval," and Roberts had loudly protested a right to same-sex marriage, they had also seen firsthand the evolving acceptance of LGBTQ employees. Both men knew that much of corporate America already had instituted workplace protections.

It turned out that there was a solid 6–3 vote with Roberts and Gorsuch to interpret Title VII as covering LGBTQ employees. The only three voting in dissent from the start were Justices Thomas, Alito, and Kavanaugh. As chief, Roberts had the power to decide who would write the opinion for the Court. (The chief justice makes the assignment when he is in the majority; if he is in the minority, dissenting, the senior associate justice in the majority makes the assignment.) Roberts chose Gorsuch, which other justices later told me set the course going forward. It meant that the majority opinion would be focused on the text of Title VII's ban on discrimination "because of . . . sex." And under a pure textualist approach, it was simply impossible to declare that Title VII's "because of sex" test applied to sexual orientation and *not* to gender identity.[10]

The chief justice had not previously signed a gay rights decision and had never been a strong proponent of the textualist approach that Gorsuch espoused. Roberts also had struggled during oral arguments with the issue of how a company could establish policies for shared bathrooms for "a transgender man transitioning to a woman." But he was persuaded to join a Title VII interpretation that accommodated contemporary America. He and Gorsuch set aside tangential concerns and agreed that the plain language of Title VII covered discrimination against gay and transgender workers. Even if an employer had other additional reasons for the firing, if the employee was LGBTQ, the discrimination was "because of sex." Roberts and Gorsuch realized that they need go no further to elaborate on other possible scenarios and religious objections. Liberal justices Ginsburg, Breyer, Sotomayor, and Kagan were already poised to rule that Title VII broadly covered gay and transgender workers.

The justices' 6–3 vote was taken privately, as usual without law clerks or other administrative staff in the room. Their law clerks would learn the vote soon enough, as they helped research and draft decisions, but they took a vow of confidentiality, and it was rare that outsiders ever got word of the outcome before a case was announced. So it was stunning that hints of the 6–3 vote in the LGBTQ cases began to leak relatively early to some journalists. It was apparent that some right-wing insiders were unhappy with the path the cases were taking and hoped outside pressure might change things. A *Wall Street Journal* editorial on November 21 shined a dark light on the possible direction of the dispute. It was headlined "The Supreme Court's Textualism Test: Kagan Tries to Lure Gorsuch and Roberts Off the Scalia Method."[11]

The editorial opened by suggesting that conservative justices, perhaps *all* justices, wanted "to claim the honor" of the late Justice Scalia's brand of textualism, and then warned that Gorsuch and Roberts could be enticed toward a false textualist interpretation. The *Journal*'s editorial page editors were not the only ones who responded to the leak. Writing in *National Review,* Princeton University professor Robert George argued that the Congress of 1964 would not have expected Title VII to ban discrimination because of sexual orientation, and he suggested that Gorsuch would be wise enough to shun that interpretation. "Did generations of Americans miss something hidden in plain sight? Justice Elena Kagan thinks so. And she believes she can prove it with a knockdown 'textualist' argument." Professor George went on to suggest that Kagan's argument would likely be dismantled by Gorsuch based on his true understanding of textualism. To some commentators on the right, Roberts was already a possible defector in a high-profile dilemma. He had memorably joined the left wing in the 2012 Obamacare dispute and more recently in 2019 against Trump's plan to add a citizenship question to the census. But the possibility that Gorsuch might be breaking ranks in a LGBTQ controversy shook conservatives.[12]

The *Wall Street Journal* editorial reinforced a belief among close Court watchers that Kagan was savvy enough to make a textualist argument and play to her colleagues' interests. She was, in some respects, an old-fashioned dealmaker. Among her mentors was Abner Mikva, a onetime Chicago politician who became a legal scholar and judge and then served as White House counsel to Bill Clinton. Mikva gave Kagan her first job, as she said in a tribute, her "first chance in the law."[13]

The rumors about internal Court developments also reached the Trump solicitor general's office, which had argued for a limited reading of Title VII. The leak represented such a departure from the norm of secrecy that government lawyers were not ready to believe what they were hearing. They thought it might be just talk. Francisco had written in the government's brief, "The ordinary meaning of 'sex' is biologically male or female; it does not include sexual orientation." Trump administration lawyers also warned that a different test could lead to prohibitions on separate male and female bathrooms, dress codes, and physical fitness standards.[14]

But Gorsuch disagreed. And in early February 2020, I learned, he privately shared the first draft of his opinion with his colleagues. He wrote that employers violated Title VII if they relied in any way on an individual employee's sex when deciding whether to fire him or keep him on. If an employer discriminated against someone on the basis of sexual orientation, the employer necessarily was treating the person worse based in part on that individual's sex. Within a few days, the four liberal justices individually told Gorsuch they were with him. Roberts soon followed. The quick endorsement demonstrated that the majority vote from October was holding to produce a decision covering gay and transgender workers.[15]

When one justice joins an opinion, or offers a suggested change, Court protocol dictates that he or she notify all the other justices. So the dissenting justices knew that Gorsuch's majority was still intact. His usual allies were frustrated. I learned that on the day that Alito received a copy of Gorsuch's first draft, delivered electronically and also on paper by a marshal's aide to his chamber in pre-pandemic tradition, Alito sent a private memo to his colleagues saying that he would be writing a dissenting opinion. Alito believed that Gorsuch had gotten the case wrong and that he was doing a disservice to Scalia's textualist tradition. Alito began gathering past cases and outside academic views to counter Gorsuch's approach. He cited commentary by Harvard Law dean John Manning, a former Scalia clerk, saying that judges should ascribe to the words of a statute "what a reasonable person conversant with applicable social conventions would have understood them to be adopting." In his slashing opinion, Alito wrote that Scalia would have condemned Gorsuch's interpretation and been in disbelief that the Congress of 1964 would have enacted a statute covering LGBTQ interests.[16]

Gorsuch considered himself a leading practitioner of the textualist

and originalist methods and had laid out his approach in his book
*A Republic, If You Can Keep It,* published a year earlier. The former
Denver-based U.S. appeals court judge described his textualist approach as starting "with dictionary definitions, rules of grammar, and
the historical context in which a law was adopted to see what its language meant to those who adopted the law." Such an approach usually
led Gorsuch to relatively narrow constructions of civil rights and liberties. In the case at hand, his approach was leading to a more expansive
result.[17]

Justice Thomas thought that Alito had the better argument and told
him he would join his opinion. Kavanaugh agreed that Gorsuch's approach was misguided and that any new interpretation of Title VII
should be in the hands of Congress. But Kavanaugh was considering
writing his own dissenting opinion explaining his views. Meanwhile,
as the drafting process continued, no one in the majority asked Gorsuch for any substantial amendment to his opinion, and none planned
to pen a separate concurrence. The liberals were simply pleased that
Title VII would cover gay and transgender employees. Roberts, too,
felt no need to say anything more. They were ready to let Gorsuch
speak, alone, for the majority.

By now, in the spring of 2020, they were all in various forms of
pandemic isolation, dealing with each other through telephone calls,
emails, and packages delivered to their homes by Court police officers. Some had left the Washington region. Breyer and his wife,
Joanna, joined an adult daughter and her three children at the family home in Cambridge, Massachusetts. Alito had retreated with his
wife, Martha-Ann, to the Jersey shore.

As they sent around copies of their draft opinions, the severest strains
emerged between Gorsuch and Alito, who was also irked by Gorsuch's
claim that he was taking a humble, modest approach. (Gorsuch often
referred to his moves as modest. During his 2017 Senate confirmation hearing, he testified to "the modest station we judges are meant
to occupy.")[18] By this point, they were no longer seeing each other,
and nearly everything was being expressed through written drafts and
memos. Alito said of Gorsuch's majority opinion in the LGBTQ dis-

pute, "If today's decision is humble, it is sobering to imagine what the Court might do if it decided to be bold." Regarding Scalia and his patented textualist method, Alito added, "No one should be fooled. The Court's opinion is like a pirate ship. It sails under a textualist flag, but what it actually represents is a theory of statutory interpretation that Justice Scalia excoriated—the theory that courts should 'update' old statutes so that they better reflect the current values of society."[19]

Kavanaugh, in the end, opted against signing Alito's dissenting opinion and instead wrote his own. In a public move reminiscent of his private note to Judge Furman in the census case, Kavanaugh used his opinion to try to soften his vote, to make sure his audience understood that he respected LGBTQ interests. "Notwithstanding my concern about the Court's transgression of the Constitution's separation of powers," he wrote, at the end of a dissent that stretched to twenty-eight pages, "it is appropriate to acknowledge the important victory achieved today by gay and lesbian Americans. Millions of gay and lesbian Americans have worked hard for many decades to achieve equal treatment in fact and in law. They have exhibited extraordinary vision, tenacity, and grit—battling often steep odds in the legislative and judicial arenas, not to mention in their daily lives. They have advanced powerful policy arguments and can take pride in today's result. Under the Constitution's separation of powers, however, I believe that it was Congress's role, not this Court's, to amend Title VII."

That passage underscored a difference between Alito and Thomas, on one hand, and Kavanaugh, on the other. Alito and Thomas would say what they thought and let the chips fall where they may. Kavanaugh appeared aware of lingering public disapproval from his 2018 hearings and often added appeasing passages to his opinions.

In their final negotiations through circulated draft opinions, Gorsuch and the five others in the majority held firm to their interpretation of the extent of Title VII coverage, irrespective of the expectations in 1964. "If we applied Title VII's plain text only to applications some (yet-to-be-determined) group expected in 1964," Gorsuch wrote, "we'd have more than a little law to overturn." He referred to the 1998 Supreme Court case *Oncale v. Sundowner Offshore Services*, in which the Court sided with a male worker on a rig who had brought a Title VII case after being singled out for harassment by male coworkers. "How many people in 1964 could have expected that the law would turn out to protect male employees? Let alone to protect them from harassment by other male employees? As we acknowledged at the time, 'male-on-male sexual harassment in the workplace was assuredly not the principal evil Congress was concerned with when it enacted Title VII.' Yet the Court did not hesitate to recognize that Title VII's plain terms forbade it. Under the employer's logic, it would seem this was a mistake." Scalia himself had written in *Oncale* that a statutory prohibition can "often go beyond the *principal evil* to cover reasonably comparable evils."[20]

Gorsuch acknowledged that employers were worried that the Court's ruling would affect situations beyond Title VII, and suddenly make it impossible to enforce sex-segregated bathrooms. He emphasized that no other laws or practices were before the justices, and that under Title VII itself, "we do not purport to address bathrooms, locker rooms, or anything else of the kind."[21]

His treatment of religious liberty was similarly brief, yet more substantive. "We are also," he wrote, "deeply concerned with preserving the promise of the free exercise of religion enshrined in our Constitution; that guarantee lies at the heart of our pluralistic society. But worries about how Title VII may intersect with religious liberties are nothing new; they even predate the statute's passage." He cited the First Amendment's guarantee of free exercise of religion and the 1993 Religious Freedom Restoration Act. That law prevented the federal government from substantially burdening a person's exercise of religion. Gorsuch wrote that there could be instances when the 1993 act would eclipse Title VII's prohibition on sex discrimination: "Because RFRA operates as a kind of super statute, displacing the normal operation of other federal laws, it might supersede Title VII's commands in appropriate cases."[22]

The decision spoke to the ideal of equality in America and reflected a coalition built around a flexible, rather than a more rigid, kind of textualism. And the justices did it without Anthony Kennedy, who had been closely identified with gay legal rights. The decision in *Bostock v. Clayton County* was a reminder that the Court always moves on. Scalia and Kennedy had their distinctive methods and legacies. The justices who remained on the bench borrowed from them and made their own way.

While Gorsuch separated himself from his usual partners on the right in the trio of LGBTQ cases, it did not appear to be the start of a new pattern. He still agreed far more with Thomas and Alito than with the liberal justices. The *Wall Street Journal* took a final jab that June, even as it, too, suggested that Gorsuch's vote was not a larger reflection of where he was headed. "An alien appears to have occupied the body of Justice Neil Gorsuch as he wrote [the] opinion in *Bostock v. Clayton County*, which sometimes happens when the Justices breathe the rarified air of the Supreme Court building. But perhaps he'll snap out of his living Constitution trance if he's shown his own previous work."[23]

Professor Karlan fielded the opposite sentiment from the Stanford Law community, former students, and lawyers who had helped with the case. During an interview with her fellow professor Joseph Bankman, Karlan, who is bisexual, said people had reached out "to give me personal thanks because a member of their family is gay or lesbian or bisexual or transgender, or a close friend of theirs is." She added,

> You know this, Joe, as well as I do—that our work plays a huge part in our lives. Yesterday was commencement at the law school and it reminded me of this famous line of Senator Paul Tsongas's from a commencement speech where he said nobody on their deathbed ever says they wish they'd spent more time at work. But that's actually not true. For many people, the time they spend at work is an extremely meaningful part of their lives and who they are. And so the idea that you should be treated fairly on the job, well, that's essential, as you say, to who we are.[24]

In the same 2019–2020 session, the justices took up an abortion rights case from Louisiana. Abortion disputes, like gay rights cases, usually came down to a single vote, and this one had also been Kennedy's. Tension churned around the case, within the marble walls and outside, throughout the country. On March 5, the day it was put to oral arguments, throngs of protesters gathered in front of the Court. There was a strong sense that *Roe v. Wade*, then nearing a half-century old, was in peril with two new Trump appointees. The landmark ruling had given women a constitutional right to end a pregnancy, as part of the privacy interests embodied in Fourteenth Amendment's protection for individual liberty. The Supreme Court had repeatedly affirmed the right to abortion, most notably in 1992's *Planned Parenthood of Southeastern Pennsylvania v. Casey*. Yet new state regulations and litigation kept coming to the justices. A significant number of religious conservatives considered abortion wrong, the equivalent of infanticide, and their political muscle dating to the Reagan administration had grown only stronger with Trump in the White House. Trump's selection of Supreme Court justices had spurred states to ramp up their effort to target abortion providers and diminish access to the procedure. His administration was backing Louisiana in the new case.

The last major abortion dispute had arisen in 2016, also in a presidential election year. Kennedy had cast the deciding vote in *Whole Woman's Health v. Hellerstedt* to strike down strict Texas regulations on physicians and health clinics performing abortions. The majority ruled that a physician-credentialing requirement and a mandate for hospital-grade facilities were excessive and put an undue burden on women seeking abortions. Texas's difficult-to-meet rules had led to the closure of clinics, and the Supreme Court majority said that the regulations unconstitutionally impinged on women's access to abortion. The new Louisiana case involved a similar mandate requiring physicians to have "admitting privileges" at a local hospital within thirty miles of an abortion clinic. Such credentials allow physicians to perform surgery and provide other medical care at a hospital. But because abortion was considered a routine outpatient procedure, clinic physicians usually skipped applying for these hospital privileges. In addition, some hospital boards were reluctant to credential abortion providers.

The Texas and Louisiana statutes stemmed from a national pattern of Republican-led states imposing additional regulations on abortion clinics—known as Targeted Regulation of Abortion Providers

(TRAP) laws—beyond the usual outpatient protections. Legislators often highlighted patient safety when proposing these regulations, but the real purpose of many of the TRAP laws was to limit women's access to abortion. The Guttmacher Institute and other abortion rights supporters argued that ramped-up requirements on facilities and physicians actually diminished patient care because they reduced the number of abortion clinics in a state, forcing women to travel farther distances to be treated. Such requirements tended to fall heaviest on poor women and those in rural regions.

In *Whole Woman's Health v. Hellerstedt,* the majority had ruled that *Casey* required a rigorous standard—tied to evidence of a regulation's burdens and benefits—for states imposing constraints on abortion clinics and their physicians. The question as the justices took up the Louisiana case was: What would a Court without Kennedy, and with two appointees of President Trump, who had campaigned against *Roe v. Wade,* do to decades of reproductive rights precedent?

The U.S. district court judge who first heard the Louisiana case in a six-day trial ruled against the state after determining that the admitting-privileges requirement, designed for physicians who performed surgery at hospitals, would reduce the number of qualifying clinic doctors and put an undue burden on women. Physicians in the state had been denied privileges, the judge said, partly because hospital criteria discouraged the granting of privileges to abortion providers. After Louisiana appealed, the U.S. Court of Appeals for the Fifth Circuit rejected the district court judge's findings and upheld the law. Now, June Medical—three abortion clinics and two physicians—had appealed to the justices.

The Trump administration joined Louisiana to fight the clinics' appeal. The president had continued to speak out against *Roe v. Wade,* as he had during the 2016 campaign. In late January 2020, just six weeks before the Supreme Court was scheduled to hear the Louisiana case, Trump became the first president to personally address the annual March for Life in Washington, D.C. Unlike past GOP presidents, who'd had an audio message piped to the crowd on the National Mall, Trump wanted to greet the marchers himself.

On that cold, gray January 24, Trump declared, "Unborn children have never had a stronger defender in the White House." He said religious liberty was "under attack" in the United States and shouted, "We are stopping it!" Trump told the crowd he had appointed so far some 180 federal judges and "two phenomenal Supreme Court Justices, Neil Gorsuch and Brett Kavanaugh."[25]

When the justices first announced they would take up the Louisiana dispute, Trump had referred to possible pressure from the Left on Kavanaugh, telling a Florida audience: "What they're trying to do is turn his vote liberal. But he's a much tougher guy than that. I hope."[26] Kavanaugh, as a lawyer in the George W. Bush administration and then as an appellate court judge, had argued for a narrow view of women's reproductive rights. But Kavanaugh also had testified during his 2018 confirmation hearing that he had not prejudged the issue, and Senator Susan Collins, a Maine Republican who cast a key vote for Kavanaugh's confirmation, did so only after she said he promised he would respect the *Roe v. Wade* precedent.

The 2020 March for Life demonstrators cheered Trump's speech. Bundled in hats and scarves, they then walked up Constitution Avenue toward the Supreme Court, with antiabortion signs in the air, some touching on the vaccine controversy that would become even more intense with COVID-19: "I am the Pro-Life Generation"; "Women's Rights Begin in the Womb"; "You Can't be Pro-Life and Pro-Vaccine"; and "Vaccines Are Made from Aborted Fetal Cells." As they passed the Department of Justice building on Constitution Avenue, Attorney General Barr and Solicitor General Francisco were out on a fifth-floor balcony off the solicitor general's suite. The pair stood smiling and waving, each with his left hand gripping the balcony rail, right hand high in the air. Some in the crowd below waved up to the lead Trump lawyers.

When the justices heard the Louisiana case on March 4, extra chairs were tucked into all the nooks and crannies of the courtroom for more than a hundred news reporters and about three hundred other spectators. Julie Rikelman, representing June Medical, told the justices in the new dispute, "This case is about respect for the Court's precedent. Just four years ago, the Court held in *Whole Woman's Health* that the Texas admitting privileges law imposed an undue burden on women seeking abortions. The Louisiana law at issue here . . . is identical to the Texas law and was expressly modeled on it." Louisiana solicitor general Elizabeth Murrill, representing the Louisiana Department of Health and Hospitals, avoided the precedent and told the justices that the state's admitting-privileges requirement "was justified."[27]

The justices disagreed over the standards from past cases for assessing abortion regulations. In *Whole Woman's Health v. Hellerstedt*, the Court had said that judges must "consider the burdens a law imposes on abortion access together with the benefits those laws confer." The justices said that lower courts should rely heavily on evidence and factual findings. The 2016 precedent, interpreting the Supreme Court's 1992 *Casey* milestone, put a premium on expert evidence, testimony, and depositions, as judges weighed the asserted benefits against the burdens of the law. The liberals remained committed to that approach, but Chief Justice Roberts suggested in remarks during the Louisiana case that the essential inquiry for courts was whether women's right to end a pregnancy was truly burdened, irrespective of the state's asserted benefit. That inquiry would become central to his opinion in the case.

Alito, emerging as one of the strongest abortion rights opponents, initiated a tense exchange as he suggested that abortion providers wanted women to terminate pregnancies so that the providers would profit. He asked Rikelman, "Would you agree with the general proposition that a party should not be able to sue ostensibly to protect the rights of other people, if there is a real conflict of interest between the party who is suing and those whose rights the party claims to be attempting to defend?" Rikelman, the longtime litigation director for the New York–based Center for Reproductive Rights, pushed back. "No, Your Honor, not if that party is directly regulated by the law in question. And, in fact, this Court has allowed third-party standing in cases where the state argued that the third parties were protected by the law and in a sense protected from the plaintiffs."

"Really?" Alito countered, as he pressed the notion that health clinics should not even be able to sue on behalf of pregnant women because they could have a conflict of interest with them—for example, over heightened safety standards. "That's amazing. You think that if the plaintiff actually has interests that are directly contrary to those of the—those individuals on whose behalf the plaintiff is claiming to sue, nevertheless that plaintiff can have standing?" Rikelman offered an example outside of the context of reproductive rights. "This Court has allowed an attorney to bring third-party claims against a statute that capped attorneys' fees in favor of clients."

"Well, that's amazing," Alito said again.

I know you think that the admitting privileges requirement serves no safety purpose, but suppose that the regulation that was being challenged was one that a lot of people might think really did serve a safety purpose. Let's say we're in a state where physicians' assistants can perform abortions, and an abortion clinic wants to challenge the training requirements for physicians' assistants. It just thinks those are too onerous and there's no justification for them. Now, if they're wrong about that, it implicates the interests of the women who may want to get an abortion, but you would say the clinic nevertheless can sue on behalf of those women?

Rikelman was emphatic. "This Court has squarely held in many cases that a plaintiff directly regulated by the law can sue, and those cases make sense for at least two reasons, Your Honor. First, because a plaintiff should not be subject to severe penalties under an unconstitutional rule. And, second, if the plaintiff is the one directly regulated, then they're—it makes sense that they are the appropriate plaintiff."

Ginsburg interjected, troubled by Alito's premise that the clinics' interests conflicted with the women's. "In this case, is there anything like the conflict that Justice Alito had mentioned? Is there a conflict?"

"No, Your Honor," Rikelman replied, "there is not even a plausible conflict in this case because this Court already held that admitting privileges served no medical benefit, and the district court here, after a trial, specifically found that this law would serve no benefit and, in fact, would harm the health of women in Louisiana."

Ginsburg also stressed in her remarks that abortion was generally a safe procedure that could be undertaken without hospital care. She called it "far safer than childbirth."

Breyer, who tried to bring down the temperature, acknowledged the recurring differences. "I understand there are good arguments on both sides," he said. "Indeed, in the country people have very strong feelings and a lot of people morally think it's wrong and a lot of people morally think the opposite is wrong. . . . I think, personally, the Court is struggling with the problem of what kind of rule of law do you have in a country that contains both sorts of people." Outside the building, protesters reflected that conflict but in an exaggerated fashion. Appearing at a lectern set up by abortion rights advocates, Senate Democratic leader Chuck Schumer declared, "From Louisiana, to Missouri, to Texas, Republican legislatures are waging war on women, all women. And they're taking away fundamental rights. I want to tell you, Gorsuch. I want to tell you, Kavanaugh, you have released the whirlwind and you will pay the price. You won't know what hit you if you go forward with these awful decisions." Schumer's warning exceeded the usual political rhetoric and the chief justice was not going to let it pass. "Justices know that criticism comes with the territory," Roberts said in a statement, "but threatening statements of this sort from the highest levels of government are not only inappropriate, they are dangerous. All Members of the Court will continue to do their job, without fear or favor, from whatever quarter."[28]

Two days after oral arguments, the justices took a closed-door vote on the abortion case. (They did not know it at the time, but that March 6 session would be their last together for nearly eighteen months, because of the COVID-19 pandemic.) Seated at the head of the conference table, Roberts was ready to vote against the Louisiana law, based on the precedent from the Texas case. He had dissented in that dispute, and he still disagreed with the majority's decision. But he said he felt bound by the precedent that the Fifth Circuit ignored. Still, Roberts adopted a narrower rationale than in the 2016 ruling, giving state legislators greater deference and thereby making it easier for them to justify restricting abortion. It was the first time, nonetheless, that he voted to strike down an abortion regulation. And it was Roberts's vote that set the direction of the case.

Going next in order of seniority, Justice Thomas, who had long argued that the Court should reconsider *Roe v. Wade*, voted to uphold the Louisiana law. No hedging, no equivocation. If it were up to him, the Court would reverse *Roe v. Wade* outright. Next around the table to vote were Justices Ginsburg and Breyer, both of whom said they would invalidate the Louisiana law and affirm the Court's balancing approach from 2016. Justice Alito was next, and he joined Thomas in dissent. Sotomayor and Kagan were with Ginsburg and Breyer against Louisiana. Then it was time for Justices Gorsuch and Kavanaugh to cast their first votes on a high court abortion case that had been heard on the merits. Both men sided with Louisiana. It was another 5–4 ruling on abortion, narrowly invalidating the credentialing requirement but with no majority for a single standard.

As things stood, the future of *Roe v. Wade* seemed secure. Roberts, the key vote at the moment, showed regard for abortion rights precedent. Sure, his rationale would make it easier for states to restrict access to the procedure through clinic and physician rules. But at that point in spring 2020, it was difficult to imagine that in less than two years—in December 2021 in a Mississippi case—the justices would take a private vote in that same small conference room, distinguished by a black marble fireplace, a portrait of Chief Justice John Marshall above it, to reverse a half century of cases on the right to privacy.

Justice Breyer began drafting the main Court opinion in the Louisiana case. As in *Whole Woman's Health v. Hellerstedt*, he emphasized that the law's burdens outweighed any medical benefits. Breyer's leading role in abortion cases, arising from his moderate liberalism on the subject, dated to 2000's *Stenberg v. Carhart*. He was able to hold a sometimes-shaky five-justice majority together. In 2016, he kept Kennedy's vote in the Texas case by heavily relying on Kennedy's writing in *Casey*. Breyer's modus operandi was persuasion through citation. He was also willing to pay heed to both sides, as he did during the March oral arguments.

Now, in 2020, Breyer's opinion laying out why the Louisiana law lacked health benefits for pregnant women was signed by only a plurality of the Court, four justices. Roberts was drafting a separate opinion concurring in the judgment but trying to alter the standard for assessing future abortion conflicts. "Nothing about *Casey* suggested that a weighing of costs and benefits of an abortion regulation was a job for the Court," he wrote, meaning that states would no longer have to demonstrate that a regulation actually enhanced the health or safety of a pregnant woman. His judicial test was focused on the burden of the regulation. To the chief justice, the only question to ask was whether a state regulation posed a "substantial obstacle" to a woman's right to end a pregnancy.

Roberts's brethren on the far right dissented. "*Roe* is grievously wrong for many reasons," Thomas wrote in a solo dissenting opinion, "but the most fundamental is that its core holding—that the Constitution protects a woman's right to abort her unborn child—finds no support in the text of the Fourteenth Amendment." Justice Alito, writing a separate dissent that was joined in part by Thomas, Gorsuch, and Kavanaugh, said, "The majority bills today's decision as a facsimile of *Whole Woman's Health v. Hellerstedt* . . . and it's true they have something in common. In both, the abortion right recognized in this Court's decisions is used like a bulldozer to flatten legal rules that stand in the way."

Kavanaugh initially sought a possible off-ramp, before supporting Louisiana's law and voting with the dissenters. I learned that he sent a series of private memos to his colleagues questioning whether they had sufficient facts about how the physician requirement affected clinic doctors. He proposed that they return the case for more lower-court findings and postpone a ruling on the merits of the law. Kavanaugh asserted that it was not clear that physicians would be unable to obtain credentials and that abortion clinics would shutter—a point that conflicted with the trial judge's findings after the six-day hearing. In the short term, Kavanaugh wanted to avoid the difficult abortion rights issue; in the long term, he was proposing a more demanding approach for any challenge to a restriction diminishing women's access to abortion.[29]

Kavanaugh might have thought that Roberts in particular would have been open to shelving the issue in an election year. But Roberts held fast to what must have been a difficult vote. From his early years in Washington, he had worked, under presidents Reagan and George H. W. Bush, for greater restrictions on abortion, and had even advocated the reversal of *Roe v. Wade*. But he had shown that as chief justice he could shatter expectations. In falling back on stare decisis, he said that regard for precedent, and by extension his opinion, was "grounded in a basic humility that recognizes today's legal issues are often not so different from the questions of yesterday and that we are not the first ones to try to answer them." Further—here he quoted Edmund Burke's *Reflections on the Revolution in France* (1790) in his opinion—"because the 'private stock of reason . . . in each man is small . . . individuals would do better to avail themselves of the general bank and capital of nations and of ages.'"[30]

Still, the chief justice who was perpetually involved in his own balancing act continued to stress that the 2016 Texas case had been wrongly decided and signaled to lower courts that states deserved greater latitude on regulations. The resolution was another sign of Roberts's power. The law came down to what he wrote.

On March 12, 2020, the Supreme Court had tacked a brief announcement to its website that it would be closed to the public as of 4:30 P.M. that day. Much of America realized that same day that life had to change because of COVID-19. The Capitol, the White House, and Washington, D.C., museums announced closures. The Metropolitan Museum of Art in New York closed that day, too, as did Broadway theaters. The theaters said it was just for a month. The day before, the World Health Organization had declared the COVID-19 outbreak a pandemic. President Trump, after downplaying the virus for weeks, went on national television to announce that the nation was suddenly at a critical moment in fighting the virus. Infections were multiplying across the globe.

The consensus was that a pause was necessary, and a *pause* is exactly what many people, including the justices, thought would occur. As with the Broadway announcement, Supreme Court officials initially believed that the new precautions would have to be taken for only a few weeks, maybe months, but never more than a year, let alone more than two years.

On March 13, Justice Kavanaugh decided to continue with a scheduled flight to Louisville for a judicial investiture for his protégé Justin Walker, joining Mitch McConnell and Don McGahn to celebrate Walker's district court appointment. As the days and weeks wore on, however, the justices canceled engagements. They passed up annual luncheons with their former law clerks and long-scheduled international trips for the summer recess. A majority of the justices were sixty-five or older, so they seemed at greater risk. Ginsburg, who turned eighty-seven on March 15, a few days after the Court closed its doors, was struggling with her fourth major occurrence of cancer. Sotomayor separately faced a higher risk because of the diabetes she had endured since childhood. Like many Americans, they were all suddenly relegated to their own four walls, not knowing when they would be back together again.

COVID altered their procedures in overt ways and their thinking about cases in a subtler regard. Most obvious were the practical consequences. Until the pandemic, the Supreme Court had only one way of hearing oral arguments: in person, in its courtroom. The justices had long refused to televise hearings or live stream the audio from the hour-long sessions. Roberts repeatedly dismissed suggestions that the oral arguments could be televised, saying in one 2018 appearance that cameras could disrupt "what we think is a very important and well-functioning part of the decision process." In a separate 2019 speech, Roberts said, "The courtroom is a very special place. Maybe part of what makes it special is that you don't see it on television."[31]

But in spring 2020 they had to figure out a way to hold remote hearings. They had twenty scheduled cases remaining for the 2019–2020 session when the pandemic hit. Roberts decided to put ten of the cases to telephonic arguments, live streamed to the public, and hold over the other ten until the following term. It was the first live stream the Court had ever offered. The justices did not actually vote on the plan, which caused some grumblings in their ranks. This was one of those instances, I discovered, when Roberts's internal critics thought he was acting peremptorily, dictating the manner of arguments without considering the sentiment of all. The solution was not ideal for anyone—the justices; the lawyers, who could not see their inquisitors face-to-face; or journalists and the public, who usually could understand more about the Court and its response to a case in the flesh. But this solution was better than the alternative of no oral arguments of any sort.

Because the Court eschewed any visual component, Roberts changed the format for questioning once they shifted to the telephonic arrangement. Instead of the customary practice of justices freely jumping in to ask questions, building on lines of argument, Roberts decided that they would ask questions in order of seniority, as if in a congressional hearing. It was a practical choice. The lawyers at the other end of the phone line, making their case, needed to know who was asking the question. The chief gave each justice three minutes for questions to each lawyer. In the early rounds, he had to cut several of them off to keep some semblance of the schedule.

The coronavirus pandemic also brought the justices a new set of controversies, arising from prisoners' rights in confined quarters and questions of religious liberties with mandatory church and synagogue closures. It also meant the return of a green-card controversy that had arisen in January 2020, when the Trump administration imposed a new income-related test for immigrants trying to become permanent residents. Among the factors considered for green-card status were age, health, education, and financial status. A provision of the Immigration and Nationality Act dictated that an immigrant who was "likely at any time to become a public charge" could not be admitted to the United States as a permanent legal resident.[32] In determining whether someone would be "primarily dependent on the Government for subsistence" and therefore inadmissible, officials had previously excluded noncash public benefits.[33] Under the Trump administration, however, the Department of Homeland Security changed the rules in 2019 to include, as grounds for inadmissibility, the receipt of noncash benefits such as the Supplemental Nutrition Assistance Program (food stamps), housing vouchers, and some forms of Medicaid. Anyone who even occasionally applied for Medicaid or other noncash assistance could be deemed a "public charge" and lose the chance to obtain permanent legal status. The administration had been carefully laying the groundwork, with Trump dribbling out various public-charge tweets. On August 12, 2019, two days before Homeland Security issued its "Inadmissibility on Public Charge Grounds" rule, Trump retweeted "@TeamTrump" on the subject: "President @realDonaldTrump is ensuring that non-citizens do not abuse American's public benefits."[34]

Several cities, states, and social service providers sued, concerned about a loss of federal assistance for needy families and costs that local governments might have to pick up. Lower-court judges blocked the new policy from taking effect while litigation progressed through the courts. But after the Trump administration appealed, the Supreme Court dissolved those injunctions, by 5–4 votes in January and February 2020, in the justices' first pre-COVID handling of the dispute. As had happened with similar orders on the Court's so-called shadow docket, no full briefing or oral arguments were held, and the justices in the majority offered no explanation for their action.[35]

The Court naturally had a need to hear some cases on an expedited timetable, particularly in capital cases or when a hotly contested lower-court order was scheduled to take effect. Yet when the justices resolved disputes outside their usual "merits" docket, without full briefing and oral arguments, their consideration necessarily became more secretive. The justices often responded to emergency requests with one-sentence orders, without making the vote of the nine public. In 2015, William Baude, a University of Chicago law professor who had been a law clerk to Roberts, referred to the array of cases that fell outside of the justices' usual merits calendar as the "shadow docket"; his description was so apt that it stuck and became widely used by law professors, journalists, and even justices themselves. In 2017, Trump administration lawyers discovered they could take full advantage of this "shadow docket" route and regularly tried to win the Court's intervention to block intermediate orders against its policies while relevant lower-court litigation was underway. Trump lawyers were successful enough in this practice—ensuring that challenged policies could take immediate effect—that some dissenting justices questioned whether their emergency calendar was being abused.[36]

Among dissenters in the controversy over the new "public charge" rule, only Sotomayor expressed her views. "It is hard to say what is more troubling," she wrote, in response to the conservative majority's February order, "that the Government would seek this extraordinary relief seemingly as a matter of course, or that the Court would grant it." She said she was especially troubled that the majority's pattern in these emergency-docket cases was benefitting one litigant over others: the Trump administration.

"Today's decision follows a now-familiar pattern," Sotomayor said. "The Government seeks emergency relief from this Court, asking it to grant a stay where two lower courts have not. The Government insists—even though review in a court of appeals is imminent—that it will suffer irreparable harm if this Court does not grant a stay. And the Court yields."[37]

Now, in April, the controversy over who should be deemed a public charge returned to the justices. New York state officials, battling one of the toughest COVID-19 infection spots nationwide, feared that immigrants were avoiding federal health care benefits to protect their status as green-card applicants. The administration had issued guidance on March 13 saying that immigrants could indeed obtain care to prevent or treat coronavirus without affecting public-charge determinations. But some federal rules contradicted that assurance, and the overall guidance was far from clear. New York state attorneys said that green-card applicants were being frightened away from treatment, imperiling the state's response to the crisis. They asked the Supreme Court in April to lift or modify its original order endorsing the Trump administration's policy. At minimum, state lawyers and immigrant rights advocates wanted the Court to say that a district court judge would not be barred from hearing another request for a modification of the rules.

Liberal justices who had dissented from the earlier actions concerning green-card applicants believed that the pandemic had transformed the situation, and they hoped that the conservative majority would be more interested in offering relief to immigrants who needed government health care and other public assistance amid the crisis. But Roberts spoke strongly against any modification of the Court's earlier stance, justices later revealed to me. He was not persuaded that the new administration guidance was confusing or that immigrants would threaten their green-card applications if they sought or obtained COVID-19 care. The four other conservatives were with him, as they had been when the policy first came to the Court. As Roberts prepared a standard memo to be circulated to all colleagues, his bottom line was that the administration had a strong hand and that the Court should discourage further litigation against the "public charge" rule. Dissenting liberals weighed their alternatives and what leverage they might have. They knew Roberts's aversion to 5–4 outcomes and the appearance of partisanship, especially on a Trump policy.

Some justices also privately admitted that they worried that if the green-card plea was rejected, the high court would appear oblivious to the thousands becoming ill and dying from the coronavirus. A few weeks earlier, in an April election dispute from Wisconsin, the five-justice conservative majority had prevented an extension of time for mail-in voting by six days. The majority had discounted health worries about voters having to go in-person to the polls and allowed restrictions on ballots-by-mail.[38]

Liberal justices wanted a district court judge to be able to clarify the pandemic rules for green-card applicants, and they strategized to figure out how to keep the case alive so that the challengers could make their arguments anew in the lower court. Roberts hoped to avoid any suggestion that the Court majority was open to the district court judge's imposing a new order on the Trump administration. Yet the chief justice had an interest in reducing internal tensions and avoiding another 5–4 decision. So in the end, liberals kept their dissent quiet and Roberts agreed to a modest compromise with the denial of the New York request: "This order does not preclude a filing in the District Court as counsel considers appropriate," the order said, falling short of actual referral to the district court for a new hearing related to COVID-19 medical care but not prohibiting one, either.[39]

For the Court's left wing, it was a modest behind-the-scenes victory, nothing comparable to the milestone for LGBTQ employees, yet an incremental concession that gave the four in the minority some satisfaction.

That was how cases between the two sides were negotiated: at the margins, with liberals coaxing and bargaining for whatever they could get from individual justices on the right. The LGBTQ and abortion rights cases and even the green-card dispute gave the minority hope that some equilibrium in the law would be preserved—provided, of course, that the Court's makeup did not change.

*Chapter 8*

---

# THE CHIEF AT THE HEIGHT
# OF HIS POWER

Congress had long tried to write legislation that would protect un-documented immigrants who were brought to the United States as children and who, over time, attended school and obtained jobs. The idea was that these young people, many of whom had arrived in America as babies, had gotten educations and were now contributing to society. They knew no other home. But legislation, first introduced in 2001 and known as the Development, Relief and Education for Alien Minors (DREAM) Act, had stalled. So in 2012 the Obama administration set up a temporary program to protect these so-called Dreamers from deportation and allow them work permits. Among other requirements, they had to have arrived before age sixteen and been in the United States for at least five years, and have no criminal record. The program, Deferred Action for Childhood Arrivals (DACA), was intended to be temporary and offered no path to citizenship.[1] By 2019, when the Supreme Court reviewed DACA, some seven hundred thousand immigrants were covered by the deferred-deportation and work-permit policy. They attended college and served in health and social services fields, the hospitality and retail trades, and the construction industry. They became small business entrepreneurs. The controversy for the Court arose because President Trump wanted to rescind DACA as part of his broader effort to keep immigrants, especially Hispanics coming across the southern border, out of the country.

This was a great threat to the hundreds of thousands of people who, having made life-changing decisions based on DACA, would be uprooted. They had enrolled in academic programs and committed to employers, believing that they would not suddenly be deported. A large network for young immigrants, United We Dream, pointed out how many of the beneficiaries were pursuing advanced degrees. "Right after receiving DACA's protection," the advocacy group and fifty other organizations wrote in an amici brief, "Luke H. submitted his applications for doctoral programs in chemistry. Now in his sixth year at the University of Chicago, he worries that—if allowed to stand—DACA's rescission could prevent him from completing his dissertation, jeopardizing years of hard work, and leaving his future uncertain." United We Stand also pointed to Jin Park, the first DACA recipient to earn a Rhodes Scholarship. He had arrived from South Korea when he was seven years old. His father worked in restaurants and his mother worked in beauty salons as he earned an education. At the time of the case, he was twenty-three, having graduated from Harvard with degrees in molecular and cellular biology, and was preparing to study global health science and epidemiology at the University of Oxford. Others had less celebrated personal histories but were nonetheless counting on the program as they began raising their own families and—with the advantage of work permits and driver's licenses—were able to commit to jobs or take on the responsibility for driving family members to school and medical appointments.[2]

Beyond the compelling human stories, the controversy threw into stark relief the clash between Donald Trump and Barack Obama. Trump's 2016 campaign against the Democratic presidential candidate, Hillary Clinton, began with his visceral opposition to then-president Obama. Trump was at the center of the racist "birther" movement demanding that Obama produce a birth certificate to prove that he was born in the United States. (Obama was born in Hawaii to a white mother from Kansas and a Black father from Kenya who met at the University of Hawaii.) In April 2011, at the White House Correspondents' Association dinner, as Obama stood at a microphone on the dais, he hit back at Trump. Then the host of *Celebrity Apprentice*, Trump sat in the glittery Washington Hilton ballroom with hundreds from the media elite and heard himself mocked for his birth-certificate stunt and TV gimmicks. Some Trump allies and commentators believed that the public humiliation helped drive him to the 2016 presidential run. Trump's political adviser Roger Stone told PBS's *Frontline*, "I think that he is kind of motivated by it: . . . 'Maybe I'll just run. Maybe I'll just show them all.'"[3]

After his election, Trump began slashing Obama initiatives and reversing his administration's legal positions in court. The Supreme Court majority tended to side with Trump. As a whole, the justices were unconcerned with the switch in administration positions, which marked a departure from the scrutiny they'd given the Obama lawyers who had abandoned their GOP predecessors' arguments.[4]

To be sure, the inscrutable Roberts also had the capacity to change direction and vote in ways that surprised even his own colleagues. That happened when the justices took up the controversy over DACA recipients. The dispute arose in the 2019–2020 session along with a series of other major cases that tested the depth of executive power, including Trump's ability to shield his personal business documents from subpoena. Adding to the tensions among the branches at this time, the nation was in the throes of another presidential election season.

Presidents and agency officials have wide latitude to rescind the practices of past administrations and to institute new ones, but they must abide by Administrative Procedure Act (APA) requirements. An administration cannot rescind a policy in a way that would be considered "arbitrary and capricious." The strictures of the APA had foiled Commerce Secretary Wilbur Ross in the controversy over whether a citizenship question could be added to the 2020 census form. And now California, New York, and other states, along with immigrant rights advocates, contended that the Trump administration had bypassed procedural requirements as it tried to roll back DACA.

The retrenchment officially began when Elaine Duke, then the acting secretary for the Department of Homeland Security, issued a

September 2017 memo that deemed DACA unlawful and likely to be struck down by federal courts. She echoed a declaration put out a day earlier by Attorney General Jeff Sessions. But Sessions and Duke were only inferring the fate of DACA from prior indeterminate federal court action on a related program, Deferred Action for Parents of Americans and Lawful Permanent Residents (DAPA). Two years after the creation of DACA, President Obama had announced that the Department of Homeland Security would similarly suspend deportation for certain undocumented parents of U.S. citizens and parents of lawful permanent residents. Unlike the original DACA program, the policy related to parents was never fulfilled because of a lower court's injunction against it.

A district court judge in Texas initially blocked the DAPA framework intended to postpone deportation for immigrant parents without papers. Affirming the order, the U.S. Court of Appeals for the Fifth Circuit asserted that such a policy initiative, covering some four million immigrants who would otherwise be subject to deportation and denied work permits, was Congress's domain, not that of an administrative agency. But the final step of this litigation was inconclusive. When the Supreme Court heard the Obama administration's appeal on DAPA in spring 2016, it deadlocked 4–4, affirming the lower-court ruling but issuing no opinion that would set national precedent. The bench had only eight justices at the time because of Antonin Scalia's death. It was a very real question whether the fate of the immigrant-parent policy gave Sessions and Duke sufficient grounds to end the child-related version.[5]

President Trump, however, had been winning on his immigration agenda at the high court, and the 5–4 conservative-liberal split seemed set in concrete. The justices by 5–4 had upheld his travel ban in 2018 in a decision written by Roberts that highlighted the president's discretion on immigration matters. Then in 2019, the administration successfully used the "shadow docket" to persuade Roberts and the four other conservatives to intervene in litigation centered on Trump's vow to build a wall with Mexico at the southern border.

Congress had refused to appropriate the full funding Trump wanted for the barrier, creating a standoff between the two branches and, at one point, a thirty-five-day government shutdown. Trump ended up signing a budget to end the shutdown. But he then declared a national emergency so that his administration could transfer $2.5 billion in Department of Defense funds to the Department of Homeland Security for his wall. The Sierra Club and the Southern Border Communities Coalition sued to block the transfer of funds, arguing that the "reprogramming," as it was called, unconstitutionally violated rules for appropriations. A U.S. district court judge sided with the challengers and blocked the administration's attempt to move the funds to the Department of Homeland Security.

The U.S. Court of Appeals for the Ninth Circuit rejected the Trump administration's request to lift the injunction. The appeals court said that the Sierra Club and the Southern Border Communities Coalition would likely succeed on the merits of their claim regarding the use of appropriations because the administration clearly breached the will of Congress. "As for the public interest," the panel of the U.S. Court of Appeals for the Ninth Circuit wrote, "we conclude that it is best served by respecting the Constitution's assignment of the power of the purse to Congress, and by deferring to Congress's understanding of the public interest as reflected in its repeated denial of more funding for border barrier construction."[6]

After administration lawyers went to the high court for relief in *Trump v. Sierra Club*, Roberts, along with Justices Thomas, Alito, Gorsuch, and Kavanaugh, constituted the majority for the unsigned order on July 26, 2019, putting a hold on the lower-court decisions. The action exemplified the pattern of conservative justices ruling on such Trump emergency requests, at night (this time on a Friday evening) and without sufficient explanation. "Wow! Big VICTORY on the Wall," Trump wrote on Twitter the same night, adding, "Big WIN for Border Security and the Rule of Law!" The four liberal justices (Ginsburg, Breyer, Sotomayor, Kagan) dissented. In mid-2019, they were still collectively trying to put a good face on the matter. They wrote no heated dissent. There was still some pretense that the two ideological camps were trying to work together. As

Trump expressed unrestrained glee at the right-wing action, liberal justices held their fire.[7]

Still, these 5–4 cases fortified the partisan character of the Court. Roberts, of course, continued to say otherwise. "The point is that when you live in a politically polarized environment, people tend to see everything in those terms," he told an audience of two thousand at the Temple Emanu-El Streicker Center in New York before the 2019–2020 term began. "That's not how we at the Court function, and the results in our cases do not suggest otherwise." This was his single, strongest message in off-bench speeches. But, in fact, the Court's 5–4 cases did regularly reflect its partisan divisions. It was as if the smooth-tongued star advocate Roberts thought that if he made the assertion often enough, people would believe it.[8]

Roberts was the justice best positioned to counteract the predictable 5–4 split. He had earlier acknowledged that as chief, he carried a separate weight and sometimes voted differently than he would if he were one of the eight associate justices. "I feel some obligation to be something of an honest broker among my colleagues and won't necessarily . . . go out of my way to pick fights," he told judges at a 2018 Fourth Circuit annual conference. And even as justices went into the DACA immigration case with a record of supporting Trump's immigration initiatives, Roberts had been signaling personal concern about the Court appearing too partisan in its alignment with the Republican president.[9] The chief justice was growing impatient with the administration. As was seen in the dispute over adding a citizenship question to the 2020 Census, Roberts favored executive authority, but not when corners were cut or rationale contrived.

To try to end DACA, Trump had enlisted Attorney General Sessions, who wrote the memorandum declaring that the Obama administration had put the policy in place without proper statutory authority. Sessions said that the absence of a date for termination of the DACA program unconstitutionally circumvented immigration law. He pointed to the previous court action on the related program that suspended deportation for immigrant parents without documentation. The case against DAPA was the flip side of the current challenge to DACA.

The DAPA complaint was initiated by Texas and twenty-five other GOP-led states, against Obama policy; the pending DACA case was brought by California, New York, and Democratic-led states against Trump's administration. Even though the eventual Supreme Court action in the case of *United States v. Texas* in 2016 was inconclusive and set no national precedent, DHS acting secretary Duke had said in her memorandum adopted from the Sessions guidance, "Taking into consideration the Supreme Court's and the Fifth Circuit's rulings in the ongoing litigation, and the September 4, 2017 letter from the Attorney General, it is clear that the June 15, 2012 DACA program should be terminated." She summarily adopted Sessions's rationale and failed to explore the potential hardships to young immigrants or the costs to employers and the broader economy if DACA ended.[10] In news conferences, Trump officials insisted that they were essentially forced to abandon DACA because it was legally invalid. They acted as if they had no choice, but they later, with less fanfare, amended their explanation.

While the blue-state litigation was pending in federal courts, Kirstjen Nielsen, who took over as Homeland Security secretary, elaborated on the Duke memo to try to give the switch deeper legal grounding. Nielsen stressed that Congress, not agency officials, should be setting policy for deferred deportations. "Even if a policy such as DACA could be implemented lawfully through the exercise of prosecutorial discretion," she wrote in a June 22, 2018, public memo, "it would necessarily lack the permanence and detail of statutory law. DACA recipients continue to be illegally present, unless and until Congress gives them permanent status." Nielsen specifically said, however, that she was elaborating on the Duke rationale, not creating new grounds to justify the rescission. (This legalistic point, apparently designed to avoid restarting the litigation, would ultimately thwart the administration's case.)[11]

For the Supreme Court's oral arguments in November 2019, hundreds of Dreamers and their supporters filled the wide sidewalk at the base of the columned building, between the two imposing seated marble figures—to the left, *Contemplation of Justice*, and to the right,

*Authority of Law.* The demonstrators held up signs that said "Build Bridges, Not Walls," "Defend DACA," and "Dreamers Belong Here." Some had walked more than two hundred miles over three weeks from New York City to Washington, D.C., to build support for preservation of DACA.[12]

Inside the courtroom and up first at the lectern was Solicitor General Noel Francisco, who relied heavily on the high court's prior action in the case regarding deferred deportations for parents. He said that the Department of Homeland Security had reasonably determined that DACA was illegal. "DACA was a temporary stopgap measure that, on its face, could be rescinded at any time," he said. Referring to the Immigration and Nationality Act, he added, "When you adopt this kind of broad and historically unprecedented program, you need to at least locate the authority to do so somewhere in the INA."[13]

Justice Elena Kagan responded, "They located the authority in INA's grant of broad discretion over national immigration enforcement policy." The questioning quickly escalated, and at one point, as Kavanaugh tried to enter the fray, he and Kagan stepped on each other's questions. "Go ahead," they said to each other simultaneously. Interjected Francisco, "I'll take either one, Your Honor." The moment provoked a rare bit of laughter among the justices.

Francisco's main point was that Congress had repeatedly declined to give Dreamers a path to lawful U.S. residence and that DACA effectively created "a shadow INA." Francisco drew a line between the government's power to set deportation priorities and outright allowing "violations of the INA by hundreds of thousands of individuals to whom Congress has repeatedly declined a pathway to lawful status."

Theodore Olson represented the DACA program's young beneficiaries. The challengers thought that the conservative Court might be particularly receptive to the former solicitor general from the George W. Bush administration, whose GOP bona fides dated to the Reagan years. Olson, it just so happened, had been one of the internal antagonists of former EPA administrator Anne Gorsuch as she tangled with congressional committees. By this point, it was forgotten history to most people, but Justice Gorsuch's late mother had put it all down in her book, writing of that tumultuous 1982–1983 period, "As the weeks wore on I found it harder and harder to deal with 'my' lawyers from the Justice Department. Teddy Olson in particular was wearing on my nerves. I have a problem with pomposity, and he was decidedly a pompous person." She had plenty of other choice words largely relegated to the annals of administration grudge matches. The advocates who had sought out Olson to defend DACA knew of that history but doubted it would be determinative in whether Justice Gorsuch was with or against them.[14]

Now, at the counsel table in the well of the courtroom with Olson, was a lawyer who represented DACA's success. Luis Cortes Romero, born in Mexico and brought to the United States when he was a year old, had earned a University of Idaho College of Law degree and practiced in Washington State. He had connected with the ACLU and other lawyers trying to keep the DACA program alive after he had begun helping a young man in Tacoma picked up by U.S. Immigration and Customs Enforcement despite having registered with DACA. Cortes Romero had been able to get in on the ground floor of arguments to support DACA, working with a team that included prominent law professors and star appellate advocates.[15]

During the arguments, Olson emphasized the violation of federal procedural safeguards and told the justices that the DACA termination "triggered abrupt, tangible, adverse consequences and disruptions in the lives of 700,000 individuals, their families, employers, communities and [the] Armed Forces." California solicitor general Michael Mongan, who stood up next, added force to the argument that the Trump administration had failed to take account of the "dramatic costs" ending the program would have on DACA immigrants and their employers.[16]

Roberts hinted that he might be concerned about how the sudden rollback could affect hundreds of thousands of people who had relied on DACA. Still, the chief seemed daunted by the sheer size of the program. When Mongan told the justices that the government had in the past adopted "class-based discretionary relief policies," Roberts said,

"Well, that history is not close to the number of people covered by DACA." Mongan acknowledged that past relief covered fewer undocumented people. Added Roberts, "Fifty thousand people, right?" That in fact represented less than 10 percent of the immigrants covered by DACA. Some commentators predicted after arguments that the Supreme Court would approve the Trump move. Based on the Court's track record, that was understandable.[17]

But Roberts was actually poised to cast the key vote, with the four liberal justices, against the administration when the Court privately deliberated after arguments. It was November 2019, and the justices were at their usual rectangular table, with briefs and three-ring binders on carts around them. Seated at the head of the table and casting the first vote, Roberts rejected the Trump rollback, to the surprise of some of his colleagues who knew he had previously voted in private against the DAPA immigrant-parent program. His view in this new case was far from a full-throated endorsement of liberal policy. He simply believed that the Trump administration had failed to sufficiently justify the recission and then engaged in invalid post hoc rationalizations. Roberts made his decision clear to his colleagues at the outset, not in the final weeks of deliberations, as had occurred in the census case a year earlier as he switched positions to doom the administration's citizenship-question plan.[18]

If some of Roberts's colleagues were surprised by his views around the private conference table, outside advocates were even more in the dark. Administration lawyers believed that the case was going their way, and attorneys backing DACA were not counting on Roberts. They continued to worry about the fate of the program, and when the COVID-19 pandemic erupted saw another opportunity to try to make their case to the justices. On March 27, as America was shutting down to protect against the virus, a group of plaintiffs wrote a letter to clerk Scott Harris asking him to alert the Court to DACA recipients' contributions to fighting the pandemic. An estimated 27,000 DACA recipients worked in health care, as nurses, physician assistants, and home aides. Lawyers for the young immigrants emphasized in their letter to the Court that "healthcare providers on the frontlines of our nation's fight against COVID-19 rely significantly upon DACA recipients to perform essential work."[19]

I later found out that by that point in March Roberts was nearly done with the first draft of his opinion siding with those challengers. Most of his colleagues had abandoned their chambers and were trying to avoid the early spread of the COVID-19 virus. As he finished his first draft, to be circulated to the others via computer, Roberts made plain that he believed Acting Secretary Duke in her memo had merely parroted Attorney General Sessions's view, violating the APA's protection against "arbitrary and capricious" changes. Roberts faulted Duke for simply adopting Sessions's line without contributing her own analysis of what was really a two-part dilemma, involving work permits for young immigrants and, separately, the exemption from any deportation order. Roberts added that when Duke confronted that dilemma, she should have considered "reliance interests"—DACA had allowed recipients to enroll in college, start businesses, earn professional licenses, and buy homes—in the deferred deportation policy dating to 2012. He also referred to the consequences to employers who'd invested time and money in training DACA recipients, citing a "friend of the court" brief submitted on behalf of 143 U.S. business associations and companies that estimated that hiring replacements would cost employers $6.3 billion.[20]

Roberts rejected the administration's plea to factor in the subsequent memo justifying the phaseout issued by Secretary Nielsen. Roberts believed that the public depended on contemporaneous explanations, not "*post hoc* rationalizations." He wrote that while Secretary Nielsen had purported to explain the Duke memorandum, her reasoning failed to align with Duke's. "Acting Secretary Duke rested the rescission on the conclusion that DACA is unlawful. Period," Roberts wrote in his final opinion. "By contrast, Secretary Nielsen's new memorandum offered three 'separate and independently sufficient reasons' for the rescission . . . only the first of which is the conclusion that DACA is illegal." Roberts highlighted the importance of procedural requirements and agency accountability. "Permitting agencies to invoke belated justifications . . . can upset 'the orderly functioning of the [APA] process of review' . . . forcing both litigants and courts to chase a moving target. Each of these values would be markedly undermined were we to allow DHS to rely on reasons offered nine months after Duke announced the rescission and after three different courts had identified flaws in the original explanation."

Roberts's view may have been informed by an innovative argument raised by a former law clerk to Kagan. Making the kind of calculated appeal that was Kagan's signature, Benjamin Eidelson, a Harvard law professor and co-counsel for those challenging the rescission, offered a narrow approach that threaded the needle between DACA and the prior DAPA dispute, and that, in fact, Roberts began adopting into his decision. Eidelson had been the lead author of one of the briefs for the challengers to the rescission. In that brief and in an op-ed in the *New York Times* published two weeks before oral arguments, he urged the justices essentially to separate the deferred deportation element of the policy from other benefits such as work permits. That way, the argument went, the Court could target the administration's failure to explain why specific, additional benefits associated with deferred deportation warranted wholesale rescission. Eidelson's arguments were subtle but plainly aimed at the justice whose vote was crucial, and as he closed his op-ed, he made his case directly: "As Chief Justice John Roberts has said, if it's not necessary to decide more in a case, it's necessary not to do so."[21]

Out of public view, as the justices continued negotiations, three of the four liberals responded enthusiastically to Roberts's draft opinion siding with the challengers. Ginsburg, Breyer, and Kagan were pleased to have any win in the immigration case. Sotomayor, however, initially held off. She was dismayed that the chief justice was ready to shut the door to arguments that the administration had violated the Constitution's equal protection guarantee as it tried to end DACA, based on Trump's racist comments about Mexican immigrants. She waited a couple of weeks after Roberts had sent around his draft opinion and then told the chief she would join part of it but write a separate statement explaining why the challengers' constitutional claim should be able to go forward in lower courts.

Beyond the anti-immigrant comments that Trump had made in his 2015 presidential announcement speech ("They're rapists. And some, I assume, are good people") and during his presidential run in 2016, when he declared that Mexican immigrants were criminals, drug dealers, and "the bad ones," once in office, he compared undocumented immigrants to "animals." "These aren't people, these are animals," Trump said in 2017, stating that they were responsible for "the drugs, the gangs, the cartels, the crisis of smuggling and trafficking, and MS-13." Referring to the gang that the FBI had identified as actually having relatively few new immigrant members, Trump said, "We are throwing MS-13 out of here so fast."[22] To ignore such statements, Sotomayor told her colleagues, represented a "blinkered approach." She said that they revealed Trump's motive for the rescission of DACA. "Taken together," Sotomayor wrote in her opinion, "the words of the President help to create the strong perception that the rescission decision was contaminated by impermissible discriminatory animus."[23]

Roberts believed that the statements Sotomayor cited were not sufficiently "contemporary" to shed light on the decision to end the DACA program, and that at any rate, the "relevant actors" were Duke and Sessions, not Trump. Sotomayor said that all she wanted was a chance for DACA advocates to make their case when the controversy returned to lower courts. She said that they at least should be able to detail their facts that plausibly alleged discriminatory animus. None of her fellow liberals agreed to the extent that they would try to convince Roberts to expand his opinion. They were gratified that he was even finding that the Department of Homeland Security had failed to sufficiently consider the potential hardships for those who were relying on DACA.

This was compromise—and its associated costs and benefits—at the reconstituted Supreme Court. It was a center-right bench that hung on the vote of Roberts. The liberals generally accepted any victory, even when limited.

In his opinion, Roberts gave the administration another opportunity to properly phase out the DACA program and demonstrate that it could fulfill the federal procedural requirements of a policy change.

"We do not decide whether DACA or its rescission are sound policies," he wrote. "The wisdom of those decisions is none of our concern. We address only whether the agency complied with the procedural requirement that it provide a reasoned explanation for its action." His bottom line: the administration could eliminate the program as it chose, but it had to do it properly. Quoting Oliver Wendell Holmes from a century earlier, Roberts wrote, "Justice Holmes famously wrote that 'men must turn square corners when they deal with the Government.' But it is also true, particularly when so much is at stake, that 'the Government should turn square corners in dealing with the people.' The basic rule here is clear: An agency must defend its actions based on the reasons it gave when it acted. This is not the case for cutting corners to allow DHS to rely upon reasons absent from its original decision."[24]

As much as the DACA decision left Sotomayor frustrated, the conservative justices were even more dismayed. They believed that the majority had intervened in a matter best left to Congress and, as a result (in the words of Thomas), "given the green light for future political battles to be fought in this Court rather than where they rightfully belong—the political branches." Some conservative justices privately complained to me that Roberts seemed motivated by public opinion and institutional worries rather than law and facts. Republican critics outside were publicly blunt. "John Roberts again postures as a Solomon who will save our institutions from political controversy and accountability," Arkansas Republican senator Tom Cotton said in a statement. "If the Chief Justice believes his political judgment is so exquisite, I invite him to resign, travel to Iowa, and get elected. I suspect voters will find his strange views no more compelling than do the principled justices on the Court."[25]

From Trump, the response was terse. He tweeted, "Do you get the impression that the Supreme Court doesn't like me?" Still, his administration was going to get a second chance to try to roll back the program. DACA recipients had only a temporary reprieve, and all involved were looking ahead to the November 2020 election and whether Dreamers' fate would be in the hands of Trump or his Democratic challenger, Joe Biden.[26]

The justices were isolated from each other at this point in the pandemic and barely getting out among friends. On Sunday, June 21, Roberts walked over to the country club near his Maryland home. He was on the grounds when he blacked out, fell, and hit his head. Then sixty-five, he was taken by ambulance to a local hospital and kept overnight for observation. He declined to publicly disclose the incident until, more than two weeks later, the *Washington Post* got a tip about the fall and was ready to write about the injury. The Court's public information office issued a statement that said Roberts's physicians believed the fall was the result of light-headedness caused by dehydration. The Court's spokeswoman said that doctors did not believe the fall was caused by a seizure. Roberts had suffered two publicly reported earlier epileptic seizures. In 2007, just two years after becoming chief justice, he blacked out while on a dock at his vacation home in Maine, fell, and hit his head. The Court's public information office said that he had had a "benign idiopathic seizure" arising from an unknown cause. His first reported seizure dated to 1993, when he was working in the U.S. solicitor general's office and had been out golfing.

The Court's police staff, which provides full-time security to the justices, had been preoccupied in these months by the health of Ginsburg, who was undergoing cancer treatment, and by Sotomayor, who felt especially vulnerable to COVID-19. The officers had protocols for when any of the nine fell ill, including aliases for the hospital. Some justices were more difficult to look after because of their age, relative frailty, or sheer demanding personality. Roberts was not known to be one of them. He returned to his regular duties within days and soon delivered another 5–4 decision involving the Trump administration. This time it left the four liberals in dissent. The dispute involved the Consumer Financial Protection Bureau and stoked the conservative majority's desire to reduce federal regulatory power. For oral arguments, Leonard Leo, the Federalist Society leader, had secured a prime seat in the courtroom. He sat with Maureen Scalia, the widow of the late justice, and one of the Scalia sons, John, in a section for justices' special guests.[27]

Roberts, with the backing of the four other conservatives, invalidated the CFPB's structure of a single director who could not be easily removed at the will of the president—a structure Congress had favored to ensure the consumer agency's independence. Kagan wrote for the four liberal dissenters in the case. As often happened when she squared off against Roberts, her opinion countered the substantive arguments while also crackling with pop references and rhetorical flourishes. Here, she made use of a well-known animated film on public television, with her own asides: "What does the Constitution say about the separation of powers—and particularly about the President's removal authority? (Spoiler alert: about the latter, nothing at all.) The majority offers the civics class version of separation of powers—call it the Schoolhouse Rock definition of the phrase," she said, referring to the educational series's description of a three-ring government: "Ring one, Executive. Two is Legislative, that's Congress. Ring three, Judiciary." Such a framework is good as far as it goes. "The problem," she chided, "lies in treating the beginning as an ending too—in failing to recognize that the separation of powers is, by design, neither rigid nor complete." Her point was that the Court majority was locked into an artificial model of congressional authority that neglected to account for modern-day economic challenges.[28]

The last decisions to be hashed out during the difficult 2019–2020 session of isolation were personal to Trump. The Manhattan district attorney and investigators in the House of Representatives were trying to subpoena the president's financial records from a set of years before he came to office. Lower federal courts in New York and Washington, D.C., had rejected Trump's assertions of immunity and executive privilege. Judges had ruled that the accounting and banking records had to be turned over to the respective investigators. As Trump appealed, he was backed by the Department of Justice.

The paired cases traced to business activities Trump had engaged in before becoming president, as New York prosecutors sought nearly a decade's worth of documents related to possible fraud on the part of the Trump Organization. Separately, committees of the House of Representatives, led by Democrats, who took power after the 2018 elections, were trying to obtain accounting and banking records as they developed ethics legislation to tighten money-laundering pro-hibitions.

Unlike past presidents, Trump declined to divest or used blind trusts for his global finances, which opened him to possible conflicts of interest. House committees issued a grand jury subpoena to Mazars USA and also subpoenaed Deutsche Bank and Capital One. Trump intervened to try to block the institutions from providing information and to challenge the power of the House to issue the subpoenas in the first place. His lawyers contended that the subpoenas lacked any legitimate legislative purpose.

At the Supreme Court, the cases had been scheduled for March 2020 in the courtroom, but once COVID-19 hit they were postponed, then rescheduled for a May teleconference. It had only been a few months earlier, in February, that Trump had eluded conviction in the Senate impeachment trial related to his alleged conditioning of secu-rity aid to Ukraine on that country's investigation of U.S. Democrats. A year before that, Robert Mueller had opted not to charge Trump with any crimes related to the Russian election interference.

Trump remained defiant. His administration had also successfully stalled testimony from his top aides, including Don McGahn, for var-ious cases. A panel of the U.S. Court of Appeals for the District of Columbia Circuit (D.C. Circuit) endorsed Don McGahn's refusal to comply with a House subpoena in February, siding with the Trump administration's arguments that federal judges lacked jurisdiction to intervene in that House subpoena fight. U.S. appellate judge Thomas Griffith wrote that U.S. district court judge Ketanji Brown Jackson had given "short shrift" to separation-of-powers principles when she ruled for the House. "In this case," Griffith wrote, "the dangers of ju-dicial involvement are particularly stark. Few cases could so concretely present a direct clash between the branches."[29] But soon after, the full D.C. Circuit threw out the Griffith panel decision and agreed to re-hear the McGahn case. This was right around the time the justices were taking up the Trump documents controversy.

The cases intersected to an extent behind the scenes among the jus-tices. I learned that Kavanaugh privately offered a suggestion based on the view that the Supreme Court lacked jurisdiction to hear the House documents disputes, just as the D.C. Circuit panel led by Judge Griffith had concluded in the McGahn controversy. Before the scheduled Supreme Court oral arguments in the Trump cases, in a memo to his eight colleagues, Kavanaugh raised the possibility that the House case could be covered by the "political question" doctrine or otherwise outside the jurisdiction of federal judges. That "political question" doctrine holds that certain disputes are better thrashed out between the political branches, with the leverage of appropriations and appointments, rather than resolved by judges.

As the justices dealt with each other that April through a series of calls and memos, Kavanaugh persuaded them to ask lawyers for the House and for Trump for supplemental filings on whether the doctrine applied or whether any other grounds would prevent the Court from deciding the case. A few justices believed the request in vain because the dispute involved Trump as a private individual. They also thought it was too close to the scheduled arguments. But Roberts agreed with Kavanaugh that they should at least air the issue.[30]

It was difficult for most outsiders to know at that point how seriously the justices were weighing the "political question" doctrine. If the justices ended up accepting the notion that the House subpoena case was too political to resolve, the Court would be undercutting congressional power and helping presidents who wanted to avoid legislative oversight. House and Senate investigative committees would be prevented from turning to federal judges to enforce subpoenas against the president and his aides. The result would ultimately enhance executive power, as Kavanaugh and other conservatives had encouraged over the years. And the adoption of this theory would have benefitted McGahn and other White House aides.

Lawyers for Trump and the House contended in their supplemental filings that the "political question" doctrine would not apply to the controversy, and both sets of litigants urged the justices to face the separation-of-powers issues at hand. The justices themselves soon abandoned their interest in the possibility, so much so that it was never raised during oral arguments.

When the telephonic arguments were held in May, most of the justices were still based in home offices. Their sentiment regarding Trump, pro and con, emerged over the phone lines. Thomas characterized the House committee subpoenas directed at Mazars as attacks on the Trump presidency. Their real motive, Thomas suggested, was "to remove the President from office." Ginsburg voiced scorn for Trump's repeated efforts to keep his tax records hidden.[31]

During the hearing, liberal justices emphasized that if Congress wanted to fulfill its legislative mission and update ethics laws, it first needed to investigate arguably unethical behavior and obtain evidence. Conservatives were more worried about protecting the presidency, whether from members of Congress harassing a president of the opposite party or from potentially hundreds of local prosecutors nationwide.

Roberts wanted to lift the issues beyond Trump. All the justices had to consider the future interests of the executive branch, of Congress, and of state prosecutors seeking records—from any president. They were aware that although this case involved a Republican, it could be only a matter of years, or even mere months, before a Democratic president was being investigated by a Republican-controlled congressional committee.

History was in the air. Past separation-of-powers battles—*United States v. Nixon* in 1974 and *Clinton v. Jones* in 1997—had yielded unanimous decisions. In 1974, the justices had rejected Richard Nixon's attempt to withhold Oval Office tapes connected to the Watergate cover-up based on executive privilege. The Court ruled that fundamental due process and the need for evidence in a criminal trial overrode Nixon's interests. In 1997, the Court rejected Bill Clinton's claim of presidential immunity as he tried to postpone a civil lawsuit by Paula Jones, who said he had sexually harassed her when he was Arkansas governor.

When the justices voted on the new pair of cases after oral arguments, such unanimity and consensus eluded them. In their private telephonic conference, the *Trump v. Vance* case produced a 5–4 split, I later learned, to affirm the lower-court judgment against Trump.

Separately, on the House dispute known as *Trump v. Mazars*, the justices fractured in their legal rationales, although a solid six at the start wanted to throw out the D.C. Circuit decision that had afforded Congress expansive power to issue subpoenas for Trump's financial documents. Those early votes were not publicly revealed. Roberts said that he would write the opinions for both cases and proceeded to try to produce greater common ground. They were of utmost importance, and it was predictable that Roberts would want to hold on to them. More than Chief Justice William Rehnquist, Roberts kept the prime cases for himself. As he began trying to bring together as many votes as possible, he was in regular telephone contact with his colleagues. Over the course of two months, he coaxed and compromised for two 7–2 opinions. Only Thomas and Alito declined to sign on to the majority judgment in each case.

Of the two cases, the New York grand jury controversy was, in some respects, easier because of Trump's extreme assertion of presidential immunity. That notion flouted all precedent. Roberts relied at the outset on the writings of the great chief justice John Marshall, when he presided over the treason trial of Aaron Burr and permitted a subpoena against President Thomas Jefferson. Befitting Roberts's interest in history (he had considered earning a Ph.D. in history before turning to law school), he opened with a flourish: "In the summer of 1807, all eyes were on Richmond, Virginia. Aaron Burr, the former Vice President, was on trial for treason. Fallen from political grace after his fatal duel with Alexander Hamilton, and with a murder charge pending in New Jersey, Burr followed the path of many down-and-out Americans of his day—he headed West in search of new opportunity." After elaborating on the subpoena for President Jefferson, Roberts wrote that Marshall had determined that no citizen, not even the president, "is categorically above the common duty to produce evidence when called upon in a criminal proceeding." The Roberts decision relied on that principle to hold that Trump was not absolutely immune from state criminal subpoenas seeking his private papers and that prosecutors were not required to show a heightened standard of need.[32]

Roberts said that standard of need, as proposed by the Department of Justice, would impede the grand jury's ability to acquire all information for an investigation. If the proceedings were delayed, he said, prosecutors would be deprived of investigative leads that the evidence might yield, allowing memories to fade and documents to disappear. Overall, the decision meant that the president would have no special protection from a subpoena but could raise the same defenses as anyone else subjected to a grand jury investigation.

Thomas and Alito dissented. Alito's writing showed some of the ill feelings the case engendered, as well as his own background as a U.S. attorney (1987–1990 in New Jersey). He knew how prosecutors might be encouraged to pursue a president. Alito rejected Trump's arguments for complete immunity but believed there should be a heightened standard of review. He threw back at Roberts lines from his majority opinion in the Trump case and also revived Roberts's 2019 opinion against Commerce Secretary Wilbur Ross. "It is not enough to recite sayings like 'no man is above the law' and 'the public has a right to every man's evidence,'" Alito wrote. "These sayings are true—and important—but they beg the question. The law applies equally to all persons, including a person who happens for a period of time to occupy the Presidency. But there is no question that the nature of the office demands in some instances that the application of laws be adjusted at least until the person's term in office ends." Then, in a phrase that ironically echoed Roberts's opinion in the census questionnaire controversy, Alito wrote, "As for the potential use of subpoenas to harass, we need not 'exhibit a naiveté from which ordinary citizens are free.'"

Thomas, in his dissent, agreed that the president lacked absolute immunity from the subpoena and that a heightened standard was not required, but he based his reasoning on a different legal rationale, and he faulted the majority for failing to address whether the subpoena could actually be enforced against Trump.

Roberts had added in a footnote, "The daylight between our opinion and Justice Thomas's 'dissent' is not as great as that label might suggest. . . . We agree that Presidents are neither absolutely immune from state criminal subpoenas nor insulated by a heightened need standard." It was a window into Roberts's preoccupation with showing the greatest unity possible, suggesting that the chief justice believed that Thomas, and possibly Alito, could have concurred and helped provide the high court with an appearance of greater harmony. Neither colleague was prepared to take that step.

The two Trump appointees, Kavanaugh and Gorsuch, turned what could have been a partial dissent into a concurring opinion. They agreed that the president lacked absolute immunity from a state criminal subpoena but argued for greater protection against enforcement of a subpoena because of Trump's responsibilities as head of the executive branch. They would have required that the New York grand jury or any state prosecutors meet the standard of *United States v. Nixon* and show a "demonstrated, specific need."

In the consolidated House cases, Roberts again labored to minimize the differences among justices. At the outset, even the liberals were splintered. Roberts partnered behind the scenes with Breyer as he developed a rationale and cited Breyer's opinion from a 2014 separation-of-powers dispute (involving presidential appointments made when the Senate was in recess) for the proposition that judges should not become needlessly involved in the "working arrangements" of the two political branches. As former lead counsel to Democratic senator Ted Kennedy of Massachusetts on the Senate Judiciary Committee in the 1970s, Breyer brought singular legislative experience to the justices' private conferences. Other justices had, obviously, experience in the executive branch, Roberts having served in the Ronald Reagan and George H. W. Bush administrations, Kagan for Bill Clinton and Barack Obama, and Kavanaugh for George W. Bush.

The majority's final decision spurned Trump's claim that the House lacked authority to issue the subpoenas. It declared as a threshold matter that Congress had the power to subpoena information for its legislative mission. Yet the Roberts majority then went on to largely reverse the D.C. Circuit opinion and find that House lawyers had not sufficiently demonstrated that they needed the Trump records. Highlighting the separation-of-powers imperative, Roberts laid out a balancing approach to test the validity of the legislative purpose asserted. If other sources (beyond the White House) could reasonably provide Congress the information it needed, he said, Congress should turn to those sources. He warned against using subpoenas to gain an institutional advantage over the executive, "a rival political branch."[33]

Six justices, including Gorsuch and Kavanaugh, joined Roberts, and, in an act of solidarity, no one broke off to write a concurring statement. Those seven justices found it in their interest to speak in a single voice. The House would have to better justify its need for the Trump documents to ensure that the request did not burden the president.

Only Thomas and Alito dissented. Thomas argued that Congress lacked any power to issue the subpoenas as part of its legislative mission. In his separate dissent, Alito said that he would not find such subpoenas categorically barred, even though "legislative subpoenas for a President's personal documents are inherently suspicious." Again, it seemed that Alito was not so far from the majority, whose test effectively blocked the House from obtaining the Trump documents.

At the moment, however, Trump could only see what he lost, and as he took to Twitter, his reaction rang of his prior objections to perceived affronts: "Courts in the past have given 'broad deference'. BUT NOT ME!" In a separate tweet, he brought up his past travails: "This is all a political prosecution. I won the Mueller Witch Hunt, and others, and now I have to keep fighting in a politically corrupt New York. Not fair to this Presidency or Administration!"[34]

Both decisions allowed Trump to continue challenging the document requests. In the New York grand jury litigation, the Roberts majority said that the president could return to lower courts to raise further arguments on New York State grounds. That process delayed for several more months the grand jury's ability to obtain evidence and ensured that none of the materials would be released before the November election. The House fight dragged on longer.

Yet for the chief justice, then completing his fifteenth session, this was no small feat in the public eye. In a pair of cases involving the most polarizing president in modern history, in an election year with tensions heightened because of COVID-19 isolation, he had managed to pull together seven of the nine justices. The Court had preserved the separation of powers without diminishing presidential power. It had followed history and shown its independence from Trump. Roberts had employed every tool he possessed, from a chief's power to assign opinions (and keep important ones for himself) to his place at the ideological center to the persuasive skill he had developed when he used to stand before the bench as an appellate advocate. He craved control, and in this moment it seemed there was nothing he couldn't achieve. He was in the majority more than any justice for the full 2019–2020 session, for 97 percent of the cases. The Court's direction and America's law, it appeared, rested in his hands.[35]

# Chapter 9

-----

# A DEATHBED WISH

Justice Ruth Bader Ginsburg walked slowly from her desk to a set of upholstered chairs beside a coffee table. She carried a single sheet of paper that contained a quotation she believed important for the subject at hand. It was early January 2020, in the middle of what would be her last term on the Court. The fireplace was lit, the wood crackling. She asked an assistant whether there was anything tasty in the office refrigerator. Told that there was some leftover strawberry cheesecake, Ginsburg waved her hand to dismiss the possibility: "Too sweet." Nearing eighty-seven, she had enjoyed the winter holidays and was feeling especially fine. She had just had one of her regular medical checkups. "I'm cancer-free, and that's good," she told me, settling into her armchair. The discussion detoured into opera and New York art galleries, among her passions. But then she focused on the topic she wanted to discuss, her interest in procedural rules that limit a court's decision. She looked down to the sheet of paper she held and recited a quote that she called a "favorite," from the 1943 case *McNabb v. United States*. Justice Felix Frankfurter had written, "The history of liberty has largely been the history of observance of procedural safeguards."[1]

Ginsburg and her colleagues on the left had achieved a few surprising victories on a Court controlled by conservatives by appealing to safeguards that dictated who can sue, when, and in which courts. The seemingly dry area of the law offered an effective way to keep some cases from being heard and to slow the momentum of the Court majority. A procedural rule, for example, was about to derail a case that could have expanded Second Amendment rights in 2020 and prevented cities and states from enforcing certain gun control laws.

The New York State Rifle and Pistol Association had sued New York City over a law that prohibited the transportation of guns to firing ranges or second homes outside the city. The association wanted to use the case to win a decision enlarging individual gun rights. The New York regulation was especially strict, and the challengers thought that they would find a sympathetic Supreme Court. Defenders of gun control agreed with that assessment and feared that if the high court considered the case, the justices would take Second Amendment rights well beyond their 2008 decision that first declared an individual right to bear arms. That earlier landmark involved handgun use in the home for self-defense. As the litigation moved through the court system, New York State officials, seeking to prevent a Supreme Court showdown, took a step to void the city ordinance. The state legislature passed a law preempting the city prohibition. Suddenly, as the Supreme Court considered the case, an overriding question was whether it was moot. Oral arguments were held in December 2019, at the end of a record-breaking year for mass shootings.[2]

Paul Clement, who had become a repeat advocate for the justices and was nearing his 100th appearance before them, represented the New York State Rifle and Pistol Association. Ginsburg jumped into the questioning. "The city has now been blocked by a state law," she said. "The state says: City, thou shalt not enforce the regulations. So what's left of this case?" Ginsburg's view was that there was no live controversy to be resolved, and certainly not one that could expand *District of Columbia v. Heller*, the Court's 2008 decision—written by Scalia, for whom Clement had earlier clerked—declaring an individual right to possess guns at home.[3]

But the rifle association wanted to keep the case going to establish that bans in New York and elsewhere on carrying firearms outside the home were unconstitutional. Clement was straightforward about what his clients sought: "a declaration that the transport ban is and always was unconstitutional." Ginsburg was not alone in her view that the case was moot; five other justices, including Chief Justice Roberts, agreed in the end that the case should be dismissed.[4]

Ginsburg took cases one by one, just as she was taking her health month by month. Some liberals, including those who had served in the Barack Obama administration, had hoped that she would retire earlier, while Obama was still in the White House. In 2013, Obama had invited her for a private luncheon at the White House. When I learned of the invitation, I asked Ginsburg afterward whether she thought he was fishing for retirement news. "I don't think he was fishing," she told me. When asked why she thought he had invited her, she said, "Maybe to talk about the Court. Maybe because he likes me. I like him."[5]

Once she rebuffed retirement calls, Ginsburg thought she had to hang on only through the November 2016 presidential election and a change in the White House. Like much of America, she presumed Hillary Clinton would beat Donald Trump. Once the opposite happened, her new goal became the November 2020 election, a desire that took on more urgency as President Trump appointed new justices in 2017 and 2018. Ginsburg continued to undergo regular scans for cancer, and she managed to stay healthy enough three years into the Trump presidency.

As it turned out, a few weeks after our January conversation in her chambers she received disturbing news. A scan showed lesions on her liver, and a biopsy revealed that they were malignant. Ginsburg's physicians recommended immunotherapy. But within a few months, it became clear that approach would not succeed, and on May 19, she began chemotherapy. The public was in the dark about those developments. Some of her colleagues were unaware of her health situation, too. Because of the coronavirus pandemic, they were unable to see or spend time with her during what would be her final months of life. Health restrictions prevented the justices from using their courtroom for spring oral arguments. They also had to abandon their lunches together on argument days. Such gatherings let the justices catch up on personal news—to cheer a family graduation or celebrate the birth of a grandchild. The justices also usually set aside time to toast a colleague's birthday with a glass of wine.[6]

Nearly everyone stopped seeing Ginsburg—fellow justices, the tight-knit appellate bar, news reporters, the public. She had to cancel speeches and other scheduled appearances. How she looked and sounded had become a national preoccupation. It was widely understood that if Ginsburg had to retire, a potential third Trump appointment would tip the Court and the law in America even further to the right. As it happened, nearly every month in 2020 brought new trials for Ginsburg's health. But she lived as if no day would be her last, and she regularly scheduled events months and even years ahead. Justice John Paul Stevens, whom she had eulogized in the summer of 2019, was her model.[7]

She loathed confinement, and exercise sessions with her longtime personal trainer, Bryant Johnson, helped to keep her fit physically and her spirits up. She was determined to continue the routine at the start of the COVID-19 pandemic and asked Court police officers to drive her to the Court building so that she could follow her gym regimen and attend to work in her chambers. A large basketball court and extensive weight-lifting equipment occupied the top floor of the Court building, but like her colleagues, Ginsburg used a small justices-only weight room on the ground floor. She spoke publicly enough about it all (the push-ups, the planks, the hours on the elliptical machine) that these workouts became as well known as her medical history.

With the pandemic underway, she shrugged off the risk of contracting the virus, as well as the District of Columbia's stay-at-home order. Johnson told the news outlet Law360, "Everybody's been shut down. The only reason why I didn't shut the justice down is because, hey, she ain't having it. . . . If she wants to train, that's the least I can do." After Law360 ran its story about Ginsburg's flouting of COVID-19 precautions and there was a great public outcry about risks to her health, Ginsburg relented. She began using hand weights and a yoga mat in her Watergate apartment. As the weeks wore on, Ginsburg undertook other mildly surreptitious activities, including dinners with a small circle of friends.[8]

Her closest staff became consumed with keeping her as healthy as possible, as she tried to live as fully as possible. Hundreds of thousands of Americans were becoming infected, and hospitals across the country were overflowing. Beds, respirators, masks, and other pieces of personal protective equipment were in short supply. A widely available vaccine was nearly a year off.

As Ginsburg underwent a new round of chemotherapy in May, she developed a painful gallbladder condition. She felt the sharp aches as she was participating by phone in oral arguments on May 5, during the first week of the justices' new teleconference format. The technology was still a bit tricky for the nine. Releasing the mute button became a challenge for some. Others just kept talking beyond their allotted time, asking more questions of a lawyer at the other end of a phone line. Chief Justice Roberts struggled to smooth out the sessions, which were a poor substitute for in-person arguments but at least gave the justices a way to hold hearings during the pandemic. After the May 5 arguments, as Ginsburg's pain intensified, she was taken to Sibley Memorial Hospital in Washington for tests and learned that a gall-stone had migrated to her cystic duct and caused an infection. She was transferred to Johns Hopkins Hospital in Baltimore, where she underwent treatment for acute cholecystitis.[9]

The Supreme Court was scheduled to hear a major women's health dispute the next day, on May 6, and Ginsburg insisted on participating. She arranged for Court technicians to connect her to the rest of the justices through a telephone hookup at the hospital. Ginsburg was not bound by convention or intimidated by her medical travails. Of all the justices, she was most open through the years regarding her health care and allowed the Court's public information office to detail her ill-nesses and treatment. Maybe it was because of all the sickness she had seen from a young age, dating to the early deaths of her sister and her mother. Rather than hide from the vicissitudes of life, or exhibit any squeamishness, Ginsburg spoke publicly about her illnesses. She took even odd mishaps in public stride. In October 2009, she scheduled a flight to London, just months after she had recovered from her first episode of pancreatic cancer. To ensure that she slept on the plane, she took a prescription sleeping pill along with two over-the-counter cold pills. Before the plane took off, the combination of pills knocked her out and she fell from her seat. She was taken by ambulance to Washington Hospital Center and kept overnight. A few weeks earlier, Ginsburg had been briefly hospitalized while feeling faint in her office after receiving an iron infusion treatment. Then seventy-six, she remarked to reporters, "Just call me Calamity Jane."[10]

The women's health dispute Ginsburg wanted to hear from her hospital room developed from Affordable Care Act (ACA) rules for contraceptive coverage. Under Obama administration policy, religious organizations were automatically exempt from providing such coverage, and certain other church-affiliated employers could apply for exemptions. But the extent of the exclusions and the paperwork required to qualify for them had been subject to continual litigation.

The Supreme Court's first review of the issue occurred in the 2014 *Burwell v. Hobby Lobby Stores.* The case involving the Oklahoma-based arts-and-crafts retailer, run by evangelical Christians, tested whether corporations could assert a right of religious freedom to obtain exemptions from the ACA's requirement to provide insurance for contraceptive coverage to their employees. Hobby Lobby and Conestoga Wood Specialties, a Pennsylvania-based cabinet manufacturer owned by Mennonites, sought exemptions based on a 1993 law, the Religious Freedom Restoration Act, which said that the federal government could not substantially burden the exercise of religion unless the action reflected a compelling interest and was the least restrictive way of serving that interest. (Hobby Lobby and Conestoga Wood Specialties said that their owners believed that life began at conception, and argued that some methods of contraception interfered with fertilization.)

The conservative majority ruled that the two for-profit corporate retailers could avoid the contraceptive coverage under the Religious Freedom Restoration Act. The Obama administration had argued that a corporation could not "exercise religion," and that Hobby Lobby and Conestoga Wood therefore were ineligible for an exemption. The 2014 ruling marked the first time the justices had found that secular corporations held religious rights. Justice Alito, to whom Roberts had assigned the opinion, wrote that Congress when it adopted the 1993 religious freedom law had not intended to exclude people who ran their businesses as for-profit entities. He said the Court would not question the grounds for religious beliefs, disregarding the views of some medical groups that had disputed the characterization of some contraceptive methods as abortifacients.

Ginsburg described that 2014 decision as one of "startling breadth" and warned that there may be no "stopping point" for exemptions. She slammed the ability of corporations to deny no-cost contraception to their employees and covered relatives, saying that the majority's decision allowed discrimination against legions of women. Just as Ginsburg clung to Frankfurter's quote about the benefits of civil procedure, she was fond of a comment she plucked from a 1919 *Harvard Law Review* article regarding free speech and free exercise claims. As she summarized her position in the Hobby Lobby case and wrote for the four liberal justices: "With respect to free exercise claims no less than free speech claims, '[y]our right to swing your arms ends just where the other man's nose begins.'"[11] She fought an uphill battle. Conservatives on the Roberts Court had been expanding religious exemptions, especially in cases brought by Christians.

A new round of litigation had begun over the so-called contraceptive mandate when the Trump administration came to office and further extended exemptions based on religious and moral objections. Rather than religious conservatives objecting, as had happened with Obama-era policy, state officials concerned about the threat to women's health care initiated litigation. In one of two paired cases the justices were to hear, the Little Sisters of the Poor, a group of Roman Catholic nuns who operated homes for the elderly and had objected to the Obama administration's rules, intervened anew to support Trump.

From the hospital, Ginsburg used her allotted time to deliver more of a speech about Congress's interest in reproductive health care than to question the lawyers arguing the case. "The glaring feature of what the government has done in expanding this exemption is to toss to the winds entirely Congress's instruction that women need and shall have seamless, no-cost, comprehensive coverage," she said. "This leaves the women to hunt for other government programs that might cover them, and for those who are not covered by Medicaid or one of the other government programs, they can get contraceptive coverage only from paying out of their own pocket, which is exactly what Congress didn't want to happen." Ginsburg's voice sounded a little tinny, but her message was clear.[12]

"In this area of religious freedom, the major trend is not to give everything to one side and nothing to the other side," she continued. "We have had a history of accommodation, tolerance here, respect for the employer's workers and students who do not share the employer's or the university's objections to contraceptives. And every time we have dealt with this subject, we have assumed that there would be a way to provide coverage that would not involve any cost-sharing by the individual." She provided a litany of cases the justices had taken up on the issue, beginning with *Burwell v. Hobby Lobby Stores*.

In the dispute at hand, the government estimated that between 70,500 and 126,400 women would lose access to contraceptive services based on the wider religious and moral exemptions. With Solicitor General Noel Francisco on the telephone line but barely getting a word in as Ginsburg spoke, and the minutes ticking away, Ginsburg repeated her key point: "You have just tossed entirely to the wind what Congress thought was essential, that is, that women be provided these services, with no hassle, no cost to them. Instead, you are shifting the employer's religious beliefs, the cost of that, on to these employees who do not share those religious beliefs. . . . The women end up getting nothing."

Paul Clement, who had represented the Little Sisters of the Poor since the start of the government's employer birth-control requirement, was back before the justices in this case. By now it was his 102nd Supreme Court argument, but it was his first telephonically. Since no one could see him in his home office, the Wisconsin native wore a bespoke Green Bay Packers jersey emblazoned with the number 100 on the back, a gift he had received for his 100th argument three months earlier.[13] "At the end of the day," Ginsburg said to him, raising the same issue she had for Francisco, "the government is throwing to the wind the women's entitlement to seamless [coverage], [at] no cost to them. It is requiring those women to pay for contraceptive services."

"Well, Justice Ginsburg," Clement responded, "first, I would echo what the Solicitor General said in pointing out that Congress itself did not even specify that contraceptions would be included in the preventative health mandate. . . . they didn't impose the preventative mandate." Ginsburg tried to pick up where she had left off, but Roberts interrupted, to move the questioning along.

The deeper context in the dispute involved the Court's divide over protections for religious conservatives, with the justices predictably split.[14] They voted on the Obamacare birth-control cases at the end of May, again by telephone and, as always, privately. Ginsburg was back home in her Washington, D.C., apartment for that teleconference. Roberts, Thomas, Alito, Gorsuch, and Kavanagh sided with the administration's effort to broaden the exemptions for employers with religious and moral objections to birth control coverage. Ginsburg and Sotomayor were ready to fully dissent. Breyer and Kagan voiced mixed regard for the administration's position. They believed that some flexibility existed for health regulators. The Trump team may not have followed the rules of the Administrative Procedure Act, but Breyer and Kagan believed it had the discretion under the Affordable Care Act to set its own policy. So the vote was 5–2–2.

Roberts assigned the opinion for the majority to Thomas. Ginsburg began writing the dissent. Kagan handled a concurring opinion for herself and Breyer, questioning whether the Trump position would survive the federal requirements for reasoned decision-making. An agency would flunk the test, they believed, if it lacked a satisfactory explanation for its action and sufficient connection between an identifiable problem and a solution.

Ginsburg was known for quickly producing opinions and for pushing others to move faster on their assignments. It was a bit of an inside joke that she was always asking for updates on when exactly drafts of opinions she had assigned would be sent around. This time, however, I learned that she thought that Roberts was setting unrealistic deadlines. Usually, the justices could finish all the cases for an annual session by late June. But between the pandemic and the late-argued May cases, decisions were running behind. Roberts eased up on the deadlines, and the justices went into the second week of July.

For Ginsburg, her last written opinion for the tumultuous 2019–2020 session would also be the last of her legal career and life. It was fitting that what she was writing reflected her commitment to sexual and religious equality. When Thomas circulated his first draft for the majority, she saw that he was emphasizing that the administration had the statutory authority to craft religious and moral exemptions. He also adopted an especially sympathetic tone toward the religious group that had been challenging the ACA's contraceptive coverage rules from the start. "For over 150 years," Thomas wrote in his opinion released to the public, "the Little Sisters have engaged in faithful service and sacrifice, motivated by a religious calling to surrender all for the sake of their brother. . . . But for the past seven years, they—like many other religious objectors who have participated in the litigation and rulemakings leading up to today's decision—have had to fight for the ability to continue in their noble work without violating their sincerely held religious beliefs." In her final dissent responding to the majority, Ginsburg wrote, "Today, for the first time, the Court casts totally aside countervailing rights and interests in its zeal to secure religious rights to the nth degree. . . . This Court leaves women workers to fend for themselves, to seek contraceptive coverage from sources other than their employer's insurer, and, absent another available source of funding, to pay for contraceptive services out of their own pockets."[15]

That she was on the losing side yet again underscored the fate for progressive views over the course of her nearly three-decade tenure. This was a new Court. Still, her presence as a fourth liberal meant something in how far the Court would go to restrict women's reproductive rights. During this same 2019–2020 session, the justices had struck down the Louisiana abortion regulation by a narrow 5–4 vote, with Roberts joining those on the left. Without Ginsburg, the law likely would have been upheld.

The day before the decision in *Little Sisters of the Poor v. Pennsylvania* was publicly released, Ginsburg had had another scan. The July 7 procedure showed a reduction of her liver lesions and no new disease. She seemed to be tolerating the chemotherapy well and planned to continue the biweekly treatments. She was still able to do the job "full steam," she said when she made her health news public a few days later.[16] The presidential election was four months away, and Trump faced a formidable challenge from former vice president Joe Biden. There was a sense among Court followers, Democratic and Republican, that she might just hang on until the end of the year.

But through the summer her hospital visits actually became more frequent. As she coped with the cancer, she was still fighting off infections. On July 14, a week after the encouraging scan related to the liver lesions, she had another setback. She began experiencing fever and chills and was again taken to Sibley Memorial and transferred to Johns Hopkins, for an endoscopic procedure to clean out a bile duct stent. She stayed at the hospital for a few more days for intravenous antibiotic treatment.[17]

She was getting weaker. Her children, Jane and James, along with grandchildren, took turns coming into Washington to help care for her. Her closest aides brought her filings from the Court. Emergency petitions related to presidential election rules were flowing in, and she wanted to keep up. In late July, she traveled to New York City to Sloan Kettering for a procedure, returning to her Washington home a few days later.[18]

During August, Ginsburg's presence was still felt among her colleagues as she cast votes on emergency election cases and dropped a birthday greeting to Justice Breyer, who turned eighty-two on the fifteenth. She officiated a wedding for family friends on her apartment patio. COVID made it too risky to be inside. She and her daughter streamed a performance by the son of one of her former clerks, David Post. Sam Post, a composer, had adapted an aria from Mozart's *Marriage of Figaro*. "A good show indeed," she wrote to David. "Jane and I enjoyed watching. Of course, I delighted in Sam's rendition of 'Voi che sapete.' Looking forward to brighter days when this eerie time ends."[19]

In early September, she had to go to Johns Hopkins for treatment of yet another infection. She returned home on September 11. Unlike other emergency hospital visits, this one was not made public, and I learned about it from Court sources. Perhaps Ginsburg's new reluctance to provide information was because it was apparent to the justice and those close to her that she had little time left. That was difficult to accept. She had come back from all the other ordeals. The presidential election was fifty days off.

On September 16, Ginsburg's staff reached out to Eric Motley, vice president of the Aspen Institute and a close friend of the justice, who was to be wed on September 18 at her apartment. An aide told Motley that the ceremony, to be held in her small courtyard, would have to be postponed. No reason was given. "They said we need to push it back, let's look at some other days," Motley later told me. Over the next forty-eight hours, family members arrived in Washington to be at Ginsburg's side. When her granddaughter Clara Spera sat with her, the justice said she wanted Clara to take down a message. "My most fervent wish is that I will not be replaced until a new president is installed," she said as Clara typed it into her laptop. Clara relayed the message to Nina Totenberg of National Public Radio, a friend of Ginsburg's, who made it public later.[20]

Justice Ginsburg died on Friday, September 18. The Court's public information office put out the news at 7:27 P.M. eastern time. It was not wholly unexpected, of course, but its arrival in journalists' in-boxes still managed to startle: "Associate Justice Ruth Bader Ginsburg died this evening surrounded by her family at her home in Washington, D.C., due to complications of metastatic pancreas cancer." Rosh Hashanah was just beginning, and many of Ginsburg's friends were in the middle of services, on Zoom because of the pandemic, as word began to circulate. Over the next few days, people brought flowers and candles to the Supreme Court building. Some carried signs that said "May Her Memory Be a Movement." Young girls wore Ginsburg-style white lace collars.

There was widespread mourning and extensive recounting on television and front pages of Ginsburg's pioneering career as a women's rights advocate. There was also a sense among Republicans of a Trump bonanza. He would get a third appointment to the Supreme Court, and Amy Coney Barrett was ready. Trump would cement a particular kind of GOP dominance. Gorsuch, Kavanaugh, and Barrett, all screened by the Federalist Society, were unlike the earlier generation of

Republican appointees—Sandra Day O'Connor and Anthony Kennedy, or even as recently as 2005, John Roberts.

Trump had interviewed Barrett in 2018 when he was looking for a Kennedy successor, and although he had chosen Kavanaugh then, it was widely understood within the administration and among the tight circle of Federalist Society supporters that Barrett could be next, particularly if Ginsburg left the bench. "I helped recommend her to the president for the Seventh Circuit," Don McGahn said later of Barrett, "so I'm a big fan of hers."[21]

Barrett, forty-eight at the time Trump selected her for the high court, was born and raised in New Orleans, the eldest daughter in a family of six children. Her father was a Shell Oil Company executive, her mother a homemaker. In her youth and as an adult raising her own family, Barrett belonged to a small, insular Christian community group known as People of Praise. The group was not part of the organized Roman Catholic Church, although most of its members, like Barrett, were Roman Catholics. Her husband, Jesse Barrett, had also been raised in a People of Praise community. Members formed "covenants" by which they served each other not just spiritually but also materially and financially.[22]

Barrett graduated from Rhodes College, and after Notre Dame Law School clerked for D.C. Circuit Court judge Laurence Silberman. Silberman, a Reagan appointee and one of Justice Scalia's oldest friends, then recommended her to Scalia for a clerkship at the high court. She went on to work for two years in private law practice, returning to Notre Dame to teach in 2002. Her outspokenness against abortion extended to her signing a 2006 statement that ran in a South Bend newspaper decrying *Roe v. Wade*'s "barbaric legacy."[23] In 2013, on the fortieth anniversary of *Roe*, she joined a public statement calling for "the unborn to be protected in law."[24] Among Barrett and her husband's seven children were two whom they had adopted from Haiti, and one who had Down syndrome, the last of their biological children.

Once appointed by Trump to the U.S. appeals court for the Seventh Circuit, Barrett bolstered her conservative bona fides with votes against reproductive rights and in favor of the Second Amendment.

Her record was the opposite of Ginsburg's, and she notably pressed for expansion of the Court's *District of Columbia v. Heller* decision. Barrett dissented when the Seventh Circuit in a 2019 Wisconsin case ruled that federal and state laws barring convicted felons from possessing a firearm did not violate the Second Amendment. In that case, *Kanter v. Barr,* Barrett said that the ban on felons was not rooted in historical precedent. Invoking her originalist approach, which mirrored Scalia's, she wrote, "History is consistent with common sense: it demonstrates that legislatures have the power to prohibit dangerous people from possessing guns. But that power extends only to people who are *dangerous.* Founding-era legislatures did not strip felons of the right to bear arms simply because of their status as felons." She added that the court majority failed to "'put the government through its paces'" and "instead treats the Second Amendment as a 'second-class right, subject to an entirely different body of rules than the other Bill of Rights guarantees.'" That last phrase came from the Supreme Court's opinion in *McDonald v. City of Chicago,* the 2010 case that declared that the individual gun rights established in *District of Columbia v. Heller* extended to the states.[25]

Separately, Barrett criticized the Supreme Court decisions upholding the Affordable Care Act, particularly the 2012 case in which Chief Justice Roberts cast the fifth vote to sustain Obamacare. She argued in a 2017 book review for a law journal that he had "pushed the Affordable Care Act beyond its plausible meaning to save the statute."[26]

Her opinions and other writings had held the attention of the Trump judicial machinery, and the day after Ginsburg's death, Chief of Staff Mark Meadows and White House counsel Pat Cipollone called Barrett to talk about the vacancy. The next day, they telephoned again and asked her to come to Washington. Barrett then met with Trump, Meadows, Cipollone, and Vice President Pence. Trump offered her the Supreme Court nomination that day, on September 21. It was seventy-two hours after Ginsburg's death. They kept the offer quiet for a week.[27]

More publicly that week of September 21, the nation witnessed a torrent of tributes to Ginsburg. For two days, her casket rested at the top of the Supreme Court steps, outdoors because of the COVID-19 pandemic rather than in the Great Hall according to the usual practice. Thousands of mourners paid their respects, including President Trump and First Lady Melania, and former president Bill Clinton (who had appointed Ginsburg) and Hillary Clinton. Many more people, tens of thousands, stood in line to have an opportunity to view the flag-draped casket.

The former women's rights lawyer and four-decade jurist then marked a final milestone. Ginsburg became the first woman and the first Jewish person to lie in state at the Capitol.[28] At the close of the week, on September 25, a military honor guard marched the casket down the marble steps of the building. Women from the Senate and the U.S. House of Representatives lined the steps, well spaced in the pandemic, like four long ribbons stretched out on the expansive marble. The spare but elegant tableau seemed fitting for the diminutive, effective force that was Ginsburg.

Soon after, a hearse carrying Ginsburg's remains pulled away from the U.S. Capitol, and top advisers to President Trump began slipping word to news reporters that the president had chosen Judge Barrett as the successor. President Trump formally announced his choice of Barrett on September 26 in a Rose Garden ceremony. The event, held before a COVID vaccine was available, with hundreds of Trump and Barrett supporters crammed into the Rose Garden without masks, was later proved to have widely spread the coronavirus. Among those who revealed shortly after September 26 that they had COVID-19 were the president and Melania Trump. It was not clear whether they had contracted the disease prior to the event or were already sick. Many White House guests became infected, including the Rev. John Jenkins, president of the University of Notre Dame.[29]

Judge Barrett and her family attended unmasked. White House officials said that Barrett had previously been infected so may not have been as vulnerable to the disease as others were. The health concerns prompted by the event reinforced Trump's irrational and chaotic response to the pandemic. From the start, he had denied its severity. Among his suggested "cures": that people inject bleach to fight off the virus. The suggestion had been issued five months before, on April 23, 2020, at a White House coronavirus briefing. It followed a presentation by William Bryan, the acting undersecretary of the U.S. Department of Homeland Security's Science and Technology Directorate, to whom Trump had briefly ceded the lectern. Bryan described government research that indicated that the virus weakened under exposure to sunlight and could be rapidly killed in saliva "or respiratory fluids" by bleach. When Trump regained the lectern, he inexplicably encouraged Bryan and other health officials to study the option of injecting bleach and other disinfectants into patients' bodies. His comments caused an immediate spike in calls to poison control centers across the country as patients began dabbling in potentially deadly self-inflicted home treatments. The makers of Clorox and Lysol issued warnings against ingesting bleach. The White House never explained how Trump had made the leap from the research outlined by Bryan to the idea of directly administering bleach, which the president referred to as "almost a cleaning."[30]

Senate Majority Leader McConnell and many other GOP senators declined to attend the Barrett unveiling. They wanted to avoid a health risk that could interfere with winning the votes for this third Trump nominee to the Supreme Court. (An exception to such caution was Republican senator Mike Lee of Utah, who tested positive for the virus after attending the White House event, then two weeks later participated in-person, without a mask, in Barrett's Senate Judiciary Committee hearings, drawing a rebuke from Democrats who said he was threatening the health of colleagues.)

It was just thirty-eight days until the November 3 election, and McConnell had long been laying the groundwork with fellow GOP senators to make short work of a third Trump confirmation no matter when it came. The blatant incongruity between his actions in late 2020 and his monthslong stalling of President Obama's 2016 nomination of Judge Merrick Garland mattered not. Back then, the Kentucky Republican, in blocking all action on Garland to succeed Scalia following his death in February 2016, had declared that February was too close to a November presidential election for the matter to be handled. For Trump appointee

Barrett, the Senate was ready to vote in a month. McConnell claimed there was a difference: the White House was controlled by a Republican, just as the Senate was controlled by Republicans. McConnell had the power to do what he wanted, by virtue of the Senate majority, even though the hypocrisy was hard to ignore.[31]

After the obstruction on the Scalia vacancy, the race to fill the Ginsburg seat accelerated public cynicism regarding the Senate confirmation process. Progressives concerned about the substantive turn at the Court increased their calls for structural reform of the bench, either through the addition of more seats to counteract the conservative dominance or through term limits. That was a long-shot hope. Key Democrats in Congress and the Democratic presidential candidate, Joe Biden, opposed the idea. During his campaign, Biden declined to support so-called court packing, but with the pressure after Ginsburg's death, he agreed if elected to appoint a commission to study the Court, which he described as "getting out of whack." But Biden cautioned, "The last thing we need to do is turn the Supreme Court into just a political football, whoever has the most votes gets whatever they want. Presidents come and go. Supreme Court justices stay for generations."[32]

The Supreme Court was supposed to be above politics, but it was increasingly entangled with them. Barrett's nomination was hastened by Trump and McConnell, and at the Supreme Court, the chief justice's administrative team insisted that Ginsburg's staff clear out of her chambers immediately after the justice's September burial service. That demand upset many Court employees. They were aware that in the weeks before Ginsburg's death, her staff had labored to ensure she always had case documents at hand, whether in the hospital or at home. Then, after her death, they had helped with the funeral arrangements. They were exhausted and still in mourning. But they had to help move boxes of Ginsburg's files and other office possessions down to a dark, windowless theater space on the ground floor (where, before COVID, tourists used to watch a film about Court operations) and sort through the chambers' contents there.

Barrett's confirmation was still about a month away, but to nearly everyone, it was a fait accompli.

As she introduced herself to senators and a televised audience on her first day of the Senate hearings, October 12, she referred to her seven children and her husband, Jesse, a lawyer: "I am used to being in a group of nine—my family." She spoke of how Justice Scalia had influenced her. "More than the style of his writing . . . it was the content of Justice Scalia's reasoning that shaped me. His judicial philosophy was straightforward: A judge must apply the law as written, not as the judge wishes it were."[33] By the third day of the hearing, an exultant Lindsey Graham, chairman of the Senate Judiciary Committee, declared, "The is the first time in American history that we've nominated a woman who's unashamedly pro-life and embraces her faith without apology." Barrett declined to reveal her position on *Roe v. Wade*, telling senators that she had no agenda to overrule abortion precedent: "I have an agenda to stick to the rule of law and decide cases as they come," she said.[34]

While Barrett aligned herself with the originalist method of Scalia, she told senators, "I want to be careful to say that if I'm confirmed you would not be getting Justice Scalia, you would be getting Justice Barrett. And that's so because originalists don't always agree and neither do textualists." Describing her originalist approach, she told senators, "All judges and justices take account of history and the original meaning. It's just that some weight it differently, whereas originalists would give it dispositive weight when it's discernible."[35]

She brought no prepared notes to the hearing and, when asked by Texas Republican senator John Cornyn what was before her, held up a blank notepad. The message, her supporters said, was her agility in answering tough questions. Yet the empty notepad also presented a metaphor for her refusal to offer information about her legal views. She declined to elaborate on her principles beyond basic conservatism.

Barrett revealed discipline in all aspects of her answers and presentation. For most of her testimony, she kept her hands neatly on her lap. Her gestures were minimal. She sidestepped her prior public opposition to abortion rights and referred to the 2006 statement condemning *Roe*'s "barbaric legacy" as something she signed "quickly on my way out of church."

She suggested that she would adhere to *Roe* as precedent, although she avoided saying whether she believed it was correctly decided. "What I said was that *Roe* held that the Constitution protects a woman's right to terminate a pregnancy, that *Casey* reaffirmed that holding and indeed many cases after *Casey* have affirmed that holding again." *Planned Parenthood of Southeastern Pennsylvania v. Casey*, which affirmed *Roe*, said that governments may not put an "undue burden" on a woman's ability to obtain an abortion. "If a question comes up before me about whether *Casey* or any other case should be overruled," Barrett said, "I will follow the law of *stare decisis* . . . applying it as the Court has articulated it, applying all of the factors: reliance, workability, being undermined by later facts in law." She was cagey about her regard for the precedential value of *Casey*.

Barrett separately declined to endorse *Griswold v. Connecticut*, the 1965 case that had led to *Roe v. Wade* by establishing a personal privacy right for couples who would use contraception. Her refusal to express support for the landmark case set her apart from Republican nominees of an earlier era, such as Roberts in 2005, who had said, "I agree with the *Griswold* Court's conclusion that marital privacy extends to contraception and availability of that. The Court since *Griswold* has grounded the privacy right discussed in that case in the liberty interest protected under the [Constitution's] Due Process Clause."[36]

Delaware senator Chris Coons followed up with Barrett. "Well, just for the benefit of those watching, Judge Barrett, as I think you well know, your predecessors talked about *Griswold* in detail. Chief Justice Roberts said he agreed with the *Griswold* Court's conclusion. He shared your view that he's comfortable commenting because it doesn't appear to be an area that would ever come before the Court. Justice Alito, Justice Kavanaugh said essentially the same thing, that they'd agree." Coons said he wanted to press her "one more time" on whether she remained unwilling to say that "at least *Griswold* is not wrong." She demurred. "I think *Griswold* isn't going anywhere unless you plan to pass a law prohibiting couples or all people from using birth control." She said she regarded the question as "entirely academic" but acknowledged that the case "does lie at the foundation of" *Roe*.

Coons wanted to make sure the audience understood the importance of the *Griswold* precedent: "It anchors a lot of modern liberty interests and personal and family autonomy," he said. "It was also extended to support same-sex intimacy in *Lawrence v. Texas,* and ultimately that same-sex couples have an equal right to marry in *Obergefell.*" Scalia had dissented in those two gay rights rulings, and Coons said, "I'm trying to help viewers understand what it means to replace a Justice Ginsburg with someone who may more closely follow Justice Scalia's approach."[37]

California senator Kamala Harris, then running on the Democratic ticket for the vice presidency, laid out Barrett's past statements against abortion rights and said: "I would suggest that we not pretend that we don't know how this nominee views a woman's right to choose and make her own health care decisions." Louisiana Republican senator John Kennedy happened to follow Harris in the Senate Judiciary Committee order and took issue with Harris's approach. He said to Barrett, "Now, my colleagues say, and Senator Harris said, that even though you have a personal opinion about abortion, that you will violate your oath to put aside those personal feelings and fairly decide abortion cases. Is that true?"

Barrett responded, "That, I gather, was the thrust of what she was saying to me, yes."

"Is she right?" Kennedy asked, presumably asking about the proposition that Barrett would not set aside her personal feelings on abortion. Barrett answered with conviction: "No, she is not right."[38]

Barrett was positioned to be the sixth Catholic on the nine-member bench. Republican presidents had been disproportionately turning to socially conservative Catholics as appointees. Until the death of Ginsburg, the high court was made up of five Catholic justices (Roberts, Thomas, Alito, Sotomayor, Kavanaugh), three Jewish justices (Ginsburg, Breyer, and Kagan) and one practicing Episcopalian justice (Neil Gorsuch, who had been raised a Catholic).

Barrett's Catholicism had been an issue in her 2017 hearing for the appellate court because of her past writings. She had coauthored, with John Garvey, a 1998 law review essay that had explored Catholic doctrine and asserted that Catholic judges opposed to capital punishment should generally recuse themselves rather than impose the death penalty on a convict. Barrett and Garvey had referred in their essay to Justice William Brennan's answer to senators during his 1957 confirmation hearing about his Catholic faith. Brennan had said, "what shall control me is the oath that I took to support the Constitution and laws of the United States" and "that oath and that alone . . . governs." For their part, Barrett and Garvey added: "We do not defend this position as the proper response for a Catholic judge to take with respect to abortion or the death penalty."[39]

Nothing Barrett said in 2020 altered the math in the Senate. Republicans had 52 members, and she won all of them, and not a single Democrat. That 52–48 vote marked the first time since 1869 that a president had nominated someone who was then confirmed without any support from the opposition party.[40]

Immediately after the Senate vote on October 26, Trump staged another Rose Garden celebration. Justice Thomas, the only Supreme Court justice who attended, conducted the ceremonial swearing-in. Trump then ushered Barrett up to a small balcony above the Rose Garden. Flanked by American flags, Trump and Barrett waved to the crowd below. Only eight days before the presidential election, the ceremony took on the appearance of a campaign event.

The celebration also foreshadowed a new era. As Fatima Goss Graves, president of the National Women's Law Center, said of Ginsburg when the change in the law was becoming clear, "There's no way she would have wanted the Court to be in the place that it is today. But we can't go back and change that fact."[41]

---

## Chapter 10

# *BUSH V. GORE* AND TRUMP V. BIDEN

Twenty years before the litigation over the election between Donald Trump and Joe Biden, the country was riven by the Supreme Court case of *Bush v. Gore.* The results on Election Day 2000 in Florida were too close to call, and that stalled the determination of a winner in the tight national contest between then-Texas governor George Bush and then–vice president Al Gore. Florida's twenty-five electoral votes were needed to put one of them over the top. The slim margin between the two candidates in Florida led to an immediate automatic recount and then laborious manual tallies. That ordeal left Americans with images of Florida officials trying to discern ballot chads, "dimpled" and otherwise; young Republicans in button-downs, ties, and blazers disrupting the Miami-Dade recounts (the so-called Brooks Brothers riot); and a jittery secretary of state certifying a 537-vote margin for Bush, from six million votes cast. After thirty-six days of uncertainty regarding whether Bush or Gore could claim Florida's decisive Electoral College votes, the Supreme Court by a 5–4 vote stopped the recounts and ensured that Florida's twenty-five votes went to Bush. Americans were torn by the Supreme Court's role in deciding the election, just as they had been divided between candidates Bush and Gore. The ruling left Democrats in despair. Justice Antonin Scalia, who was with the majority for the decision favoring Bush, told critics with his characteristic bluster, "Get over it!"[1]

But for many Americans, the anguish of a one-vote-margin Supreme

Court decision along ideological, if not political, lines endured. The decision was a perennial topic at Senate confirmation hearings for justices. Nominees avoided revealing their personal views, but as Elena Kagan told senators in 2010 regarding election integrity, "It's hard to think of a more important question in a democratic system." In 2020, *Bush v. Gore* and the issue of election integrity shadowed litigation between the Trump and Biden campaigns. And as traumatic as *Bush v. Gore* was to the nation in 2000, Trump-torn America was headed for worse.[2]

The nation was more polarized, and the coronavirus pandemic raged. Then in late spring, America's cities erupted with massive demonstrations calling for racial equality and police accountability. The protests followed the May 25 police killing of George Floyd in Minneapolis. Floyd, an African American, was arrested for allegedly buying cigarettes with a counterfeit twenty-dollar bill. A white police officer, Derek Chauvin, knelt on Floyd's neck for more than nine minutes, having pinned him to the ground after handcuffing him and positioning him facedown. "I can't breathe," Floyd cried out as he lost consciousness. According to Minneapolis Police Department supervisors, Floyd had no pulse for the final two minutes that Chauvin held his position. His death was ruled a homicide, and Chauvin was convicted of murder. Another white officer present pleaded guilty to a state charge of aiding and abetting second-degree manslaughter; he and two officers at the scene who assisted Chauvin by sitting on Floyd, one Black and the other Hmong American, were convicted on federal counts of willfully violating Floyd's right to medical care, and the two were convicted of failing to stop Chauvin as Floyd lay dying. (Chauvin also pleaded guilty to a federal civil rights charge.)[3]

In the aftermath, Trump continued his disparagement of the Black Lives Matter movement. He wrote on Twitter on May 29 of demonstrators protesting police brutality: "Those THUGS are dishonoring the memory of George Floyd, and I won't let that happen. Just spoke to Governor Tim Walz and told him the Military is with him all the way. Any difficulty and we will assume control but, when the looting starts, the shooting starts." Twitter took the unusual step of limiting users' ability to view the tweet, the language of which recalled racist

1960s police tactics, saying the post violated Twitter's rules against "glorifying violence."[4]

The volatility of the times shook American democracy. Little seemed predictable, and—most crucially for the Supreme Court in the public mind—it was not clear that if the election were again thrown to the Court, the justices would rule in a way the country would accept.

Trump exacerbated suspicions that the Supreme Court would fail to serve as a neutral arbiter. When he insisted on speeding up the Senate consideration of his third Court nominee, the election was on his mind. "I think this will end up in the Supreme Court, and I think it's very important that we have nine justices," he declared after the death of Justice Ruth Bader Ginsburg and as election-related lawsuits boiled up from the states. He had always suggested that the Supreme Court should, and would, rescue him, whether on his immigration policy or in subpoena fights. Now, he intimated, the fate of his second term would be in the hands of the justices, a conservative supermajority bolstered by his three appointees.[5]

It was no coincidence that three of the sitting justices in 2020 had worked for Republican candidate Bush in 2000: Chief Justice John Roberts and Justices Brett Kavanaugh and Amy Coney Barrett. Roberts had been nearest the center of the *Bush v. Gore* litigation. That was to have been expected, given his age, experience, and prior connections with the Reagan and George H. W. Bush administrations. Roberts had advised Theodore Olson, Bush's lead lawyer in the Supreme Court litigation. Olson recalled Roberts's support for his strategy of bringing a federal constitutional claim to end the Florida recounts that threatened Bush's lead, a novel approach criticized by some fellow conservatives at the time. "I remember John saying, 'I think you can win,'" Olson told the Miller Center oral history project years later, "and it gave me a lot of confidence to hear someone I respected as much as John Roberts saying, 'You're not crazy. There's something to what you're saying.'"[6]

When the Supreme Court ruled on December 12, 2000, for Olson's theory, the majority declared that Florida counties' recount standards varied too widely to be fair and to meet the constitutional guarantee of equal protection. Three justices in the five-member majority (Chief Justice William Rehnquist, joined by Antonin Scalia and Clarence Thomas) offered an additional rationale that would have strengthened the power of state legislatures to control presidential election battles. This rationale, which became known as the "independent state legislature" theory, failed to draw a Court majority in 2000. Under the approach, a state court lacks the authority to find that a state legislature's electoral practices violate the state's constitution. The theory could, if taken to the extreme, lead some legislators to try to reverse valid election results. Federal constitutional protections guaranteeing equal protection of the law and due process would still apply to any election contest.

The theory in 2000 centered on Article II, Section 1, of the U.S. Constitution, which dictates, "Each State shall appoint, in such Manner as the Legislature thereof may direct, a Number of Electors, equal to the whole Number of Senators and Representatives to which the state may be entitled in Congress." In his *Bush v. Gore* concurrence, Rehnquist focused on the word "Legislature," saying that in the context of the full provision, the wording conveys "the broadest power of determination" and "leaves it to the legislature exclusively to determine the method" for appointing presidential electors. That approach failed to take account of state constitutional dictates that define and bind legislative authority. And, if carried to the utmost, it would make individual legislators kingmakers of a sort, able to name the electors who would then decide which presidential candidate received the state's electoral votes, irrespective of who the people had chosen at the polls. Based on his analysis, Rehnquist said federal judges, as well as state judges, must defer to legislative determinations on election practices. "This inquiry does not imply a disrespect for state *courts* but rather a respect for the constitutionally prescribed role of state *legislatures*," Rehnquist wrote in the Florida election controversy. He took issue with the Florida supreme court's extension of a seven-day deadline set by the state legislature to certify the election results.

Anthony Kennedy and Sandra Day O'Connor, the two other justices who made up the *Bush v. Gore* majority that cut off the Florida recounts, had declined to join the Rehnquist opinion empowering legislatures. Rehnquist acknowledged that his approach seemed at odds with conservative principles. "In most cases, comity and respect for federalism compel us to defer to the decisions of state courts on issues of state law," he wrote. "But there are a few exceptional cases in which the Constitution imposes a duty or confers a power on a particular branch of a State's government. This is one of them."[7]

The independent state legislature theory, shunned by the Court majority and dormant for years, took on new life in the Trump election cases, a legacy of his reelection bid. Four Supreme Court justices ended up endorsing the theory that would give state legislatures exclusive authority over how presidential elections were conducted. In the future, if there were a fifth vote, that could lead to state legislatures substantially influencing who becomes president. The theory could favor Republican presidential candidates, because the GOP controlled the legislatures in battleground states in the early 2020s.

The bloodier and more immediately consuming legacy of the Trump reelection bid was the January 6 assault on the Capitol, of course. Trump had held a rally at the Ellipse, a park south of the White House, before Congress was scheduled to certify the Electoral College count of Biden's 306 votes. (Trump had received 232 votes.) "All of us here today do not want to see our election victory stolen by emboldened radical-left Democrats, which is what they're doing. And stolen by the fake news media. That's what they've done and what they're doing," he said, falsely portraying the situation. "We will never give up. We will never concede. It doesn't happen. You don't concede where there's theft involved."

Trump urged people at the rally to march to the Capitol to fight for their country. "We fight like hell," he said. "And if you don't fight like hell, you're not going to have a country anymore." Trump's supporters then trudged down Pennsylvania Avenue to the Capitol. With baseball bats, knives, bear spray, and other weapons, they produced the worst assault on the building since the War of 1812. The riot left five people dead and more than a hundred police officers injured.[8] One of the more chilling results of the insurrection was a spate of law-enforcement suicides that followed. An on-duty U.S. Capitol Police officer of fifteen years' standing took his life days after, as did a D.C. police officer injured in the riot. In the months following, two Metropolitan Police Department officers who had either helped secure the Capitol or assisted in enforcing the curfew established in the aftermath committed suicide.[9]

The Democratic-controlled House of Representatives impeached Trump—a second time—for his role in fomenting the insurrection. The GOP-controlled Senate acquitted him, again for the second time. A special House select committee on January 6 then spent nearly two years trying to hold the instigators responsible. It emerged that Clarence Thomas's wife, Ginni, had attended the Trump rally. (She had not marched to the Capitol.) Texts the committee collected from Trump's former chief of staff Mark Meadows revealed, however, that Ginni Thomas had been pressing Meadows to keep up the legal effort to reverse the results of the election: "Help This Great President stand firm, Mark!!!" she wrote. "You are the leader, with him, who is standing for America's constitutional governance at the precipice. The majority knows Biden and the Left is attempting the greatest Heist of our History."[10]

The entire 2020 presidential election cycle was darkened by the COVID-19 pandemic. People feared going into public spaces, including the polls set up in community and civic centers. Businesses operated remotely. Workers handled their jobs via home computers and cell phones. Trump was still appearing at campaign rallies, but Biden scaled back. The Democratic National Convention, scheduled to bring together fifty thousand delegates and backers in Milwaukee, went virtual in August 2020. The Republican convention was switched from its planned Charlotte location to Jacksonville, Florida, because of the Trump team's rejection of North Carolina's COVID-19 social distancing and safety protocols.

Voters requested mail-in ballots at record rates. The U.S. Postal Service was overwhelmed, and some absentee ballots reached voters late or not at all. At the polls, workers struggled to keep voters socially distanced and masked while they waited in lines. As litigation over deadlines and accommodations came to the high court, the majority generally ruled against deadline extensions for absentee ballots and against accommodations such as curbside drop-offs. The Court's decisions largely favored Republican interests; in dissent, the four liberals (after Ginsburg's death, just three on the left) protested that the majority was disenfranchising millions of voters.

A spring Wisconsin dispute, the first major case to reach the Supreme Court in the primary season, demonstrated the chaos on the ground and the Court's divisions. In the days leading up to the state's April 7 primary, officials were crushed by hundreds of thousands of requests for absentee ballots. The Democratic National Committee, working with state Democrats, persuaded a federal district judge to extend the deadline for the receipt of absentee ballots by six days because of the increased demand in voting by mail. Over Republican National Committee opposition, a U.S. appellate court upheld the deadline extension. Republicans then appealed to the Supreme Court, arguing that no extension was necessary and that the federal district judge who added the six days to the deadline had overstepped his authority.

The Supreme Court under Chief Justice Roberts had its own record of curtailing voting rights that laid the groundwork for its response to 2020. The Court majority had been dismantling federal protections and favoring greater state control in this area of the law, including with the 2013 *Shelby County v. Holder* decision. Five years later, the same conservative, Roberts-led bloc upheld an Ohio voter-purge law (for residents who had not cast a ballot for at least four years) and separately sided with Texas as it defended a district map that a lower-court judge found had disadvantaged Latinos in the state.[11]

The new Wisconsin case in the spring of 2020 similarly provoked the Court majority's resistance to federal judicial involvement in state elections. The high court dissolved the district court order that had allowed absentee ballots mailed and postmarked after the April 7 election day to be counted if they were received by April 13. Justices in the majority said that the lower-court judge had wrongly intervened too close to a scheduled election. The Court's opinion was joined by Roberts, Thomas, Alito, Gorsuch, and Kavanaugh. They tried to minimize the opinion by declaring that the dispute centered on "a narrow, technical question about the absentee ballot process."[12]

Liberal justices seized on that assertion. "That is wrong," wrote Ginsburg for the dissenters.

> The question here is whether tens of thousands of Wisconsin citizens can vote safely in the midst of a pandemic. . . . With the majority's stay in place, that will not be possible. Either they will have to brave the polls, endangering their own and others' safety. Or they will lose their right to vote, through no fault of their own. That is a matter of utmost importance—to the constitutional rights of Wisconsin's citizens, the integrity of the State's election process, and in this most extraordinary time, the health of the Nation.

The two sets of justices disputed each other's version of the facts, a dimension that characterized much of the Roberts Court's action on voting rights in 2020. The dueling camps contradicted each other's recitations of what happened in lower-court proceedings in the Wisconsin case, and each side implied bad faith on the part of the other. The conservative majority, for example, declared that the Democratic challengers had not even sought the extra days. "Importantly, in their preliminary injunction motions," the conservatives wrote, "the plaintiffs did not ask that the District Court allow ballots mailed and postmarked after election day, April 7, to be counted. That is a critical point in the case." But the challengers *had* asked for the extra six days after health conditions worsened and it was clear that the people of Wisconsin were increasingly requesting absentee ballots. As Ginsburg noted in her dissent for the liberals, "although initially silent, the plaintiffs specifically requested that [deadline extension] remedy at the preliminary-injunction hearing in view of the ever-increasing demand for absentee ballots."[13]

The majority also asserted that courts should not interfere with election rules on the eve of an election, based on the 2006 case of *Purcell v. Gonzalez*, which held that federal judges should avoid intervening lest they disrupt the state's administration of an election and cause voter confusion. But the Supreme Court's own decision did just that, on the night before the polls were to open, by reversing a system in place under the district court order. The majority seemed to want it both ways, concluding: "The Court's decision on the narrow question before the Court should not be viewed as expressing an opinion on the broader question of whether to hold the election, or whether other reforms or modifications in election procedures in light of COVID-19 are appropriate. That point cannot be stressed enough." But that emphasis brought only more attention to the paradox of interfering in a way that forced more people to leave their homes and stand in line to vote during the pandemic. The two sides differed strikingly over how the COVID crisis should alter their legal analysis. The majority used as its touchpoint "an ordinary election" and the distribution of ballots. Dissenters wrote that such a comparison to normal times "boggles the mind."

Many Wisconsin residents had no alternative to voting in person, since absentee ballots were delayed in the mail. The *Milwaukee Journal Sentinel* criticized the state Republicans who brought the case. "They claim to be standing up for democracy, but Tuesday's election will be the most undemocratic in the state's history, in addition to putting at risk everything we've gained from the past three weeks of staying home and keeping our distance."[14]

In the months that followed in 2020, political parties and candidates, state legislators, and courts at all levels fought over absentee ballot deadlines and in-person accommodations. Sticking with the pattern of the Wisconsin case, the five Republican Supreme Court appointees largely sided with the challengers to various deadline extensions and accommodations, while the four Democratic appointees backed the states and others seeking accommodations.

A Florida case in July exemplified the pattern. The majority endorsed a sudden lower-court order that prevented thousands of former convicts in Florida from participating in a primary election because they had not paid off fines, fees, and other penalties. Florida voters in 2018 had approved a measure to amend the state constitution to restore voting rights to people with felony convictions as long as they had finished all terms of their sentences. A subsequent law adopted by state legislators had said all fines and financial penalties had to be paid up, too. Advocates for the poor challenged the constitutionality of that condition, and a U.S. district court judge ruled that it violated the equal protection guarantee. Just before the Florida primary, the U.S. Court of Appeals for the Eleventh Circuit intervened to restore the payoff requirement. The change arguably violated the *Purcell v. Gonzalez* principle that electoral rules not be altered close to an election. But the Supreme Court, in a one-sentence order that offered no explanation of its reasoning, let the new Eleventh Circuit order stand. Sotomayor dissented on behalf of the liberal wing. She wrote that the majority's move "continues a trend of condoning disfranchisement," noting that the Florida decision diverged from the majority's move in the earlier Wisconsin case, when it disallowed a change in absentee ballot deadlines because it supposedly was too close to Election Day.[15]

As the November 3 general election drew close, judges in Pennsylvania, Michigan, and Wisconsin faced new litigation related to ballot deadlines. Four years earlier, Trump had won the presidency because of roughly eighty thousand votes cast in his favor in those three states. Biden appeared to be recapturing what was once thought to be a "blue wall" for Democrats, and the candidates were battling it out in those states nearly one vote at a time.

When a new Wisconsin case reached the Supreme Court in late October, the specter of *Bush v. Gore* truly loomed, as justices demonstrated a new interest in preventing judges from reviewing legislative election rules. The case began when Wisconsin Democrats won a deadline extension from a U.S. district court judge for the submission of absentee ballots for the general election. The ballots would still have to be postmarked by November 3, the judge said, but they could be received as late as November 9 because of mail delays. Republicans immediately appealed and won at the U.S. Court of Appeals for the Seventh Circuit. When the Democratic National Committee sought relief from the Supreme Court, the justices refused to revive the district court judge's order. Over dissent from the remaining three liberals (Breyer, Sotomayor, and Kagan), the Court rejected the Democratic

National Committee's argument for an extension of time for Wisconsin absentee ballots.[16]

Chief Justice Roberts criticized the district court's "federal intrusion on state lawmaking processes." Then Gorsuch, joined by Kavanaugh, went further, deriding the district court judge's pandemic concerns and pressing the independent state legislature theme: "Why did the district court seek to scuttle such a long-settled tradition in this area? COVID. Because of the current pandemic, the court suggested, it was free to substitute its own election deadline for the State's." Gorsuch invoked a version of Rehnquist's view from 2000 of the supremacy of legislatures in administering presidential elections. He did not cite the late chief justice or *Bush v. Gore* but flatly declared, "The Constitution provides that the state legislatures—not federal judges, not state judges, not state governors, not other state officials—bear primary responsibility for setting election rules." He said that legislatures deserved deference because they were close to the people and responsive to their needs.[17]

Kavanaugh then penned a solo statement, lifting directly from Rehnquist's theory and declaring in a footnote, "Under the U.S. Constitution, the state courts do not have a blank check to rewrite state election laws for federal elections. Article II expressly provides that the rules for Presidential elections are established by the States 'in such Manner as the *Legislature* thereof may direct.' . . . [A] state court may not depart from the state election code enacted by the legislature." Like Gorsuch, Kavanaugh said that state legislatures deserve deference in setting the rules for presidential elections, and Kavanaugh added, "As Chief Justice Rehnquist persuasively explained in *Bush v. Gore* . . . the text of the Constitution requires federal courts to ensure that state courts do not rewrite state election laws." That was only the second time a justice had ever cited *Bush v. Gore* in its twenty-year history (Thomas had referred to it passingly in a footnote in a 2013 Arizona dispute), and Kavanaugh's new reference seemed to imply that Rehnquist had expressed the Court's holding. But Rehnquist had failed to draw a majority.[18]

Striking a separate provocative note, Kavanaugh discounted the unusual circumstances of the pandemic and mail disruptions. He warned of "chaos and suspicions of impropriety that can ensue if thousands of absentee ballots flow in after election day and potentially flip the results of the election." Kagan, in dissent, took issue particularly with that part of Kavanaugh's opinion. "There are no results to 'flip' until all valid votes are counted," she wrote. "And nothing could be more 'suspicious' or 'improper' than refusing to tally votes once the clock strikes 12 on election night," she wrote. "To suggest otherwise, especially in these fractious times, is to disserve the electoral process." She also faulted the majority for imposing deadlines from pre-pandemic life: "Today, mail ballots often travel at a snail's pace, and the elderly and ill put themselves in peril if they go to the polls. So citizens—thousands and thousands of them—who have followed all the State's rules still cannot cast a successful vote. And because that is true, the ballot-receipt deadline that once survived constitutional review no longer does."[19]

Two days later, the justices deadlocked and left intact a Pennsylvania state court's deadline extension for mail-in ballots. (Barrett had just been sworn in as a justice, but she declined to participate.) The three justices on the far right, however, issued a warning regarding state legislative power. "The provisions of the Federal Constitution conferring on state legislatures, not state courts, the authority to make rules governing federal elections would be meaningless if a state court could override the rules adopted by the legislature simply by claiming that a state constitutional provision gave the courts the authority to make whatever rules it thought appropriate for the conduct of a fair election," Alito wrote, joined by Thomas and Gorsuch.[20]

Even with the cloud of COVID and additional controversy over state electoral rules, voter participation reached record levels in November 2020. The American electorate cast nearly 158.4 million ballots, for a turnout 7 percentage points higher than in 2016. Several states were too close to call for days, and it was not until Saturday, November 7, that former vice president Biden was able to declare victory.[21]

Trump, from the morning after the election and on, claimed without grounds that he had won. He tried to assert on November 4 that because ballots were still being counted, some sort of fraud had occurred. "We were getting ready to win this election. Frankly, we did win this election. We did win this election." He vowed to go to the Supreme Court to stop the tallies ("We want all voting to stop") and be assured his victory.[22]

Under many states' procedures, properly postmarked mail-in ballots could be counted for a set period after Election Day. By any measure, Trump never won the requisite 270 electoral college votes. Biden called for patience, saying, "It's not my place or Donald Trump's place to declare who's won this election. That's the decision of the American people."[23]

Former White House counsel Don McGahn weighed in the day after the election as he was being interviewed by the *Washington Post*'s Robert Costa as part of a streamed *Washington Post Live* segment. "Let's be honest," McGahn told Costa. "We went to bed last night and the president was up seemingly in all the states that mattered. We woke up this morning, he still seemed to be up in the states that mattered. And as the day goes on, he seems to be losing ground. So that's not the kind of thing that really should give anybody confidence in the system."[24]

But the ballots still coming in and being counted were valid. When Costa followed up with McGahn regarding Trump's claim that he had definitely won, McGahn, who said he had voted for Trump over Biden, responded, "He's certainly passionate about winning. And when you look at the results last night it certainly looked like he won . . . So, you know, he has to explore options and if one of [them] is litigation, he should do that." State election officials had predicted from the start that the count would take extra time because the pandemic had caused more people to vote by mail. Trump had disparaged voting by mail, of course, since more of those ballots tended to be cast by Democrats and, as counting continued, results turned bluer throughout the country.

Costa also asked McGahn about the importance of having Justice Barrett on the Court for election-related litigation. The former White House counsel was evasive, saying it depended on the case that went up to the Court and adding, "I think at the end of the day, knowing her record, she's going to call the balls and strikes as she sees it in accordance with established law." The clichéd response obscured the stakes of the moment. Trump's allies were trying to enlist the justices in a case that would deliver him a second term.[25]

Trump lacked sound arguments, but that did not diminish GOP expectations or, alternatively, the fear among Democratic lawyers that somehow valid election results would be subverted. Three former U.S. solicitors general from Democratic administrations teamed up to prepare for Trump legal arguments or ploys that would use the resources of the federal government. Former SGs Seth Waxman and Walter Dellinger (who had served in the Clinton administration) and Donald Verrilli (from the Obama administration) stayed in contact by email and text and met daily over Zoom. (The pandemic still made in-person sessions difficult.) They enlisted networks of election-law specialists and appellate attorneys as they produced white papers that could be turned into pleadings and briefs, as warranted. They tried to envision all manner of disruption, including an attempt to cancel the election altogether. Nothing, they believed, was outside the realm of possibility, as they considered ways that Trump might prevent the certification by Vice President Pence of the Electoral College counts on January 6 or impede Biden's January 20 inauguration. "But the one scenario we didn't envision was a mob running wild in the Capitol itself," Verrilli told me later.[26]

When Trump spoke to his supporters on the Ellipse on January 6, he focused on Pence: "I hope Mike is going to do the right thing. . . . Because if Mike Pence does the right thing, we win the election." Trump claimed, falsely, that Pence had the power to reject the certification of the Biden victory. The president made plain the pressure he was exerting on Pence. "All Vice President Pence has to do is send it back to the states to recertify and we become president and you are the happiest people."

Trump then told the audience, "I actually, I just spoke to Mike." Trump said that he had urged the vice president to show "courage" and warned if he failed, "then we're stuck with a president who lost the election by a lot and we have to live with that for four more years. We're just not going to let that happen." Trump often fixated on "courage," yet in a confusing way that deprived the word of its usual meaning. When he contracted the coronavirus, he suggested it was an act of political courage, saying, "As your leader, I had to do that."[27]

But Pence had no authority under the Constitution to reject the certification. One of the outside legal experts he had turned to, as Trump's legal squad pressured him, was former U.S. court of appeals judge J. Michael Luttig, who said Pence was duty-bound to accept the Electoral College counts as tallied by members of Congress. Luttig later connected the January 6 riot and independent state legislature theory, writing in 2022, "The Republicans' mystifying claim to this day that Trump did, or would have, received more votes than Joe Biden in 2020 were it not for actual fraud, is but the shiny object that Republicans have tauntingly and disingenuously dangled before the American public for almost a year and a half now to distract attention from their far more ambitious objective." Luttig asserted that Trump's allies had promoted the independent state legislature argument at the Supreme Court with the goal of persuading the justices to interpret the Electoral College process and the Electoral Count Act (1877) so that the vice president would reject enough swing-state counts to give Trump the presidency. And now, Luttig wrote, "Trump and Republicans are preparing to return to the Supreme Court, where this time they will likely win the independent state legislature doctrine, now that Amy Coney Barrett is on the Court and ready to vote."[28]

Back in 2020, Trump had relied on a band of loyalists whose legal arguments were universally rejected in the courts. Among his allies were Rudy Giuliani, the former New York mayor; John Eastman, a Chapman University constitutional law professor; Sidney Powell, a former federal prosecutor in Texas; and Cleta Mitchell, a conservative election-law attorney who had warned without evidence of rampant fraud at the polls.

Mitchell participated in a January 2, 2021, call with Trump and Meadows as the president implored Georgia secretary of state Brad Raffensperger to "find" some 11,780 votes—to reverse the actual results, which favored Biden. (A few days later, Mitchell resigned from

Foley & Lardner, the D.C. law office where she was a partner, following criticism of her involvement in the call. She attributed her departure to "a massive pressure campaign . . . mounted by leftist groups.") Beyond the call with Raffensperger, Trump and his surrogates sought out officials in swing states to try to turn things around.

His allies' efforts eventually met with the kind of retribution that Trump himself seemed to elude. Rudy Giuliani's law license was temporarily suspended in New York in 2021, and in May 2022 he went before the House select committee investigating the January 6 insurrection. Eastman faced an ethics investigation by the State Bar of California, resigned from Chapman, and was forced to turn over records to the House's January 6 committee. The House of Representatives voted to hold Mark Meadows, the former White House chief of staff, in contempt of Congress for defying a subpoena from the January 6 committee. (As one of the last acts of the House panel, in October 2022, it voted to subpoena Trump for testimony and documents related to the attack on the Capitol.)[29]

The president and his aides had spent four years undermining U.S. rights and legal norms, and as Trump was losing in 2020, he challenged the voting rights especially of Blacks, Hispanics, and other racial minorities. Trump claimed that voter fraud was rampant in Detroit. He then said that he had won Michigan, which prompted Biden, who in fact had about 150,000 more votes than Trump, to say, "We won Michigan. It's going to be certified. . . . It's hard to fathom how this man thinks."[30]

Trump's claims of fraud were debunked in one lawsuit after another. In one late-November Pennsylvania dispute that reached the U.S. Court of Appeals for the Third Circuit, Judge Stephanos Bibas expressed the fear that the Trump team was undermining public trust. "Free, fair elections are the lifeblood of our democracy," Bibas, who had been appointed by Trump, wrote. "Charges of unfairness are serious. But calling an election unfair does not make it so. Charges require specific allegations and then proof. We have neither here." Other lower-court judges struck similar themes about the breathtakingly misguided arguments that Trump and his lawyers pushed. They wanted ballots invalidated wholesale and results decertified. When U.S. district court judge Timothy Batten in Georgia—appointed by George W. Bush—dismissed a complaint brought by Sidney Powell, he described the request as "perhaps the most extraordinary relief ever sought in any federal court in connection with an election. They want this Court to substitute its judgment for that of two and a half million Georgia voters who voted for Joe Biden, and this I am unwilling to do." Two days later in Wisconsin, when U.S. district court judge Pamela Pepper, an appointee of Barack Obama, threw out a Trump campaign challenge to Biden's state victory, she wrote, "Federal judges do not appoint the president in this country. One wonders why the plaintiffs came to federal court and asked a federal judge to do so."[31]

During these desperate last weeks of 2020, Trump was pressing on all fronts. He drew on a theme that he would shortly reprise for the January 6 insurrection, declaring, on December 8, "Let's see whether or not somebody has the courage—whether it's a legislator or legislatures, or whether it's a justice of the Supreme Court or a number of justices of the Supreme Court—let's see if they have the courage to do what everybody in this country knows is right." He tried to reach Leonard Leo, who had significantly influenced the president's judicial appointments. Leo declined to take the calls.[32]

A last-ditch Trump-backed case reached the justices within one day of the twentieth anniversary of *Bush v. Gore*. It was led by Republican Texas attorney general Ken Paxton and attempted to outright reverse the will of the voters in Pennsylvania, Georgia, Michigan, and Wisconsin—all states that had gone for Biden. (Paxton had no complaint with results in Texas, which Trump had carried.) Paxton was joined by eighteen other Republican state attorneys general and 126 GOP members of Congress. They had not gone first to any lower court, but rather filed an "original jurisdiction" claim, asserting that states had made unlawful changes to their election procedures enabling voter fraud. On the morning of December 11, as the country awaited Supreme Court action, Trump posted on Twitter, "If the Supreme Court shows Great Wisdom and Courage, the American People will win perhaps the most important case in history and our Electoral Process will be respected again!"[33]

But the Supreme Court threw out the case. Its unsigned order said, "Texas has not demonstrated a judicially cognizable interest in the manner in which another State conducts its elections." Trump had pulled the justices down in the dirt with him at various points over the previous four years, but not this time. The meritless claims he supported with Attorney General Paxton drew not a single vote, as the Court acted just three days before the Electoral College was scheduled to meet to cast votes for Biden as the election winner. The justices, including the three Trump appointees, separated themselves from such Trump partisans as Giuliani. Not a single justice was publicly receptive to Trump's assertions of election irregularities at this critical point before the Electoral College count. No one dissented from the unsigned Court order, and only Alito and Thomas wrote a short additional statement saying they would have allowed Texas to file the case but would not have granted its claims.[34]

Twenty years earlier, the presidential election contest was marked by narrow votes, down to the one-vote margin of the *Bush v. Gore* ruling. But in 2020, the final Supreme Court action against Trump's election claims was not even close.

Writing later, Richard Hasen, an election law expert, warned that Trump's schemes might nonetheless work in the future. "Although the federal judiciary was largely unsympathetic to Trump's baseless election challenges in 2020, this historical fact was contingent on judges maintaining some fidelity to judicial independence," Hasen wrote. "Such independence is not guaranteed in the future given the fact that the President is in the unique position of picking who will adjudicate future challenges." Hasen observed that Trump had directed many public pleas at the justices he had placed on the bench, such as Barrett, and he wrote, "A future President may learn from Trump's 2020 failure and seek to identify more explicitly partisan candidates for the Supreme Court."[35]

A future Supreme Court may be more receptive to claims that could undermine the will of the people at the polls, too. Thomas, especially, showed sympathy for Trump's claims of fraud, and he, along with Alito, Gorsuch, and Kavanaugh, stood poised to accept the independent state legislative theory that could collapse judicial safeguards.[36] In a North Carolina case in March 2022, those four justices expressed a desire to take up the question of state legislative authority in elections. "There can be no doubt that this question is of great national importance," Alito wrote. "We will have to resolve this question sooner or later, and the sooner we do so, the better."

And it was soon. Just three months later, in June 2022, the justices announced they would hear that North Carolina case of *Moore v. Harper*, centered on an extreme partisan gerrymander drawn by the state legislature. The North Carolina supreme court ruled that the map violated the state constitution's coverage for free elections, equal protection, and free speech and assembly. Republicans argued that the independent state legislature theory, in this situation tied to the Constitution's Elections Clause (as opposed to the Electors Clause in the case of *Bush v. Gore*), should have prevented the state court from reviewing the legislature's map. The Elections Clause dictates that "The Times, Places and Manner of holding Elections for Senators and Representatives, shall be prescribed in each State by the Legislature thereof." A decision in the weighty Supreme Court case was expected by mid-2023, in time to influence state rules in the 2024 cycle and, perhaps, the outcome of a presidential election.

As the new controversy returned the justices to the theory of complete legislative power advanced in *Bush v. Gore* by Chief Justice Rehnquist, it also evoked a warning from Justice Kennedy about the danger to democracy of usurping state constitutional protections.

"It seems to me essential to the republican theory of government that the constitutions of the United States and the states are the basic charter," Kennedy had said during *Bush v. Gore* oral arguments, "and to say that the legislature of the state is unmoored from its own constitution, and it can't use its court . . . [is] it seems to me a holding which has grave implications for our republican theory of government."

## Chapter 11

# THE SUPERMAJORITY

The trauma of the January 6 assault on the Capitol hung in the air for Joe Biden's inaugural, on January 20, 2021. About twenty thousand members of the National Guard had been deployed to help with security at the Capitol and patrol the streets of Washington. Attendance on the elevated platform at the West Front of the Capitol was limited because of pandemic social distancing. But even with the fearful atmosphere, the inaugural offered plenty of showstopping highlights: Lady Gaga, wearing a navy cashmere jacket with a large gilded dove-of-peace brooch and a skirt of red silk faille, sang the national anthem. And Amanda Gorman, at twenty-two the youngest-ever inaugural poet, read "The Hill We Climb," which she said she had finished the night after the Capitol rampage.[1]

"When day comes, we ask ourselves: / Where can we find light / In this never-ending shade? / The loss we carry, a sea we must wade," she said, as her words reflected the despair of the moment along with its hopes: "And yet the dawn is ours before we knew it / Somehow, we do it / Somehow, we've weathered and witnessed / A nation that isn't broken, but simply unfinished." Gorman's energy was evident even as she arrived and began taking photos with dignitaries on the platform, including some of the justices. When Gorman left the stage, she then playfully bumped elbows with Elena Kagan.

Sonia Sotomayor swore in Kamala Harris, the nation's first Black vice president and the first of Asian descent. Per custom, Chief Justice

John Roberts swore in Biden. In Biden's inaugural address, the seventy-eight-year-old president called for unity and healing. "We must end this uncivil war," he said, between red and blue states, conservatives and liberals. Former president Trump refused to attend.

The justices' oral arguments and private conferences were still being conducted by teleconference. The nine were vaccinated, but their staffs were not yet. (The vaccine became widely available in the spring of 2021.) Rounds of infection broke out among staffers in the chief justice's chambers and elsewhere through the building, sending employees into renewed isolation. Amy Coney Barrett flew back and forth from her home in Indiana for her early months of Court work. She eventually sold the family's South Bend house and settled with her family in a Virginia suburb. She attended Mass at Saint James, where Father Paul Scalia, the son of her mentor Antonin Scalia, was pastor.

As the remaining eight soon reoriented around a new colleague, they dealt with a new administration. Three weeks after President Biden entered the White House, the U.S. solicitor general's office wrote a letter to the Court saying that it was changing the federal government's position in a pending case involving Obamacare. Trump had run against the Affordable Care Act in 2016 and, once elected president, had attempted to persuade Congress to kill it. When he failed on the legislative front, the president tried through litigation. His administration had urged the justices in the pending case to invalidate the entire Affordable Care Act. The dispute traced back to 2017, when Congress zeroed out the tax penalty for the plank of Obamacare that had required all Americans to obtain health insurance or pay a penalty. That insurance mandate had been the subject of an important 2012 Supreme Court case, in which the justices narrowly upheld the mandate, with Roberts writing that it was permissible under Congress's taxing power. The decision construing the individual insurance requirement as a tax was key to the constitutionality of the entire ACA at the time.

Republican state officials who initiated the lawsuit argued that without the tax penalty, the insurance mandate lacked its constitutional mooring. They said that it should be invalidated, a course of action that would take the entire nearly thousand-page law down with it. Trump's solicitor general, Noel Francisco, had supported the effort. But now, with Biden in the White House, the Department of Justice was altering positions. "Following the change in Administration . . . the United States no longer adheres to the conclusions in the previously filed brief," Deputy Solicitor General Edwin Kneedler wrote to the justices in February 2021, asserting that even though Congress had reduced the payment amount to zero in 2017, it had preserved the mandate as a choice between two options.[2]

This switch by the Biden administration was not surprising. The GOP states' lawsuit rested on shaky legal ground. It was unlikely that the new high court, even with Barrett seated, would be persuaded. But there were other switches of the government's legal position in the works, and they were riskier propositions. Trump was gone, but his justices constituted one-third of the bench. And just as his audacious views were capturing more of mainstream America, the right-wing agenda was alive at the Supreme Court. Three of the justices in the new conservative supermajority—Thomas, Alito, and Gorsuch—were writing daring opinions impugning decades of precedent. The question was whether the remaining conservatives—Roberts, Kavanaugh, and Barrett—would put any brake on their zeal.

U.S. appellate judge Merrick Garland, the would-be ninth justice, returned to the national stage. President Biden chose Garland to be the new attorney general. As Biden unveiled Garland's nomination at the White House, the nominee referred to the Trump-inspired destruction that had occurred while the Electoral College votes were being tallied and said, "The rule of law is not just some lawyer's turn of phrase. It is the very foundation of our democracy. The essence of the rule of law is that like cases are treated alike, that there is not one rule for Democrats and another for Republicans, one rule for friends and another for foes." Garland, sixty-eight at the time, said he would try to restore confidence in the Justice Department that Trump had undermined. For his part, President Biden told Garland, "You won't work for me. You are not the president's or the vice president's lawyer. Your loyalty is not to me. It's to the law, the Constitution." A year earlier, as Trump was seeking leniency for his friend and political strategist Roger Stone, who was convicted of lying under oath and threatening a witness, the president had asserted that he, not the attorney general, was effectively the nation's highest law enforcement officer.[3]

Garland, who had been an appellate judge since 1998, was familiar to the justices, as was Elizabeth Prelogar, the new Biden administration solicitor general. Prelogar had clerked for Ginsburg and then Kagan and had served as an assistant solicitor general from 2014 to 2019, arguing cases before the justices and separately working on special counsel Robert Mueller's investigation of Russian election interference. A native of Idaho, she had studied in Saint Petersburg as a Fulbright fellow and was fluent in Russian.[4]

Clearly Biden was also a known quantity: many of the justices had faced questions from him as nominees when he was a senator. He had chaired the Senate Judiciary Committee and set the tone for confirmations, including at the 1991 hearing for Clarence Thomas. During his 2020 presidential campaign, Biden was still fending off criticism for his clumsy handling of Anita Hill as a witness. Thomas's defenders said that Biden had turned the confirmation into a circus, and that Hill's charges had been less than credible. Thomas's critics said that Biden had failed to give Hill's claims a fair airing, had kept women with similar complaints from testifying, and had seemed as woefully unschooled in the matter of sexual harassment as many of his colleagues. "Can you tell the committee what was the most embarrassing of all the incidents you have alleged?" he asked at one point.[5]

Biden also presided over the relatively low-key hearings for Ginsburg in 1993 and Breyer in 1994. A little more than a decade later, in 2005 and 2006, Biden, still on the Senate Judiciary Committee, hammered George W. Bush's nominees John Roberts and Samuel Alito over their narrow views on privacy and racial remedies. He then voted against both of the men.

The Supreme Court supermajority presented a hurdle for the Biden administration as it began replacing Trump policies. The new Court makeup also dislodged Roberts's control and offered the five justices

on the hard right new opportunities for overhauling the law. For decades before Ginsburg's death and replacement by Barrett, there were
four liberal justices fending off a new conservatism, and those on
the left were often able to secure a crucial fifth vote. That meant that
even as the Court became more conservative, coalitions at the center of
the bench were able to preserve abortion rights and racial affirmative
action, as just two examples. Centrist conservatives also ensured that
federal regulatory authority, while curtailed, remained largely intact.
The new Court dynamic threatened to return the bench to the pre–
New Deal era, before Congress instituted—and the Court upheld—
protections for labor, public health and safety, the economy, and the
environment.

Roberts had been the critical fifth vote after Justice Anthony Kennedy retired. Now conservatives did not need him for a majority. Yet if
the justices on the left persuaded Roberts to their side, that gave them
only four votes. They needed another justice to prevail as a majority and
make a difference in the law. This new math diminished the chief justice's leverage at the center. It foretold a less effective, personally difficult
role for a man who had risen from first in class to first among equals.

The new dynamic was seen almost immediately in the area of religious liberty, where the right wing already had made significant
advances. Even before Barrett's appointment, promoted by outside
religious conservatives because of her positions on faith and the law,
the Court had permitted more prayer in public settings, greater government funding of religious education, and broader exceptions to the
Affordable Care Act's birth control coverage.

A new series of challenges arose when COVID-19 hit the country and state and local governments imposed a series of capacity
limits on large gatherings to try to control the spread of the virus.
The coronavirus was transmitted through airborne particles and
droplets, so religious settings, with people in close quarters, chant-
ing and singing, were considered especially fraught. Some churches
and synagogues, however, claimed such restrictions on gatherings
constituted an infringement on the free exercise of religion. The
absence of Ginsburg transformed this line of cases.

The first round of such challenges had arrived before Ginsburg's death, which meant that Roberts was at the center and controlling the outcome with his vote. He had cast the decisive vote to uphold California's capacity limits on public gatherings imposed by Governor Gavin Newsom. (Attendance at places of worship was limited to 25 percent of building capacity or a maximum of one hundred attendees.) Roberts observed at the time (a vaccine was not yet available) that public safety should be the domain of "politically accountable officials" who run states and cities. In this he leaned partly on a 1905 decision, *Jacobson v. Massachusetts*, that endorsed state power during a smallpox outbreak. Two months later Roberts cast the decisive vote to leave in place Nevada's capacity limits on churches.[6]

Within weeks of Barrett's October confirmation, her vote transformed the outcome in a controversy over New York's COVID-19 restrictions at churches and synagogues. By a 5–4 vote, the Court threw out New York State's capacity limits at religious services. The Court's order came just before midnight on the Wednesday evening before Thanksgiving 2020. Roberts, now dissenting, and Gorsuch, in the majority, engaged in rancorous cross-claims about a legal precedent.

"We may not shelter in place when the Constitution is under attack," Gorsuch wrote about limits for religious services. "Things never go well when we do." He then upbraided Roberts for his earlier opinion in the California case of *South Bay United Pentecostal Church v. Newsom* and for his citation of *Jacobson v. Massachusetts*, calling the California opinion "mistaken from the start. To justify its result, the concurrence reached back 100 years. . . . But *Jacobson* hardly supports cutting the Constitution loose during a pandemic." Gorsuch said that the 1905 case was irrelevant. Roberts protested in the new case that he had not actually relied on the *Jacobson* precedent, causing Gorsuch to declare in response, "That was the first case *South Bay* cited on the substantive legal question before the Court, it was the only case cited involving a pandemic, and many lower courts quite understandably read its invocation as inviting them to slacken their enforcement of constitutional liberties while COVID lingers." Roberts fired back that Gorsuch was himself making more of the case than he had intended when he'd originally cited it. Gorsuch's discussion of the 1905 case "occupies three pages" of his writing in the New York dispute, Roberts noted, while he himself had given it "exactly one sentence." Added Roberts, "It is not clear which part of this lone quotation [from *Jacobson*] today's concurrence finds so discomfiting." With Roberts in dissent were Breyer, Sotomayor, and Kagan. Sotomayor wrote a separate dissenting opinion, joined only by Kagan, warning, "Justices of this Court play a deadly game in second guessing the expert judgment of health officials about the environments in which a contagious virus, now infecting a million Americans each week, spreads most easily."[7]

A few months later, another COVID-19 case came down to the same 5–4 vote, with another midnight order and another set of opinions exposing the fissures among the justices. The majority, again with Barrett's fifth vote, blocked California's limits on Bible study sessions and prayer meetings held in homes. (The state had prohibited gatherings of people from more than three households.) Roberts sided with the liberals in dissent, although he did not sign their opinion criticizing the majority for ignoring scientific findings regarding transmission of the virus.

The unsigned majority opinion in this new California case, *Tandon v. Newsom*, criticized the state for treating activities in some secular establishments, including retail stores, more permissively than those in homes. Issued late on a Friday night and relatively brief (only four pages), it introduced a new level of favoritism for religious activities and government accommodation.

In dissent, Kagan said that the majority was misguided in comparing secular and religious activities. Kagan noted that the judges in the lower-court cases had explained that activities (like shopping) in less intimate settings than a home "do pose lesser risks for at least three reasons. First, 'when people gather in social settings, their interactions are likely to be longer than they would be in a commercial setting,' with participants 'more likely to be involved in prolonged conversations.' . . . Second, 'private houses are typically smaller and less ventilated than commercial establishments.' . . . And third, 'social distancing and mask-wearing are less likely in private settings and enforcement is more difficult.'" Kagan said the Court should respect California's distinctions regarding health risks, concluding, "The law does not require that the State equally treat apples and watermelons."[8]

Outside critics of the majority's decision such as Jim Oleske, a professor at Lewis & Clark Law School, focused on the Court's implicit abandonment of a principle from a 1990 case, *Employment Division v. Smith*, which had said that as long as laws were neutral and generally applied, they could be upheld, irrespective of how they might affect religious practices. The approach taken in the new California dispute, *Tandon v. Newsom*, dictated that any secular exemption required a comparable religious exemption. Exacerbating the outside criticism was that the Court decided *Tandon v. Newsom* without a full briefing or oral arguments, on the "shadow docket," after the religious challengers sought immediate relief from the California capacity regulations.

It just so happened that a separate case that was fully briefed during the 2020–2021 session could have offered the justices an opportunity to more directly assess the future of the *Employment Division v. Smith* case. But the majority sidestepped the question, as Roberts generated a compromise. That case, a conflict between LGBTQ interests and religious liberty, arose from the city of Philadelphia's suspension of a foster-care contract with Catholic Social Services (CSS). The city suspended the contract when the agency would not certify same-sex couples as foster parents. CSS's refusal was grounded in its religious beliefs and its view of marriage as being between a man and a woman. When the justices agreed to hear the CSS appeal, they said that they would use the case to reconsider *Employment Division v. Smith*, which many religious adherents argued had failed to sufficiently protect them from regulation.

The possibility that the high court would grant religious conservatives even more opportunities to challenge neutral regulations, particularly those intended to fight discrimination, drew inordinate attention to the case. But in the end, a majority passed up the direct reconsideration of *Smith*, even as it ruled against the city. "Our task," Roberts wrote,

> is to decide whether the burden the City has placed on the religious exercise of CSS is constitutionally permissible. *Smith* held that laws incidentally burdening religion are ordinarily not subject to strict scrutiny under the Free Exercise Clause so long as they are neutral and generally applicable. . . . This case falls outside *Smith* because the City has burdened the religious exercise of CSS through policies that do not meet the requirement of being neutral and generally applicable.

Roberts construed the contract between the city and CSS as including "a system of individual exemptions," meaning it gave government officials discretion and could not be regarded as generally applied. That differentiated the Philadelphia case from situations covered by the *Smith* precedent, when laws incidentally burden religion and do not demand the strictest judicial scrutiny. In the Philadelphia dispute, Roberts wrote, Philadelphia's system of individual exemptions required it to have a "compelling reason" to exclude CSS, and it did not. He wrote that the city impinged on the agency's free exercise of religion by forcing it either to certify same-sex couples as foster parents or to change its mission in violation of its religious beliefs.[9]

Justices Barrett and Kavanaugh signed on to the Roberts compromise. In a concurring opinion by Barrett, joined by Kavanaugh and Breyer, the newest justice agreed that, because of the nature of the Philadelphia regulation, there was no need to revisit *Smith*. "We need not wrestle with" larger questions of religious liberty, she wrote. "There would be a number of issues to work through if *Smith* were overruled." The three liberals, Breyer, Sotomayor, and Kagan, also fully joined the Roberts opinion, presumably satisfied that he held back the rightward push on religion. Alito filed an unusually lengthy seventy-seven-page opinion concurring only in the Court's judgment, which led some law professors to speculate that he might have had a majority for his views but lost it. Justices told me later that was never the case. From the start, a majority wanted a narrow decision.

Alito and Gorsuch suggested in separate opinions that Roberts had engaged in a sleight of hand to avoid core legal issues. "After receiving more than 2,500 pages of briefing and after more than a half-year of post-argument cogitation," Alito wrote, joined by Thomas and Gorsuch, "the Court has emitted a wisp of a decision that leaves religious liberty in a confused and vulnerable state." Gorsuch added, in a separate concurring opinion, "From start to finish, it is a dizzying series of maneuvers." He also adopted a characteristic tone of reproach as he referred to the Barrett concurrence, writing, "We hardly need to 'wrestle' today with every conceivable question that might follow from recognizing Smith was wrong. . . . the Court should overrule it now, set us back on the correct course, and address each case as it comes."[10]

Such were the new ruptures. Liberals Breyer, Sotomayor, and Kagan were willing to go along with the Roberts majority to avoid further erosion of precedent, and the real battle was among the controlling six over how fast and how far. Clashes over religion were one of the most defining of the Roberts Court, and even when it moved incrementally, it was always in the same direction: to favor adherents who wanted exemptions from antibias laws, or more opportunities for government funding, or more prayer or signs of religion in schools and other public places.

Another Roberts Court compromise on that same June 2021 day arose from the competing legal stances of the Trump and Biden administrations. Despite the seemingly high stakes in the third-round attack on the ACA, the test was limited because the challengers' claims were arguably baseless. (The final 7–2 vote would demonstrate that.) Trump had denounced the law since its passage in 2010. As a New York real estate developer, he had called the ACA "a total disaster," a criticism he embellished when he attained the presidency, improbably adding tones of the Judith Viorst children's classic *Alexander and the Terrible, Horrible, No Good, Very Bad Day:* "We eliminated Obamacare's horrible, horrible, very expensive and very unfair, unpopular individual mandate. A total disaster." In 2012, he had criticized Roberts for casting the crucial vote upholding the law, saying in a Twitter post, "Congratulations to John Roberts for making Americans hate the Supreme Court because of his BS." In 2016, in an ABC television interview, Trump said, "Justice Roberts could've killed Obamacare and should've, based on everything—should've killed it twice." By 2017, his predictions had escalated and reached peak wish fulfillment: "It implodes by itself." But as president, Trump failed to persuade the Republican-dominated Congress to repeal the law.[11]

The case underway in early 2021 had been brought by Texas and seventeen other Republican-led states. Administration lawyers usually believe that they have an obligation to defend a law if reasonable arguments can be made. But in this situation, the Trump administration refused to defend the law and ended up taking the most extreme position with the Republican attorneys general: that the Supreme Court should strike down the law. That would have included the Medicaid expansion for poor people and marketplace options for those not covered by employee plans, along with provisions that prevented insurance companies from charging people higher premiums because of their health history or excluding people with preexisting conditions such as cancer.[12]

There was a threshold issue, however: to establish legal standing, litigants must show that they have been harmed. Texas and the other states argued that the ACA burdened them by bringing more people into state-administered coverage programs, and the individual plaintiffs who joined the case cited the minimum-coverage mandate. But the Court said neither group had valid grounds for their complaint. "We proceed no further than standing," Justice Stephen Breyer, to whom Roberts had assigned the Court's opinion, wrote. "Neither the individual nor the state plaintiffs have shown that the injury they will suffer or have suffered is 'fairly traceable' to the 'allegedly unlawful conduct' of which they complain."

Trump appointees Kavanaugh and Barrett joined the Breyer opinion. Even Thomas, who had twice before voted against the ACA, agreed with Breyer's bottom line. Thomas said that the "fundamental problem" was that none of the plaintiffs had "identified any unlawful action that has injured them." Only Justices Alito and Gorsuch fully dissented, and their opinion largely replayed broader grievances with the sweeping law. "Today's decision is the third installment in our epic Affordable Care Act trilogy," Alito wrote, "and it follows the same pattern as installments one and two. In all three episodes, with the Affordable Care Act facing a serious threat, the Court has pulled off an improbable rescue." Still, the new lopsided ruling (prior cases had come down to 5–4 and 6–3) reinforced the reality that Obama's signature domestic achievement was now entrenched in the law and society.[13]

The Obamacare dispute was eclipsed in importance by the two final decisions of the 2020–2021 session, which went to the core of American democracy in the vein of earlier cases such as *Citizens United* (lifting limits on corporate and labor union expenditures in campaigns), *Shelby County v. Holder* (ending preclearance for new election rules in states with a history of discrimination), and *Rucho v. Common Cause* (greenlighting extreme partisan gerrymandering in the states).

The more potentially far-reaching of the two final cases began in Arizona and involved a section of the Voting Rights Act barring practices that racially discriminate. This provision of the landmark act, known as Section 2, had become even more essential to the right to vote in 2013, after the justices eroded the protections of Section 5 in *Shelby County*. With Section 5 gone, states enacted a rash of new rules for casting ballots that could be challenged only after they took effect under the VRA's Section 2.

The new Arizona case had the potential to make it more difficult to sue for discrimination under Section 2. It tested how to prove a racially discriminatory impact, at a time when Republican legislatures were increasingly adopting restrictions that appeared to reduce access to the polls for Black, Hispanic, and Native American voters. The Arizona laws in question required ballots cast at the wrong precinct to be tossed out and, separately, criminalized the third-party collection of absentee ballots. The latter provision would affect nursing home residents, who might rely on people other than relatives to collect their ballots, or people in remote tribal areas of Arizona, where residents sometimes used neighbors or tribal leaders to deliver mail. The U.S.

Court of Appeals for the Ninth Circuit had invalidated both regulations, highlighting the state's history: "For over a century, Arizona has repeatedly targeted its American Indian, Hispanic, and African American citizens, limiting or eliminating their ability to vote and to participate in the political process."[14]

But the six-justice bloc on the right reversed and toughened the standard for bringing Section 2 claims. Roberts assigned the majority opinion to Alito, who laid out five "guideposts" for claims, including the burden imposed on voters and the strength of the state's interest in a restriction, such as to prevent fraud. "Having to identify one's own polling place and then travel there to vote does not exceed the 'usual burdens of voting,'" he wrote, in *Brnovich v. Democratic National Committee,* referring to the rule that required ballots cast in the wrong place be discarded. He accentuated state interests in fighting fraud in elections as he minimized concern for disparities in a regulation's impact on various racial groups. "To the extent that minority and non-minority groups differ with respect to employment, wealth, and education, even neutral regulations, no matter how crafted, may well result in some predictable disparities in rates of voting and noncompliance with voting rules," he wrote. "But the mere fact there is some disparity in impact does not necessarily mean that a system is not equally open or that it does not give everyone an equal opportunity to vote."[15]

Dissenters condemned the decision and placed it squarely with *Shelby County* in its weakening of the 1965 Voting Rights Act. "What is tragic here," Kagan declared, "is that the Court has (yet again) rewritten—in order to weaken—a statute that stands as a monument to America's greatness, and protects against its basest impulses." She recalled Chief Justice Roberts's declaration, in *Shelby County,* that "things have changed dramatically" in the country.

"Maybe some think that voter suppression is a relic of history and so the need for a potent Section 2 has come and gone," Kagan wrote, but "Congress gets to make that call. Because it has not done so, this Court's duty is to apply the law as it is written. The law that confronted one of this country's most enduring wrongs; pledged to give every American, of every race, an equal chance to participate in our democracy;

and now stands as the crucial tool to achieve that goal. That law, of all laws, deserves the sweep and power Congress gave it. That law, of all laws, should not be diminished by this Court." Her words in *Brnovich* recalled her mournful 2019 dissent in *Rucho v. Common Cause*, when the majority had said that federal judges could do nothing about extreme gerrymandering

In the second important ruling on the last day of the session, *Americans for Prosperity v. Bonta*, Roberts took the lead as the majority struck down a California donor-disclosure law for certain tax-exempt charities in the state. California had required such entities to turn over to state officials information that the nonprofits submitted to the Internal Revenue Service listing the names and addresses of major donors. The Americans for Prosperity Foundation, affiliated with the politically formidable Koch family, and the Thomas More Law Center, a Christian advocacy group, argued in a lawsuit that the disclosure demand would chill free association under the First Amendment and ultimately lessen donations. The state countered that the disclosure of the names of major donors would prevent fraud and assist the state in the administration of its own tax laws. Roberts, joined by his conservative colleagues, agreed with the challengers that the law violated the First Amendment right to free association.

"The upshot is that California casts a dragnet for sensitive donor information from tens of thousands of charities each year," Roberts wrote, "even though that information will become relevant in only a small number of cases involving filed complaints." Dissenting justices contended that the ruling took a step toward ending disclosure rules in the campaign finance context and could lead to shady anonymous contributions in campaigns. "Today's analysis marks reporting and disclosure requirements with a bull's-eye," Sotomayor said. "Regulated entities who wish to avoid their obligations can do so by vaguely waving toward First Amendment 'privacy concerns.'"[16]

Ian Millhiser of *Vox* went further, in a piece that captured the sentiment of liberals beyond the Court. He noted that before the ruling in *Americans for Prosperity v. Bonta*, the Court had found most disclosure laws valid, and he predicted that such regulations would, after the ruling, be presumed unconstitutional, giving wealthy donors "far more ability to shape American politics in secret."[17]

On the Court, new interpersonal conflicts were emerging. They were not revealed merely in quiet conversations with a few outsiders. They were laid bare in public opinions. And the pattern reflected more than the usual criticism of fellow justices' legal reasoning. It extended to an impugning of motives. For example, in *Torres v. Madrid*, a police abuse case, Gorsuch suggested that his colleagues were kowtowing to policing concerns and the Black Lives Matter movement. He wrote that in siding with a New Mexico woman shot by police while fleeing the scene, the majority had ignored the legal principles in the case because of what he described euphemistically as "new policing realities." He also said the Court might have been following an "impulse" to provide some relief. (Gorsuch was joined in the dissent by Thomas and Alito.) Roberts, who had written the majority opinion, countered that "the dissent speculates that the real reason for today's decision is an 'impulse' to provide relief . . . or maybe a desire 'to make life easier for ourselves.' . . . There is no call for such surmise."

In another instance, Sotomayor denounced Kavanaugh's legal reasoning in a case finding that juveniles could be sentenced to life without parole even without a determination that the offender was irreparably corrupt. She said that her colleague was "fooling no one" with his "egregious" and "twist[ed]" interpretation of decisions. The 6–3 decision along familiar ideological lines effectively undermined precedent from 2012 and 2016 requiring an assessment of incorrigibility. Sotomayor declared that the Kavanaugh majority conclusion "would come as a shock" to the justices who had signed earlier precedent saying that life in prison could be justified only for "the rarest children, those whose crimes reflect 'irreparable corruption.'" Kavanaugh, who wanted to minimize public differences, wrote, "We simply have a good-faith disagreement with the dissent over how to interpret [past cases]. That kind of debate over how to interpret relevant precedents is commonplace." In a separate dispute, Kagan accused Kavanagh of engaging in judicial "scorekeeping" as he tried to turn one of her earlier opinions against her. In the case at hand, Kagan dissented as Kavanaugh wrote for the majority that a 2020 Supreme Court decision forbidding nonunanimous jury verdicts in criminal cases could not be applied retroactively to people already convicted under such jury practices and seeking to challenge their convictions. Kavanaugh wrote that Kagan should not be able to "impugn today's majority for supposedly shortchanging criminal defendants" because she had dissented in the original case. As Kagan rejoined, she distinguished between the legal issues of the two disputes and said, "Judges should take cases one at a time, and do their best in each to apply the relevant legal rules. . . . No one gets to bank capital for future cases; no one's past decisions insulate them from criticism. The focus always is, or should be, getting the case before us right."[18]

Justice Breyer, liberal like Kagan but lacking her cutting style, was the product of a far less polarized era. He shrugged off disagreeable personalities and nostalgically recalled his time as a Senate staffer in the 1970s, working on bipartisan compromises. Breyer was widely respected, but by 2021, some Democrats wanted the 1994 Clinton appointee to step down. He was well into his eighties, and Democrat Biden was in the White House, positioned to make the first nomination since President Obama was denied the chance to fill the Scalia vacancy. Biden had promised to appoint the first African American woman justice, and the notion of a younger liberal energized progressives. They were still consumed by the fallout from Ruth Bader Ginsburg's decision against retirement when a Democratic president was in the White House. The 6–3 makeup was grim for liberals, but there was always the possibility that it could get worse—that Breyer would hold out and Biden would miss the chance to name a successor. Liberal advocates pressured Breyer with op-eds in major newspapers and even resorted to a billboard truck flashing "Breyer, Retire" that circled the Capitol Hill area.[19]

In July 2021, after the voting rights and donation-disclosure cases, Breyer left town with no retirement announcement and headed to the family cottage in Plainfield, New Hampshire, where he had vacationed for decades. About seventy miles northwest of Manchester, the town was a small hamlet secluded in the white pines, without a single stoplight. In mid-July, when I visited him there, Breyer settled into a booth at a little country store to talk about his time on the Court and what he was weighing regarding retirement.[20]

He believed that he had another year on the bench because the Senate would remain majority Democrat through at least 2022. That was a gamble of sorts. Democrats held a slim one-vote margin, and only with Vice President Harris presiding to break a tie. Republican leader Mitch McConnell had proved his ruthlessness when it came to judges. But Breyer found personal satisfaction with his new seniority on the left. Because of the Court's reverence for rank and order, he was now, without Ginsburg, the first of the liberals to speak in the justices' private sessions, following Roberts and the longer-serving Thomas. Breyer thought that gave him a new ability to set the tone of negotiations and work toward compromise. He honestly felt that he could make a difference in one more year, as the justices prepared to take up cases on abortion rights and gun control. Breyer, it would turn out, was wrong.

Breyer minimized the obvious political and ideological issues that separated the nine. He insisted that disputes were based primarily on justices' differing views of the structure of the Constitution and how statutes should be interpreted. His tendency to put a good face on the situation infuriated liberals. Breyer was in many ways clinging to a world that no longer existed. His closest friends on the Court had been those at the center, such as Justice Sandra Day O'Connor. But there was no one comparable to O'Connor or Justice Anthony Kennedy or, before them, Justice Lewis Powell. The middle had evaporated.

Later that summer, while Breyer was mulling his future and his colleagues were still in their far-flung vacation locales, the Court acted on two emergency requests from the Biden administration that demonstrated the majority's lack of deference to the new president, in contrast to what was given Trump. In one of the cases, the justices prevented the Biden administration from discontinuing a Trump policy that sent Central American migrants seeking asylum to Mexico as they awaited U.S. hearings. By a 6–3 vote, the Court declined a request to lift a lower-court order that required the administration to continue

Trump's Migrant Protection Protocols, known informally as the "Remain in Mexico" policy. Biden lawyers, who were asking the Court at this point only to block the lower-court order, argued that the policy exposed asylum seekers who had traveled from Central America to new dangers—there had been widespread reports of kidnapping, rape, and murder among those forced to wait in Mexico.[21]

The second emergency request from the Biden administration arose from a freeze on evictions originally imposed by Congress to help struggling renters who had lost jobs during the pandemic. The eviction moratorium had expired at the end of July; Congress had failed to enact new legislation; and the U.S. Centers for Disease Control and Prevention had extended the moratorium for counties with high rates of COVID-19 transmission for another two months to try to lessen economic hardships and avoid further spread of the virus among renters forced to move.[22]

Millions of Americans were behind on their monthly rents. Congress had appropriated more than $46 billion to help renters and landlords, but the funds were only slowly getting to needy people.[23] The threat of widespread evictions persisted. In defending the administrative extension of the moratorium, the government pointed to a new surge in infections caused by a COVID variant known as Delta. "The trajectory of the pandemic has since changed—unexpectedly, dramatically, and for the worse," government lawyers told the Court, as they urged the justices to respect the views of policymakers charged with protecting the public health.

But the Court sided with landlords who had brought the case, *Alabama Association of Realtors v. Department of Health and Human Services*, and said that the CDC simply lacked the authority to extend the eviction moratorium. Rejecting the administration's arguments that it had validly acted under a 1944 public health law, the conservative majority said that the law covered "measures like fumigation and pest extermination," not anything as drastic as eviction policy. The three liberal dissenters insisted that the 1944 law applied to eviction moratoria and that there was no reason to back away from that interpretation—especially as COVID-19 continued to kill people. By

August 2021, when the Supreme Court considered the case, COVID deaths worldwide had reached nearly 4.5 million. U.S. deaths from COVID, then clocking in at over 630,000, would reach nearly one million eight months later. The lineup among justices was familiar: in the majority were Roberts, Thomas, Alito, Gorsuch, Kavanaugh, and Barrett; in dissent were Breyer, Sotomayor, and Kagan.[24]

Tracking COVID had by then become a horrifyingly predictable exercise. The trend of disease and death was only upward. "On applicants' [the landlords'] last trip to this Court," wrote the dissenting justices, "they argued that the 'downward trend in COVID-19 cases and the effectiveness of vaccines' left 'no . . . public-health rationale for the [CDC's then-operative eviction] moratorium.' . . . These predictions have proved tragically untrue." The three liberals urged their conservative colleagues to take more time with the case and to hear oral arguments rather than summarily rejecting the Biden administration's position. Such entreaties went unheeded as the Court continued to demonstrate just how much the justices wanted the federal government out of American life.

Perhaps chastened by criticism from within and beyond the Court, the majority agreed to hear arguments, rather than act summarily from their emergency docket, in *National Federation of Independent Business v. OSHA*, a later consequential case concerning the Biden administration's effort to stop the spread of COVID-19. The Occupational Safety and Health Administration (OSHA) had issued a new rule directing employers with one hundred or more workers to institute either a vaccine requirement or weekly COVID-19 testing. OSHA, represented by Department of Justice lawyers, said that the directive flowed from its statutory authority to protect employees from "grave danger" through exposure to new hazards and harmful agents. It was challenged by the National Federation of Independent Business (NFIB) and officials from twenty-seven states.

On January 7, the day the case was to be heard, the justices were using their courtroom. But only a few spectators were allowed in, among them the lawyers involved in the case, judicial clerks, and a limited number of journalists. It was a sign of the deterioration of relations among the justices that as the Delta variant of COVID was making its way across the country, mask protocol became its own kind of federal case. When the justices entered the courtroom, Gorsuch was the lone one without a mask and Sotomayor remained in her chambers, ready to participate through an audio feed. The two justices usually sat next to each other in the tall black leather chairs.

Gorsuch declined to respond to later news media queries about why he shunned the mask, and numerous commentators chalked it up to ideological views. That such sentiment could imperil the health of Gorsuch's colleagues did not go unremarked upon. National Public Radio's Nina Totenberg reported that "according to Court sources, Sotomayor did not feel safe in close proximity to people who were unmasked," and Totenberg added that "Roberts, understanding that, in some form asked the other justices to mask up." After Totenberg's report, Gorsuch and Sotomayor issued an unusual joint statement: "Reporting that Justice Sotomayor asked Justice Gorsuch to wear a mask surprised us. It is false. While we may sometimes disagree about the law, we are warm colleagues and friends." But that was strange wording: Totenberg had not reported that Sotomayor had asked Gorsuch to wear a mask; she had reported that Roberts had. I later learned that the chief justice was surprised by Sotomayor and Gorsuch's joint public statement. Their move suddenly put attention on him and his wishes. A few hours later, the chief justice issued his own statement, itself an extraordinarily rare occurrence. Roberts said simply that he had not asked any justice to wear a mask and that he would say nothing more on the matter. Totenberg stood by her reporting that Roberts "in some form asked the other justices to mask up." It was not difficult to believe that the chief justice had implicitly encouraged his colleagues to wear masks as they sat in close proximity. Sotomayor had indeed spoken privately to him and other colleagues about her health concerns. Whatever happened behind the scenes, the justices' conflicting accounts underscored their broader lack of transparency and tendency to close ranks against the news media, even as they plunged into the mask wars of the political arena.

During oral arguments in the OSHA case, Solicitor General Prelogar described COVID-19 as "the deadliest pandemic in American history" and spoke of the "particularly acute workplace danger" it posed. She said that OSHA had "studied the science" of the virus's transmission and "found that workers are exposed to danger when they're inside together for as little as 15 minutes." But most of the justices suggested by their questions that OSHA had overstepped its authority, and that a vaccine requirement that could affect an estimated eighty million workers should be left to Congress or state authorities. Chief Justice Roberts was wary of the government's position. He repeated the claim made by Scott Keller, an NFIB lawyer, that COVID-19 transmission was "not a workplace issue [but] an out-in-the world issue." Keller said OSHA should at least distinguish among workplaces and consider the heightened risk in certain industries such as health care.[25]

The Court ultimately agreed with the NFIB that OSHA had exceeded its statutory authority. The majority's unsigned decision narrowly construed OSHA's power over "occupational" safety: "Although COVID-19 is a risk that occurs in many workplaces, it is not an occupational hazard in most. COVID-19 can and does spread at home, in schools, during sporting events, and everywhere else that people gather. That kind of universal risk is no different from the day-to-day dangers that all face from crime, air pollution, or any number of communicable diseases. Permitting OSHA to regulate the hazards of daily life—simply because most Americans have jobs and face those same risks while on the clock—would significantly expand OSHA's regulatory authority without clear congressional authorization."[26]

The Court described the OSHA rule covering workplaces of one hundred or more as a "blunt instrument" that "draws no distinctions based on industry or risk of exposure to COVID-19. Thus, most lifeguards and linemen face the same regulations as do medics and meatpackers." The majority's emphasis reflected a traditionally conservative interpretation, and the urgency of a pandemic failed to temper its disregard for regulatory solutions.

Three of the justices on the right wing then wrote their own opinion demonstrating they would go further to rein in agency power and expressing greater fears of federal encroachment on American life.

Gorsuch, joined by Thomas and Alito, said that regulatory agencies should act only through "a clear grant of authority from Congress." Congress may sometimes be "tempted to delegate power to agencies" to avoid being held accountable for unpopular policies, Gorsuch observed. But he warned, "If Congress could hand off all its legislative powers to unelected agency officials, it would dash the whole scheme of our Constitution and enable intrusions into the private lives and freedom of Americans by bare edict rather than only with the consent of their elected representatives."

The three dissenting justices, Breyer, Sotomayor, and Kagan, countered that OSHA had established that COVID-19 posed distinct risks to workers across all sectors of industry and the economy. "COVID-19 spreads more widely in workplaces than in other venues because more people spend more time together there," they wrote. In what would amount to the ringing of a public-health alarm bell, they added: "In the face of a still-raging pandemic, this Court tells the agency charged with protecting worker safety that it may not do so in all the workplaces needed. As disease and death continue to mount, this Court tells the agency that it cannot respond in the most effective way possible." In a separate case decided the same day, *Biden v. Missouri,* the Court did allow the secretary of health and human services to impose a vaccine mandate on workers at hospitals, nursing homes, and other places that received federal Medicare and Medicaid funding. That policy covered an estimated ten million health care workers. Roberts and Kavanaugh joined Breyer, Sotomayor, and Kagan for the majority in the case. Dissenting were Thomas, Alito, Gorsuch, and Barrett.[27]

Eugene Scalia, the eldest son of the late justice and a former secretary of labor under Trump, viewed the OSHA decision as "a significant setback" for an agency that fell within the Labor Department's authority. But Scalia also suggested that the Biden administration had it coming. In a *Wall Street Journal* column, Scalia contended that the administration overreached in attempting to invoke "emergency" authority to impose the vaccine requirement on large employers, especially in light of the Roberts Court's antiregulatory emphasis. "Now the court's decision limits OSHA's reach to places where the virus poses 'special' danger because of 'particular' features of the job or work-place," wrote Scalia, whose own conservative instincts were to reduce job-safety mandates. "OSHA will have to proceed more narrowly and cautiously than before its ill-fated rule—a reminder that when an agency stretches its power too far, it can end up with less authority than it had before." Coming to the case with his own predisposition, Scalia nonetheless accurately sized up the new Court: "All of President Trump's appointees are arguably more interested than the justices they replaced in articulating a jurisprudence that constrains federal agen-cies' ability to assume responsibilities ordinarily performed by Con-gress, or by the courts."[28]

Richard Lempert, a University of Michigan law professor and a senior fellow in governance studies at the Brookings Institution, con-nected the OSHA case to other Roberts Court patterns, including decisions curtailing voting rights. He noted that the Supreme Court since the mid-1930s had generally deferred to the other branches of government on policy. "The Justices' decisions were influenced by their political values, but there were places they would not go," he wrote in a column for the Brookings Institution. "The current Court major-ity, however, seems willing to go almost anywhere their politics takes them. They defer to state legislatures that seek to limit voting rights or gerrymander legislative seats, and declare obsolete Congressional laws designed to protect the ballot."[29]

Dissenting justices in the OSHA case had also struck an ominous note. "And then, there is this Court," they had written. "Its Members are elected by, and accountable to, no one. And we lack the background, competence, and expertise to assess workplace health and safety issues."

*This Court.* The bench was almost unrecognizable, particularly if one were comparing the current collection of justices to any grouping since the post–New Deal era. This was the era shaped by the Trump effect. Modern-day conservatives, particularly his three appointees, differed from their earlier counterparts. Past GOP-appointed justices, even with their aversion to big government and interest in protecting busi-ness, often deferred to regulators overseeing their specialized fields.

The late Justice Scalia, in fact, had early in his tenure been a strong proponent of the idea that judges should defer to agencies' interpretations of their authority under federal statutes. Fellow Reagan appointee Anthony Kennedy endorsed regulatory power, including in a 2007 case finding that the Environmental Protection Agency can regulate greenhouse gas emissions from new cars and trucks.[30]

The contrast with conservatives of the past was not limited to disputes over federal power. The new right wing seemed determined to transform the law, especially regarding reproductive rights and religious liberty.

Two weeks after the OSHA ruling was issued, Breyer formally announced that he would step down at the end of the 2021–2022 session. Having prolonged his decision and shaken Democrats about the possible risk of GOP Senate interference, he chose an early point in the Court calendar to make it official. This would give Biden sufficient time to make a choice before the next term began. For good measure, Breyer said in his announcement that he would not leave until his successor was fully confirmed.[31]

There had already been so much disruption. It was difficult to fathom what would happen next, how much else could seemingly change overnight.

## Chapter 12

# "ZERO. NONE."

The justices were trying to act as if nothing were wrong. Chief Justice John Roberts smiled as he greeted lawyers, judges, and other luminaries in the Great Hall of the Supreme Court for a May 2, 2022, ceremony honoring the memory of the late justice John Paul Stevens. The chief chatted with Attorney General Merrick Garland, who once upon a time might have been a justice himself. Roberts then took his front-row seat, next to Clarence Thomas and Stephen Breyer, who was accompanied by his wife, Joanna. As always, the justices were positioned in order of seniority. Behind Roberts were the more-junior justices and some spouses, including Amy Coney Barrett, at the time the newest justice, with her husband, Jesse Barrett. Sonia Sotomayor had been talking cheerfully with them. Only one of the nine was not yet present, Samuel Alito.[1]

The memorial, arranged by Supreme Court lawyers for Stevens, who had died in July 2019, had been postponed during the pandemic. COVID-19 was still a threat, and some people still wore masks to avoid infection, but scheduling the Stevens event for this first Monday in May seemed safe, and overdue. The Court had just finished its April oral argument session, the last for the annual term. It appeared that the justices could get a breather. It was happenstance, then, that a few days before the Stevens observance they received the news that a ninety-eight-page first-draft opinion in an abortion rights case had somehow been leaked. It was in the hands of Politico and about to be made public by the news entity. The justices had immediately begun some damage control—trying to ensure that their internal computer system was secure—but they were at a loss for how the breach had occurred and unsure of exactly when the draft of *Dobbs v. Jackson Women's Health Organization* would be published.

Virtually everyone else in the Great Hall that Monday afternoon was unaware of the suspense surrounding this most important case of the annual session, arguably the most important case in decades, a case that had the potential to change everything for women and for the Court's standing in America. Alito had written and circulated the draft opinion, which was dated February 10, to his colleagues some three months before. Earlier, just after December oral arguments in the dispute, the nine had voted privately on *Dobbs*. Five justices on the far-right wing had the majority. But it was a close vote, effectively 5–1–3, with Roberts in the middle, voting to uphold a Mississippi fifteen-week abortion ban but stopping short of reversing the 1973 case of *Roe v. Wade*. And with the fractious subject of abortion, there was inevitably a question of whether that (still private) five-justice majority would hold. Less than a week earlier, on April 26, a *Wall Street Journal* editorial had speculated that there was a majority to overturn *Roe* based on the December oral arguments, but the paper warned of a "ferocious lobbying campaign" and the possibility that Roberts might lure one of the conservatives in the majority away for a compromise decision. All internal debate was closely held at this point, and what I had been able to learn from my sources indicated that Roberts had *not* made progress with a compromise position that would preserve some right to abortion. But the *Wall Street Journal* editorial could not be dismissed. Its writers, who appeared to favor the reversal of *Roe*, were connected through mutual friends to the conservative justices. In the past, such as in the *Bostock* LGBTQ case, the *Journal* had obtained early, reliable information. Their editorial could not help but provoke questions among close Court watchers about whether Roberts was indeed making headway that the *Wall Street Journal* hoped to stanch.[2]

Alito finally entered the Great Hall. Arriving from the rear, he walked quickly up the center row, between the sets of chairs, toward the elevated speaker's platform. He was directed to his place, at the far right of the front row, next to Stephen and Joanna Breyer. U.S. solicitor general Elizabeth Prelogar then opened the memorial, leading the way for former law clerks and Stevens's granddaughter Hannah Mullen, a Georgetown University Law clinical fellow, to pay tribute to the justice whose portrait graced the front of the room, beside the elevated speaker's platform, which was set off by two large elegant vases of flowers.

After the memorial events—which included a private session in the courtroom where Stevens's accomplishments were read aloud and the bar resolutions in memory and appreciation of the justice's life, work, and service were accepted—the justices went their separate ways.[3] They were not scheduled to be together for another ten days, at which point they would meet in a private conference on pending cases. Several hours passed that Monday night.

Politico's story and the accompanying first-draft *Dobbs* opinion were published online at 8:32 P.M., just as the outlet's emailed "Breaking News" alert blasted across computer screens. The alert echoed the first lines of the story: "The Supreme Court has voted to strike down the landmark *Roe v. Wade* decision, according to an initial draft majority opinion written by Justice Samuel Alito circulated inside the court and obtained by POLITICO. . . . '*Roe* was egregiously wrong from the start,' Alito writes."[4]

The news was shocking in every way, in the sheer substance of what the justices apparently were about to declare and in the manner in which it was disclosed. Never before had such an extensive first-draft opinion been leaked and published at such an early stage of negotiations. The document that Politico posted appeared real, as astonishing as it was. (Roberts confirmed the draft's authenticity the next day.) A Supreme Court majority was about to obliterate a constitutional right.

The draft was stridently written, an audacious dismissal of a fundamental right granted nearly a half century earlier. Alito's historical sources were both strange (reaching back to English law that treated a woman who undertook abortion as a "murderess") and limited: "Until the latter part of the 20th century, there was no support in American law for a constitutional right to obtain an abortion. Zero. None." Further, Alito's rejection of *Roe*'s right to privacy, because it was not explicitly enumerated in the Constitution, necessarily cast doubt on such rights as access to contraceptives (as the Court had granted in 1965); interracial marriage (as enshrined in 1967); and same-sex marriage (as declared in 2015).[5]

Even with a Russian invasion of Ukraine then preoccupying the United States and the rest of the world, television and newspaper sites interrupted their scheduled programming that May 2 evening to announce the disclosure of the draft opinion and the potential consequences. Women's rights advocates were not alone in voicing objections. The Alito draft proposed to erase a swath of privacy protections. Protesters began gathering in front of the Court building, then moved, over the next days, to the justices' homes. Court officials erected an eight-foot-high fence and placed concrete blocks around the building. "AREA CLOSED: By order of Supreme Court Marshal," read the signs on the fence.

The Supreme Court had first granted the constitutional right to abortion in a case that began with a Texas carnival worker who said she was raped and wanted to end the pregnancy. By a 7–2 vote, the justices struck down a Texas law that criminalized the procedure and ruled that the Fourteenth Amendment's due process guarantee of personal liberty covered a woman's right to end a pregnancy. The bench at the time was dominated by Republican appointees whose approach to the law ran the ideological spectrum. Justice Harry Blackmun, a former in-house attorney at the Mayo Clinic and lower-court judge appointed by President Richard Nixon in 1970, wrote the opinion. After weeks of discussions with his colleagues over the interests of the woman, her physician, and the fetus, Blackmun wrote that women must have the choice to abort a fetus up to the point of viability—that is, when the fetus could live outside the womb. Signing that 1973 decision were Chief Justice Warren Burger, another Nixon appointee, and Justices William O. Douglas (appointed by Franklin D. Roosevelt), William Brennan (Dwight Eisenhower), Potter Stewart (also Eisenhower), Thurgood Marshall (Lyndon B. Johnson), and Lewis F. Powell Jr. (Nixon); dissenting were Byron R. White (John F. Kennedy) and William Rehnquist (Nixon).[6]

That seven-justice majority had not come easily. Because of illnesses and retirements, *Roe v. Wade* had to be argued twice, and Justice Brennan wrote in his personal account of *Roe*, available in his papers at the Library of Congress, that initially "it looked extremely doubtful that there would be a majority for the position that restrictive abortion laws are unconstitutional." Brennan, it should be noted, was the only Catholic justice at the time. He recorded in his history of the case that within a week of the January 22 ruling, "the letters were coming in at the rate of 2000–3000 a day and continued to do so at least a month. I, the only Catholic on the Court, and Justice Blackmun, the author of the opinion, received the bulk of the mail. The rhetoric and tone of the majority of the letters was extremely vitriolic."[7]

The religious makeup of the 1973 Court contrasted with that of the bench in 2022, when six of the nine sitting justices were Catholic (Roberts, Thomas, Alito, Sotomayor, Kavanaugh, and Barrett) and a seventh justice had been raised Catholic (Gorsuch). As Republican presidents sought out nominees averse to *Roe*, they gravitated toward Catholic jurists.

Opposition to *Roe* in the 1970s came largely from Catholics who believed that life began at conception and that abortion was akin to murder. President Nixon hadn't even commented publicly on the decision, an indication of how little abortion rights were then knotted with politics. In time, the religious coalition broadened. Evangelicals mobilized as part of the Moral Majority during the 1980 election of Ronald Reagan. Republican presidents continued to capitalize on the issue, and Donald Trump took it the furthest with his 2016 campaign vow to appoint Supreme Court justices who would roll back abortion rights.

In 1992, the Court affirmed the central holding of *Roe* by a 5–4 vote in the case of *Planned Parenthood of Southeastern Pennsylvania v. Casey*. With five Republican appointees in the majority, the Court endorsed the viability line, estimated at about twenty-three weeks.[8] The justices who crafted the controlling plurality opinion—Sandra Day O'Connor, Anthony Kennedy, and David Souter—wrote that government could not put an "undue burden" on women seeking abortion before the fetus could live on its own. They said an undue burden exists when a state places "substantial" obstacles in a woman's path. On the day *Casey* was announced, O'Connor said from the bench, "Some of us as individuals find abortion offensive to our most basic principles of morality, but that can't control our decision. Our obligation is to define the liberty of all, not to mandate our own moral code." Souter voiced consideration for individual choices and the Court's own reputation, asserting that "countless people . . . have organized intimate relationships and made choices that define their views of themselves and their places in society in the two decades since [*Roe*] was handed down." Of the institution that he had joined just two years earlier, following his appointment by George H. W. Bush, Souter said, "Like the character of an individual, the legitimacy of the Court must be earned over time."[9]

The first Bush administration, notwithstanding the Souter appointment, had continued Reagan's opposition to abortion (with the help of then–deputy U.S. solicitor general John Roberts).[10] Pressures from those administrations added to internal tensions and shifting votes in 1992. On May 29, one month before the final ruling would be announced, Kennedy, who became the crucial fifth vote to uphold *Roe,* penned a note to Blackmun that said, "I need to see you as soon as you have a few free moments. I want to tell you about some developments in Planned Parenthood v. Casey, and at least part of what I say should come as welcome news."[11]

That history offered a reminder that decisions in momentous cases could be in flux until the final weeks.

The first test of abortion rights with two of the Trump appointees, Gorsuch and Kavanagh, had occurred in 2020 in a Louisiana dispute. Gorsuch and Kavanaugh dissented in that case, *June Medical Services v. Russo,* along with Thomas and Alito, as the justices again reinforced the right of a woman to end a pregnancy without undue government burden. The majority struck down a Louisiana credentialing requirement for physicians that would have closed clinics in the state. Roberts cast the deciding vote based on precedent from a similar 2016 Texas case, even as he applied a legal rationale that enhanced the ability of states to reduce access to abortion through restrictions on clinics and physicians.[12]

The Court might have remained 5–4 on whether to overrule *Roe*, as it had been for decades, with the decision upheld even as states obtained greater latitude for regulation. But everything changed after Ruth Bader Ginsburg died and Amy Coney Barrett was sworn in to replace her. Barrett's succession occurred as Mississippi officials were appealing a lower-court decision against the state ban on abortion at fifteen weeks of pregnancy. The state had lost in lower courts because the prohibition directly clashed with the constitutional guarantee embodied in *Roe* and *Casey*. Signed by Republican governor Phil Bryant in 2018, the law had no exceptions for incidents of rape or incest.

The fate of Mississippi's appeal was tightly bound up with the death of the liberal Ginsburg and the elevation of the conservative Barrett. Mississippi officials first filed their petition for certiorari in *Dobbs v. Jackson Women's Health Organization* on June 15, 2020, when Ginsburg was still serving. (The name of Thomas Dobbs, Mississippi's top health officer, was automatically used in the lawsuit.) Jackson Women's Health Organization, which had started the challenge to Mississippi's prohibition, submitted its response to the Dobbs petition later that summer, urging the justices not to take up the case. Lawyers for the abortion providers noted that lower appeals court judges had been following the strictures of *Roe* and *Casey*, striking down all previability bans.[13]

With the filings from the two sides complete, the Supreme Court on September 2 placed *Dobbs* on the schedule for the justices' private September 29 conference. That September 29 session would have offered the justices their first opportunity to either accept the appeal or reject the case. At that early-September point, the petition might have been denied. The Court had never agreed to take up a dispute over fetal viability. There was a presumption in the lower courts, as seen in the Fifth Circuit that ruled against Mississippi, that the viability firewall was established precedent.

There would have been, perhaps, sentiment among four justices (Thomas, Alito, Gorsuch, and Kavanaugh) to reexamine the underpinnings of *Roe* and *Casey*. But while it took four votes to grant a petition for full briefing and oral arguments, it required five to actually decide a case. The justices on the far right were simply not guaranteed a fifth vote. Roberts, the only other member of the Court who had expressed opposition to abortion rights, had just voted to strike down Louisiana's tough regulation of physicians who performed abortion. There was no sign inside that the chief justice wanted to reconsider *Roe v. Wade* wholesale. In fact, it was the opposite. Trump was still in office, and Roberts was trying to defuse politically charged cases.

All such calculations became meaningless on September 18, the day Ginsburg died, eleven days before the justices would have had their first opportunity to vote on the petition. The Court necessarily rescheduled it, and the first private session with Barrett in place was October 30. But Barrett, who had been sworn in just four days earlier, declined to participate in several cases around this time, including on early matters related to the 2020 presidential election.

Barrett wanted more time to weigh the *Dobbs* petition, not just weeks, but months. Not since 1992 had the justices heard an appeal that directly challenged the principle that states were forbidden from banning abortions before the fetus could live outside the womb. Yet there was something bigger stirring, driven by the sense among anti-abortion advocates that their moment might have finally arrived with Barrett's appointment.

Of the other longer-serving justices, only Thomas had outright said he wanted to reverse *Roe*, asserting that the Court's abortion-related jurisprudence had "spiraled out of control." Still, Alito, Gorsuch, and Kavanaugh had sufficient records to suggest they might be bolder if their numbers were stronger. Barrett's appointment brought home that prospect.[14]

Months passed, and the justices continued to postpone word on whether they would take up the *Dobbs* case or deny it. As Barrett kept her cards close, some conservative colleagues described her as "nervous" about how to proceed, while liberals inside thought, perhaps, that she was justifiably torn about how far the Court should go. All hesitancy ended in May 2021, after the Mississippi petition had been rescheduled more than twenty times. The Court issued an order on May 17 stating that it would hear the state's appeal. But the Court said that it was confining its consideration to just one question: "whether all pre-viability prohibitions on elective abortions are unconstitutional." Secondary questions Mississippi had raised, as well as the fundamental issue of a constitutional right to abortion in the early weeks of pregnancy, were supposedly off the table.[15]

Still, even with the limited question, the potential consequences of the case were colossal. *Roe*'s viability standard was nearly fifty years old. As the Court in 1973 had tried to balance a woman's interests with those of the fetus, it had chosen viability, because, the majority wrote, "the fetus then presumably has the capability of meaningful life outside the mother's womb. State regulation protective of fetal life after viability thus has both logical and biological justifications."[16]

Advocacy groups on both sides debated its significance—most abortions in America occurred in the first trimester, well before twenty-three weeks. Yet abortion rights supporters believed that if the line were breached in a case involving a fifteen-week prohibition, it would be just a matter of time before bans were permitted down to ten weeks or even six weeks. Mississippi attorney general Lynn Fitch and solicitor general Scott Stewart were already moving past such scenarios. They urged the Supreme Court in new filings to eviscerate the abortion right completely. They argued that *Roe* and *Casey* were "egregiously wrong" (language that Alito later echoed in his opinion) and should be wholly reversed.[17]

As spring turned to summer in 2021, other Republican-run states were inspired by the presence of Barrett and the new makeup of the Court. The Texas legislature passed a law that banned abortions at the first sign of cardiac activity, roughly six weeks. Officials added a cunning twist to their "heartbeat law," delegating the enforcement of the ban to private citizens. It was a way to insulate state officials from lawsuits and try to ensure that judges would not block enforcement of the law. The provision empowered private citizens to sue anyone who performed an abortion or assisted a woman in ending her pregnancy. Any person who won such a case could obtain at least $10,000 in damages.[18]

It was a sign of what was to come in the Mississippi case that when Whole Woman's Health and other abortion providers asked the Supreme Court to try to prevent the Texas law from taking effect on September 1, the five-member far-right bloc denied the appeal. After subsequent oral arguments and briefing, the five justices held to their position that most state officials were shielded from clinic lawsuits. Gorsuch wrote the opinion, joined by Thomas, Alito, Kavanaugh, and Barrett. Their action, compromising the role of the high court itself to preserve constitutional rights, forced Texas women seeking to end a pregnancy to continue traveling to neighboring states for care, provided they even had the resources.

Dissenting in the December 10 ruling, issued more than three months after the Court had allowed Texas's Senate Bill 8 (SB 8) to take effect, Justice Sotomayor wrote sharply of the consequences to women in the second-most-populous state, saying that "the law has threatened abortion care providers with the prospect of essentially unlimited suits for damages, brought anywhere in Texas by private bounty hunters, for taking any action to assist women in exercising their constitutional right to choose. The chilling effect has been near total. . . . The Court should have put an end to this madness months ago, before S. B. 8 first went into effect."[19]

But for the majority, this was not madness. Five justices wanted an end to *Roe*, irrespective of the years of precedent and irrespective of what they had told senators during their confirmation hearings. They were ready to seize the moment. Roberts, the sixth conservative, was losing leverage in this area of the law—a surprising development for a jurist who had been a critic of abortion rights and a lifelong Catholic whose wife, Jane, had provided pro bono legal counsel to Feminists for Life.

The Texas SB 8 case was just the first step. That same December, the justices heard arguments in the Mississippi case unencumbered by the procedural complications of the Texas law. Roberts tried to offer a compromise during the arguments, suggesting that the Court uphold the fifteen-week ban, lifting the viability standard, but preserve some right to abortion in the early weeks of pregnancy. He suggested that the fetal-viability line had been arbitrarily imposed and should not be viewed as part of *Roe*'s core holding. He deemed the references to viability as more of a legal aside, "dicta." As much as he was ready to diminish *Roe* to stop its outright demise, his proposition required at least one of the five other conservatives to join him for a majority (with the liberals who did not want to overturn any of *Roe* but would provide the votes to stop its total reversal).[20]

There would be no takers. During arguments, Kavanaugh, who on other occasions had inched toward Roberts in a middle ground, signaled he wanted state legislatures to assume control of abortion rights. He presented a vision of the Constitution devoid of an abortion right, in his words "neither pro-life nor pro-choice." Barrett separately questioned whether any burden women experienced in carrying a pregnancy to term would be ameliorated by state laws allowing women to bring newborns as foundlings to fire stations, hospitals, or other designated locations.

"Why don't the safe haven laws take care of that problem?" Barrett asked. "It seems to me that it focuses the burden much more narrowly. There is, without question, an infringement on bodily autonomy, you know, which we have in other contexts, like vaccines. However, it doesn't seem to me to follow that pregnancy and then parenthood are all part of the same burden."

Julie Rikelman, who had been the lead lawyer against a Louisiana abortion restriction in 2020, was back before the Court, representing the Jackson Women's Health Organization of Mississippi. She responded to Barrett that a woman's right to privacy in abortion encompassed "bodily integrity" as well as "decisional autonomy and specifically decisions relating to childbearing, marriage and procreation.

"Even if some of those laws are new since *Casey*," Rikelman said,

the idea that a woman could place a child up for adoption has, of course, been true since *Roe,* so it's a consideration that the

Court already had before it when it decided those cases and adhered to the viability line. But, in addition, we don't just focus on
the burdens of parenting, and neither did *Roe* and *Casey*. Instead,
pregnancy itself is unique. It imposes unique physical demands
and risks on women and, in fact, has impact on all of their lives, on
their ability to care for other children, other family members, on
their ability to work. And, in particular, in Mississippi, those risks
are alarmingly high. It's 75 times more dangerous to give birth in
Mississippi than it is to have a pre-viability abortion, and those
risks are disproportionately threatening the lives of women of
color.

Rikelman had been born in Kiev, Ukraine, and immigrated to the
United States in 1979 as a child. She graduated from Harvard College in 1993 and then obtained her law degree there in 1997. She
had been the litigation director at the Center for Reproductive Rights
since 2011, after earlier working for law firms in Alaska and New
York and then becoming a counsel and vice president for litigation
for NBCUniversal. (Soon after the case was resolved at the Supreme
Court, President Biden nominated her to the Boston-based U.S. appellate court.)[21]

In the *Dobbs* case, Rikelman was fighting a losing battle, as were the
liberals. Sotomayor recalled the politics that had brought the Court
to this moment. She referred to remarks from Mississippi sponsors
of the abortion ban that implied they believed the new Court would
welcome the abortion prohibition. "Will this institution survive the
stench that this creates in the public perception that the Constitution
and its reading are just political acts?" Sotomayor asked, adding, "I
don't see how it is possible."

Mississippi solicitor general Scott Stewart answered Sotomayor, "I
think the concern about appearing political makes it absolutely imperative that the Court reach a decision well grounded in the Constitution, in text, structure, history, and tradition, and that carefully goes
through the *stare decisis* factors that we've laid out."

"*Casey* did that," Sotomayor responded.

"No, it didn't, Your Honor, respectfully," Stewart said.

The *Casey* court had examined constitutional history and explored the factors that would justify adherence to—or conversely, the reversal of—precedent. It chose steadfastness, writing, "The promise of constancy, once given, binds its maker for as long as the power to stand by the decision survives and the understanding of the issue has not changed so fundamentally as to render the commitment obsolete."[22] The justices in 1992 committed themselves to a vision of the Constitution enshrined by the Court nearly three decades earlier. Mississippi solicitor general Stewart simply did not share that vision.

Breyer and Kagan emphasized regard for precedent. "Usually there has to be a justification, a strong justification in a case like this beyond the fact that you think the case is wrong," said Kagan. "And I guess what strikes me when I look at this case is that, you know, not much has changed since *Roe* and *Casey.*" She observed that *Roe* had long divided Americans, with some people believing it "wrong" and others believing it "right"—a point that the Court in 1992 acknowledged and predicted would endure.

Stewart, a former law clerk to Justice Thomas who served as a deputy assistant attorney general in the Trump Department of Justice, countered that the intervening decades had only worsened the situation. *Roe* and *Casey,* he maintained, "adopt a right that purposefully leads to the termination of now millions of human lives."

After the arguments, the five justices on the right were ready to abolish *Roe.* I had learned of the vote from Court sources, but I continued to contemplate the possibility of switched votes and shifting views, as had happened in past abortion cases. The evidence, however, bore out how solid those five votes were. The leaked Alito draft was produced in about two months, relatively quickly for such a substantial case. And the justices who joined him before the ninety-eight-page document became public never wavered after the leak; perhaps they never wavered *because* of the disclosure. The Politico leak published in May cemented not only the vote count but also the acceptance of Alito's unsparing denigration of the justices who wrote *Roe* and *Casey* and his selective use of history.

Chief Justice Roberts, however, persisted. I learned that he continued for weeks to privately lobby fellow conservatives to save some element of a constitutional right to abortion.

As the end of the 2021–2022 session neared and the justices tried to meet their traditional end-of-June deadline, tensions were higher than usual because of the breach. The day after publication of the draft, Roberts had launched an investigation, appointing Marshal Gail Curley to oversee the search for a culprit. "To the extent this betrayal of the confidences of the Court was intended to undermine the integrity of our operations," Roberts vowed, "it will not succeed. The work of the Court will not be affected in any way."[23] But the new cloud of suspicion unnerved the justices' law clerks, who came under the most scrutiny. I learned that the marshal's team asked all the clerks to sign affidavits declaring that they had not leaked the document. Her staff also began trying to obtain cell phone details from clerks' private phones, which prompted alarm and drove some clerks with privacy worries to seek outside legal advice. (Labor attorneys and law professors described the measures as heavy-handed, even hypocritical, but not out of legal bounds.) Law clerks serve for a single term. Competition for these coveted spots (four per chamber) is fierce, and those selected are regarded within the profession as the elite of the elite. Most hold degrees from Ivy League law schools and have had experience as clerks for prominent lower-court judges.[24]

Perhaps it was logical to focus aggressively on the law clerks, who, unlike the full-time employees, would be leaving in July after the session ended. But they were not necessarily the only possible source of the disclosure. The draft document had been circulated among the justices' offices electronically and on paper. The marshal later had a team search the cell phones and laptops of full-time employees in the justices' chambers. Investigators apparently continued to hit dead ends.

The leak had the effect of surfacing the distrust among justices. Thomas, who usually spoke about how well the justices got along, told a Dallas audience in late May that the justices couldn't help but be looking over their shoulders, wondering who was responsible for the disclosure of the *Dobbs* draft. He pointedly contrasted relations with the Court atmosphere before 2005, when Roberts came on: "We actually trusted each other. We may have been a dysfunctional family, but we were family, and we loved it." Asked about the celebrated close friendship of the late Ginsburg and Scalia, Thomas said, "This is not the Court of that era. I sat with Ruth Ginsburg for almost 30 years. And she was actually an easy colleague for me. You knew where she was." It was a revealing comment from a justice who himself was known inside the Court for abhorring the kind of cagey negotiations Roberts often undertook.[25]

Amid the tensions from the unsolved disclosure and continued conflicts in the substance of cases, the justices tried for some sense of normalcy. Roberts followed through with a scheduled reunion of his current and previous law clerks on the first Saturday night in June. Kagan continued to break away for a few rounds of golf. Other justices kept up scheduled speaking engagements, barely referring to the leak.

All of the justices were aware of how much had changed in less than two years, since Barrett had succeeded Ginsburg. Thomas, who had often been a solo dissenter, was prevailing across the board. Both he and Alito were only in their early seventies, but they felt a sense of urgency, as if their time were limited. They were running the tables and taking advantage of the majority that they had. Breyer, Sotomayor, and Kagan were palpably frustrated in discussions with law clerks and in a few outside appearances, such as with lower-court judges. Just two years earlier, they had been at the center of major rulings for abortion rights, LGBTQ protections, and the preservation of the young immigrant "Dreamer" program. Just one year earlier, they had managed to be part of some compromises; for example, on religious liberties and Obamacare. Now they expected to win nothing.

Beyond the extraordinary abortion case underway, the justices were in the final weeks of negotiations over two important controversies regarding the separation of church and state and a dispute that would expand the Second Amendment right "to keep and bear arms." In the backdrop of the latter were ongoing mass shootings. In May alone, a gunman killed ten people in a Buffalo supermarket, and another shooter killed nineteen children and two teachers at an elementary school in Uvalde, Texas. Such episodes did not deter a six-justice majority, led by Thomas, in broadly expanding the 2008 *District of Columbia v. Heller* case that first proclaimed an individual right to bear arms. A five-justice majority had said then that the right extended to handguns in the home for self-defense.[26]

For more than a decade since, Thomas and other conservatives had sought to go further on Second Amendment rights but had lacked the backing of a majority. "It is extremely improbable that the Framers understood the Second Amendment to protect little more than carrying a gun from the bedroom to the kitchen," Thomas wrote in 2020, as the Court declined a dispute over a New Jersey gun restriction.[27]

But Barrett bolstered the conservative majority, enabling Thomas to carry out his vision of the Second Amendment. He was joined by all his colleagues on the right wing, including Roberts—a sign that there was new strength in numbers. The case, *New York State Rifle & Pistol Association v. Bruen,* marked the first time the justices declared a right to carry a weapon outside the home. The majority also adopted a new framework for reviewing gun laws, discarding a balancing approach that had been employed by lower courts. Whether gun restrictions can stand, Thomas wrote, must be measured by the nation's history, not by a state's assertion of urgent public safety interests. He said that the Second Amendment "requires courts to assess whether modern firearms regulations are consistent with the Second Amendment's text and historical understanding" dating to the late eighteenth century. Thomas acknowledged that the Court was lifting up the Second Amendment over other constitutional rights by discarding the usual deference to legislative interests, explaining, "The Second Amendment 'is the very product of an interest balancing by the people' and it 'surely elevates above all other interests the right of law-abiding, responsible citizens to use arms' for self-defense."[28]

Dissenters, the three liberals as usual, argued that neither the Constitution nor the 2008 *Heller* decision demanded such regard for Second Amendment rights. In a practical vein, Breyer, joined by Sotomayor and Kagan, warned that "firearms in public present a number of dangers, ranging from mass shootings to road rage killings, and are responsible for many deaths and injuries in the United States." Alito, who like Thomas had been pushing for greater gun rights for years, wrote a separate statement that acerbically addressed a list of mass shootings compiled by Breyer. "How does the dissent account for the fact that one of the mass shootings near the top of its list took place in Buffalo?" he asked with astounding bluntness about the recent tragedy. "The New York law at issue in this case obviously did not stop that perpetrator."

Disputes over the separation of church and state similarly broke along 6–3 lines. One of the cases extended the 2017 decision in *Trinity Lutheran Church of Columbia v. Comer,* when Roberts began setting down pieces toward a decision requiring states that subsidize private education to include schools that promote religious beliefs. The new controversy from Maine developed, as the 2017 Missouri case had, at the intersection of the First Amendment's two religion clauses, prohibiting the government's "establishment of religion" and the "free exercise thereof." The disputed Maine program provided money for students to attend private schools in areas that lacked a public high school, but it excluded sectarian institutions, defined in part as those "associated with a particular faith or belief system and which, in addition to teaching academic subjects, promotes the faith or belief system with which it is associated." In the opinion by Roberts, the Court struck down the Maine exclusion, saying it breached the free exercise of religion. The Court denied the state's establishment concerns, declaring, "A State's antiestablishment interest does not justify enactments that exclude some members of the community from an otherwise generally available public benefit because of their religious exercise."[29]

Roberts contended that the new ruling flowed fully from principles applied in earlier cases. But that was not quite right, because the earlier cases concerned the mere "status" or "character" of a church entity that claimed bias, not how the public funds were to be used. In the case five years earlier, Roberts had said that Missouri unconstitutionally excluded the Trinity Lutheran Church's Child Learning Center based on its religious status from the grant program for playground surfaces made from recycled tires. He had asserted that his rationale was narrow and had added a footnote that the case "involves express discrimination based on religious identity with respect to playground resurfacing." Roberts repeated the status-versus-use distinction in 2020's *Espinoza v. Montana Department of Revenue,* when he wrote that states may not bar a school from participating in a student-aid program solely because of a school's religious character.

Unlike those cases, the Maine issue tested whether government was constitutionally required to provide funds that would be used for religious education. And Roberts demonstrated that he was never committed to the earlier distinction. "In *Trinity Lutheran* and *Espinoza,* we held that the Free Exercise Clause forbids discrimination on the basis of religious status," he wrote. "But those decisions never suggested that use-based discrimination is any less offensive to the Free Exercise Clause."

Dissenting liberals questioned what was to come when states suddenly "must" pay for religious education. Wrote Breyer, "Does that transformation mean that a school district that pays for public schools must pay equivalent funds to parents who wish to send their children to religious schools? Does it mean that school districts that give vouchers for use at charter schools must pay equivalent funds to parents who wish to give their children a religious education?" Breyer contended that the Roberts majority paid "almost no attention to the words" of the First Amendment's first clause prohibiting establishment of religion, "while giving almost exclusive attention to the words in the second" guaranteeing the free exercise of religion.

Sotomayor wrote a separate statement recalling her sentiment of five years earlier. "I warned in *Trinity Lutheran* . . . that the Court's analysis could 'be manipulated,'" she said. Her message: "This Court should not have started down this path five years ago."

Less than a week later, in yet another case reinforcing the pattern benefitting religious conservatives, the six-justice majority sided with a Washington State high school football coach, Joseph Kennedy, who was suspended after he continued to pray at midfield after games. The Court overturned a lower-court decision that had accepted the Bremerton School District's establishment concerns, that observers would think the public school district had impermissibly endorsed religion or exposed student athletes to coercion. The majority again put an emphasis on the First Amendment's "free exercise" guarantee over the prohibition on government "establishment of religion."[30]

The Court discarded the traditional "endorsement" standard, while also minimizing the possibility of student coercion. Gorsuch, writing for the majority, said that Kennedy was engaged in a personal religious observance—not acting as a school employee—when he prayed after the game. In disciplining the coach, the majority said, the school district infringed free speech and free exercise rights. The Court was concerned about "censorship and suppression," and said judges resolving such religious-discrimination claims should look to "historical practices" and focus on the original meaning of First Amendment protections.

The breadth of the decision was likely to encourage more challenges by religious adherents and increase displays of religion in schools and other public places—a point that troubled dissenting liberals. They said that prayer led by any school official "strikes at the core of our constitutional protections for the religious liberty of students and their parents." In the dissenting opinion, written by Sotomayor, the three on the left contended that the majority had misconstrued the facts of the case and the disruptive effect of Kennedy's prayers on the field. They said that the coach's conduct was far from solitary, and they included in their opinion photos of Kennedy surrounded by kneeling players. They said that the majority's decision would dilute religious liberty protections and decades of precedent forbidding school-sponsored prayer, dating as far back as *Engel v. Vitale* (1962).

At the same time that the supermajority prevailed on culture-war issues of guns and religion, it moved ahead on a pattern important to corporate America and conservatives seeking less government regulation of American life. The decision in *West Virginia v. Environmental*

*Protection Agency* further fulfilled an enduring agenda item of former White House counsel Don McGahn. "There is a coherent plan here," McGahn had told an audience of the Conservative Political Action Conference in 2018, "where actually the judicial selection and the deregulatory effort are really the flip side of the same coin."[31]

The justices, again by a 6–3 vote, curtailed federal regulatory authority over climate change initiatives in a decision with implications for environmental protection, public health, and consumer safety efforts. Written by Roberts, the ruling built on decisions from 2020, invalidating the structure of the Consumer Financial Protection Bureau, and early 2022, throwing out the Occupational Safety and Health Administration's vaccine requirement for large employers.

In the new decision, the Roberts majority ruled that an Environmental Protection Agency (EPA) program to limit carbon dioxide emissions at coal-fired power plants went beyond the agency's authority under the 1970 Clean Air Act. Roberts allowed that limiting emissions and forcing a transition from coal to provide electricity might be a "sensible" way to address the climate change crisis. "But it is not plausible that Congress gave EPA the authority to adopt on its own such a regulatory scheme in" the Clean Air Act, he said. Crucially, Roberts said that regulations that raise "major questions," as in the climate-change case at hand, should face greater judicial scrutiny and be permitted only if an agency can "point to clear congressional authorization" for its action. In such situations, he said, courts "expect Congress to speak clearly if it wishes to assign to an agency decisions of vast economic and political significance." The decision represented yet another departure from the principle that a court should defer to agencies' interpretations of their statutory authority, as spelled out in the 1984 *Chevron v. Natural Resources Defense Council* decision.

Gorsuch, who had long argued against the principle of agency deference embodied in *Chevron*, wrote a concurring opinion that commended the approach expressed in Roberts's requirement of "clear congressional authorization" for agency action yet added his own stamp. With a possible reference to former president Barack Obama's mantra in the face of congressional inaction ("I've got a pen, and I've got a phone"), Gorsuch said, "When Congress seems slow to solve problems, it may be only natural that those in the Executive Branch might seek to take matters into their own hands. But the Constitution does not authorize agencies to use pen-and-phone regulations as substitutes for laws passed by the people's representatives."

Such was the attitude that originally drew McGahn to Gorsuch. The former White House counsel had told a 2020 audience that he was aware that Gorsuch, even as a lower U.S. appellate judge, had questioned so-called Chevron deference, and McGahn added, "Ironically, or maybe not ironically, the EPA administrator at the time of *Chevron* was Neil Gorsuch's mother. She tussled with the bureaucracy. It did not end well." (One of the consolidated cases leading to the *Chevron v. Natural Resources Defense Council* ruling indeed began during the Anne Gorsuch stewardship; it was called *Natural Resources Defense Council v. Gorsuch*.)[32]

The liberal justices dissented from the new EPA case. They observed that the Court had been obstructing the 2015 Clean Power Plan from the start, when in an unprecedented move the justices blocked the program in 2016 while it was still being reviewed in lower courts. Kagan, joined by Breyer and Sotomayor, wrote, "The Court today prevents congressionally authorized agency action to curb power plants' carbon dioxide emissions. The Court appoints itself—instead of Congress or the expert agency—the decision-maker on climate policy. I cannot think of many things more frightening."[33]

The leaked draft in the *Dobbs* case had put people on notice. But the actual decision, issued on June 24, managed to be breathtaking nonetheless. The bloc that had come together just twenty months earlier, with the appointment of Barrett, definitively overturned a half century of women's abortion rights in the United States. The sweep of the decision was on its own remarkable. Among the few modest changes Alito made from the draft was elimination of the flip commentary: "Zero. None." But those words remained immortal because of the strikingly abrasive way Alito had first declared, in his draft, that there was no support for a right to abortion in the Constitution and because that attitude still pervaded the final opinion.[34]

As he denigrated *Roe* and *Casey,* Alito wrote that

> the Constitution makes no reference to abortion, and no such right is implicitly protected by any constitutional provision, including the one on which the defenders of *Roe* and *Casey* now chiefly rely—the Due Process Clause of the Fourteenth Amendment. That provision has been held to guarantee some rights that are not mentioned in the Constitution, but any such right must be "deeply rooted in this Nation's history and tradition" and "implicit in the concept of ordered liberty." The right to abortion does not fall within this category.

The abortion right differs from other rights within the Fourteenth Amendment's protection of "liberty," Alito said, "because it destroys what those decisions called 'fetal life' and what the law now before us describes as an 'unborn human being.'" Alito contended that the reasoning of the opinion would not extend to other due process rights, such as same-sex marriage. But Thomas wrote separately—and alone—calling for future reconsideration of cases such as *Obergefell v. Hodges* (a right to same-sex marriage), *Lawrence v. Texas* (the right of same-sex couples to engage in intimate sexual acts), and *Griswold v. Connecticut* (the right to obtain contraceptives).

Since 1973, when the court by a 7–2 vote cemented a right to privacy for the abortion choice, fifteen new justices had joined the bench. All but six of them had endorsed *Roe* to some extent. Five of those made up the majority in *Dobbs.* They separated themselves from their predecessors by highlighting the interests of the fetus, rather than a women's right to choose what happens to her pregnancy.

Despite their protestations on behalf of precedent during their confirmation hearings, all three Trump appointees were with Alito and Thomas. They could not have reached a majority if any one of the three had pulled away. Roberts, in an opinion concurring only in the judgment, said he agreed that the Mississippi fifteen-week ban should be upheld, yet "the Court's decision to overrule *Roe* and *Casey* is a serious jolt to the legal system—regardless of how you view those cases."[35]

The chief justice's effort to persuade even just one colleague to join his compromise was difficult at the outset, but the May leak of the draft opinion and public revelation of the votes made the endeavor all but impossible. He usually negotiated in private, without anyone beyond the Court knowing how votes were initially cast. Even after the leak, Roberts pressed on, perhaps hoping he still had a chance with Kavanaugh, who in the past had been open to Roberts's persuasion. They shared Catholic roots, Ivy League educations, and GOP administration experience. Their homes in Maryland were so close to each other that once the *Dobbs* draft leaked and protests began, demonstrators could visit both homes on the same evening.[36]

Roberts himself had previously switched votes late in deliberations on other cases. After the leak, in late May and early June, the justices on the far right feared Roberts could disrupt their majority, so they pressed their colleagues to try to hasten release of the final decision in the *Dobbs* case, lest anything suddenly threaten their majority. Their fears were likely for naught. Kavanaugh stuck with his vote to reverse *Roe*.

In the end, the sixty-seven-year-old chief justice finishing his seventeenth session also confessed to a lack of confidence, writing, "Both the Court's opinion and the dissent display a relentless freedom from doubt on the legal issue that I cannot share. . . . I am not sure, for example, that a ban on terminating a pregnancy from the moment of conception must be treated the same under the Constitution as a ban after fifteen weeks."

The three liberals wrote a rare joint dissenting opinion insisting that the Court had "betray[ed] its guiding principles." As much as Breyer, Sotomayor, and Kagan lamented the fate of the Court itself, they said they felt more sorrow "for the many millions of American women who have today lost a fundamental constitutional protection." The dissenters warned where the majority might go next: "No one should be confident that this majority is done with its work," they wrote. "The right *Roe* and *Casey* recognized does not stand alone. To the contrary, the

Court has linked it for decades to other settled freedoms involving bodily integrity, familial relationships, and procreation."

At another time, at least one of them might have read portions of a dissent from the bench in a courtroom filled with spectators. But the Court building was closed, the justices shielded from public view, releasing their opinions electronically. The voice of the majority was on a computer screen or printout, as was the voice of the dissent. Yet the force of each was undeniable. The 2022 *Dobbs* decision was destined to become among the most consequential ever, paired with the 1973 *Roe v. Wade*. Perhaps most notable among other such historical pairings, the 1954 *Brown v. Board of Education* decision, which ended the "separate but equal" doctrine and began the desegregation of schools, was tied to *Plessy v. Ferguson,* the 1896 decision that upheld and decreed separate accommodations for Black and white people.

Starkly, where *Brown* ensured rights, *Dobbs* eliminated them.

Among those joining religious conservatives in praise for the ruling was Senate GOP leader Mitch McConnell, who had shaped the current Court more than nearly anyone. He deemed the decision "courageous and correct" and said, "Millions of Americans have spent half a century praying, marching, and working toward today's historic victories for the rule of law and for innocent life. I have been proud to stand with them throughout our long journey and I share their joy today."[37]

Abortion opponents had waited a long time, to be sure. But the Trump appointees brought speed, allowing Alito to write for the majority, as he turned away Roberts's plea for more time, "It is far better—for this Court and the country—to face up to the real issue without further delay."

With the *Dobbs* decision as its capstone, the justices reordered every part of American life as the session came to a close, evoking dissenters' reference in an earlier case to the "restless and newly constituted Court." This was the Court of the future, too. The three Trump appointees were still in their fifties. Thomas was seventy-four and Alito seventy-two, and both could serve another decade.[38]

On the last day of the session, June 30, at noon, eighty-three-year-old Justice Breyer officially retired. He was then succeeded by fifty-one-year-old Ketanji Brown Jackson, the nation's first African American woman justice. Her appointment, following a fellow liberal and the justice for whom she once served as a law clerk, did not displace the conservative supermajority at all.

Yet this was a pivotal moment in the Court's 233-year history. Jackson, whom President Biden had first put on the D.C. Circuit appellate court, spoke when she was selected for the high court of the pioneers who had proceeded her. She observed that she shared a birthday with Constance Baker Motley, the first Black woman appointed as a federal judge. President Lyndon Johnson named Motley, who died in 2005, to a U.S. district court seat in 1966. "We were born exactly 49 years to the day apart. Today, I proudly stand on Judge Motley's shoulders."[39]

Jackson had served as a federal public defender, and not since Thurgood Marshall, who helped found the NAACP Legal Defense Fund, had an appointee had significant experience representing criminal defendants. She was still working out her appellate approach, telling senators during her confirmation hearing, "Unlike some judges who come to appellate work from academia and who have some overarching theory of the law, I approach cases from experience, from practice and consistent with my constitutional obligations. So my philosophy is one in which I look at cases impartially, consistent with my independence as a judicial officer."[40] If Jackson were to sit on the high court as long as Breyer did, she would still be a justice in 2050.

Breyer had remained on the bench a year longer than progressive advocates had wanted. He thought he could make a difference on abortion rights, on gun control, and on any one of the major religion or regulatory authority rulings. Instead, he was left to dissent. It was a bleak moment for the justice, who had joined a far different Court in 1994. That was two years after *Planned Parenthood v. Casey*, when the earnest reconsideration—and then affirmation—of *Roe* made it nearly impossible to imagine a future reversal.

But in late 2022, greater erosion of rights seemed inevitable. The justices had already announced that in upcoming months they would reexamine voting rights and possibly accord state legislatures greater power over elections; consider an end to university affirmative action;

and weigh another challenge to a state civil rights law forbidding businesses that provide wedding-related services from discriminating against same-sex couples.

The Court had no middle, no center to hold. Conservatives were galvanized by their number. And Donald Trump, who had demonstrated so little respect for the law, truth, and democracy, had changed the balance for at least a generation.

# EPILOGUE

For months after the 2022–2023 session ended, the Supreme Court justices refused to acknowledge that their decisions had unsettled American life and undermined public trust in the judiciary. Chief Justice John Roberts insisted that criticism of the Court, as revealed in numerous opinion polls and commentary about the legitimacy of the judiciary, merely reflected public disagreement with the bottom-line judgments. Samuel Alito, who had written the Court's opinion reversing *Roe v. Wade*, made light of public criticism in July, but as condemnation continued into the autumn, Alito warned that "saying or implying that the Court is becoming an illegitimate institution or questioning our integrity crosses an important line."[1]

Other conservative justices avoided public events or spoke only to like-minded, friendly groups. By their choices, the justices fortified the country's red-versus-blue political polarization. Amy Coney Barrett appeared at an invitation-only conference organized by business executives in Big Sky, Montana. Her attendance continued a pattern of speeches at traditionally conservative venues. Her first major public appearance had been with Senate Republican powerhouse Mitch McConnell in Louisville.[2]

Similarly, when Alito first emerged on a public stage after issuing the decision ending *Roe*, he spoke at an event sponsored by Notre Dame Law School's Religious Liberty Initiative in Rome. He offered a studied defense of Supreme Court support for religious conservatism, and as such reinforced his opinion in *Dobbs v. Jackson Women's Health Organization*, which favored fetal life over a woman's right to choose whether to carry an early pregnancy to term. Alito referred to the actual decision only briefly—and, as was his way, caustically. "I had the honor this term of writing, I think, the only Supreme Court decision in the history of that institution that has been lambasted by a whole string of foreign leaders," Alito quipped. He continued to draw criticism in the fallout from the *Dobbs* decision and its early leak. The *New York Times* reported in November 2022 that a former antiabortion leader had told Chief Justice Roberts after the *Dobbs* disclosure that Alito had in 2014 privately revealed early information about the outcome of a case involving religious rights and the Affordable Care Act's contraceptive regulation. Alito denied the claim and Roberts declined to respond to reporters' questions. Related coverage in the *Times* and elsewhere pointed out the tight relationships between evangelical leaders and conservative jurists, reinforcing an appearance of the justices catering to their own people.[3]

Elena Kagan, one of the remaining liberals and a continual dissenter, became a lone voice from within the Court questioning its legitimacy. She told audiences that the Court should not presume to have public respect; rather, it had to earn "its legitimacy . . . by what it does, by the way it behaves." And she warned, "If over time the Court loses all connection with the public and with public sentiment, that's a dangerous thing for democracy."[4]

The justices' rejection of decades-old decisions and their plunging public approval ratings were part of a larger narrative about the breakdown of democracy. Scholars and commentators increasingly pointed to the gap between officials who held power and the interests of a majority of Americans.[5]

Roberts evaded the real issue. "I don't understand the connection between opinions that people disagree with and the legitimacy of the Court," he said, dismissing concerns about the Court's diminished stature. But people were not questioning the Court's legitimacy simply because they disagreed with opinions. It was because the decisions abandoned entrenched precedent and appeared to reflect individual justices' partisan alliances. The overhaul of constitutional privacy rights, which grabbed people's attention more than any other decision, had occurred in two short years. The justices had endorsed abortion rights in 2020 when they struck down a Louisiana regulation on physicians who performed abortions. What changed between 2020 and 2022 was the partisan makeup of the bench: Ruth Bader Ginsburg, a Democratic appointee, was succeeded by Barrett, the third appointee of a Republican president who had promised voters in 2016 that he would appoint justices who would end the protections of *Roe*.

Conservatives, of course, had pursued that goal for decades. Ronald Reagan ran for the presidency in 1980 against *Roe*, and his 1987 attempt to appoint Robert Bork, an originalist who disavowed *Roe* outright, became a milestone in confirmation battles. It took Trump and a team of men loyal to the memory of Bork to avenge the Senate rejection and carry out Bork's vision.

In 2023, the Trump appointees were still in their fifties. The only other one of the nine that youthful was the newest justice, Ketanji Brown Jackson.

Before the 2022–2023 session began, Jackson, fifty-two, underwent a formal investiture. Artifacts of history imbued the September 30 ceremony, from the use of a black horsehair chair that had belonged to Chief Justice John Marshall, to the parchment scroll on which Jackson's presidential commission was printed. She was the first Black woman ever to sit in the ceremonial chair and then take a seat on the elevated bench to hear and decide cases. Amid the pomp of the ritualistic occasion, with hundreds of friends, family, and colleagues gathered in the courtroom (a first for the post-pandemic era) and President Joe Biden in attendance, excitement was in the air.[6]

As Roberts administered the oath to Jackson, and she repeated the vow to "do equal right to the poor and to the rich," Justice Alito stood directly behind Jackson, by virtue of his seniority and position next to the chief justice. Alito was smiling. Everyone was smiling.

In that moment, one might have forgotten the divisions, the public disapproval, and the consequences of the Court's decisions to American life. But too much had changed too recently for that. Jackson's nomination, representing groundbreaking diversity after 233 years of history, did surely alter the image of the Court. Yet equally indelible was the transformation of the law itself, brought on by a majority laying waste to precedents and, indeed, offering no one confidence that it was done with its work.

# ACKNOWLEDGMENTS

Since I began writing about the Supreme Court, I've had a quiet mental refrain for my audiences: *This is your Supreme Court.* I've tried to focus on the consequences of decisions in American life. Through the years, another line has crept into my thinking as I've labored to understand what's really happening inside the chambers and been met with the Court's institutional resistance toward the press and public. That attitude is, as I was long ago admonished, *If we had wanted you to know that, we would have told you.* So, I am especially grateful to the individual justices and other insiders who privately inform my understanding of the Court's workings. I am also indebted to a stable of former law clerks and regular Supreme Court advocates who have provided trusted, confidential guidance over the years.

The exciting part of these book endeavors is the research and reporting. More challenging is putting it all together, especially against the backdrop of contemporary news developments and the continued turmoil of the post-Trump world. Colleagues and lawyers lent their expertise, including Priscilla Alverez, Marcia Coyle, Garrett Epps, Richard Hasen, Liz Hayes, and Jared Roberts. Law professor Dan Ortiz at the University of Virginia and Dean Erwin Chemerinsky at the University of California, Berkeley, generously read drafts of chapters. Toni Locy provided superb research, as did Jamie Ehrlich. Janet Byrne, editor extraordinaire, did more than anyone to refine the final manuscript before submission. To the shudders of my family (see below), I said I'd write another book just to work with Janet again.

I am appreciative of the leadership at CNN, where I've worked full time since 2017, for the unrivaled enthusiasm toward my extracurricular book projects, beginning with Chairman and CEO Chris Licht. I am most indebted to Virginia Moseley, executive vice president of editorial; Adam Levine, vice president for Washington news gathering; and Dan Berman, assistant managing editor for CNN politics, who expertly guides my daily Court analyses. Washington Bureau Chief Sam Feist, a fellow Georgetown Law alum, is also a source of inspiration. Other editors and producers to whom I am grateful for leadership are Rachel Smolkin, Allison Hoffman, and Laura Smitherman. I couldn't ask for a harder-working team of colleagues on the Supreme Court beat, beginning with Ariane de Vogue, CNN's Supreme Court reporter; Jessica Schneider, justice correspondent; and Stephen Vladeck, a law professor with expertise in the Court's "shadow docket."

Other friends at CNN provided constant encouragement, beginning with officemate Kristin Fisher and Washington Bureau colleagues Dana Bash, David Chalian, Marshall Cohen, Jennifer Dargan, Mary Kay Mallonee, Christi Parsons, Evan Perez, Abby Phillip, Katelyn Polantz, Mark Preston, Manu Raju, Paula Reid, John Robinson, Tierney Sneed, Whitney Wild, and Jeff Zeleny. Anchor Jake Tapper is in a category of his own, as a friend and adviser over the years.

At the Supreme Court, public information officer Patricia McCabe is a model of professionalism. And I learn daily from my colleagues on this beat: legal commentators Linda Greenhouse, Dahlia Lithwick, and Mark Joseph Stern, and the full-time press corps of Robert Barnes, Jess Bravin, Shannon Bream, Andrew Chung, Jan Crawford, Devin Dwyer, John Fritze, Jessica Gresko, Amy Howe, Lawrence Hurley, Ken Jost, Brent Kendall, Adam Liptak, Tony Mauro, Steven Mazie, Nicole Ninh, Kimberly Robinson, David Savage, Mark Sherman, Greg Stohr, Nina Totenberg, Mark Walsh, and Pete Williams.

The Library of Congress manuscript division remains one of my favorite places, and I cannot overstate my gratitude to historian Ryan Reft, who specializes in documents related to judicial, domestic policy, and political affairs.

This book would never have arrived between two covers without the prescient eye of Mauro DiPreta, executive editor of William Morrow at HarperCollins. Well before the Supreme Court took its sharpest rightward turn, Mauro saw the value in tracing where it was headed and shepherded this project through the consequential 2021–2022 session. I am thankful for his leadership and that of Liate Stehlik, president and publisher of the Morrow Group. Allie Johnston, a first-rate editorial assistant, kept all the pieces moving through the production process, overseen by senior production editor Dale Rohrbaugh. I am grateful to Allison Carney, marketing director, and Megan Wilson, publicity director, for their commitment and superb promotion of this book.

Special long-term gratitude goes to Gail Ross, my agent of nearly twenty years. For this book, she steered me back to the HarperCollins umbrella, home of my first Supreme Court biography, on Sandra Day O'Connor. Like Mauro, Gail understood just how consequential these past five years would be to the law in America.

I work on my books in a cluttered spare bedroom that long ago lost the bed and is now filled with files, books, papers, and countless Post-its scribbled with reminders and mantras. Toward the end of this project, I wrote on one little slip, "Don't Lose Something Valuable." It was meant to refer to key interview notes and documents amid the heaps. But just as soon as I wrote it down, I thought, *That's not about research materials. That's about my family and friends.* Plainly, I am captivated by the Court. But I wouldn't be able to spend so much time researching and writing about it, at night and on weekends, without the sustenance (and indulgence) of the people closest to me. Friends who have been a wellspring of support for my writing life include Fred Barbash, Debby Baum, Canera Pagano, Michael Pagano, Pam Fessler, Liz Halloran, Sue Long, Mark Patrick, Ronald Weich, and Elder Witt. John Shiff-man and Jack Shafer, pals from my days at Reuters, remain wiseacres but excellent advisers.

Somehow, my large sprawling family of eight younger brothers and sisters, their spouses, the nieces and nephews, and my own children and stepchildren have remained with me, offering love and patience even when I test them. They ask, "When will this one be done?" But they also ask about the justices and what is happening to the law at this historic time. On our weekly Zoom calls that began during the pandemic and continued even after we were able to visit one another in person again, daughters Elizabeth and Susannah unfailingly inquired about the Court and the status of this book.

Yet, of everyone in my big family, the person who is most intellectually engaged with all corners of American legal culture happens to be the one who bears the greatest brunt of my book projects: Clay Lewis, my husband. We have been together for nearly thirty-five years. I write about the Court and its effect on the lives of all Americans. Clay's daily presence in mine—his questions, care, and love—sustains me above all else. And for that I am grateful beyond words.

# NOTES

## Prologue: Unmasked

1. Bethany Irvine, "Why 'Heartbeat Bill' Is a Misleading Name for Texas' Near-Total Abortion Ban," *Texas Tribune*, September 2, 2021, https://www.texastribune.org/2021/09/02/texas-abortion-heartbeat-bill.

2. *Whole Woman's Health v. Jackson*, no. 21A24, September 1, 2021, order and opinions, https://www.supremecourt.gov/opinions/20pdf/21a24_8759.pdf; *Whole Woman's Health v. Jackson*, no. 21-463, October 22, 2021, https://www.supremecourt.gov/orders/courtorders/102221zr_986b.pdf; *United States v. Texas*, no. 21A85, October 22, 2021, order and opinions, https://www.supremecourt.gov/opinions/21pdf/21a85_5h25.pdf.

3. "Texas Abortion Patients' Attempts to End Their Pregnancy on Their Own Is Higher Than the National Rate, New Study Finds," press release, Texas Policy Evaluation Project, University of Texas at Austin, January 9, 2020, https://sites.utexas.edu/txpep/files/2020/01/TxPEP-self-managed-abortion-release.pdf.

4. *Whole Woman's Health v. Jackson*, no. 21-463, September 23, 2021, petition for certiorari, https://www.supremecourt.gov/DocketPDF/21/21-463/193539/20210923145031873_WWH%20v%20Jackson%20-%20petition%20for%20cert%20before%20judgment.pdf.

5. Such moves would be contrary to the holding of *District of Columbia v. Heller*, 554 U.S. 570 (2008), which enshrined a new Second Amendment right, and contrary to the First Amendment protections in *Citizens United v. Federal Election Commission*, 558 U.S. 310 (2010).

6. Mary Ramsey, "Justice Amy Coney Barrett Argues US Supreme Court Isn't 'A Bunch of Partisan Hacks,'" *Louisville Courier Journal*, September 12, 2021, https://www.courier-journal.com/story/news/politics/mitch-mcconnell/2021/09/12/justice-amy-coney-barrett-supreme-court-decisions-arent-political/8310849002.

7. Adam Liptak, "Alito Responds to Critics of the Supreme Court's 'Shadow Docket,'" *New York Times*, September 30, 2021, https://www.nytimes.com/2021/09/30/us/politics/alito-shadow-docket-scotus.html.

8. Joan Biskupic, "In the Shadows: Why the Supreme Court's Lack of Transparency Could Cost It in the Long Run," CNN, September 2, 2021, https://www.cnn.com/2021/09/01/politics/transparency-analysis-supreme-court-abortion/index.html; Joan Biskupic, "Dissension at the Supreme Court as Justices Take Their Anger Public," CNN, October 1, 2021, https://www.cnn.com/2021/10/01/politics/supreme-court-unhappy-justices/index.html.

9. "Legal Recruiter Jane S. Roberts Joins Macrae," press release, Macrae, March 5, 2019, https://www.macrae.com/news-master/givecustomname-776r2; Aleksi Tzatzev, "Meet the Fascinating Spouses Behind the Nation's Supreme Court Justices," *Business Insider*, October 23, 2012, https://www.businessinsider.com/spouses-of-the-supreme-court-justices-2012-10; Lloyd Grove, "The Courtship of Joanna Breyer," *Washington Post*, July

11, 1994, https://www.washingtonpost.com/archive/lifestyle/1994/07/11/the-courtship-of-joanna-breyer/554b7d14-f842-4170-b42e-7666d0722497.

10. Author interview with Stephen Breyer, October 13, 2021; Sotomayor opinion concurring in part and dissenting in part, *United States v. Texas,* 595 U.S. ____ (2021), Sotomayor concurring in part and dissenting in part, https://www.supremecourt.gov/opinions/21 pdf/21a85_5h25.pdf.

11. *Whole Woman's Health v. Jackson,* no. 21-463, November 1, 2021, transcript, https://www .supremecourt.gov/oral_arguments/argument_transcripts/2021/21-463_6kgm.pdf, and *United States v. Texas,* no. 21-588, November 1, 2021, transcript, https://www.supreme court.gov/oral_arguments/argument_transcripts/2021/21-588_m648.pdf.

12. *Whole Woman's Health v. Jackson,* no. 21-463, November 1, 2021, transcript; Kagan was referring to the 1908 case of *Ex parte Young* (209 U.S. 123), which permitted federal judges to block state officials' enforcement of laws that were challenged as unconstitutional while the validity of those laws was tested in court.

13. *United States v. Texas,* transcript.

14. Author interviews with Supreme Court sources with firsthand knowledge of internal debate over Texas's Senate Bill 8 (SB 8); for accounts of Kavanaugh's and Barrett's remarks during arguments, see Joan Biskupic, "Inside the Court: A Historic Three Hours That Could Decide the Future of Abortion Rights," CNN, November 1, 2021, https:// www.cnn.com/2021/11/01/politics/supreme-court-texas-abortion-kagan-analysis /index.html; and Adam Liptak, "Supreme Court Hints That It May Allow Challenge to Texas Abortion Law," *New York Times,* November 1, 2021, https://www.nytimes. com/2021/11/01/us/politics/texas-abortion-law-supreme-court.html; see also Mark Joseph Stern, "What I Got Wrong about Brett Kavanaugh and Abortion," Slate, December 14, 2021, https://slate.com/news-and-politics/2021/12/brett-kavanaugh-dobbs-sb8 -abortion-texas.html.

15. *Dobbs v. Jackson Women's Health Organization,* no. 19-1392, December 1, 2021, transcript, https://www.supremecourt.gov/oral_arguments/argument_transcripts/2021/19-1392_ gfbi.pdf.

16. *Whole Woman's Health v. Jackson,* 595 U.S. ____ (2021), https://www.supremecourt.gov /opinions/21pdf/21-463_new_8o6b.pdf; Thomas wrote an opinion concurring in part and dissenting in part, stating: "In my view, petitioners may not maintain suit against any of the governmental respondents under *Ex parte Young,* 209 U. S. 123 (1908). I would reverse in full the District Court's denial of respondents' motions to dismiss and remand with instructions to dismiss the case for lack of subject-matter jurisdiction."

17. *Whole Woman's Health v. Jackson,* 595 U.S. ____ (2021), https://www.supremecourt.gov /opinions/21pdf/21-463_new_8o6b.pdf.

18. President Carter, who served from 1977 to 1981, had not a single opportunity to appoint a justice; President Clinton (1993–2001) appointed two justices, and President Obama (2009–2017) appointed two justices.

19. In addition to Roosevelt's eight new appointments, he elevated Associate Justice Harlan Fiske Stone to chief justice. President Nixon appointed a total of four justices; President Reagan named three new justices and elevated Associate Justice William Rehnquist to chief justice.

## Chapter 1: "Inside the Castle"

1. The text of Trump's speech is in the 115 Cong. Rec. S364 (daily ed. January 20, 2017) (statement of the president), https://www.govinfo.gov/content/pkg/CREC-2017-01-20/pdf/CREC-2017-01-20-pt1-PgS362-4.pdf.

2. C-SPAN was among the news organizations that posted video of the inaugural event. See "Inaugural Luncheon Gathering," C-SPAN, January 20, 2017, https://www.c-span.org /video/?422125-1/president-trump-vice-president-pence-honored-inaugural-luncheon;

"Supreme Court Justices Arrive at Capitol," YouTube video, posted by AP Archive, January 25, 2017, https://www.youtube.com/watch?v=bSBeSA_guVI.

3.  Trump had the greatest number of Supreme Court appointments in a single term since Nixon. Of Reagan's three appointments in his second term, one involved the elevation of William Rehnquist from associate justice to chief justice; Nixon's four new appointments in his first term were of Warren Burger, Harry Blackmun, Lewis Powell, and Rehnquist.

4.  Donald Trump (@realdonaldtrump), September 18, 2018, 11:45:38 P.M. EST, https://www.thetrumparchive.com/?searchbox=%22The+Supreme+Court+is+one+of+the+main+reasons+I+got+elected+President%22.

5.  Exec. Order No. 13769, 82 Fed. Reg. 8977 (February 1, 2017) https://www.federalregister.gov/documents/2017/02/01/2017-02281/protecting-the-nation-from-foreign-terrorist-entry-into-the-united-states. For a list of the countries, see Exec. Order No. 13780, 82 Fed. Reg. 13209 (March 6, 2017), https://www.federalregister.gov/documents/2017/03/09/2017-04837/protecting-the-nation-from-foreign-terrorist-entry-into-the-united-states. For reporting on the removal of the language from Trump's campaign website, see Christine Wang, "Trump Website Takes Down Muslim Ban Statement after Reporter Grills Spicer in Briefing," CNBC, May 8, 2017, https://www.cnbc.com/2017/05/08/trump-website-takes-down-muslim-ban-statement-after-reporter-grills-spicer-in-briefing.html.

6.  Michael D. Shear, Nicholas Kulish, and Alan Feuer, "Judge Blocks Trump Order on Refugees Amid Chaos and Outcry Worldwide," *New York Times*, January 28, 2017, https://www.nytimes.com/2017/01/28/us/refugees-detained-at-us-airports-prompting-legal-challenges-to-trumps-immigration-order.html.

7.  *Hawai'i v. Trump*, 245 F.Supp.3d 1227 (D. Haw. 2017).

8.  *Washington v. Trump*, temporary restraining order, February 3, 2017, U.S. District Court, Western District of Washington at Seattle, http://cdn.ca9.uscourts.gov/datastore/general/2017/02/03/17-141_TRO_order.pdf.

9.  The second tweet was a day earlier, on February 4. Donald Trump (@realdonaldtrump), February 4, 2017, 8:12:02 A.M. EST, https://www.thetrumparchive.com/?searchbox=%22so-called+judge%22, and February 5, 2017, 3:39:05 P.M. EST, https://www.thetrumparchive.com/?searchbox=https://www.thetrumparchive.com/?searchbox=%22Just+cannot+believe+a+judge%22.

10.  Bybee dissenting opinion in *Washington v. Trump*, 847 F.3d 1151, 36 (9th Cir. 2017): "Even as I dissent from our decision not to vacate the panel's flawed opinion, I have the greatest respect for my colleagues," http://cdn.ca9.uscourts.gov/datastore/opinions/2017/03/17/17-35105_Amd_Order.pdf.

11.  Donald Trump (@realdonaldtrump), April 26, 2017, 6:20:00 A.M. EST, https://www.thetrumparchive.com/?searchbox=%22First+the+Ninth+Circuit+rules+against+the+ban%22.

12.  The Trump University case eventually settled for $25 million, approved by Judge Curiel and the Ninth Circuit. Steve Eder and Jennifer Medina, "Trump University Suit Settlement Approved by Judge," *New York Times*, March 31, 2017, https://www.nytimes.com/2017/03/31/us/trump-university-settlement.html; Maura Dolan, "U.S. Appeals Court Refuses to Scuttle $25-Million Trump University Settlement," February 6, 2018, *Los Angeles Times*, https://www.latimes.com/local/lanow/la-me-trump-university-20180206-story.html.

13.  "Donald Trump Campaign Rally in San Diego, California," May 27, 2016, https://www.c-span.org/video/?410129-1/donald-trump-campaigns-san-diego-california. Curiel's orders came in the long-running case of *Makaeff v. Trump University*, early context at *Makaeff v. Trump University*, 715 F.3d 254 (9th Cir. 2013), https://cdn.ca9.uscourts.gov/datastore/opinions/2013/04/17/11-55016.pdf.

14.  "Donald Trump Rails against Judge's 'Mexican Heritage,'" CNN, https://www.cnn.com/videos/politics/2016/06/03/donald-trump-judge-mexican-trump-university-case-lead-sot.cnn.

15. Arnold Schwarzenegger (@Schwarzenegger), June 6, 2016, 7:40 P.M., https://twitter
.com/Schwarzenegger/status/739965267501977600.

16. David Boucher, Joey Garrison, and Joel Elbert, "Trump in Nashville: 'Time for Us to
Embrace Our Glorious National Destiny,'" *Tennessean*, March 15, 2017.

17. Donald Trump (@realdonaldtrump), June 5, 2017, 6:25:02 A.M. EST, https://www.the
trumparchive.com/?searchbox=%22People%2C+the+lawyers+and+the+courts%22.

18. Paired orders granting the Trump administration's request to block lower-court action
against the travel ban and allow it to take effect during the litigation: *Trump v. Hawaii*, no. 17A550, December 4, 2017, https://www.supremecourt.gov/orders/court
orders/120417zr_4gd5.pdf; *Trump v. International Refugee Assistance*, no. 17A60, December 4, 2017, https://www.supremecourt.gov/orders/courtorders/120417zr1_j4ek.pdf.

19. Yates disclosed that the FBI had interviewed Flynn about the matter. Flynn had been
head of the military's Defense Intelligence Agency in the Obama administration, until
he was dismissed in 2014. Robert S. Mueller III, *Report on the Investigation into Russian Interference in the 2016 Presidential Election*, vol. 2, p. 31 (Washington, D.C.: U.S.
Department of Justice, March 2019), https://www.justice.gov/archives/sco/file/1373816
/download; See also, Ryan Lizza, "Why Sally Yates Stood Up to Trump," *The New Yorker*,
May 22, 2017, https://www.newyorker.com/magazine/2017/05/29/why-sally-yates-
stood-up-to-trump.

20. "Watch Lester Holt's Extended Interview with President Trump," NBC News, May 11,
2017, https://www.nbcnews.com/nightly-news/video/pres-trump-s-extended-exclusive-
interview-with-lester-holt-at-the-white-house-941854787582.

21. Mueller, *Report*, vol. 1, p. 11.

22. "The Atlantic City Lineage of Trump's White House Counsel," NJ.com, December
4, 2016, https://www.nj.com/politics/2016/12/the_atlantic_city_lineage_of_trumps_
white_house_co.html.

23. Clifford Hall, "Former White House Official Don McGahn: 'I Know How Tough the
Life of a Musician Is—I Respect Them for What They Do,'" *Guitar World*, August 10,
2020, https://www.guitarworld.com/features/former-white-house-official-don-mcgahn-
i-know-how-tough-the-life-of-a-musician-is-i-respect-them-for-what-they-do.

24. Biographical details from Joan Biskupic, *American Original: The Life and Constitution
of Supreme Court Justice Antonin Scalia* (New York: Sarah Crichton Books, 2009); for
the lack of an autopsy, see Lawrence K. Altman, "Scalia Autopsy Decision Divides Pa-
thologists," *New York Times*, February 20, 2016, https://www.nytimes.com/2016/02/21
/health/antonin-scalia-autopsy.html.

25. "HLS Reflects on the Legacy of Antonin Scalia," *Harvard Law Bulletin*, Spring 2016,
https://today.law.harvard.edu/feature/hls-reflects-legacy-justice-scalia.

26. *Obergefell v. Hodges*, 576 U.S. 644 (2015); *District of Columbia v. Heller*, 554 U.S. 570
(2008).

27. Alito joined the bench in January 2006, four months after Roberts became chief justice.

28. Author interviews with Leonard Leo, November 16, 2020, May 4, 2021, March 11, 2022;
Mitch McConnell, *The Long Game: A Memoir* (New York: Sentinel, 2019), 263; "The
American People Should Have a Voice in the Selection of the Next Supreme Court
Justice," press release, Mitch McConnell, February 22, 2015, https://www.republican
leader.senate.gov/newsroom/remarks/the-american-people-should-have-a-voice-in-
the-selection-of-the-next-supreme-court-justice.

29. See Neil Gorsuch with Jane Nitze and David Feder, *A Republic, If You Can Keep It* (New
York: Crown, 2019), 4. Gorsuch refers to press reports involving a friend, Judge Thomas
Hardiman (unnamed in the book), as he was trailed near his Pennsylvania home.

30. "Acting Attorney General Boente Issues Guidance to Department on Executive Order,"
press release, U.S. Department of Justice, January 30, 2017, https://www.justice.gov/opa
/pr/acting-attorney-general-boente-issues-guidance-department-executive-order.

31. In his confirmation hearings, Sessions had testified that he had not communicated with Russians during the campaign, but senators had doubts and delayed his confirmation for attorney general. There was some ambiguity to Sessions's statement regarding possible contact, and it turned out that he had interacted with Kislyak at the Republican National Convention and at a campaign event at the Mayflower Hotel in Washington. Robert Farley, "Did Sessions 'Lie'?," FactCheck.org, March 2, 2017, https://www.factcheck.org/2017/03/did-sessions-lie. In September 2016, in a conversation with the Russian ambassador to the United States, Sergey Kislyak, Attorney General Sessions criticized Russian aggression in Ukraine and discussed NATO. Sessions and his aides told Mueller that Russian meddling in the election did not come up in that meeting. Kislyak attempted to meet with Sessions after Trump's election victory during the transition, but that meeting never occurred. Mueller eventually concluded: "The evidence is not sufficient to prove that Sessions gave knowingly false answers to Russia-related questions in light of the wording and context of those questions." Mueller, *Report*, vol. 1, p. 198.

32. "Full Transcript and Video: Trump Picks Neil Gorsuch for Supreme Court," *New York Times*, January 31, 2017, https://www.nytimes.com/2017/01/31/us/politics/full-transcript-video-trump-neil-gorsuch-supreme-court.html.

33. See Gorsuch's Senate Judiciary Committee questionnaire detailing the dates for his Trump contacts. https://www.judiciary.senate.gov/imo/media/doc/Neil%20M.%20Gorsuch%20SJQ%20(Public).pdf; Maureen Scalia's large yard sign, author interviews with Leonard Leo, November 16, 2020, and October 26, 2022.

34. Charlie Savage and Julie Turkewitz, "Neil Gorsuch Has Web of Ties to Secretive Billionaire," *New York Times*, March 14, 2017, https://www.nytimes.com/2017/03/14/us/politics/neil-gorsuch-supreme-court.html.

35. Charlie Savage, "Neil Gorsuch Helped Defend Disputed Bush-Era Terror Policies, *New York Times*, March 15, 2017, https://www.nytimes.com/2017/03/15/us/politics/neil-gorsuch-torture-guantanamo-bay.html.

36. Ariane de Vogue, "Meet Neil Gorsuch, Fly-Fishing Scalia Fan," CNN, February 1, 2017, https://www.cnn.com/2017/01/31/politics/neil-gorsuch-antonin-scalia.

37. Neil M. Gorsuch, *The Future of Assisted Suicide and Euthanasia* (Princeton, NJ: Princeton University Press, 2006).

38. Leonard Leo contacts with Neil Gorsuch detailed in Gorsuch's Senate Judiciary Committee questionnaire, which lists the dates for his Trump contacts, https://www.judiciary.senate.gov/imo/media/doc/Neil%20M.%20Gorsuch%20SJQ%20(Public).pdf; "Donald F. McGahn II: The Legal & Regulatory Landscape in the Era of Trump," YouTube video, posted by Widener Law Commonwealth, February 25, 2020, https://www.youtube.com/watch?v=N-Jo6iH0PpY; Don McGahn at Princeton University conference, "The Politics of Judicial Nominations in an Age of Mistrust," March 6, 2020 (author was a conference participant).

39. Neil A. Lewis, "Barbara Olson, 45, Advocate and Conservative Commentator," *New York Times*, September 13, 2001, https://www.nytimes.com/2001/09/13/us/barbara-olson-45-advocate-and-conservative-commentator.html.

40. "13th annual Barbara K. Olson Memorial Lecture," YouTube video, posted by The Federalist Society, November 13, 2013, https://www.youtube.com/watch?v=VI_c-5S4S6Y.

41. David Enrich, *Servants of the Damned* (New York: HarperCollins, 2022), 226.

42. *Gutierrez-Brizuela v. Lynch*, 834 F.3d 1142 (10th Cir. 2016), https://casetext.com/case/gutierrez-brizuela-v-lynch.

43. Anne M. Burford with John Greenya, *Are You Tough Enough?* (New York: McGraw-Hill, 1986); Lois Romano and Jacqueline Trescott, "The Rise and Fall of Anne Burford," *Washington Post*, March 10, 1983, https://www.washingtonpost.com/archive/lifestyle/1983/03/10/the-rise-and-fall-of-anne-burford/30f4a9c9-b2d1-4348-9c56-6e5708a3d68a; Adam Liptak, Peter Baker, Nicholas Fandos, and Julie Turkewitz, "In Fall of Gorsuch's Mother,

a Painful Lesson in Politicking," *New York Times,* February 4, 2017, https://www.nytimes.com/2017/02/04/us/politics/neil-gorsuch-supreme-court-nominee.html.

44. Philip Shabecoff, "House Charges Head of E.P.A. with Contempt," *New York Times,* December 17, 1982, https://www.nytimes.com/1982/12/17/us/house-charges-head-of-epa-with-contempt.html.

45. Burford, *Are You Tough Enough?,* 225; David Hoffman and Cass Peterson, "Burford Quits as EPA Administrator," *Washington Post,* March 10, 1983, https://www.washingtonpost.com/archive/politics/1983/03/10/burford-quits-as-epa-administrator/49ef0add-f834-4bef-8fd5-35f13d1f2abd.

46. Burford, *Are You Tough Enough?,* 225.

47. Douglas Martin, "Anne Gorsuch Burford, 62, Reagan E.P.A. Chief, Dies," *New York Times,* July 22, 2004, https://www.nytimes.com/2004/07/22/us/anne-gorsuch-burford-62-reagan-epa-chief-dies.html.

48. Gorsuch, *A Republic, If You Can Keep It,* 13–14.

49. "Legal & Regulatory Landscape in the Era of Trump."

50. "Blumenthal Meets with Supreme Court Nominee Judge Neil Gorsuch," press release, Richard Blumenthal, February 8, 2017, https://www.blumenthal.senate.gov/newsroom/press/release/blumenthal-meets-with-supreme-court-nominee-judge-neil-gorsuch; Arnie Seipel and Ted Robbins, "Trump Slams Senator Who Revealed Gorsuch's Criticism of Remarks on Judges," NPR, February 8, 2017, https://www.npr.org/2017/02/08/514195859/gorsuch-calls-trump-tweets-about-judges-demoralizing-and-disheartening.

51. Ashley Parker, Josh Dawsey, and Robert Barnes, "Trump Talked about Rescinding Gorsuch's Nomination," *Washington Post,* December 19, 2017, https://www.washingtonpost.com/politics/trump-reportedly-considered-rescinding-gorsuchs-nomination/2017/12/18/ad2b3b68-e1c7-11e7-9eb6-e3c7ecfb4638_story.html.

52. *Confirmation Hearing on the Nomination of Hon. Neil M. Gorsuch to Be an Associate Justice of the Supreme Court of the United States,* 115 Cong. 66 (2017) (statement of Neil Gorsuch), https://www.govinfo.gov/content/pkg/CHRG-115shrg28638/pdf/CHRG-115shrg28638.pdf.

53. *Thompson R2-J School District v. Luke P,* 540 F.3d. 1143 (10th Cir. 2008), https://ca10.washburnlaw.edu/cases/2008/08/07-1304.pdf.

54. *Endrew F. v. Douglas County School District,* 580 U.S. ____ (2017), https://www.supremecourt.gov/opinions/16pdf/15-827_0pm1.pdf.

55. National Education Association, "Judge Neil Gorsuch's Record on Students with Disabilities," 2017, https://cqrcengage.com/nea/file/ocMxYuLUmcR/NEA-on-Gorsuch-and-IDEA.pdf.

56. *Confirmation Hearing on the Nomination of Hon. Neil M. Gorsuch,* 278.

57. Ariane de Vogue, Ashley Killough, and Theodore Schleifer, "Gorsuch Forced to Defend Decision in Frozen Trucker Case," CNN, March 21, 2017, https://www.cnn.com/2017/03/21/politics/neil-gorsuch-frozen-trucking-case-al-franken/index.html.

58. Committee on the Judiciary, U.S. House of Representatives, Washington, D.C. Interview of Don McGahn, June 4, 2021, https://judiciary.house.gov/uploadedfiles/mcgahn_interview_transcript.pdf.

59. Author learned of the incident in 2017 and confirmed the details in interviews (2020–2022) with Supreme Court sources who had firsthand knowledge.

60. Adam Liptak, "Neil Gorsuch Speech at Trump Hotel Raises Ethical Questions," *New York Times,* August 17, 2017, https://www.nytimes.com/2017/08/17/us/politics/gorsuch-speech-trump-hotel-ethics.html.

61. Josh Gerstein, "Gorsuch Takes Victory Lap at Federalist Dinner," November 16, 2017, Politico, https://www.politico.com/story/2017/11/16/neil-gorsuch-federalist-society-speech-scotus-246538; Debra Cassens Weiss, "'Judges Wear Robes, Not Capes,' Gor-

such Says in Federalist Society Speech," *ABA Journal,* November 17, 2017, https://www
.abajournal.com/news/article/judges_wear_robes_not_capes_gorsuch_says_in_federal
ist_society_speech.

62. Among other early choices were Michigan supreme court justice Joan Larsen, for the
Columbus-based Sixth Circuit, and University of Pennsylvania law professor Stephanos Bibas, for the Philadelphia-based Third Circuit. Both were former Supreme Court law clerks
and Federalist Society stalwarts and within judicial possibilities for any Republican president.

63. Amy C. Barrett and John H. Garvey, "Catholic Judges in Capital Cases," *Marquette
Law Review* 81 (1997–1998): 307, https://scholarship.law.nd.edu/law_faculty_scholar
ship/527; Joan Biskupic, "Why Republicans and Democrats Are Asking about Amy
Coney Barrett's Faith," CNN, October 11, 2020, https://www.cnn.com/2020/10/11
/politics/religion-barrett-feinstein-cruz-hearing-supreme-court/index.html; "A Conversation with Amy Coney Barrett," Hillsdale College, Washington, D.C., May 21, 2019,
https://www.hillsdale.edu/conversation-with-amy-coney-barrett.

64. Reuters, "The 'Dogma' Question That Made Amy Coney Barrett a Conservative
Hero," *New York Times,* September 25, 2020, https://www.nytimes.com/video/us
/politics/100000007357319/amy-barrett-supreme-court.html.

65. "A Conversation with Amy Coney Barrett."

66. The Department of Justice nominee was Eric Dreiband. There also was Michigan supreme court justice Joan Larsen, nominated to a U.S. appellate seat. See "Feinstein Speaks
on Dreiband Nomination," press release, Committee on the Judiciary, United States Senate, September 6, 2017, https://www.judiciary.senate.gov/press/dem/releases/feinstein-
speaks-on-dreiband-nomination.

67. Trump comments on Charlottesville, via ABC news, August 12, 2017, https://twitter
.com/abc/status/896455567027326976.

68. "Trump Condemns 'Repugnant' Hate Groups, Including KKK, Neo-Nazis," ABC News,
August 14, 2017, https://abcnews.go.com/Politics/video/trump-condemns-repugnant-
hate-groups-including-kkk-neo-49209623.

69. Angie Drobnic Holan, "In Context: Donald Trump's 'Very Fine People on Both Sides'
Remarks," PolitiFact, April 26, 2019, https://www.politifact.com/article/2019/apr/26
/context-trumps-very-fine-people-both-sides-remarks.

70. Michael Burke, "Biden: Trump 'Assigns Moral Equivalence' to 'Dark Forces' of Hate,"
The Hill, October 30, 2018, https://thehill.com/homenews/campaign/413870-biden-
trump-assigns-moral-equivalence-to-dark-forces-of-hate.

71. Eric Bradner and Maeve Reston, "Joe Biden Takes Trump Head-On over Charlottesville in Announcement Video," CNN, April 25, 2019, https://www.cnn.com/2019/04/25
/politics/joe-biden-charlottesville-trump-2020-launch/index.html.

72. Video, "Trump Calls for Police to Be 'Rough' with Suspects," *Los Angeles Times,* August
2, 2017, https://www.latimes.com/94241089-132.html.

73. Joan Biskupic, "Why Joe Arpaio Was Found Guilty," CNN, August 24, 2017, https://
www.cnn.com/2017/08/24/politics/why-joe-arpaio-was-found-guilty/index.html.

74. "Statement of ABA President Hilarie Bass Re: Pardon of Former Arizona Sheriff Joe Arpaio," press release, American Bar Association, August 25, 2017, https://www.american
bar.org/news/abanews/aba-news-archives/2017/08/statement_of_hilarie0.

## Chapter 2: "Nobody on That Court Is Like Anybody Else on That Court"

1. The history and modern controversy over Supreme Court expansion is covered in Presidential Commission on the Supreme Court of the United States, *Final Report* (Washington, D.C., December 2021), https://www.whitehouse.gov/wp-content/uploads/2021/12
/SCOTUS-Report-Final-12.8.21-1.pdf.

2. "Supreme Court Visitor Entrance," press release, Supreme Court of the United States, May
3, 2010, https://www.supremecourt.gov/publicinfo/press/pressreleases/pr_05-03-10; Ste-

phen Breyer, joined by Ruth Bader Ginsburg, "Statement Concerning the Supreme Court's Front Entrance," *Supreme Court Journal* (May 3, 2010): 831, https://www.supremecourt .gov/orders/journal/jnl09.pdf#page=807; author interviews with John Paul Stevens, October 1, 2010, and October 27, 2011; author interview with Antonin Scalia, August 1, 2012.

3.   Justice Lewis F. Powell Jr., "How *U.S. v. Nixon* Changed Presidential Power," interview by Bill Moyers, June 25, 1987, https://billmoyers.com/content/justice-lewis-f-powell.

4.   The Senate confirmed Ginsburg 96–3 and Breyer 87–9 before Roberts's 2005 nomination; the nominees who followed him were Alito, Sotomayor, Kagan, Gorsuch, Kavanaugh, Barrett, and Jackson.

5.   John Roberts to James Moore, December 22, 1968, copy obtained from La Lumiere School.

6.   Roberts's biographical details drawn from Joan Biskupic, *The Chief: The Life and Turbulent Times of Chief Justice John Roberts* (New York: Basic Books, 2019).

7.   Roberts appeared at the New England School of Law in Boston on February 3, 2016, "Inside the Supreme Court," C-SPAN, https://www.c-span.org/video/?404131-1 /discussion-chief-justice-john-roberts.

8.   Roberts's legal preparation and strategic approach from Biskupic, *The Chief*; for intense preparation before arguing a case, see especially 119–20.

9.   For more information on the John Quincy Adams sofa, see the History, Art, and Archives website of the U.S. House of Representatives, https://history.house.gov/Collection /Detail/43080.

10.   *National Federation of Independent Business v. Sebelius,* 567 U.S. 519 (2012).

11.   Biskupic, *The Chief,* 221–48.

12.   Ibid., 245.

13.   *Shelby County v. Holder,* 570 U.S. 2 (2013). For further discussion of Roberts and race, see ibid., 249–74.

14.   Eli Rosenberg and Abby Ohlheiser, "Ruth Bader Ginsburg Was Seen in Public Monday. Conspiracy Theorists Still Insist She's Dead," *Washington Post,* February 6, 2019, https://www.washingtonpost.com/technology/2019/02/06/ruth-bader-ginsburg-was-seen-public-monday-conspiracy-theorists-still-insist-shes-dead; Daniel Moritz-Rabson, "Former White House Adviser Continues Fueling QAnon Theory That Ruth Bader Ginsburg Is Dead," *Newsweek,* February 15, 2019, https://www.newsweek.com /sebastian-gorka-promotes-qanon-conspiracy-ruth-bader-ginsburg-dead-1333440; Bill McCarthy, "Viral Photo, Flight Logs Don't Prove Chief Justice John Roberts Went to Jeffrey Epstein's Island," *Politifact,* December 21, 2020, https://www.politifact.com/fact checks/2020/dec/21/facebook-posts/no-viral-photo-doesnt-show-chief-justice-john-robe; Josh Dawsey and Felicia Sonmez, "Trump Mocks Kavanaugh Accuser Christine Blasey Ford," *Washington Post,* October 2, 2018, https://www.washingtonpost.com /politics/trump-mocks-kavanaugh-accuser-christine-blasey-ford/2018/10/02/25f6f8aa-c662-11e8-9b1c-a90f1daae309_story.html.

15.   *Obergefell v. Hodges,* 576 U.S. 644 (2015), https://www.supremecourt.gov/opinions /14pdf/14-556_3204.pdf.

16.   Author interview with Anthony Kennedy, April 14, 2014; author interview with Ruth Bader Ginsburg, July 11, 2016, regarding Roberts conferring first with Kennedy on assignments; author interviews with other justices in 2021 and 2022 after the six-justice conservative majority was in place.

17.   Author interview with Anthony Kennedy, April 14, 2014. (The baby boom birth years are roughly 1946–1964.)

18.   Clarence Thomas, *My Grandfather's Son: A Memoir* (New York: HarperCollins, 2007), 100; see also 94, 107, 142, 231–32.

19.   For Thomas's testimony before the U.S. Senate on October 11, 1991, see "Flashback: Clarence Thomas responds to Anita Hill," YouTube video, posted by CNN, April 13, 2016, https://www.youtube.com/watch?v=ZURHD5BU1o8.

20. Joan Biskupic, "The Quotable Words of Supreme Court Justice Clarence Thomas," CNN, October 24, 2021, https://www.cnn.com/2021/10/24/politics/clarence-thomas-through-the-years/index.html; *Created Equal: Clarence Thomas in His Own Words*, dir. Michael Pack, 2020, https://www.justicethomasmovie.com.

21. Justice Clarence Thomas speech to National Bar Association, July 29, 1998, C-SPAN, https://www.c-span.org/video/?109490-1/supreme-court-justice-speech.

22. *Grutter v. Bollinger*, 539 U.S. 306 (2003), https://supreme.justia.com/cases/federal/us/539/306/case.pdf.

23. Author interview with Clarence Thomas, February 21, 2014.

24. Among former law clerks to Thomas who became judges were Gregory Katsas and Neomi Rao, both appointed to the D.C. Circuit; David Stras, to the Eighth Circuit; and Allison Jones Rushing, to the Fourth Circuit. See also Emma Green, "The Clarence Thomas Effect," *The Atlantic*, July 10, 2019, https://www.theatlantic.com/politics/archive/2019/07/clarence-thomas-trump/593596.

25. See remarks on *stare decisis*, e.g., in Ariane de Vogue, "Thomas Says Government Institutions Shouldn't be 'Bullied' Following Leak of Draft Opinion on Abortion," CNN, May 7, 2022, https://www.cnn.com/2022/05/06/politics/clarence-thomas-stare-decisis-roe-v-wade-leak.

26. Ginni Thomas speech, "Post-Election Analysis and Future of Conservatism," C-SPAN, November 9, 2016, https://www.c-span.org/video/?418304-1/conservative-activists-discuss-post-election-priorities.

27. Jane Mayer, "Is Ginni Thomas a Threat to the Supreme Court?," *The New Yorker*, January 21, 2022, https://www.newyorker.com/magazine/2022/01/31/is-ginni-thomas-a-threat-to-the-supreme-court.

28. Chief Justice John Roberts, "Year-End Report on the Federal Judiciary," Public Information Office, Supreme Court of the United States, December 31, 2011, https://www.supremecourt.gov/publicinfo/year-end/2011year-endreport.pdf; Joan Biskupic, "John Roberts Can't Do Anything about Clarence Thomas," CNN, March 30, 2022, https://www.cnn.com/2022/03/30/politics/john-roberts-clarence-ginni-thomas-supreme-court/index.html.

29. *National Federation of Independent Business v. Dept of Labor, OSHA*, no. 21A247, January 7, 2022, transcript, https://www.supremecourt.gov/oral_arguments/argument_transcripts/2021/21a244_7k47.pdf.

30. *Confirmation Hearing on the Nomination of Samuel A. Alito, Jr., to Be an Associate Justice of the Supreme Court*, 109th Cong. 54 (2006) (statement of Samuel Alito), https://www.govinfo.gov/content/pkg/GPO-CHRG-ALITO/pdf/GPO-CHRG-ALITO.pdf;1972 yearbook: https://pr.princeton.edu/pictures/a-f/alito_samuel_anthony/htm/02nassau_herald_text.htm.

31. George W. Bush, *Decision Points* (New York: Crown, 2010), 102.

32. Nina Totenberg, "Roberts Slams 'Pep Rally' Scene at State of Union," March 10, 2010, NPR, https://www.npr.org/templates/story/story.php?storyId=124537470; Robert Barnes, "Supreme Court Splits Openly on Worker Protection Suits," *Washington Post*, June 24, 2013, https://www.washingtonpost.com/politics/supreme-court-splits-openly-on-worker-protection-suits/2013/06/24/c9b1eb62-dcf7-11e2-bd83-e99e43c336ed_story.html; Garrett Epps, "Justice Alito's Inexcusable Rudeness," *The Atlantic*, June 24, 2013, https://www.theatlantic.com/national/archive/2013/06/justice-alitos-inexcusable-rudeness/277163; Joan Biskupic, "Supreme Court's Ginsburg Vows to Resist Pressure to Retire," Reuters, July 4, 2013, https://www.reuters.com/article/us-usa-court-ginsburg/exclusive-supreme-courts-ginsburg-vows-to-resist-pressure-to-retire-idUSBRE9630C820130704.

33. "Address by Justice Samuel Alito [2020 National Lawyers Convention]," YouTube video, posted by The Federalist Society, November 25, 2020, https://www.youtube.com/watch?v=VMnukCVIZWQ; Thomas statement respecting the denial of certio-

rari, joined by Alito, *Kim Davis v. David Ermold,* 592 U.S. _____ (2020), https://www
.supremecourt.gov/opinions/20pdf/19-926_5hdk.pdf.

34. "Address by Justice Samuel Alito."

35. *Weinberger v. Wiesenfeld,* 420 U.S. 636 (1975), https://supreme.justia.com/cases/federal
/us/420/636/#tab-opinion-1951259.

36. Author interview with Ruth Bader Ginsburg, July 11, 2016; Timothy S. Robinson,
"US Circuit Judge Harold Leventhal Dies at 64," *Washington Post,* November 21, 1979,
https://www.washingtonpost.com/archive/local/1979/11/21/us-circuit-judge-harold-
leventhal-dies-at-64/876e8fae-8444-4f31-a2ee-0ebff5d669c9.

37. "Justice Ginsburg: 'I'm Fine Being Linked to the Notorious BIG,'" NBC News video,
February 23, 2017, https://www.nbcnews.com/video/ruth-bader-ginsburg-explains-
origins-of-the-notorious-rbg-883729987755; Irin Carmon and Shana Knizhnik, *Notorious RBG* (New York: Dey Street, 2015); Tyler Aquilina, "See Kate McKinnon's Best
Moments as Ruth Bader Ginsburg on *Saturday Night Live,*" *Entertainment Weekly,*
September 19, 2920, https://ew.com/tv/kate-mckinnon-best-moments-as-ruth-bader-
ginsburg-on-saturday-night-live; Joan Biskupic, "Ruth Bader Ginsburg: 'For So Long,
Women Were Silent,'" CNN, January 22, 2018, https://www.cnn.com/2018/01/21
/politics/ruth-bader-ginsburg-sundance-film-festival/index.html.

38. Author interview with Ruth Bader Ginsburg, July 11, 2016.

39. David Mack, "Ruth Bader Ginsburg Made a Cameo Onstage in an Opera," *BuzzFeed,*
November 14, 2016, https://www.buzzfeednews.com/article/davidmack/ruth-bader-
ginsburg-made-a-camero-on-stage-in-an-opera.

40. Veronica Toney, "Ruth Bader Ginsburg Makes Her Washington National Opera Debut
with a Role Mirroring Her Real Life," *Washington Post,* November 13, 2016, https://
www.washingtonpost.com/news/reliable-source/wp/2016/11/13/ruth-bader-ginsburg-
makes-her-washington-national-opera-debut-with-a-role-mirroring-her-real-life; Jay
Gabler, "Ruth Bader Ginsburg Makes Politically Pointed Operatic Debut," Minnesota
Public Radio, https://www.classicalmpr.org/story/2016/11/14/ruth-bader-ginsburg-
opera.

41. Author interview with Ruth Bader Ginsburg, July 31, 2014.

42. Stephen Breyer appearance over Zoom with National Asian Pacific American Bar Association, November 4, 2020, https://www.cand.uscourts.gov/about/interview-with-
justice-breyer.

43. *Parents Involved in Community Schools v. Seattle School District No. 1,* 551 U.S. 701 (2007),
https://supreme.justia.com/cases/federal/us/551/05-908/index.pdf.

44. Cristian Farias, "Noel Francisco, Trump's Tenth Justice," *New York Review of Books,*
August 9, 2018, https://www.nybooks.com/daily/2018/08/09/noel-francisco-trumps-
tenth-justice; *Janus v. American Federation of State, County and Municipal Employees,* no. 16-1466, February 26, 2018, transcript, https://www.supremecourt.gov/oral
_arguments/argument_transcripts/2017/16-1466_bocf.pdf.

45. Sonia Sotomayor, *My Beloved World* (New York: Knopf, 2013); Greg Stohr, "Sotomayor's
Book Advances from Knopf Exceed $3 Million," *Bloomberg,* June 7, 2013, https://www
.bloomberg.com/news/articles/2013-06-07/sotomayor-s-book-advances-from-knopf-
surpass-3-million.

46. *Schuette v. Coalition to Defend Affirmative Action,* 572 U.S. 291 (2014), https://www
.supremecourt.gov/opinions/13pdf/12-682_8759.pdf. For an example of Sotomayor questioning colleagues' candor, see dissent in *Jones v. Mississippi,* 593 U.S. _____
(2021): "The Court is fooling no one" (https://www.supremecourt.gov/opinions/20pdf
/18-1259_8njq.pdf).

47. "Supreme Court Justice Kagan at University of Colorado Law School," C-SPAN, October 22, 2019, https://www.c-span.org/video/?465467-1/supreme-court-justice-kagan-
university-colorado-law-school.

48. *Citizens United v. Federal Election Commission,* 558 U.S. 310 (2010), https://supreme
.justia.com/cases/federal/us/558/08-205/index.pdf; Dahlia Lithwick, "Unprecedented:
Watching the Supreme Court Make Its Campaign Finance Jurisprudence Disappear,"
*Slate,* September 9, 2009, https://slate.com/news-and-politics/2009/09/watching-the-
supreme-court-make-its-campaign-finance-jurisprudence-disappear.html.

49. "Justice Elena Kagan at the Aspen Ideas Festival," YouTube video, posted by The Aspen
Institute, June 29, 2013, https://www.youtube.com/watch?v=DC_PVDsYK9g; Garance
Franke-Ruta, "Justice Kagan and Justice Scalia Are Hunting Buddies—Really," *The Atlantic,* June 2013, https://www.theatlantic.com/politics/archive/2013/06/justice-kagan-
and-justice-scalia-are-hunting-buddies-really/277401.

50. *The Nomination of Elena Kagan to Be an Associate Justice of the Supreme Court,* 111 Cong.
144 (2010) (statement of Elena Kagan), https://www.govinfo.gov/content/pkg/CHRG-
111shrg67622/pdf/CHRG-111shrg67622.pdf.

51. *Arizona Free Enterprise Club's Freedom Club PAC v. Bennett,* 564 U.S. 721 (2011), https://
www.supremecourt.gov/opinions/10pdf/10-238.pdf; author interview with Ruth Bader
Ginsburg, June 29, 2011.

52. *Trinity Lutheran Church of Columbia, Inc. v. Comer,* 582 U.S. ___ (2017), https://www
.supremecourt.gov/opinions/16pdf/15-577_khlp.pdf.

53. Author interviews with sources who had firsthand knowledge of negotiations in the case.

54. "DeVos: Supreme Court Sends Clear Message That Religious Discrimination Cannot
Be Tolerated," U.S. Department of Education, EIN Presswire, June 26, 2017, https://
www.einnews.com/pr_news/389032448/devos-supreme-court-sends-clear-message-
that-religious-discrimination-cannot-be-tolerated#; Emma Brown, "Why Betsy DeVos
Is Cheering the Supreme Court's Church Playground Decision," *Washington Post,* June
27, 2017, https://www.washingtonpost.com/news/education/wp/2017/06/26/why-
betsy-devos-is-cheering-the-supreme-courts-church-playground-decision; Betsy DeVos
to the Hon. Nancy Pelosi, March 11, 2019, https://www2.ed.gov/policy/elsec/guid
/secletter/190311.html.

55. Three years after the Trinity Lutheran case, on June 30, 2020, in *Espinoza v. Montana
Department of Revenue,* 591 U.S. ____ (2020), the justices upheld a program providing
tuition assistance for children in private schools and dissolved any notion that the 2017
decision had limited reach (https://www.supremecourt.gov/opinions/19pdf/18-1195_
g314.pdf). The Trump administration amicus curiae brief in *Espinoza* quoted Roberts's
*Trinity Lutheran* opinion: "Discriminatory restriction is 'odious to our Constitution' and
it 'cannot stand'" (https://www.supremecourt.gov/DocketPDF/18/18-1195/116295/201
90918175731796_18-1195tsacUnitedStates.pdf).

56. *Burwell v. Hobby Lobby Stores,* 573 U.S. 682 (2014), https://supreme.justia.com/cases
/federal/us/573/13-354/case.pdf.

57. The chronology of Roberts's switches in the Affordable Care Act case is detailed in Biskupic, *The Chief,* 221–58; the chronology of the justices' switch in *Fisher v. University of
Texas at Austin* is detailed in Joan Biskupic, *Breaking In: The Rise of Sonya Sotomayor and
the Politics of Justice* (New York: Sarah Crichton Books, 2014), 191–210. For details on
Roberts's switched vote in *Department of Commerce v. New York,* see Joan Biskupic, "How
John Roberts Killed the Census Citizenship Question," CNN, September 12, 2019,
https://www.cnn.com/2019/09/12/politics/john-roberts-census-citizenship-supreme-
court/index.html.

58. *Pavan v. Smith,* 582 U.S. ____ (2017), https://www.supremecourt.gov/opinions/16
pdf/16-992_868c.pdf. Gorsuch dissented, joined by Thomas and Alito, objecting that the
majority sided with the women straightaway, without full briefing or public oral arguments. "Summary reversal is usually reserved for cases where 'the law is settled and stable,
the facts are not in dispute, and the decision below is clearly in error,'" Gorsuch asserted.
"Respectfully, I don't believe this case meets that standard." He insisted that nothing in

*Obergefell* made clear how such a birth-certificate dispute should be resolved. For internal debate during 2017 on *Pavan v. Smith* and *Masterpiece Cakeshop v. Colorado Civil Rights Commission,* author interviews with knowledge of the negotiations.

59. *Masterpiece Cakeshop v. Colorado Civil Rights Commission,* no. 16-111, December 5, 2017, transcript, https://www.supremecourt.gov/oral_arguments/argument_trans cripts/2017/16-111_f29g.pdf; *Masterpiece Cakeshop, v. Colorado Civil Rights Commission,* 584 U.S. _____ (2018), https://www.supremecourt.gov/opinions/17pdf/16-111_j4el.pdf.

60. *Fisher v. University of Texas,* 570 U.S. 297 (2013), https://www.supremecourt.gov/opinions /12pdf/11-345_l5gm.pdf; *Fisher v. University of Texas at Austin,* 579 U.S. _____ (2016), https://supreme.justia.com/cases/federal/us/579/14-981/case.pdf.

61. For *Bakke* history from Marshall files, see, Fred Barbash and Joan Biskupic, "First Black Justice Unyielding in Rights Crusade," *Washington Post,* May 25, 1993, https://www .washingtonpost.com/archive/politics/1993/05/25/1st-black-justice-unyielding-in- rights-crusade/45458d79-4026-4fe7-9e88-199e05ac92df; the cases to be resolved in the 2022–2023 session were *Students for Fair Admissions v. Harvard* and *Students for Fair Admissions v. University of North Carolina.*

62. Brennan case files, Manuscript Division, Library of Congress, https://www.loc.gov/item /mm82052266. *Regents of the University of California v. Bakke,* 438 U.S. 265 (1978). An earlier affirmative action case had been dismissed as moot, *DeFunis v. Odegaard,* 416 U.S. 312 (1974).

63. This was a difficult time for Blackmun, as author Linda Greenhouse details in her 2005 biography of the justice. He was recovering from surgery for prostate cancer. Yet, even as he struggled with the case, he never appeared ready to join with Chief Justice Burger and the others opposed to the UC-Davis program. As Greenhouse documents, Blackmun informed his colleagues on May 1, 1978, that he would vote to uphold the admissions policy. Greenhouse, *Becoming Justice Blackmun* (New York: Times Books, 2005), 131–32.

64. Bob Woodward and Scott Armstrong, *The Brethren* (New York: Simon & Schuster, 1979). Lewis chronicled his reporting on the incident, including calls to former law clerks and communications with Brennan; notes are contained in his files at the Library of Congress, Anthony Lewis Papers, Manuscript Division, Library of Congress, https://findingaids.loc.gov/exist_collections/ead3pdf/mss/2013/ms013127.pdf.

65. John Roberts to Henry Friendly, November 1, 1980, Henry Jacob Friendly Papers, Harvard University.

66. Lewis Powell, confidential memo to his file regarding the justices' participation in interviews with Woodward and Armstrong, October 7, 1977 (addressed to Warren Burger but not sent, according to a personal notation on the memo); contained in Powell Archives, Washington and Lee University Law School. See also, David J. Garrow, "*The Brethren:* Inside the Supreme Court," *Constitutional Commentary* 18, no. 2 (Summer 2001): 303–18, https://scholarship.law.umn.edu/cgi/viewcontent.cgi?article=1259&context=concomm.

67. Woodward and Armstrong, *The Brethren,* 224–25.

68. Anthony Lewis, who formerly was the *New York Times* Supreme Court correspondent and then became a columnist, contacted law clerks who had been at the Court that 1971–1972 session and took detailed notes of their accounts. See Lewis's papers at the Library of Congress, Manuscript Division, https://www.loc.gov/item /mm81075856.

69. Brennan to Lewis, January 14, 1980, Lewis papers, Manuscript Division, Library of Congress.

## Chapter 3: "Joining Us for Tonight's Ceremony Is Every Sitting Supreme Court Justice"

1. Transcript from October 19, 2016, presidential debate, moderator Chris Wallace, https://www.debates.org/voter-education/debate-transcripts/october-19-2016-debate-

transcript; details of Garza case from filings and Supreme Court opinion in *Azar v. Garza*, 584 U.S. ___ (2018).

2.   *Confirmation Hearing on the Nomination of Hon. Brett M. Kavanaugh to Be an Associate Justice of the Supreme Court of the United States*, 115 Cong. 528 (2018) (statement of Rochelle M. Garza), https://www.govinfo.gov/content/pkg/CHRG-115shrg32765/pdf/CHRG-115shrg32765.pdf.

3.   Jane Doe testimony in ACLU filing, https://www.aclu.org/legal-document/garza-v-hargan-complaint-injunctive-relief-and-damages; *Azar v. Garza*, 584 U.S. ___ (2018), https://www.supremecourt.gov/opinions/17pdf/17-654_5j3b.pdf.

4.   Bill Chappell, "Court Puts a Hold on Order That Approved Undocumented Teen's Abortion," NPR, October 19, 2017, https://www.npr.org/sections/thetwo-way/2017/10/19/558771914/court-puts-a-hold-on-order-that-approved-undocumented-teens-abortion.

5.   Joan Biskupic, "Trump Puts Faith in Religious Right," CNN, October 14, 2017, https://www.cnn.com/2017/10/14/politics/donald-trump-religious-conservatives-appeals/index.html.

6.   See, for example, *Bellotti v. Baird*, 443 U.S. 622 (1979).

7.   ORR policy prohibited the staff at a shelter from "taking any action that facilitates an abortion without direction and approval from the Director." The policy also dictated that a minor seeking an abortion must work with the government "to identify a suitable sponsor who could take custody of her in the United States." *Azar v. Garza*, 584 U.S. ___ (2018), https://www.supremecourt.gov/opinions/17pdf/17-654_5j3b.pdf.

8.   *Garza v. Hargan*, Chutkan order filed October 13, 2017, https://dockets.justia.com/docket/district-of-columbia/dcdce/1:2017cv02122/190182; see also https://www.supremecourt.gov/DocketPDF/17/17A655/24343/20171218184847765_Garza%20v%20Hargan%20Stay%20Application.pdf; Christina Caron, "Undocumented 17-Year-Old Must Delay Abortion, Court Rules," *New York Times*, October 21, 2017, https://www.nytimes.com/2017/10/21/us/texas-immigrant-abortion-appeal.html.

9.   D.C. Circuit panel decision issued October 20, 2017, in the majority were Henderson and Kavanaugh; Millett dissented. Author interview with Brigitte Amiri, June 15, 2021.

10.  For Millett's dissent, see https://s3.documentcloud.org/documents/4114096/Millett-Dissent-HHS-20171020.pdf.

11.  *Garza v. Hargan*, 874 F.3d (D.C. Cir. 2017) (en banc), https://www.cadc.uscourts.gov/internet/opinions.nsf/C81A5EDEADAE82F2852581C30068AF6E/$file/17-5236-1701167.pdf.

12.  "After a Month of Obstruction by the Trump Administration, Jane Doe Gets Her Abortion," press release, ACLU, October 25, 2017, https://www.aclu.org/press-releases/after-month-obstruction-trump-administration-jane-doe-gets-her-abortion.

13.  *Azar v. Garza*, 584 U.S. ___ (2018), https://www.supremecourt.gov/opinions/17pdf/17-654_5j3b.pdf.

14.  Michael D. Shear, "Trump Names Supreme Court Candidates for Nonexistent Vacancy," *New York Times*, November 17, 2017, https://www.nytimes.com/2017/11/17/us/politics/trump-supreme-court.html.

15.  Joan Biskupic, "Gorsuch v. Roberts: The Rookie Takes on the Chief," CNN, October 8, 2017, https://www.cnn.com/2017/10/08/politics/neil-gorsuch-john-roberts-rivalry/index.html.

16.  Linda Greenhouse, "Trump's Life-Tenured Judicial Avatar," *New York Times*, July 6, 2017, https://www.nytimes.com/2017/07/06/opinion/gorsuch-trump-supreme-court.html; Adam Liptak, "#GorsuchStyle Garners a Gusher of Groans. But Is His Writing Really That Bad?," *New York Times*, April 30, 2018, https://www.nytimes.com/2018/04/30/us/politics/justice-neil-gorsuch-writing-style.html; Mark Joseph Stern, "Feud: Elena and Neil," Slate, October 18, 2017, https://slate.com/news-and-politics/2017/10/why-rumors-of-a-gorsuch-kagan-supreme-court-clash-are-such-a-bombshell.html.

17.  *Epic Systems Corp v. Lewis*, 584 U.S. ___ (2018), https://www.supremecourt.gov/opinions /17pdf/16-285_q8l1.pdf.

18.  *Janus v. American Federation of State, County and Municipal Employees*, no. 16-1466, February 26, 2018, transcript, https://www.supremecourt.gov/oral_arguments/argument_ transcripts/2017/16-1466_bocf.pdf.

19.  Shane Goldmacher, "Trump's Hidden Back Channel to Justice Kennedy: Their Kids," Politico, April 6, 2017, https://www.politico.com/story/2017/04/donald-trump-supreme-court-236925; Adam Liptak and Maggie Haberman, "Inside the White House's Quiet Campaign to Create a Supreme Court Opening," *New York Times*, June 28, 2018, https://www.nytimes.com/2018/06/28/us/politics/trump-anthony-kennedy-retirement.html.

20.  Ivanka Trump (@ivankatrump), Instagram, February 22, 2017, https://www.instagram .com/p/BQ0jcnaFFTv.

21.  Martha Ross, "How Ivanka Enlisted Daughter Arabella in Reported White House Effort to Charm Anthony Kennedy," *Mercury News* (San Jose, CA), June 29, 2018, https:// www.mercurynews.com/2018/06/29/how-ivanka-trump-enlisted-daughter-arabella-in-reported-white-house-effort-to-charm-anthony-kennedy.

22.  McGahn at a Princeton University conference, "The Politics of Judicial Nominations in an Age of Mistrust," on March 6, 2020. (Author was a conference participant.)

23.  *Janus v. American Federation of State, County and Municipal Employees*, 585 U.S. ___ (2018), https://www.supremecourt.gov/opinions/17pdf/16-1466_2b3j.pdf.

24.  Another example was *Encino Motorcars v. Navarro* (584 U.S. ___ [2018]), in which the justices split 5–4 along the same lines to disallow overtime pay for certain automobile workers, a position pushed by the Trump administration after reversing course from Obama. Conservatives believed the law was clear. Again, Ginsburg spoke for dissenters, saying the majority compromised worker protections from the 1930 New Deal era "without even acknowledging that it unsettles more than half a century of our precedent" (https://www.supremecourt.gov/opinions/17pdf/16-1362_gfbh.pdf).

25.  Donald Trump (@realdonaldtrump), June 27, 2018, 10:11:05 A.M. EST, https://www .thetrumparchive.com/?searchbox=%22Big+loss+for+the+coffers%22.

26.  Transcript from *Kiobel v. Royal Dutch Petroleum*, no. 10-1491, October 1, 2012, https:// www.supremecourt.gov/oral_arguments/argument_transcripts/2012/10-1491rearg .pdf. In the case at hand, the Obama administration had partially reversed a stance by the George W. Bush administration regarding when the Alien Tort Statute (1789) could be invoked against governments and corporations for human rights abuses abroad.

27.  Biskupic, *The Chief*, 97–100.

28.  *Trump v. Hawaii*, 585 U.S. ___ (2018), https://www.supremecourt.gov/opinions /17pdf/17-965_h315.pdf.

29.  *Trump v. Hawaii*, Kennedy concurrence.

30.  *Trump v. Hawaii*, Sotomayor concurrence and bench announcement, which can be found at Oyez.org: https://www.oyez.org/cases/2017/17-965.

31.  Author interviews with justices; "Justice Kennedy Retirement Announcement," press release, Supreme Court of the United States, June 27, 2018, https://www.supremecourt .gov/publicinfo/press/pressreleases/pr_06-27-18.

32.  McGahn, "The Politics of Judicial Nominations in an Age of Mistrust."

33.  Shannon (Flaherty) McGahn worked for Representative Jeb Hensarling (R-TX), Representative Tom DeLay (R-TX), and Treasury Secretary Steven Mnuchin. She also served as a staff director for the House Financial Services Committee. Eventually she became a lobbyist with the National Association of Realtors.

34.  Carl Hulse, *Confirmation Bias: Inside Washington's War Over the Supreme Court* (New York: HarperCollins, 2019), 4, for prediction about Kavanaugh on the Supreme Court.

35.  Matt Zapotosky, "Prominent Appeals Court Judge Alex Kozinski Accused of Sexual Misconduct," *Washington Post*, December 8, 2017, https://www.washingtonpost.com

/world/national-security/prominent-appeals-court-judge-alex-kozinski-accused-of-sexual-misconduct/2017/12/08/1763e2b8-d913-11e7-a841-2066faf731ef_story.html.

36. Jackie Calmes, *Dissent: The Radicalization of the Republican Party and Its Capture of the Court* (New York: Twelve, 2021), 8, 421 (Calmes cites Tom Brune's August 3, 2005, *Newsday* story about Roberts work for Kavanaugh's lobbyist father).

37. "Judge Brett Kavanaugh Supreme Court Nomination Announcement," July 9, 2018, C-SPAN, https://www.c-span.org/video/?448032-1/president-trump-nominates-brett-kavanaugh-supreme-court. After he left the high court, Kennedy opted against hearing appellate cases, as Sandra Day O'Connor and David Souter had, or taking up any major book project, as John Paul Stevens had.

38. Michael D. Shear and Michael S. Schmidt, "A Coveted Lawyer's Juggling Act May Be Good, and Bad, for Trump," *New York Times*, September 2, 2018, https://www.nytimes.com/2018/09/02/us/politics/william-burck.html.

39. Seung Min Kim, "Clearinghouse for Kavanaugh Documents Is a Bush White House Lawyer, Angering Senate Democrats," *Washington Post*, August 15, 2018, https://www.washingtonpost.com/politics/clearinghouse-for-kavanaugh-documents-is-a-bush-white-house-lawyer-angering-senate-democrats/2018/08/15/224973dc-a082-11e8-b562-1db4209bd992_story.html.

40. *Swidler & Berlin v. United States*, 524 U.S. 399 (1998).

41. Author interview with Ken Starr, July 16, 2018; Joan Biskupic, "How the Clinton Sex Scandal Shaped Brett Kavanaugh and Could Give Clues on His Thoughts on Robert Mueller," CNN, August 22, 2018, https://www.cnn.com/2018/08/20/politics/kavanaugh-clinton-starr-lewinsky-memo/index.html.

42. "President Attends Swearing-In Ceremony for Brett Kavanaugh to the U.S. Court of Appeals for the District of Columbia Circuit," press release, White House, June 1, 2006, https://georgewbush-whitehouse.archives.gov/news/releases/2006/06/20060601-4.html.

43. All quotes taken from Kavanaugh transcript, *Confirmation Hearing on the Nomination of Hon. Brett M. Kavanaugh.*

44. Conservative blogger Edward Whelan put out information he believed would vindicate Kavanaugh, "compelling evidence" that would show that Kavanaugh was telling the truth: Ed Whelan (@EdWhelanEPPC), September 18, 2018, 6:37 P.M., https://twitter.com/edwhelaneppc/status/1042180930620796928. Whelan advanced the notion that Ford had mixed up the houses where the incident occurred and had misidentified the possible assailant. He posted the name of a Georgetown Prep classmate of Kavanaugh's and the floor plan of the house where he had lived. Ford issued a statement saying, "I knew them both. There is zero chance that I would confuse them." Whelan, then the president of the Ethics and Public Policy Center, apologized for publicly naming the other Georgetown Prep student and took a leave of absence from the center. His claim of mistaken identity, however, continued to be embraced by some Republicans. Matt Stevens, "Edward Whelan, Conservative Strategist, Takes Leave of Absence after Kavanaugh Tweets," *New York Times*, September 23, 2018, https://www.nytimes.com/2018/09/23/us/politics/ed-whelan-eppc.html.

45. Mitch McConnell, *The Long Game* (New York: Sentinel, 2019), 273.

46. Michael S. Schmidt, *Donald Trump v. The United States* (New York: Random House, 2020), 346.

47. Jill C. Tyson, assistant director, FBI, to the Hon. Sheldon Whitehouse and the Hon. Christopher A. Coons, June 30, 2021, https://www.whitehouse.senate.gov/imo/media/doc/20210630%20FBI%20Response%20to%20Sen%20Whitehouse%20Sen%20Coons,pdf.

48. Retired Justice Stevens's remarks about Kavanaugh's potentially disqualifying testimony, https://www.c-span.org/video/?451375-1/retired-justice-stevens-judge-kavanaughs-

hearing-performance-disqualifying; specific segment is here: https://www.youtube
.com/watch?v=PkgR50q5-L0; Susan Svrluga, "'Unfathomable': More Than 2,400 Law
Professors Sign Letter Opposing Kavanaugh's Confirmation," *Washington Post,* October 4, 2018, https://www.washingtonpost.com/education/2018/10/04/unprecedented-
unfathomable-more-than-law-professors-sign-letter-after-kavanaugh-hearing; Joan
Biskupic, "Partisanship Questions Threaten to Shadow Kavanaugh on the Court," CNN,
October 5, 2018, https://www.cnn.com/2018/10/05/politics/partisanship-questions-
shadow-brett-kavanaugh/index.html.

49.     Allie Malloy, Kate Sullivan, and Jeff Zeleny, "Trump Mocks Christine Blasey Ford's
Testimony, Tells People to 'Think of Your Son,'" CNN, October 3, 2018, https://www
.cnn.com/2018/10/02/politics/trump-mocks-christine-blasey-ford-kavanaugh-
supreme-court/index.html; "Donald Trump Makes Lewd Remarks About Women on
Video," YouTube video, posted by NBC News, October 17, 2016, https://www.youtube
.com/watch?v=fYqKx1GuZGg.

50.     "Susan Collins Announces She Will Vote to Confirm Judge Kavanaugh," press release,
Susan Collins, October 5, 2018, https://www.collins.senate.gov/newsroom/senator-
collins-announces-she-will-vote-confirm-judge-kavanaugh. Collins's floor speech appears in 115 Cong. Rec. S6587 (daily ed., October 5, 2018) (statement of Susan Collins),
https://www.congress.gov/115/crec/2018/10/05/CREC-2018-10-05-pt1-PgS6559-7
.pdf.

51.     McConnell, *The Long Game,* 275.

52.     John Paul Stevens, *Five Chiefs* (New York: Little, Brown, 2011), 207–8.

53.     "Trump Apologizes to Kavanaugh and His Family During Ceremonial Swearing-In," YouTube video, posted by CNN, October 8, 2018, https://www.youtube.com/
watch?v=KqnNN52whlw; "The Ceremonial Swearing-In of Supreme Court Justice Brett
Kavanaugh by President Donald Trump," CNN, October 10, 2018, https://www.cnn
.com/2018/10/10/politics/transcript-trump-brett-kavanaugh-swearing-in/index.html.

54.     Brooke Singman, "Meet Attorney General Barr's 'Right Hand': Kerri Kupec on Her
Journey to the Justice Department," Fox News, December 23, 2020, https://www.fox
news.com/politics/meet-barr-right-hand-kerri-kupec-justice-department.

## Chapter 4: The Triumvirate

1.      "Donald F. McGahn II: The Legal & Regulatory Landscape in the Era of Trump," You-
Tube video, posted by Widener Law Commonwealth, February 25, 2020, https://www
.youtube.com/watch?v=N-Jo6iH0PpY.

2.      McConnell and McGahn pressed for less federal regulation particularly in campaign
finance, applauding such decisions as the 2010 *Citizens United.* They teamed up in 2021
after Trump left office for a Supreme Court case brought by Texas Republican senator
Ted Cruz targeting a federal regulation that limited loans and repayments to candidates.
In a friend-of-the-court brief to the Supreme Court written by McGahn, representing
McConnell, they urged the justices not only to lift the loan limit but also to use the
case to wipe out what remained of the 2002 Bipartisan Campaign Reform Act (BCRA;
commonly known as McCain-Feingold for its leading Senate sponsors, Arizona Republican John McCain and Wisconsin Democrat Russ Feingold). The justices sided with
Cruz on the loan limitation but declined to roll back BCRA regulations as far as Mc-
Connell and McGahn had sought. *Federal Election Commission v. Cruz,* 596 U.S. _____
(2022), https://www.supremecourt.gov/opinions/21pdf/21-12_m6hn.pdf; earlier amicus curiae brief of Senator Mitch McConnell, https://www.supremecourt.gov/Docket
PDF/21/21-12/206152/20211222125801433_21-12%20merits%20tsac%20McCon
nell.pdf.

3.      For an investigative piece on Leonard Leo's fundraising efforts, see Robert O'Harrow Jr.
and Shawn Boburg, "A Conservative Activist's Behind-the-Scenes Campaign to Remake

the Nation's Courts," *Washington Post*, May 21, 2019, https://www.washingtonpost.com/graphics/2019/investigations/leonard-leo-federalists-society-courts. See also Kenneth P. Vogel and Shane Goldmacher, "An Unusual $1.6 Billion Donation Bolsters Conservatives," *New York Times*, August 22, 2022, https://www.nytimes.com/2022/08/22/us/politics/republican-dark-money.html.

4. Jack Goldsmith (@jacklgoldsmith), August 18, 2018, 4:11 P.M., https://twitter.com/jacklgoldsmith/status/1030910169453080577.

5. Iver Peterson, "Patrick T. McGahn Jr., 72, Lawyer for Casinos," *New York Times*, August 3, 2000, https://www.nytimes.com/2000/08/03/nyregion/patrick-t-mcgahn-jr-72-lawyer-for-casinos.html; Wolfgang Saxon, "Joseph McGahn, 82, Pioneer of Casinos in Atlantic City," *New York Times*, December 28, 1999, https://www.nytimes.com/1999/12/28/nyregion/joseph-mcgahn-82-pioneer-of-casinos-in-atlantic-city.html; Don Sr. obituary, https://gormleyfuneralhomellc.com/tribute/details/134/Donald-McGahn/obituary.html; lawsuit details from "Trump Sues Former Lawyer 'Paddy' McGahn," *The Press of Atlantic City*, October 6, 1995, https://pressofatlanticcity.com/trump-sues-former-lawyer-patrick-paddy-mcgahn/article_6b3f9e76-16d8-11e6-b681-2b0df4c3460a.html;

6. Don McGahn at Princeton University, "The Politics of Judicial Nominations in an Age of Mistrust," March 6, 2020. (Author was a conference participant.)

7. McGahn at Widener, February 25, 2020; Michelle Brunetti Post, "Atlantic City Native Don McGahn Gives Glimpse into White House Counsel Role," *The Press of Atlantic City*, January 23, 2020, https://pressofatlanticcity.com/politics/atlantic-city-native-don-mcgahn-gives-glimpse-into-white-house-counsel-role/article_57dcdd98-e5f8-574e-895a-50591141c4bc.html

8. McGahn at Widener, February 25, 2020.

9. See, for example, Eric Lichtblau, "In Don McGahn, Donald Trump Gets a Combative White House Counsel," *New York Times*, December 12, 2016, https://www.nytimes.com/2016/12/12/us/politics/donald-trump-white-house-counsel-donald-mcgahn.html.

10. Lichtblau, "In Don McGahn"; Ellen L. Weintraub, "Trump's Pick for White House Counsel Is Wrong for the Job," *Washington Post*, December 9, 2016, https://www.washingtonpost.com/opinions/i-worked-with-trumps-pick-for-white-house-counsel-he-doesnt-care-about-corruption/2016/12/09/76f0793c-bcac-11e6-94ac-3d324840106c_story.html; Brody Mullins and Mary Jacoby, "FEC Chairman McGahn Marches to His Own Tune," *Wall Street Journal*, October 29, 2008, https://www.wsj.com/articles/SB122523208143177711; Charles Homans, "Mitch McConnell Got Everything He Wanted. But at What Cost?," *The New York Times Magazine*, January 22, 2019, https://www.nytimes.com/2019/01/22/magazine/mcconnell-senate-trump.html.

11. McGahn at Widener, February 25, 2020.

12. McGahn "The Politics of Judicial Nominations."

13. David Enrich, *Servants of the Damned* (New York: HarperCollins, 2022), 241–42.

14. Robert S. Mueller III, *Report on the Investigation into Russian Interference in the 2016 Presidential Election*, vol. 2 (Washington, D.C.: U.S. Department of Justice, March 2019), 4, https://www.justice.gov/archives/sco/file/1373816/download; Committee on the Judiciary, U.S. House of Representatives, Washington, D.C. Interview of Don McGahn, June 4, 2021, https://judiciary.house.gov/uploadedfiles/mcgahn_interview_transcript.pdf.

15. Kenneth B. Noble, "New Views Emerge of Bork's Role in Watergate Dismissals," *New York Times*, July 26, 1987, https://www.nytimes.com/1987/07/26/us/new-views-emerge-of-bork-s-role-in-watergate-dismissals.html; Mueller, *Report*, vol. 2, pp. 85–86, https://www.justice.gov/storage/report_volume2.pdf.

16. Mueller, vol. 2, p. 1.

17. McGahn returned to Jones Day and continued to represent Majority Leader McConnell and to work for Senate candidates, including in 2020, as McConnell tried to preserve the GOP majority and his leadership post.

18. McGahn, "The Politics of Judicial Nominations."

19. Mitch McConnell, *The Long Game* (New York: Sentinel, 2019), 269.

20. A. Mitchell McConnell Jr., "Haynsworth and Carswell: A New Senate Standard of Excellence," *Kentucky Law Journal* 59 (1970–71): 43–70, https://www.govinfo.gov/content/pkg/GPO-CHRG-REHNQUIST/pdf/GPO-CHRG-REHNQUIST-4-23-1.pdf; "McConnell Honors the Life of Marlow Cook," press release, Mitch McConnell, February 4, 2016, https://www.republicanleader.senate.gov/newsroom/remarks/mcconnell-honors-the-life-of-marlow-cook. Antonin Scalia was assistant attorney general of the Department of Justice's Office of Legal Counsel from 1974 to 1977.

21. McConnell, *The Long Game*, 51, 61, 65.

22. George Lardner Jr., "The Man Who Makes Money Talk," *Washington Post*, September 7, 1997, https://www.washingtonpost.com/wp-srv/politics/special/campfin/stories/cf090797.htm. For McConnell's National Republican Senatorial Committee tenure, see the biography on his website, https://www.republicanleader.senate.gov/about.

23. McConnell, *The Long Game*, 80, 85–86.

24. 133 Cong. Rec. 28901 (daily ed., October 22, 1987) (remarks of Mitch McConnell), https://www.govinfo.gov/content/pkg/GPO-CRECB-1987-pt21/pdf/GPO-CRECB-1987-pt21-1-2.pdf.

25. "Senate Debate on Filibuster Rules," C-SPAN, November 21, 2013, https://www.c-span.org/video/?c4739176/user-clip-regret-lot-sooner.

26. Ted Barrett, "Mitch McConnell Makes Senate History as Longest-Serving Republican Leader," CNN, June 12, 2018, https://www.cnn.com/2018/06/12/politics/mitch-mcconnell-longest-serving-gop-senate-leader/index.html.

27. McConnell, *The Long Game*, 260, 262.

28. Senate Republican Conference, "Letter to President Barack H. Obama," March 2, 2009, https://web.archive.org/web/20100507163000/http:/republican.senate.gov/public/index.cfm?FuseAction=Blogs.View&Blog_ID=3c522434-76e5-448e-9ead-1ec-214b881ac&Month=3&Year=2009. McConnell's barriers to Obama's choices for the bench were reinforced by Federalist Society leaders. Leonard Leo and three other Republican lawyers, including former attorney general Edwin Meese III, wrote to McConnell within days of the Obama inaugural to urge him to apply "an unprecedented level of Senate scrutiny" to Obama's nominees for the bench. Joan Biskupic, *The Chief: The Life and Turbulent Times of Chief Justice John Roberts* (New York: Basic Books, 2019), 304.

29. Russell Wheeler of the Brookings Institution's Governance Studies Program, who has tracked judicial nominations for decades, said that the median time for Obama appeals court candidates, from nomination to confirmation, was 229 days. During George W. Bush's tenure, the median was 219 days; during Clinton's it was 139 days; and during Reagan's tenure it was 45 days. Joan Biskupic, "Amid Tension, Trump and McConnell Together on Judges," CNN, September 5, 2017, https://www.cnn.com/2017/09/05/politics/Donald-trump-mitch-mcconnell-federal-judges/index.html; also see Congressional Research Service, "Judicial Nomination Statistics and Analysis: U.S. Circuit and District Courts, 1977–2020," report no. R45622, May 18, 2021, https://crsreports.congress.gov/product/pdf/R/R45622.

30. Dates of Neil Gorsuch's contacts with officials drawn from his Senate Judiciary Committee questionnaire, https://www.judiciary.senate.gov/imo/media/doc/Neil%20M.%20Gorsuch%20SJQ%20(Public).pdf.

31. "Steven Calabresi '80, '83 J.D., David McIntosh '80 & Lee Liberman Otis '79," *Yale Alumni Magazine*, May 8, 2009, https://yalealumnimagazine.com/blog_posts/956-steven-calabresi-80-83jd-david-mcintosh-80-lee-liberman-otis-79; Michael Kruse, "The Weekend at Yale That Changed American Politics," *Politico Magazine*, September/October 2018, https://www.politico.com/magazine/story/2018/08/27/federalist-society-yale-history-conservative-law-court-219608.

32. Joan Biskupic, *American Original: The Life and Constitution of Supreme Court Justice Antonin Scalia* (New York: Sarah Crichton Books, 2009), 79.

33. "Justice Thomas Conversation at Federalist Society," January 31, 2020, C-SPAN, https://www.c-span.org/video/?468755-1/justice-clarence-thomas-conversation-federalist-society.

34. Author interviews with Leonard Leo, November 16, 2020, May 4, 2021, March 11, 2022.

35. Author interview with Leonard Leo, October 26, 2022.

36. Presidential Candidate Debates, Republican Candidates Debate in Greenville, South Carolina, The American Presidency Project, https://www.presidency.ucsb.edu/node/311440.

37. Megan Rosenfeld, "For the High Court, a New Tune," *Washington Post*, May 21, 1988, https://www.washingtonpost.com/archive/lifestyle/1988/05/21/for-the-high-court-a-new-tune/ce7397ce-d7f7-497a-9a64-9b875075caf7.

38. Author interview with Leonard Leo, March 11, 2022.

39. President Richard Nixon had campaigned against the liberalism of the Earl Warren Court, particularly its decisions favoring criminal defendants. The Reagan administration was the first of the modern era that undertook a systematic approach to changing the courts through lifetime appointments.

40. Author interviews with Leonard Leo, November 16, 2020, and March 11, 2022.

41. Jeff Greenfield, "The Justice Who Built the Trump Court," Politico, July 9, 2018, https://www.politico.com/magazine/story/2018/07/09/david-souter-the-supreme-court-justice-who-built-the-trump-court-218953.

42. Russell Wheeler, "Judicial Appointments in Trump's First Three Years: Myths and Realities," Brookings Institution, January 28, 2020, https://www.brookings.edu/blog/fixgov/2020/01/28/judicial-appointments-in-trumps-first-three-years-myths-and-realities/. Regarding the ages of judges, Wheeler noted, for example, that the average age of Trump's appellate judge choices was 47; for Obama's, it was 53. For racial demographics covering the Biden administration, Wheeler provided updated statistics to author for the period ending September 30, 2022; 21 percent of Biden's nominees were Black women, most visibly, of course, Ketanji Brown Jackson to the Supreme Court.

43. Wheeler, "Judicial Appointments."

44. Pamela A. Bresnahan to the Hon. Charles E. Grassley and the Hon. Dianne Feinstein, November 7, 2017, https://www.americanbar.org/content/dam/aba/administrative/government_affairs_office/talley-rating-letter-to-grassley-and-feinstein.pdf.

45. Aaron Blake, "That Painful Exchange Between a Trump Judicial Pick and a GOP Senator, Annotated," *Washington Post*, December 15, 2017, https://www.washingtonpost.com/news/the-fix/wp/2017/12/15/that-painful-exchange-between-a-trump-judicial-pick-and-a-gop-senator-annotated.

46. Jonah Engel Bromwich and Niraj Chokshi, "Trump Judicial Nominee Attracts Scorn after Flopping in Hearing," *New York Times*, December 15, 2017, https://www.nytimes.com/2017/12/15/us/politics/matthew-petersen-senator-kennedy.html; Karoun Demirjian, "Republican Senator Suggests Trump Is Strong-Arming Judicial Nominees Through Congress," *Washington Post*, November 29, 2017, https://www.washingtonpost.com/powerpost/republican-senator-suggests-trump-is-strong-arming-judicial-nominees-through-congress/2017/11/29/5842d74c-d51e-11e7-95bf-df7c19270879_story.html.

47. "Matthew Petersen's Letter to Trump Withdrawing His Judicial Nomination," CNN, December 18, 2017, https://www.cnn.com/2017/12/18/politics/petersen-nomination-withdrawal-letter.

48. Bryn Stole, "Kennedy: 'Incredible' Résumé, but Selection Process, Fifth Circuit Nominee's Louisiana Ties Raise Doubts," *The Advocate* (New Orleans), November 29, 2017, https://www.theadvocate.com/acadiana/news/courts/article_bb78b934-d556-11e7-87c2-8fb7330aa700.html.

49.  "John Kennedy's Opening Statement at Kyle Duncan Confirmation Hearing," C-SPAN, November 29, 2017, https://www.c-span.org/video/?c4694344/user-clip-john-kennedys-opening-statement-kyle-duncan-confirmation-hearing.

50.  Author interviews with Leonard Leo, May 4, 2021, and March 11, 2022.

51.  "Judge Justin Walker Investiture Part Four—Judge Walker Speech," YouTube video, posted by "Walker Investiture," March 13, 2020, https://www.youtube.com/watch?v=k5iUfudxuM8.

52.  Walker cited his work in his Senate Judiciary Committee questionnaire, https://www.judiciary.senate.gov/imo/media/doc/Justin20Walker20SJQ20-20PUBLIC.pdf.

53.  *Susan Seven-Sky v. Eric H. Holder, Jr.*, 661 F.3d 1 (D.C. Cir. 2011), https://caselaw.find law.com/us-dc-circuit/1585226.html.

54.  *National Federation of Independent Business v. Sebelius*, 567 U.S. 519 (2012), https://www.supremecourt.gov/opinions/11pdf/11-393c3a2.pdf.

55.  Justin Walker, "Brett Kavanaugh Said Obamacare Was Unprecedented and Unlawful," *The Federalist*, July 3, 2018, https://thefederalist.com/2018/07/03/brett-kavanaugh-said-obamacare-unprecedented-unlawful; "Judge Justin Walker Investiture Part Four"; Nomination of Justin Walker to the United States Court of Appeals for the D.C. Circuit, Questions for the Record Submitted May 13, 2020, https://www.judiciary.senate.gov/imo/media/doc/Walker%20Responses%20to%20QFRs1.pdf.

56.  "Senate Confirms Justin Walker of Kentucky to Be U.S. District Judge," press release, Mitch McConnell, October 24, 2019, https://www.republicanleader.senate.gov/newsroom/press-releases/senate-confirms-justin-walker-of-kentucky-to-be-us-district-judge.

57.  "Ratings of Article III and Article IV Judicial Nominees, 115th Congress," Standing Committee on the Federal Judiciary, American Bar Association, December 13, 2018, https://www.americanbar.org/content/dam/aba/administrative/government_affairs_office/web-rating-chart-trump-115.pdf; "Ratings of Article III and Article IV Judicial Nominees, 116th Congress," Standing Committee on the Federal Judiciary, American Bar Association, December 15, 2020, https://www.americanbar.org/content/dam/aba/administrative/government_affairs_office/webratingchart-trump116.pdf; dates from Walker Senate questionnaire; "Judge Justin Walker Investiture Part Four."

58.  "Judge Justin Walker Investiture Part Four."

59.  *On Fire Christian Center, Inc. v. Fischer*, no. 3:2020cv00264—Document 6 (W.D. Ky. 2020), https://law.justia.com/cases/federal/district-courts/kentucky/kywdce/3:2020cv00264/116558/6.

60.  Susan Davis, "Judge Says He Faced No Political Pressure from McConnell to Retire," NPR, May 5, 2020, https://www.npr.org/2020/05/05/850772809/judge-says-he-faced-no-political-pressure-from-mcconnell-to-retire; Carl Hulse, "Appeals Court Vacancy Is Under Scrutiny Ahead of Contested Confirmation Hearing," *New York Times*, May 4, 2020, https://www.nytimes.com/2020/05/04/us/politics/senate-confirmation-justin-walker.html; author interview with Thomas Griffith, June 15, 2022.

61.  Jeffrey Minear to Elizabeth Paret, circuit executive, May 8, 2020; Judge Karen Le-Craft Henderson Judicial Council order, May 15, 2020, https://www.cadc.uscourts.gov/internet/misconduct.nsf/2EDB3A1B222B45BD852585690068B236/$file/DC-20-90011.O.2.pdf.

62.  Nina Totenberg, "Federal Panel of Judges Dismisses All 83 Ethics Complaints against Brett Kavanaugh," NPR, December 18, 2018, https://www.npr.org/2018/12/18/678004085/federal-panel-of-judges-dismiss-all-83-ethics-complaints-against-brett-kavanaugh.

63.  "Chief Justice Roberts Remarks at University of Minnesota Law School," October 16, 2018, C-SPAN, https://www.c-span.org/video/?451977-1/chief-justice-roberts-stresses-supreme-courts-independence-contentious-kavanaugh-hearings.

64.  Paul LeBlanc, "Sotomayor Says Kavanaugh a Part of the Supreme Court 'Family,'" CNN, November 17, 2018, https://www.cnn.com/2018/11/17/politics/sotomayor-kavanaugh-axe-files-axelrod/index.html; Veronica Stracqualursi, "Ruth Bader Ginsburg Defends Kava-

naugh, Gorsuch as 'Very Decent and Very Smart,'" CNN, July 26, 2019, https://www.cnn.com/2019/07/26/politics/ruth-bader-ginsburg-kavanaugh-gorsuch/index.html.

65. Joan Biskupic, "Allegations Remain in Forefront for Kavanaugh, 7 Months after His Confirmation," CNN, May 3, 2019, https://www.cnn.com/2019/05/03/politics/brett-kavanaugh-christine-blasey-ford-stephen-moore-supreme-court/index.html; Kamala Harris, Christine Blasey Ford, "100 Most Influential People," *Time*, 2019, https://time.com/collection/100-most-influential-people-2019/5567675/christine-blasey-ford; Mitch McConnell, Brett Kavanaugh, "100 Most Influential People," *Time*, 2019, https://time.com/collection/100-most-influential-people-2019/5567753/brett-kavanaugh.

66. Joan Biskupic, "Justice Brett Kavanaugh Says Judges 'Owe Our Allegiance to the Constitution,'" CNN, May 7, 2019, https://www.cnn.com/2019/05/07/politics/kavanaugh-wisconsin/index.html.

67. McGahn, "The Politics of Judicial Nominations."

## Chapter 5: A Moment of Truth

1. Kagan referred to her brother's comic book passion during an appearance at Georgetown University Law Center on July 18, 2019. See "Supreme Court Justice Elena Kagan discusses John Paul Stevens, Gerrymandering, Writing and More," YouTube video, posted by Georgetown Law, July 22, 2019, https://www.youtube.com/watch?v=k21ShdZLV-A (from 55:20).

2. *Kimble v. Marvel Entertainment*, 576 U.S. 446 (2015), https://www.supremecourt.gov/opinions/14pdf/13-720_jiel.pdf.

3. *Kimble v. Marvel Entertainment*.

4. *Kisor v. Wilkie*, no. 18-15, March 27, 2019, transcript, https://www.supremecourt.gov/oral_arguments/argument_transcripts/2018/18-15_3314.pdf.

5. Dahlia Lithwick, "Does the Chief Justice Hate Elena Kagan?," *Newsweek*, July 29, 2010, https://www.newsweek.com/does-chief-justice-hate-elena-kagan-74245. For Roberts's praise for Kagan, see "A Conversation with Chief Justice Roberts," conversation with J. Harvie Wilkinson, C-SPAN, June 25, 2011, C-SPAN https://www.c-span.org/video/?300203-1/conversation-chief-justice-roberts.

6. Christi Parsons, "U. of C. Faculty Didn't Back Kagan," *Chicago Tribune*, May 30, 2010, https://www.chicagotribune.com/news/ct-xpm-2010-05-30-ct-met-kagan-chicago-20100530-story.html.

7. When Anthony Kennedy retired, Ginsburg considered taking his chambers but in the end opted against it. Justice Samuel Alito took over the Kennedy chambers in fall 2018. Information regarding previous Ginsburg falls from author interviews with Ginsburg, August 7, 2012, and July 2, 2013; "Press Release Regarding Justice Ginsburg," Supreme Court of the United States, November 8, 2018, https://www.supremecourt.gov/publicinfo/press/pressreleases/pr_11-08-18.

8. November 8, 2018, statement regarding Ginsburg's fall and fracturing of ribs, https://www.supremecourt.gov/publicinfo/press/pressreleases/pr_11-08-18; December 21, 2018, statement regarding Ginsburg's lung surgery, https://www.supremecourt.gov/publicinfo/press/pressreleases/pr_12-21-18.

9. Alan Rappeport, "Wilbur Ross, a Billionaire Investor, Is Confirmed as Commerce Secretary," *New York Times*, February 27, 2017, https://www.nytimes.com/2017/02/27/us/politics/wilbur-ross-commerce-secretary.html.

10. Facts drawn from U.S. district court decision in *State of New York v. U.S. Department of Commerce*, 351 F. Supp. 3d 502 (S.D.N.Y. 2019).

11. John Gore's aide Danielle Cutrona wrote to Wendy Teramoto, chief of staff for Secretary of Commerce Wilbur Ross, "The AG is eager to assist" (September 17, 2017).

12. Arthur Gary letter in the record compiled by Judge Furman and other courts hearing challenges to the Department of Commerce. Gary wrote that "The Department of Justice

is committed to robust and evenhanded enforcement of the Nation's civil rights laws and to free and fair elections for all Americans. In furtherance of that commitment, I write on behalf of the Department to formally request that the Census Bureau reinstate on the 2020 Census questionnaire a question regarding citizenship, formerly included in the so-called 'long form' census. This data is critical to the Department's enforcement of Section 2 of the Voting Rights Act and its important protections against racial discrimination in voting."

13. Ross's memo of March 2018 reads, in part, "As you know, on December 12, 2017, the Department of Justice . . . requested that the Census Bureau reinstate a citizenship question on the decennial census to provide census block level citizenship voting age population ('CVAP') data. . . . Having these data at the census block level will permit more effective enforcement of the Act. Section 2 protects minority population voting rights." Ross covered his earlier role by writing, "Following receipt of the DOJ request, I set out to take a hard look at the request and ensure that I considered all facts and data relevant to the question so that I could make an informed decision on how to respond."

14. There were three sets of grounds: First, the challengers asserted that the citizenship question violated the Constitution's mandate for an "actual enumeration," because the query would diminish the accuracy of the court. Second, they noted that the government was required to provide all people, not only citizens, "equal protection of the law." The citizenship question would deter some respondents, who would then not be counted in the important tabulation that leads to political representation and government funding. Third, and no less crucially, the challengers argued that the way the citizenship question was adopted violated the Administrative Procedure Act, a 1946 law that dictated the specific procedures all agencies are required to follow when changing policies.

15. For additional discussion of the "shadow docket," see pages 209–10 and 216–17.

16. *In Re Department of Commerce,* October 22, 2018, order, https://www.supremecourt.gov/opinions/18pdf/18a375_k536.pdf.

17. "In arriving at his decision as he did, Secretary Ross violated the law," Furman wrote. "And in doing so with respect to the census—one of the most critical constitutional functions our Federal Government performs . . . and a 'mainstay of our democracy'—Secretary Ross violated the public trust." *State of New York v. U.S. Department of Commerce.*

18. Ibid.

19. Joan Biskupic, "20 Years of Closed-Door Conversations with Ruth Bader Ginsburg," CNN, September 19, 2020, https://www.cnn.com/2020/09/19/politics/rbg-biskupic-ruth-bader-ginsburg-interviews/index.html.

20. The Court's action on the matter was handled through written filings, without oral arguments, and neither the conservatives nor the liberals provided any reasoning with the order that temporarily restored the rules for transgender troops.

21. *Department of Commerce v. New York,* no. 18-966, April 23, 2019, https://www.supreme court.gov/oral_arguments/argument_transcripts/2018/18-966_i4dj.pdf (Roberts: "The CVAP, Citizen Voting Age Population, is the critical element in voting rights enforcement, and this is getting citizen information").

22. *Department of Commerce v. New York,* no. 18-966, April 23, 2019, transcript, https://www.supremecourt.gov/oral_arguments/argument_transcripts/2018/18-966_5hek.pdf.

23. Author interviews with lawyers involved in the moot court.

24. *Department of Commerce v. New York,* transcript.

25. "Solicitor General Noel Francisco Delivers Remarks at the Department of Justice Asian American and Pacific Islander Heritage Month Program," Office of Public Affairs, U.S. Department of Justice, May 24, 2018, https://www.justice.gov/opa/speech/solicitor-general-noel-francisco-delivers-remarks-department-justice-asian-american-and.

26. Francisco amended the record in *Trump v. Hawaii,* for example, after he said, "Well, the President has made crystal clear on September 25th that he had no intention of imposing the Muslim ban," and that "He has made crystal-clear that Muslims in this country are great Americans and there are many, many Muslim countries who love this country, and he has praised Islam as one of the great countries of the world." (https://www.supremecourt.gov/oral_arguments/argument_transcripts/2017/17-965_l5gm.pdf, https://www.supremecourt.gov/DocketPDF/17/17-965/45303/20180501160039839_Letter2017-965.pdf, https://www.supremecourt.gov/DocketPDF/17/17-965/43794/20180418113221228_17-965rbUnitedStates.pdf). In *Babb v. Wilkie,* involving a Veterans Affairs pharmacist bringing an age-discrimination complaint against her federal employer, Francisco argued that the Age Discrimination in Employment Act barred the relief she sought, but that other legal avenues were available beyond the ADEA, including under a section of the Civil Service Reform Act. Opposing lawyer Roman Martinez, a former law clerk to Roberts, retorted, "That's a cruel joke that will be played on this Court if you accept that rationale." Martinez said that the section of the Civil Service Reform Act that Francisco cited was unenforceable. "The Solicitor General has had months to come up with a solution to this hypothetical," regarding alternative avenues for age bias, "and the best the Solicitor General can do is come up with a statutory provision that's unenforceable." The justices ordered the lawyers to submit letters explaining the discrepancy, and Francisco acknowledged the error regarding judicial relief. (See https://www.supremecourt.gov/DocketPDF/18/18-882/129698/20200123125354646_18-8822osupp2obrief2oletter.pdf, https://www.supremecourt.gov/DocketPDF/18/18-882/129713/20200123134009564_2020-01-2320No.2018-88220Babb20Supplemental20Letter2oBr.pdf; see also Erich Wagner, "Trump Administration Acknowledges Mistake in Supreme Court Age Discrimination Case," *Government Executive,* January 30, 2020, https://www.govexec.com/management/2020/01/trump-administration-acknowledges-mistake-supreme-court-age-discrimination-case/162785.)

27. Author's private interviews with Supreme Court sources throughout the 2018–2019 session.
28. *Vieth v. Jubelirer,* 541 U.S. 267 (2004), https://www.supremecourt.gov/opinions/03pdf/02-1580.pdf.
29. Michael Wines, "Thomas Hofeller, Republican Master of Political Maps, Dies at 75, *New York Times,* August 21, 2018, https://www.nytimes.com/2018/08/21/obituaries/thomas-hofeller-republican-master-of-political-maps-dies-at-75.html; see also "User Clip: Hofeller Defines Redistricting," C-SPAN, May, 27, 1991, https://www.c-span.org/video/?c4801547/user-clip-hofeller-defines-redistricting and "User Clip: Hofeller on Redistricing," C-SPAN, August 13, 2001, https://www.c-span.org/video/?c4804050/user-clip-hofeller-redistricing; and see Michael Wines, "Republican Gerrymander Whiz Had Wider Influence Than Was Known," *New York Times,* September 10, 2019, https://www.nytimes.com/2019/09/10/us/republican-gerrymander-thomas-hofeller.html; and David Daley, "The Secret Files of the Master of Modern Republican Gerrymandering," *The New Yorker,* September 6, 2019, https://www.newyorker.com/news/news-desk/the-secret-files-of-the-master-of-modern-republican-gerrymandering.
30. *Gill v. Whitford,* 585 U.S. ____ (2018), https://www.supremecourt.gov/opinions/17pdf/16-1161_dc8f.pdf.
31. *Gill v. Whitford.*
32. *Rucho v. Common Cause,* no. 18-422, March 2019, transcript, https://www.supremecourt.gov/oral_arguments/argument_transcripts/2018/18-422_3e04.pdf.
33. *Rucho v. Common Cause,* transcript.
34. Drawn from Kagan's dissent in *Rucho v. Common Cause,* 588 U.S. ____ (2019), https://www.supremecourt.gov/opinions/18pdf/18-422_9ol1.pdf.
35. *Franchise Tax Board v. Hyatt,* 587 U.S. ____ (2019), https://www.supremecourt.gov/opinions/18pdf/17-1299_8njq.pdf.

36. *Knick v. Township of Scott,* 588 U. S. ____ (2019), https://www.supremecourt.gov /opinions/18pdf/17-647_m648.pdf.

37. Evidence presented to Judge Furman on May 30, 2019, and included with Dale E. Ho to the Hon. Scott S. Harris, clerk of court, Supreme Court, May 30, 2019, https://www .supremecourt.gov/DocketPDF/18/18-966/101439/20190530142417722_2019.05 .30%20NYIC%20Respondents%20Notice%20of%20Filing%20--%20Final.pdf.

38. Author interviews with lawyers involved in the case throughout the 2018–2019 session; John A. Freedman to the Hon. Jesse M. Furman, May 30, 2019, https://www .brennancenter.org/sites/default/files/legal-work/2019-05-31-595-Plaintiffs%27%20 Unredacted%20Motion.pdf, attached to Ho to Harris. See also Michael Wines, "Deceased GOP Strategist's Hard Drives Reveal New Questions on the Census Citizenship Question," *New York Times,* May 30, 2019, https://www.nytimes.com/2019/05/30/us /census-citizenship-question-hofeller.html.

39. Joshua A. Geltzer, "Will the Legitimacy of the Supreme Court Survive the Census Case?," *New York Times,* May 31, 2019, https://www.nytimes.com/2019/05/31/opinion /census-citizenship-question-supreme-court-travel-ban.html; "Census Target: John Roberts," *Wall Street Journal,* June 2, 2019, https://www.wsj.com/articles/census-target-john-roberts-11559510039.

40. "Justice Elena Kagan Delivers Humor, Wisdom, and Inspiration at Eighth Annual John Paul Stevens Lecture," Colorado Law, November 4, 2019, https://www.colorado.edu /law/2019/11/04/justice-elena-kagan-delivers-humor-wisdom-and-inspiration-eighth-annual-john-paul-stevens.

41. Donald Trump (@realdonaldtrump), June 27, 2019, 1:37:22 P.M. EST, https://www .thetrumparchive.com/?searchbox=%22I+have+asked+the+lawyers+if+they+can+delay +the+Census%22.

42. Katie Benner, "Barr Says Legal Path to Census Citizenship Question Exists, but He Gives No Details," *New York Times,* July 8, 2019, https://www.nytimes.com/2019/07/08/ us/politics/william-barr-census-citizenship.html; William P. Barr, *One Damn Thing After Another* (New York: William Morrow, 2022), 273–79.

43. The Senate had confirmed Barr earlier that February 14, 2019, day, along a near party-line vote, 55–45.

44. Transcript, interview with William P. Barr, George W. Bush Oral History Project, Miller Center, University of Virginia, April 5, 2001, https://millercenter.org/the-presidency /presidential-oral-histories/william-p-barr-oral-history.

45. Barr's June 8, 2018, memo, is available from lawfareblog, https://www.documentcloud .org/documents/5638848-June-2018-Barr-Memo-to-DOJ-Muellers-Obstruction.html.

46. See chapter 6 for an account of Barr's misrepresentation of the report.

47. Benner, "Barr Says Legal Path to Census Citizenship Question Exists."

48. Barr, *One Damn Thing after Another,* 276–78; Michael Wines and Katie Benner, "Judge Rejects Justice Dept. Request to Change Lawyers on Census Case," *New York Times,* July 9, 2019, https://www.nytimes.com/2019/07/09/us/census-citizenship-question.html.

49. "Remarks by Attorney General William P. Barr on Census Citizenship Question," press release, U.S. Department of Justice, July 11, 2019, https://www.justice.gov/opa/speech /remarks-attorney-general-william-p-barr-census-citizenship-question.

50. *Rucho v. Common Cause,* 588 U. S. ____ (2019), https://www.supremecourt.gov/opinions /18pdf/18-422_9ol1.pdf.

51. Kagan dissenting, *Rucho v. Common Cause,* 588 U. S. ____ (2019), https://www.supreme court.gov/opinions/18pdf/18-422_9ol1.pdf. In 2016, Republican congressional candidates won ten of North Carolina's thirteen seats, with 53 percent of the statewide vote. Two years later, Republican candidates won nine of twelve seats, though they received only 50 percent of the vote.

52.  Charles Fried, "A Day of Sorrow for American Democracy," *The Atlantic*, July 3, 2019, https://www.theatlantic.com/ideas/archive/2019/07/rucho-v-common-cause-occasion-sorrow/593227; "Justice Elena Kagan Delivers Humor, Wisdom, and Inspiration."

## Chapter 6: "Justice Is Not Inevitable"

1.  "Chief Justice Roberts Remarks at University of Minnesota Law School," October 16, 2018, C-SPAN, https://www.c-span.org/video/?451977-1/chief-justice-roberts-stresses-supreme-courts-independence-contentious-kavanaugh-hearings.

2.  *East Bay Sanctuary Covenant v. Trump*, order granting temporary restraining order, https://www.cand.uscourts.gov/wp-content/uploads/cases-of-interest/east-bay-sanctuary-v-trump-jst/C18-6810-JST_Order-Granting-TRO.pdf.

3.  "Judge Vance Murder," Federal Bureau of Investigation, accessed September 19, 2022, https://www.fbi.gov/history/famous-cases/judge-vance-murder; "Alabama Executes Man for 1989 Mail-Bomb Murder of U.S. Appeals Court Judge Robert S. Vance," press release, U.S. Attorney's Office, Northern District of Alabama, April 20, 2018, https://www.justice.gov/usao-ndal/pr/alabama-executes-man-1989-mail-bomb-murder-us-appeals-court-judge-robert-s-vance-0.

4.  Jon Tigar was just four years old at the time. Brennan later acknowledged unwanted intervention from J. Edgar Hoover; the justice and the elder Tigar eventually reconciled. (Tigar went on to represent, among others, Angela Davis and the Chicago Seven and, much later, in 1997, Oklahoma City bomber Terry Nichols.) Lois Romano, "A Man of Independent Means," *Washington Post*, September 29, 1997, https://www.washington post.com/archive/lifestyle/1997/09/29/a-man-of-independent-means/efa6e2f2-dd0a-4ea5-8f92-56a66aec72fc; Seth Stern and Stephen Wermiel, *Justice Brennan: Liberal Champion* (New York: Mariner Books, 2010), 264–74.

5.  The *Washington Post* reported that Trump, speaking to reporters in the driveway at the White House, had said, "This was an Obama judge. And I'll tell you what, it's not going to happen like this anymore. Everybody that wants to sue the United States, they file their case in—almost—they file their case in the Ninth Circuit. And it means an automatic loss no matter what you do, no matter how good your case is." Trump predicted: "We will win that case in the Supreme Court of the United States." Robert Barnes, "Rebuking Trump's Criticism of 'Obama Judge,' Chief Justice Roberts Defends Judiciary as 'Independent,'" *Washington Post*, November 21, 2018, https://www.washingtonpost.com/politics/rebuking-trumps-criticism-of-obama-judge-chief-justice-roberts-defends-judiciary-as-independent/2018/11/21/6383c7b2-edb7-11e8-96d4-0d-23f2aaad09_story.html.

6.  The Court's public information office provided the statement first to the Associated Press: Mark Sherman, "Roberts, Trump Spar in Extraordinary Scrap Over Judges," Associated Press, November 21, 2018, https://apnews.com/article/north-america-donald-trump-us-news-ap-top-news-immigration-c4b34f9639e141069c08cf1e3deb6b84.

7.  Donald Trump (@realdonaldtrump), November 21, 2018, 3:51:11 P.M. EST, https://www.thetrumparchive.com/?searchbox=%22Sorry+Chief+Justice+John+Roberts%2C+but+you+do+%22.

8.  *Confirmation Hearing on the Nomination of John G. Roberts, Jr. to Be Chief Justice of the United States*, 109th Cong. 1217 (2005) (statement of John Roberts).

9.  Julie Hirschfeld Davis and Mark Mazzetti, "Highlights of Robert Mueller's Testimony to Congress," *New York Times*, July 24, 2019, https://www.nytimes.com/2019/07/24/us/politics/mueller-testimony.html.

10.  Donald Trump (@realdonaldtrump), July 24, 2019, 10:11:16 A.M. EST, https://www.thetrumparchive.com/?searchbox=%22This+has+been+a+disaster+for+the+Demo crats%22 (Trump added the words "Chris Wallace @FoxNews" at the end of his tweet); Todd Purdum, "Robert Mueller and the Tyranny of 'Optics,'" *The Atlantic*, July 25, 2019,

https://www.theatlantic.com/politics/archive/2019/07/mueller-testimony-congress-optics/594676.

11. Barr's June 8, 2018, memo may be found on lawfareblog: https://www.documentcloud.org/documents/5638848-June-2018-Barr-Memo-to-DOJ-Muellers-Obstruction.html.

12. William P. Barr to the Hon. Lindsey Graham, the Hon. Jerrold Nadler, the Hon. Dianne Feinstein, and the Hon. Doug Collins, March 24, 2019, as reprinted in "Read Attorney General William Barr's Summary of the Mueller Report," *New York Times*, March 24, 2019, https://www.nytimes.com/interactive/2019/03/24/us/politics/barr-letter-mueller-report.html; Reuters Staff, "Trump Responds to Mueller Report: 'Complete and Total Exoneration," Reuters, March 24, 2019, https://www.reuters.com/article/us-usa-trump-russia-tweet/trump-responds-to-mueller-report-complete-and-total-exoneration-idUSKCN1R50U3. For an account of Barr's decision and his motivations in getting ahead of the public Mueller report, see Michael S. Schmidt, *Donald Trump v. The United States* (New York: Random House, 2020), 351–55.

13. Robert S. Mueller III to the Hon. William P. Barr, March 27, 2019, https://int.nyt.com/data/documenthelper/796-mueller-letter-to-barr/02499959cbfa313c36d4/optimized/full.pdf.

14. "Read Trump's Phone Conversation with Volodymyr Zelensky," CNN, September 26, 2019, https://www.cnn.com/2019/09/25/politics/donald-trump-ukraine-transcript-call/index.html.

15. Karoun Demirjian, Mike DeBonis, and Matt Zapotosky, "Trump Said His Ukraine Call Was 'Perfect.' Impeachment Witness Testified Otherwise," *Washington Post*, November 19, 2019, https://www.washingtonpost.com/politics/lt-col-alexander-vindman-reveals-in-testimony-that-he-told-an-intelligence-official-about-trumps-call-with-ukrainian-leader/2019/11/19/61c46b16-0ae4-11ea-8397-a955cd542d00_story.html.

16. Danny Hakim, "Army Officer Who Heard Trump's Ukraine Call Reported Concerns," *New York Times*, October 28, 2019, https://www.nytimes.com/2019/10/28/us/politics/Alexander-Vindman-trump-impeachment.html; Jeremy Diamond, Kevin Liptak, and Katelyn Polantz, "Mulvaney Brashly Admits Quid pro Quo over Ukraine Aid as Key Details Emerge—and Then Denies Doing So," CNN, October 17, 2019, https://www.cnn.com/2019/10/17/politics/mick-mulvaney-quid-pro-quo-donald-trump-ukraine-aid; Michael D. Shear and Katie Rogers, "Mulvaney Says, Then Denies, That Trump Held Back Ukraine Aid as Quid pro Quo," *New York Times*, October 17, 2019, https://www.nytimes.com/2019/10/17/us/politics/mick-mulvaney-trump-ukraine.html; "Read Mulvaney's Conflicting Statements on Quid pro Quo," *New York Times*, October 17, 2019, https://www.nytimes.com/2019/10/17/us/politics/mulvaney-transcript-quid-pro-quo.html.

17. Mueller's team had tried without success to arrange an interview with Trump himself. Explaining why he declined to try a subpoena, Mueller said the effort would likely have been useless because any attempt to enforce the subpoena would be tied up in courts and delay his investigation for a substantial time.

18. Pat A. Cipollone to Nancy Pelosi, October 8, 2019, reprinted in "READ: White House Letter to House Democrats," CNN, October 8, 2019, https://www.cnn.com/2019/10/08/politics/wh-letter-to-pelosi/index.html.

19. U.S. House impeachment reports available here: https://intelligence.house.gov/report; https://judiciary.house.gov/the-impeachment-of-donald-john-trump/. Senate trial and the role of the chief justice: https://www.senate.gov/about/powers-procedures/impeachment.htm#:~:text=In%20the%20case%20of%20presidential,conviction%20is%20removal%20from%20office.

20. Ann E. Marimow and Jonathan O'Connell, "In Court Hearing, Trump Lawyer Argues a Sitting President Would Be Immune from Prosecution Even If He Were to Shoot Someone," *Washington Post*, October 23, 2019, https://www.washingtonpost.com/local/legal-issues/ny-based-appeals-court-to-decide-whether-manhattan-da-can-get-

trumps-tax-returns/2019/10/22/8c491346-ef6e-11e9-8693-f487e46784aa_story.html;
Jeremy Diamond, "Trump: I Could 'Shoot Somebody and I Wouldn't Lose Voters,'"
CNN, January 24, 2016, https://www.cnn.com/2016/01/23/politics/donald-trump-shoot-somebody-support/index.html.

21. *Trump v. Mazars USA,* no. 19-5142, U.S. Court of Appeals for the District of Columbia Circuit, October 11, 2019, https://www.cadc.uscourts.gov/internet/opinions.nsf/20C16C3C5721030C85258490004DE33C/$file/19-5142-1810450.pdf.

22. Chief Justice John Roberts, "2019 Year-End Report on the Federal Judiciary," Public Information Office, Supreme Court of the United States, December 31, 2019, https://www.supremecourt.gov/publicinfo/year-end/2019year-endreport.pdf.

23. "READ: Ruth Bader Ginsburg's Eulogy of John Paul Stevens," CNN, July 23, 2019, https://www.cnn.com/2019/07/23/politics/ruth-bader-ginsburg-eulogy-john-paul-stevens/index.html.

24. Linda Greenhouse, "Supreme Court Justice John Paul Stevens, Who Led Liberal Wing, Dies at 99," *New York Times,* July 16, 2019, https://www.nytimes.com/2019/07/16/us/john-paul-stevens-dead.html; Joan Biskupic, "John Paul Stevens: Unassuming but Impactful over His 99 Years," CNN, July 17, 2019, https://www.cnn.com/2019/07/17/politics/john-paul-stevens-analysis/index.html; "H-Gram Special Edition: The Passing of Associate Justice of the Supreme Court John Paul Stevens," Naval History and Heritage Command, July 22, 2019, https://www.history.navy.mil/about-us/leadership/director/directors-corner/h-grams/h-gram-special-edition-stevens.html.

25. Biskupic, "John Paul Stevens: Unassuming but Impactful."

26. "Press Release Regarding Justice Ginsburg," Supreme Court of the United States, August 23, 2019, https://www.supremecourt.gov/publicinfo/press/pressreleases/pr_08-23-19; Joan Biskupic, "20 Years of Closed-Door Conservations with Ruth Bader Ginsburg," CNN, September 19, 2020, https://www.cnn.com/2020/09/19/politics/rbg-biskupic-ruth-bader-ginsburg-interviews/index.html.

27. Joan Biskupic, "Rehnquist Departs Trying Experience," *Washington Post,* February 13, 1999, https://www.washingtonpost.com/wp-srv/politics/special/clinton/stories/rehnquist021399.htm; "A Decorated Sleeve," Harvard Law School, accessed September 19, 2022, https://exhibits.law.harvard.edu/decorated-sleeve.

28. Peter Baker and Nicholas Fandos, "Bolton Objected to Ukraine Pressure Campaign, Calling Giuliani 'A Hand Grenade,'" *New York Times,* October 14, 2019, https://www.nytimes.com/2019/10/14/us/politics/bolton-giuliani-fiona-hill-testimony.html.

29. Paul LeBlanc, "John Roberts Scolds Legal Teams after Tense Exchange: 'Those Addressing the Senate Should Remember Where They Are,'" CNN, January 22, 2020, https://www.cnn.com/2020/01/22/politics/john-roberts-scolds-legal-teams-senate-trial-chief-justice/index.html. The Swayne trial began in 1904. He was impeached by the House in December "for submitting false expense claims, making use of a private railroad car, not living in his district as required by law, and abusing the contempt powers of his court." (A collection of material related to the case is available online from the Library of Congress: https://guides.loc.gov/federal-impeachment/charles-swayne.) Early in 1905, the Senate acquitted Swayne of all charges.

30. Donald Trump (@realdonaldtrump), January 15 12:45:31 A.M. EST, https://www.thetrumparchive.com/?searchbox=%22Now+up+to+187+Federal+Judges%22, and January 24, 2020, 10:37:31 A.M. EST, https://www.thetrumparchive.com/?searchbox=%22over+the+fact+that+Republicans+are+up+to%22.

31. Dana Milbank, "John Roberts Comes Face to Face with the Mess He Made," *Washington Post,* January 23, 2020, https://www.washingtonpost.com/opinions/2020/01/23/john-roberts-comes-face-face-with-mess-he-made.

32. 116th Cong. Rec. S767 (daily ed., January 31, 2020) (statement of John Roberts), https://www.govinfo.gov/content/pkg/CREC-2020-01-31/pdf/CREC-2020-01-31-senate.pdf.

33. "2020 State of the Union Address," C-SPAN, February 4, 2020, https://www.c-span.org/video/?468549-1/2020-state-union-address.

34. "Full Transcript: Mitt Romney's Speech Announcing Vote to Convict Trump," *New York Times*, February 5, 2020, https://www.nytimes.com/2020/02/05/us/politics/mitt-romney-impeachment-speech-transcript.html.

35. "John Roberts Declares Trump Acquitted, Gavels Out Impeachment Trial," YouTube video, posted by Bloomberg Quicktake: Now, February 5, 2020, https://www.youtube.com/watch?v=JeZQe12COz4; Joan Biskupic, "John Roberts' Legacy Will Forever Be Entwined with Trump's," CNN, February 5, 2020, https://www.cnn.com/2020/02/05/politics/john-roberts-impeachment-trial/index.html.

36. *Committee on the Judiciary of the U.S. House of Representatives v. McGahn*, 407 F. Supp. 3d 35 (D.D.C. 2019).

37. "Full Transcript: Mitt Romney's Speech."

38. "President Trump Statement on Senate Acquittal," February 6, 2020, C-SPAN, https://www.c-span.org/video/?469059-1/president-trump-statement-senate-acquittal.

39. Carlton W. Reeves, "Defending the Judiciary: A Call for Justice, Truth, and Diversity on the Bench," April 11, 2019, https://www.youtube.com/watch?v=BlvzpFVDBZw; text version available through, https://lawprofessors.typepad.com/files/4-11-19-judge-reeves-speech.pdf; "Road to the White House 2016, Donald Trump Campaign Rally in San Diego, California," C-SPAN, https://www.c-span.org/video/?410129-1/donald-trump-campaigns-san-diego-california; Curiel case: *Makaeff v. Trump University*, 715 F.3d 254 (9th Cir. 2013), https://cdn.ca9.uscourts.gov/datastore/opinions/2013/04/17/11-55016.pdf.

40. Reeves speech. Regarding Curiel, Reeves said,

> I know what I heard when a federal judge was called "very biased and unfair" because he is "of Mexican heritage." When that judge's ethnicity was said to prevent his issuing "fair rulings." When that judge was called a "hater" simply because he is Latino. I heard the words of James Eastland, a race-baiting politician, empowered by the falsehood of white supremacy, questioning the judicial temperament of a man solely because of the color of his skin. I heard those words and I did not know if it was 1967 or 2017.

41. Lynn Adelman, "The Roberts Court's Assault on Democracy," *Harvard Law & Policy Review* 14 (2020): 131, 136–37, https://harvardlpr.com/wp-content/uploads/sites/20/2020/03/Adelman.pdf.

42. "Resolution of Judicial Misconduct Complaints about District Judge Lynn Adelman," Judicial Council of the Seventh Judicial Circuit, June 22, 2020, http://www.ca7.uscourts.gov/judicial-conduct/judicial-conduct_2020/07-20-90046_90044.pdf, 9.

43. Eugene Volokh, "'Resolution of Judicial Misconduct Complaints About District Judge Lynn Adelman,'" *Reason*, June 24, 2020, https://reason.com/volokh/2020/06/24/resolution-of-judicial-misconduct-complaints-about-district-judge-lynn-adelman.

44. *Shelby County v. Holder*, 570 U.S. 529, 557 (2013).

45. *League of Women Voters of Florida v. Laurel M. Lee*, 4:21cv186-MW/MAF (N.D. Fla. March 31, 2022) (the text of the ruling is available at https://www.miamiherald.com/latest-news/article259981080.ece/BINARY/Judge20WalkerE28099s20ruling.pdf).

46. Jeffrey M. Jones, "Approval of U.S. Supreme Court Down to 40%, a New Low," Gallup, September 23, 2021, https://news.gallup.com/poll/354908/approval-supreme-court-down-new-low.aspx.

## Chapter 7: Culture Wars in a Time of COVID

1. Karlan was known for her easy but well-aimed humor before the justices: As she argued a Fourth Amendment case in 2008, she said that false information from a police computer

file, relied on in the execution of a warrant, had tainted the warrant and that the evidence obtained from it should be suppressed. Chief Justice Roberts said the police were probably doing the best they could on a tight budget. Karlan replied, "There's not a Barney Fife defense to the violation of the Fourth Amendment." (Transcript of *Herring v. United States,* argued in 2008 and decided in 2009, https://www.supremecourt.gov/oral_arguments /argument_transcripts/2008/07-513.pdf.)

2.  *Bostock v. Clayton County,* no. 17-1618, October 8, 2019, transcript, https:// www.supremecourt.gov/oral_arguments/argument_transcripts/2019/17-1618_2a34 .pdf, 4–5.

3.  President Lyndon B. Johnson's Address to a Joint Session of Congress, November 27, 1963, https://www.archives.gov/legislative/features/civil-rights-1964/lbj-address.html; "Landmark Legislation: The Civil Rights Act of 1964," Art & History, United States Senate, https://www.senate.gov/artandhistory/history/common/generic/CivilRights-Act1964.htm; "On This Day, Filibuster Fails to Block the Civil Rights Act," National Constitution Center blog, June 19, 2022, https://constitutioncenter.org/interactive-constitution/blog/on-this-day-congress-passes-the-civil-rights-act.

4.  Author interviews with multiple justices and other Supreme Court sources for chronology of internal debate during 2019–2020 session.

5.  Roberts dissent in *Obergefell v. Hodges,* 576 U.S. 644 (2015).

6.  Jeffrey M. Jones, "LGBT Identification in U.S. Ticks Up to 7.1%," Gallup, February 17, 2022, https://news.gallup.com/poll/389792/lgbt-identification-ticks-up.aspx.

7.  UCLA School of Law Williams Institute, "Adult LGBT Population in the United States," July 2020, https://williamsinstitute.law.ucla.edu/wp-content/uploads/LGBT-Adult-US-Pop-Jul-2020.pdf.

8.  *Harris Funeral Homes v. Equal Employment Opportunity Commission,* no. 18-107, October 8, 2019, transcript, https://www.supremecourt.gov/oral_arguments/argument_trans cripts/2019/18-107_6j37.pdf.

9.  *Harris Funeral Homes v. Equal Employment Opportunity Commission* transcript.

10. Chronology comes from author interviews with Court sources as the case was resolved; Joan Biskupic, "Anger, Leaks and Tensions at the Supreme Court during the LGBTQ Rights Case," CNN, July 28, 2020, https://www.cnn.com/2020/07/28/politics/neil-gorsuch-supreme-court-lgbtq-civil-rights-act-alito/index.html.

11. "The Supreme Court's Textualism Test: Kagan Tries to Lure Gorsuch and Roberts off the Scalia Method," editorial, *Wall Street Journal,* November 21, 2019, https://www.wsj.com /articles/the-supreme-courts-textualism-test-11574382080.

12. Robert P. George, "Counterfeit Textualism," *National Review,* November 19, 2019, https://www.nationalreview.com/2019/11/counterfeit-textualism.

13. "Tribute to Abner Mikva: Justice Elena Kagan," Mikva Challenge blog, July 5, 2016, https://mikvachallenge.org/blog/tribute-kagan. See also Neil A. Lewis, "Abner Mikva, Lawmaker, Judge and Mentor to Obama, Dies at 90," *New York Times,* July 6, 2016, https://www.nytimes.com/2016/07/06/us/abner-mikva-lawmaker-judge-and-mentor-to-obama-dies-at-90.html.

14. Department of Justice amicus curiae brief in combined cases of *Bostock v. Clayton County* and *Altitude Express v. Zarda,* https://www.supremecourt.gov/DocketPDF/17/17-1618 /113417/20190823143040818_17-1618bsacUnitedStates.pdf.

15. Author interviews with Court sources regarding internal debate, June–July 2020.

16. Alito dissent, *Bostock v. Clayton County,* 590 U.S. ____ (2020), https://www.supremecourt .gov/opinions/19pdf/17-1618_hfci.pdf.

17. Neil M. Gorsuch with Jane Nitze and David Feder, *A Republic, If You Can Keep It* (New York: Crown, 2019), 131–32.

18. *Confirmation Hearing on the Nomination of Hon. Neil M. Gorsuch to Be an Associate Justice of the Supreme Court of the United States,* 115 Cong. 66 (2017) (statement of Neil

Gorsuch), https://www.govinfo.gov/content/pkg/CHRG-115shrg28638/pdf/CHRG-115shrg28638.pdf.

19.  Alito dissent, *Bostock v. Clayton County,* 590 U.S. ____ (2020), https://www.supreme court.gov/opinions/19pdf/17-1618_hfci.pdf.

20.  *Oncale v. Sundowner Offshore Services,* 523 U.S. 75 (1998).

21.  *Bostock v. Clayton County,* 590 U.S. ____ (2020), https://www.supremecourt.gov/opinions/19pdf/17-1618_hfci.pdf

22.  *Bostock v. Clayton County.*

23.  For the justices' voting records, see the SCOTUSblog Stat Pack, compiled by Adam Feldman, https://www.scotusblog.com/wp-content/uploads/2020/07/Justice-agreement-7.20.20.pdf; "Gorsuch vs. Gorsuch," editorial, *Wall Street Journal,* June 16, 2020, https://www.wsj.com/articles/gorsuch-vs-gorsuch-11592350714.

24.  Author interview with Pamela Karlan, May 28, 2022; "Arguing at the Court: Pam Karlan discusses Zarda and the LGBTQ+ Win for Employment Rights," Stanford Law School blog, June 18, 2020, https://law.stanford.edu/2020/06/18/arguing-at-the-court-pam-karlan-discusses-zarda-and-the-lgbtq-win-for-employment-rights.

25.  "Trump: 'Unborn Children Have Never Had a Stronger Defender in the White House,'" *Washington Post,* January 24, 2020, https://www.washingtonpost.com/video/politics/trump-unborn-children-have-never-had-a-stronger-defender-in-the-white-house/2020/01/24/104eeb22-4f35-448a-baa3-9ade1255443d_video.html; Lauren Egan, "Trump Becomes First Sitting President to Attend March for Life Rally," NBC News, January 24, 2020, https://www.nbcnews.com/politics/donald-trump/trump-becomes-first-sitting-president-attend-march-life-rally-n1122246.

26.  "Remarks on Signing an Executive Order Protecting and Improving Medicare for Our Nation's Seniors in the Villages, Florida," The American Presidency Project, October 3, 2019, https://www.presidency.ucsb.edu/documents/remarks-signing-executive-order-protecting-and-improving-medicare-for-our-nations-seniors.

27.  *June Medical Services v. Russo,* no. 18-1323, March 4, 2020, transcript, https://www.supremecourt.gov/oral_arguments/argument_transcripts/2019/18-1323_d18e.pdf.

28.  Robert Barnes and Colby Itkowitz, "Roberts Rebukes Schumer for Saying Justices Will 'Pay the Price' for a Vote against Abortion Rights," *Washington Post,* March 4, 2020, https://www.washingtonpost.com/politics/schumer-vows-kavanaugh-gorsuch-will-pay-the-price-for-vote-on-abortion-rights-case/2020/03/04/ce4ae2b4-5e5a-11ea-9055-5fa12981bbbf_story.html.

29.  Author interviews with justices and other Supreme Court sources during the 2019–2020 session; Joan Biskupic, "How Brett Kavanaugh Tried to Sidestep Abortion and Trump Financial Docs Cases," CNN, July 29, 2020, https://www.cnn.com/2020/07/29/politics/brett-kavanaugh-supreme-court-abortion-trump-documents/index.html.

30.  *June Medical Services v. Russo,* 591 U.S. ____ (2020), https://www.supremecourt.gov/opinions/19pdf/18-1323_c07d.pdf.

31.  "Chief Justice Roberts Remarks at University of Minnesota Law School," October 16, 2018, C-SPAN, https://www.c-span.org/video/?451977-1/chief-justice-roberts-stresses-supreme-courts-independence-contentious-kavanaugh-hearings; "A Conversation with Chief Justice John Roberts," interview with Belmont Law dean Alberto Gonzales, Belmont University College of Law, February 6, 2019, YouTube video, posted by Belmont University, February 7, 2019, https://www.youtube.com/watch?v=x-2vV84d6RY.

32.  Immigration and Nationality Act, June 27, 1952, and subsequent amendments, https://www.govinfo.gov/content/pkg/COMPS-1376/pdf/COMPS-1376.pdf.

33.  "Public Charge: An Overview," National Immigration Law Center, October 2013, https://www.nilc.org/issues/economic-support/public-charge-overview.

34.  Donald Trump (@realdonaldtrump), August 12, 2019, 6:28:29 P.M. EST, https://www.thetrumparchive.com/?searchbox=%22ensuring+that+non-citizens%22; "Inadmissibility on

Public Charge Grounds,"84 Fed. Reg. 41292 (August 14, 2019), https://www.federalregister
.gov/documents/2019/08/14/2019-17142/inadmissibility-on-public-charge-grounds.

35.  *Department of Homeland Security v. New York,* 589 U.S. __ (2020), https://www.supreme
court.gov/opinions/19pdf/19a785_j4ek.pdf; *Chad Wolf v. Cook County,* 589 U.S. __
(2020), https://www.supremecourt.gov/opinions/19pdf/19a905_7m48.pdf. While the
full majority declined to address the specifics of the disputes at hand, in the New York
case Gorsuch and Thomas wrote a statement taking exception to nationwide injunctions,
and in the Cook County, Illinois, case, dissenting Justice Sotomayor criticized the "now-
familiar pattern" of the Court siding with the Trump administration when it sought to
escape lower court orders.

36.  William Baude, "Forward: The Supreme Court's Shadow Docket," University of Chicago Law School, Public Law and Legal Theory Working Paper no. 508, 2015, https://
chicagounbound.uchicago.edu/cgi/viewcontent.cgi?article=1961&context=public_law_
and_legal_theory. In addition, Stephen Vladeck, a University of Texas law professor,
documented the Court's disproportionate granting of emergency relief to the Trump administration and testified before the Senate Judiciary Committee on September 29, 2021,
that such emergency requests were "a central feature of" the solicitor general's strategy
and that they "paid dividends" at the Roberts Court. "Thus," Vladeck said in a statement,
"not only was there a dramatic increase in the *demand* for shadow docket rulings from
the Court's 'Tenth Justice,' but the Justices—or at least a majority of them—were willing
to go along with it" (see "Texas's Unconstitutional Abortion Ban and the Role of the
Shadow Docket," Hearing Before the Senate Committee on the Judiciary, September
29, 2021, https://www.judiciary.senate.gov/imo/media/doc/Vladeck20testimony1.pdf).

37.  *Wolf v. Cook County,* 589 U.S. ____ (2020), Sotomayor dissenting, https://www.supreme
court.gov/opinions/19pdf/19a905_7m48.pdf.

38.  The majority's order was issued the night before the April 7 election, at a time when Wisconsin officials said they had a backlog of requests for absentee ballot requests.

39.  *Department of Homeland Security v. New York,* no. 19A785, April 24, 2020, https://www
.supremecourt.gov/orders/courtorders/042420zr_o7jp.pdf.

## Chapter 8: The Chief at the Height of His Power

1.  "Secretary Napolitano Announces Deferred Action Process for Young People Who
Are Low Enforcement Priorities," Office of the Press Secretary, U.S. Department of
Homeland Security, June 15, 2012, https://www.dhs.gov/news/2012/06/15/secretary-
napolitano-announces-deferred-action-process-young-people-who-are-low.

2.  *Department of Homeland Security v. Regents of the University of California,* amicus brief, United We Stand, https://www.supremecourt.gov/Docket
PDF/18/18-587/117839/20191002181633860_18-5872018-5882018-589_Amici
20Brief.pdf.

3.  Theories abound about the consequences of Obama's mocking of Trump at the 2011
dinner. See Patrice Taddonio, "WATCH: Inside the Night President Obama Took On
Donald Trump," *Frontline,* PBS, September 22, 2016, https://www.pbs.org/wgbh/front
line/article/watch-inside-the-night-president-obama-took-on-donald-trump; Patrice
Taddonio and Catherine Trautwein, "Before Indictment, Roger Stone Had Longtime
Ties to Trump," *Frontline,* PBS, January 25, 2019, https://www.pbs.org/wgbh/frontline
/article/roger-stone-indicted-donald-trump-russia-investigation; Amy B. Wang, "Trump
Was Mocked at the 2011 White House Correspondents' Dinner. He Insists It's Not Why
He Ran," *Washington Post,* April 19, 2018, https://www.washingtonpost.com/news/arts-
and-entertainment/wp/2017/02/26/did-the-2011-white-house-correspondents-dinner-
spur-trump-to-run-for-president.

4.  In Trump's first term, his administration won the four major cases in which his lawyers had abandoned an Obama administration's legal stance: *Epic Systems Corp. v. Lewis;*

*Husted v. A. Philip Randolph Institute; Janus v. American Federation of State, County, and Municipal Employees;* and *Lucia v. SEC.* Examples of Roberts's tough approach to Obama administration lawyers include *Kiobel v. Royal Dutch Petroleum,* no. 10-1491, October 12, 2012, transcript, https://www.supremecourt.gov/oral_arguments/argument_trans cripts/2012/10-1491rearg.pdf; and *Arizona v. United States,* no. 11-182, April 25, 2012, transcript, https://www.supremecourt.gov/oral_arguments/argument_trans cripts/2011/11-182.pdf.

5. *Texas v. United States,* 809 F.3d 134 (5th Cir. 2015), https://www.ca5.uscourts.gov /opinions5Cpub5C15/15-40238-CV0.pdf.

6. *Trump v. Sierra Club* documents, https://www.supremecourt.gov/DocketPDF/19 /19A60/107966/20190712162632881_Sierra20Club%20Stay%20Appl.%20App.%20 and%20TOC.pdf.

7. *Trump v. Sierra Club* order, July 26, 2019, https://www.supremecourt.gov/opinions /18pdf/19a60_o75p.pdf; Donald Trump (@realdonaldtrump), July 26, 2019, 6:37:00 P.M. EST, https://www.thetrumparchive.com/?searchbox=%22Big+VICTORY +on+the+Wall.+Big+WIN+for+Border+Security+and+the+Rule+of+Law%22.

8. Adam Liptak, "Politics Has No Place at the Supreme Court, Chief Justice Roberts Says," *New York Times,* September 25, 2019, https://www.nytimes.com/2019/09/25/us/politics /chief-justice-john-roberts-interview.html; Ariane de Vogue, "John Roberts Says Supreme Court Doesn't Work in a 'Political Manner,'" CNN, September 24, 2019, https:// www.cnn.com/2019/09/24/politics/john-roberts-new-york/index.html.

9. See Roberts's conversation with Judge J. Harvie Wilkinson, June 29, 2018, at the Fourth Circuit annual conference, White Sulphur Springs, West Virginia, available at https://www.c-span.org/video/?447323-1/interview-supreme-court-chief-justice- john-roberts.

10. "Memorandum on Rescission of Deferred Action for Childhood Arrivals (DACA)," Elaine C. Duke, acting secretary, Department of Homeland Security, September 5, 2017, https://www.dhs.gov/news/2017/09/05/memorandum-rescission-daca.

11. "Memorandum from Secretary Kirstjen M. Nielsen," secretary, U.S. Department of Homeland Security, June 22, 2018, https://www.dhs.gov/sites/default/files/publications /18_0622_S1_Memorandum_DACA.pdf.

12. "News and Updates," Home Is Here, November 13, 2019, https://www.homeishere march.org/news-updates.

13. *Department of Homeland Security v. Regents of the University of California,* no. 18- 587, November 12, 2019, transcript, https://www.supremecourt.gov/oral_arguments /argument_transcripts/2019/18-587_1bn2.pdf.

14. Anne M. Burford with John Greenya, *Are You Tough Enough?* (New York: McGraw-Hill, 1986), 157. (Olson had no comment on the passage.)

15. Dahlia Lithwick, "I Would Be Lying if I Said That I Wasn't Scared," Slate, June 23, 2020, https://slate.com/news-and-politics/2020/06/supreme-court-daca-lawyer.html.

16. *Department of Homeland Security v. Regents of the University of California,* transcript.

17. Mark Joseph Stern, "Supreme Court Seems Ready to Let Trump Kill DACA," Slate, November 12, 2019, https://slate.com/news-and-politics/2019/11/daca-scotus- oral-arguments.html; Adam Liptak, "Supreme Court Appears Ready to Let Trump End DACA Program," *New York Times,* November 12, 2019, https://www.nytimes .com/2019/11/12/us/supreme-court-dreamers.html; Joan Biskupic, "Fate of DACA Immigrants May Hang on Vote of Chief Justice Roberts," CNN, November 12, 2019, https://www.cnn.com/2019/11/12/politics/daca-immigration-john-roberts-supreme- court/index.html.

18. *Department of Homeland Security v. Regents of the University of California,* 591 U.S. ____ (2020), https://www.supremecourt.gov/opinions/19pdf/18-587_5ifl.pdf; Joan Biskupic, "Behind Closed Doors During One of John Roberts' Most Surprising Years on the Su-

preme Court," CNN, July 27, 2020, https://www.cnn.com/2020/07/27/politics/john-roberts-supreme-court-liberals-daca-second-amendment/index.html.

19. Michael J. Wishnie, Trudy S. Rebert, Araceli Martínez-Olguín, Mayra B. Joachin, Karen C. Tumlin, Amy S. Taylor, and Paige Austin to the Hon. Scott S. Harris, re: *Wolf v. Batalla Vidal,* no. 18-589, March 27, 2020, https://www.supremecourt.gov/Docket-PDF/18/18-589/139241/20200327101941772_20202003202720Letter20to20Court 20for2018-589.pdf.

20. "Amici Curiae Brief of 143 U.S. Business Associations and Companies," filed by Andrew J. Pincus, https://www.supremecourt.gov/DocketPDF/18/18-587/118043/20191003195845599_DACA20Amicus20Sup20Ct20Oct202019.pdf.

21. "Brief for D.C. respondents," filed by Eidelson and lawyers from Jenner and Block in *Trump v. National Association for the Advancement of Colored People,* one of the series of cases consolidated under the title of *Department of Homeland Security v. Regents of the University of California,* https://www.supremecourt.gov/DocketPDF/18/18-587/117336 /20190927152935734_18-5872015-58820and2018-58920bs20DC20Respondents.pdf; Benjamin Eidelson, "A Way Out for the Supreme Court in DACA," *New York Times,* October 27, 2019, https://www.nytimes.com/2019/10/27/opinion/daca-supreme-court .html.

22. Michelle Ye Hee Lee, "Donald Trump's False Comments Connecting Mexican Immigrants and Crime," *Washington Post,* July 8, 2015, https://www.washingtonpost .com/news/fact-checker/wp/2015/07/08/donald-trumps-false-comments-connecting-mexican-immigrants-and-crime; Otto Santa Ana et al., "Making Our Nation Fear the Powerless," in *Language in the Era of Trump: Scandals and Emergencies,* ed. Janet McIntosh and Norma Mendoza-Denton (Cambridge: Cambridge University Press, 2020), 244.

23. *Department of Homeland Security v. Regents of the University of California* 591 U.S. ____ (2020), Sotomayor concurrence (internal quotations omitted).

24. *Department of Homeland Security v. Regents of the University of California,* Roberts majority opinion.

25. *Department of Homeland Security v. Regents of the University of California,* Thomas dissent, joined by Alito and Gorsuch.

26. Donald Trump (@realdonaldtrump), June 18, 2020, 11:10:19 A.M. EST, https://www .thetrumparchive.com/?searchbox=%22Do+you+get+the+impression+that+the +Supreme+Court%22.

27. The underlying issue in the Consumer Financial Protection Bureau (CFPB) case turned on how much control presidents could assert over such independent regulatory agencies as the CFPB, the Federal Trade Commission, the Federal Communications Commission, and the Securities and Exchange Commission. Congress created the CFPB in 2010 to safeguard consumers in their financial transactions after the 2008 recession, which crippled the housing market and shrunk retirement accounts. Predatory lending practices had helped spawn the economic crisis. To ensure that the bureau would be independent and effective, its director held a five-year term and could be removed by the president only for "inefficiency, neglect of duty, or malfeasance in office." Businesses that opposed the work of the bureau argued that its structure was unconstitutional in the way it limited a president's ability to get rid of the sole director. (Most independent agencies were directed by multimember boards.)

The lawsuit that reached the Supreme Court began after the CFPB had begun scrutinizing a California-based firm, Seila Law, that provided services for people in debt. The bureau sought documents related to Seila Law's upfront fees and possible telemarketing violations. Seila Law declined to comply with the request and sued the bureau. The Trump administration backed Seila Law rather than the agency (*Seila Law v. Consumer Financial Protection Bureau,* 591 U.S. ____ [2020], Roberts opinion for the majority, https://www.supremecourt.gov/opinions/19pdf/19-7_new_bq7d.pdf).

28. Kagan concurrence, *Seila Law v. Consumer Financial Protection Bureau,* Kagan concurrence, https://www.supremecourt.gov/opinions/19pdf/19-7_n6io.pdf.

29. *Committee on the Judiciary of the U.S. House of Representatives v. McGahn,* 407 F. Supp. 3d 35 (D.D.C. 2019).

30. Author interviews with Supreme Court sources who had firsthand knowledge of the internal discussions on the Trump cases in 2019 and 2020.

31. *Trump v. Mazars,* no. 19-715, May 12, 2020, transcript, https://www.supremecourt.gov /oral_arguments/argument_transcripts/2019/19-715_h3ci.pdf.

32. *Trump v. Vance,* 591 U.S. ____ (2020), Roberts's opinion for the majority, https://www .supremecourt.gov/opinions/19pdf/19-635_o7jq.pdf.

33. *Trump v. Mazars,* 591 U.S. ____ (2020), Roberts majority opinion, https://www.supreme court.gov/opinions/19pdf/19-715_febh.pdf.

34. Donald Trump (@realdonaldtrump), July 9, 2020, 10:38:59 A.M. EST, https://www.thetrump archive.com/?searchbox=%22Courts+in+the+past+have+given%22, and 10:38:12 A.M. EST, https://www.thetrumparchive.com/?searchbox=%22now+I+have+to+keep+fighting%22.

35. For final statistics on voting patterns for the 2019–2020 session, see Adam Feldman, "Final Stat Pack for October Term 2019 (updated)," *SCOTUSblog,* July 10, 2020, https:// www.scotusblog.com/2020/07/final-stat-pack-for-october-term-2019.

## Chapter 9: A Deathbed Wish

1. Author interview with Ruth Bader Ginsburg, January 7, 2020; *McNabb v. United States,* 318 U.S. 332 (1943); Joan Biskupic, "How Ruth Bader Ginsburg Is Trying to Check the Conservative Majority," CNN, January 9, 2020, https://www.cnn.com/2020/01/08 /politics/ruth-bader-ginsburg-civil-procedure/index.html.

2. Lisa Marie Pane, "US Mass Killings Hit New High in 2019, Most Were Shootings," Associated Press, December 23, 2019, https://apnews.com/article/or-state-wire-ny-state-wire-el-paso-2019-year-in-review-tx-state-wire-4441ae68d14e61b64110db44f90 6af92; Jason Silverstein, "There Were More Mass Shootings Than Days in 2019," CBS News, January 2, 2020, https://www.cbsnews.com/news/mass-shootings-2019-more-than-days-365.

3. *New York State Rifle & Pistol Association, Inc. v. City of New York,* no. 18-280, December 2, 2019, transcript, https://www.supremecourt.gov/oral_arguments/argument_trans cripts/2019/18-280_8nka.pdf.

4. *New York State Rifle & Pistol Association, Inc. v. City of New York,* 590 U.S. ___ (2020), https://www.supremecourt.gov/opinions/19pdf/18-280_ba7d.pdf transcript.

5. Joan Biskupic, "20 Years of Closed-Door Conversations with Ruth Bader Ginsburg," CNN, September 19, 2020, https://www.cnn.com/2020/09/19/politics/rbg-biskupic-ruth-bader-ginsburg-interviews/index.html.

6. Justice Ginsburg public statement about the cancer treatment that dated to May 19, "Statement from Justice Ruth Bader Ginsburg," press release, Supreme Court of the United States, July 17, 2020, https://www.supremecourt.gov/publicinfo/press/press releases/pr_07-17-20.

7. Ruth Bader Ginsburg eulogy for John Paul Stevens, July 23, 2019, reprinted at CNN, https://www.cnn.com/2019/07/23/politics/ruth-bader-ginsburg-eulogy-john-paul-stevens/index.html.

8. Jimmy Hoover, "Supreme Court Gives RBG Space for 'Essential' Workouts," Law360, March 31, 2020, https://www.law360.com/articles/1259086/supreme-court-gives-rbg-space-for-essential-workouts.

9. "Press Release Regarding Justice Ginsburg," Supreme Court of the United States, May 5, 2020, https://www.supremecourt.gov/publicinfo/press/pressreleases/pr_05-05-20. Chief Justice Roberts ran the telephonic hearings like a congressional committee session, calling on members of the Court one by one in order of seniority.

10. The Court's public information officer called the episode "an apparent adverse reaction to a sleeping aid combined with cold medication"; Frank James, "Justice Ginsburg Out of Hospital After Passing Out on Plane," NPR, October 15, 2009, https://www.npr.org /sections/thetwo-way/2009/10/justice_ginsburg_out_of_hospit.html.

11. *Burwell v. Hobby Lobby Stores,* 573 U.S. 682 (2014), https://www.supremecourt.gov /opinions/13pdf/13-354_olp1.pdf; Zechariah Chafee Jr., "Freedom of Speech in War Time," *Harvard Law Review* 32, no. 8 (June 1919): 932, 957, https://www.jstor.org /stable/pdf/1327107.pdf.

12. *Little Sisters of the Poor Saints Peter and Paul Home v. Pennsylvania,* no. 19-431, May 6, 2020, transcript, https://www.supremecourt.gov/oral_arguments/argument_trans cripts/2019/19-431_d1o2.pdf.

13. Regarding the Green Bay Packers jersey, author interview with Paul Clement, June 17, 2022.

14. See, for example, *Town of Greece v. Galloway,* 572 U.S. 565 (2014), in which a five-justice bloc endorsed prayers before council meetings in Greece, New York, even as the prayers favored Christian beliefs over others: https://www.supremecourt.gov /opinions/13pdf/12-696_bpm1.pdf.

15. *Little Sisters of the Poor Saints Peter and Paul Home v. Pennsylvania,* 591 U.S.___ (2020), https://www.supremecourt.gov/opinions/19pdf/19-431_5i36.pdf.

16. "Statement from Justice Ruth Bader Ginsburg," press release, Supreme Court of the United States, July 17, 2020, https://www.supremecourt.gov/publicinfo/press/press releases/pr_07-17-20.

17. "Press Release Regarding Justice Ginsburg," Supreme Court of the United States, July 14, 2020, https://www.supremecourt.gov/publicinfo/press/pressreleases/pr_07-14-20.

18. "Press Release Regarding Justice Ginsburg," press release, Supreme Court of the United States, July 29, 2020, https://www.supremecourt.gov/publicinfo/press/pressreleases /pr_07-29-20.

19. Joan Biskupic and Ariane de Vogue, "Ginsburg Spent Her Final Weeks Living as If There'd Be Many More," CNN, September 25, 2020, https://www.cnn.com/2020/09/25 /politics/ruth-bader-ginsburg-final-weeks/index.html.

20. Ibid.

21. "Transcript: Post Live Election Daily with Former White House Counsel Don McGahn, Maryland Governor Larry Hogan and Biden Campaign Adviser Bob Bauer," interview by Robert Costa, *Washington Post,* November 4, 2020, https://www .washingtonpost.com/washington-post-live/2020/11/04/post-live-election-daily-with-maryland-governor-larry-hogan-biden-campaign-adviser-bob-bauer/ and https://www .washingtonpost.com/washington-post-live/2020/11/09/transcript-post-live-election-daily-with-former-white-house-counsel-don-mcgahn-maryland-governor-larry-hogan-biden-campaign-adviser-bob-bauer.

22. Emma Brown, Jon Swaine, and Michelle Boorstein, "Amy Coney Barrett Served as a 'Handmaid' in Christian Group People of Praise," *Washington Post,* October 6, 2020, https://www.washingtonpost.com/investigations/amy-coney-barrett-people-of-praise/2020/10/06/5f497d8c-0781-11eb-859b-f9c27abe638d_story.html; Ruth Graham and Sharon LaFraniere, "Inside the People of Praise, the Tight-Knit Faith Community of Amy Coney Barrett," *New York Times,* October 8, 2020, https://www.ny times.com/2020/10/08/us/people-of-praise-amy-coney-barrett.html. See also, Margaret Talbot, "Amy Coney Barrett's Long Game," *The New Yorker,* February 7, 2022, https:// www.newyorker.com/magazine/2022/02/14/amy-coney-barretts-long-game.

23. Josh Salman and Kevin McCoy, "Supreme Court Nominee Amy Coney Barrett Signed 2006 Anti-Abortion Ad in *Tribune,*" *South Bend Tribune* (IN), October 2, 2020, https:// www.southbendtribune.com/story/news/local/2020/10/02/supreme-court-nominee-amy-coney-barrett-signed-2006-anti-abortion-ad-in-tribune/43904493.

24. Senate Committee on the Judiciary, Amy Coney Barrett Confirmation Hearing, October 13, 2020, supplemental filing to the committee, https://www.feinstein.senate.gov/public/_cache/files/b/a/bad03794-30e1-41bc-af87-19b6bcea5822/C4487689BF124C929E61242AF6D56F98.amy-coney-barrett-senate-questionnaire-supplement.pdf.

25. *Kanter v. Barr*, 919 F.3d 437 (7th Cr. 2019), https://law.justia.com/cases/federal/appellate-courts/ca7/18-1478/18-1478-2019-03-15.html; *McDonald v. City of Chicago*, 561 U.S. 742 (2010), Alito plurality opinion, https://www.supremecourt.gov/opinions/09pdf/08-1521.pdf.

26. Amy C. Barrett, "Countering the Majoritarian Difficulty," *Constitutional Commentary* 61, no 32 (2017): 80, https://scholarship.law.nd.edu/law_faculty_scholarship/1318.

27. Amy Coney Barrett, questionnaire submitted to the Senate Judiciary Committee, September 29, 2020.

28. House Speaker Nancy Pelosi had wanted Ginsburg to lie in state in the Capitol Rotunda, but Senate Majority Leader Mitchell McConnell rejected that option, according to a Pelosi biography by Susan Page. He said that no precedent existed for a justice lying in the Rotunda, and that Ginsburg would instead be placed in Statuary Hall, on the House side of the building. Susan Page, *Madam Speaker: Nancy Pelosi and the Lessons of Power* (New York: Twelve, 2021), 339.

29. Others who soon became ill included former senior Trump adviser Kellyanne Conway, Tricia Scalia, former New Jersey governor Chris Christie, and Senator Mike Lee. Fr. Jenkins ended up apologizing to the Notre Dame community, and Fr. Paul Scalia apologized to his Virginia parish for showing a lack of judgment in not wearing a mask.

30. "President Trump with Coronavirus Task Force Briefing," C-SPAN, April 23, 2020, https://www.c-span.org/video/?471458-1/president-trump-coronavirus-task-force-briefing; Fox News posted Bryan's presentation as a separate clip: "Higher Temps Cut Virus Life: William Bryan on How Virus Survives," YouTube video, posted by LiveNOW from FOX, April 23, 2020, https://www.youtube.com/watch?v=gysW87xniUE; Colin Dwyer, "'Under No Circumstance': Lysol Maker, Officials Reject Trump's Disinfectant Idea," NPR, April 24, 2020, https://www.npr.org/sections/coronavirus-live-updates/2020/04/24/843571171/under-no-circumstance-lysol-maker-officials-reject-trump-s-disinfectant-idea; Katie Rogers, Christine Hauser, Alan Yuhas, and Maggie Haberman, "Trump's Suggestion That Disinfectants Could Be Used to Treat Coronavirus Prompts Aggressive Pushback," *New York Times*, April 24, 2020, https://www.nytimes.com/2020/04/24/us/politics/trump-inject-disinfectant-bleach-coronavirus.html.

31. Ginsburg died on September 18. Trump formally nominated Barrett on September 26, the Senate confirmed her on October 26, and the election was eight days later, on November 3.

32. Biden first revealed his plan for the bipartisan commission to study the Supreme Court to CBS's Norah O'Donnell in a wide-ranging interview during the campaign, "Joe Biden Makes the Case for Why He Should Be President," CBS, October 25, 2020, https://www.cbsnews.com/news/joe-biden-democratic-presidential-candidate-kamala-harris-60-mintues-interview-norah-odonnell-2020-10-25.

33. Committee on the Judiciary, Amy Coney Barrett Senate Confirmation Hearing, Barrett opening statement, October 12, 2020, https://www.judiciary.senate.gov/imo/media/doc/Barrett20Testimony.pdf.

34. Committee on the Judiciary, Amy Coney Barrett Senate Confirmation Hearing, October 13, 2020, https://www.c-span.org/video/?476316-1/barrett-confirmation-hearing-day-2-part-1; https://www.c-span.org/video/?476317-1/barrett-confirmation-hearing-day-3-part-1; Biskupic, "Amy Coney Barrett's Answers Were Murky, but Her Conservative Philosophy Is Clear," CNN, October 15, 2020, https://www.cnn.com/2020/10/15/politics/amy-coney-barrett-conservative-philosophy/index.html.

35. Confirmation Hearing on the Nomination of Amy Coney Barrett, https://www.c-span .org/video/?476316-4/barrett-confirmation-hearing-day-2-part-2.

36. *Confirmation Hearing on the Nomination of John G. Roberts, Jr. to Be Chief Justice of the United States,* 109 Cong. 207 (2005) (statement of John Roberts), https://www.gov info.gov/content/pkg/GPO-CHRG-ROBERTS/pdf/GPO-CHRG-ROBERTS .pdf.

37. "WATCH: Sen. Chris Coons Questions Supreme Court Nominee Amy Coney Barrett," YouTube video, posted by PBS NewsHour, October 14, 2020, https://www.youtube.com /watch?v=G1N6-dSBxzE; C-SPAN coverage of questioning, https://www.c-span.org /video/?476317-2/barrett-confirmation-hearing-day-3-part-2.

38. Cited remarks during the Senate Judiciary Committee of Senators Harris and Kennedy can be seen in these videos: https://www.youtube.com/watch?v=j7hUb0uH6DM and https://www.youtube.com/watch?v=iQ0C3bgzCo0.

39. Amy C. Barrett and John H. Garvey, "Catholic Judges in Capital Cases," *Marquette Law Review* 81 (1997–1998): 307, https://scholarship.law.nd.edu/law_faculty_scholarship /527. Also at this link: https://scholarship.law.marquette.edu/cgi/viewcontent.cgi? article=1443&context=mulr, with the Brennan citation at 347.

40. Sarah Binder, "Barrett Is the First Supreme Court Justice Confirmed without Opposition Support Since 1869," *Washington Post,* October 27, 2020, https://www.washingtonpost .com/politics/2020/10/27/barrett-is-first-supreme-court-justice-confirmed-without- opposition-support-since-least-1900.

41. Author interview with Fatima Goss Graves on the one-year anniversary of Ruth Bader Ginsburg's death; Joan Biskupic, "RBG's Legacy One Year after the Liberal Icon's Death," CNN, September 18, 2021, https://www.cnn.com/2021/09/18/politics/rbg- death-anniversary-analysis/index.html.

## Chapter 10: *Bush v. Gore* and Trump v. Biden

1. *Bush v. Gore,* 531 U.S. 98 (2000), https://tile.loc.gov/storage-services/service/ll/usrep/us rep531/usrep531098/usrep531098.pdf. For Scalia's reaction and an inside look at the Supreme Court justices' handling of case, see Joan Biskupic, *American Original: The Life and Constitution of Supreme Court Justice Antonin Scalia* (New York: Sarah Crich-ton Books, 2009), chapter 11; for an oral history retrospective of the 2000 *Bush v. Gore* saga in light of the 2020 election, see Eva Alvarado, David A Graham, Cullen Murphy, and Amy Weiss-Meyer, "The Bush-Gore Recount Is an Omen for 2020," *The Atlantic,* August 17, 2020, https://www.theatlantic.com/politics/archive/2020/08/ bush-gore-florida-recount-oral-history/614404. See also Lucy Morgan, "*Bush v. Gore* and 36 Days of Sheer Chaos in 2000: Could It Happen Again in Swing State Flor-ida in 2020?," *Florida Phoenix,* July 20, 2020, https://floridaphoenix.com/2020/07/20 /bush-v-gore-and-36-days-of-sheer-chaos-in-2000-could-it-happen-again-in-swing- state-florida-in-2020.

2. *The Nomination of Elena Kagan to Be an Associate Justice of the Supreme Court of the United States,* 111 Cong. 84 (2010) (statement of Elena Kagan), https://www. govinfo.gov/content/pkg/CHRG-111shrg67622/pdf/CHRG-111shrg67622 .pdf.

3. Amy Forliti, Steve Karnowski, and Tammy Webber, "3 Ex-Cops Convicted of Rights Violations in Floyd Killing," Associated Press, February 24, 2022, https://apnews.com /article/death-of-george-floyd-george-floyd-minneapolis-race-and-ethnicity-racial- injustice-ab7a1e89268ac60a58ae8a317e0b6079.

4. Barbara Sprunt, "The History Behind 'When the Looting Starts, the Shooting Starts,'" NPR, May 29, 2020, https://www.npr.org/2020/05/29/864818368/the-history-behind- when-the-looting-starts-the-shooting-starts.

5. Peter Baker, "Trump Says He Wants a Conservative Majority on the Supreme Court in

Case of an Election Day Dispute," *New York Times,* September 23, 2020, https://www
.nytimes.com/2020/09/23/us/elections/trump-supreme-court-election-day.html.

6.   Critics of the Bush legal team had thought that it would never obtain a Supreme Court
     hearing for its claim that the Florida state election recounts violated the U.S. Constitution.
     Many thought that the dispute over Florida polling practices would be settled in state courts.
     As Olson recalled years later of the justices' decision to grant his petition on behalf of Bush:
     "I was unbelievably jubilant when they granted cert[iorari], because all these people . . . were
     saying that I was an idiot for even thinking that it could possibly happen; that was vindication
     to a certain degree" (Transcript, interview with Theodore B. Olson, George W. Bush Oral
     History Project, Miller Center, University of Virginia, March 28, 2012, https://millercenter.
     org/the-presidency/presidential-oral-histories/theodore-b-olson-oral-history).

7.   *Bush v. Gore,* 531 U.S. 98 (2000).

8.   "Rally on Electoral College Vote Certification," C-SPAN, https://www.c-span.org
     /video/?507744-1/rally-electoral-college-vote-certification; House Committee on the
     Judiciary, "The Impeachment of Donald John Trump Evidentiary Record from the
     House of Representatives," Committee on the Judiciary, U.S. House of Representatives,
     https://judiciary.house.gov/the-impeachment-of-donald-john-trump; House Impeach-
     ment Managers and the House Defense, *Prosecution of an Insurrection: The Complete Trial
     Transcript of the Second Impeachment of Donald Trump* (New York: The New Press, 2022),
     124, 269; Jack Healy, "These Are the Five People Who Died in the Capitol Riot," *New
     York Times,* January 11, 2021, https://www.nytimes.com/2021/01/11/us/who-died-in-
     capitol-building-attack.html.

9.   Whitney Wild, Paul LeBlanc, and Rashard Rose, "2 More DC Police Officers Who Re-
     sponded to Capitol Insurrection Have Died by Suicide," CNN, August 3, 2021, https://
     www.cnn.com/2021/08/02/politics/dc-metropolitan-police-officer-suicide-january-6-
     capitol-riot/index.html; Robert Farley, "Fact Check: How Many Died as a Result of
     Capitol Riot?," FactCheck.org, November 1, 2021, updated March 21, 2022, https://
     www.factcheck.org/2021/11/how-many-died-as-a-result-of-capitol-riot.

10.  Ryan Nobles, Annie Grayer, Zachary Cohen, and Jamie Gangel, "First on CNN: January
     6 Committee Has Text Messages Between Ginni Thomas and Mark Meadows," CNN,
     May 21, 2022, https://lite.cnn.com/en/article/h_005d545bc02e6b923c8ad6bb21d0b752.

11.  *Shelby County v. Holder,* 570 U.S. 529 (2013); *Husted v. A. Philip Randolph Institute,* 584
     U.S. ____ (2018); *Abbott v. Perez,* 585 U.S. ____ (2018).

12.  *Republican National Committee v. Democratic National Committee,* 598 U.S. ____
     (2020), per curiam unsigned opinion by the majority; Ginsburg dissenting opinion,
     joined by Breyer, Sotomayor, and Kagan, https://www.supremecourt.gov/opinions/19
     pdf/19a1016_o759.pdf.

13.  *Republican National Committee v. Democratic National Committee.*

14.  "Editorial: Evers' Ban on In-Person Voting Was the Right Call to Ensure a Safe, Fair
     Election During Coronavirus Pandemic," *Milwaukee Journal Sentinel,* April 6, 2020,
     https://www.jsonline.com/story/news/solutions/2020/04/06/editorial-wisconsin-
     governor-tony-evers-right-stop-person-vote-during-coronavirus/2955827001. (The ref-
     erence in the headline is to Gov. Tony Evers.)

15.  *Raysor v. DeSantis,* 591 U.S. ____ (2020), https://www.supremecourt.gov/opinions/19
     pdf/19a1071_4h25.pdf. The Court's interpretation of the *Purcell* case was increasingly af-
     fecting redistricting challenges and allowing congressional maps that lower-court judges
     had ruled unlawfully discriminatory to take effect. See, for example, Michael Wines,
     "Maps in Four States Were Ruled Illegal Gerrymanders. They're Being Used Anyway,"
     *New York Times,* August 8, 2022, https://www.nytimes.com/2022/08/08/us/elections
     /gerrymandering-maps-elections-republicans.html.

16.  *Democratic National Committee v. Wisconsin State Legislature,* 592 U.S. ____ (2020),
     https://www.supremecourt.gov/opinions/20pdf/20a66_new_m6io.pdf.

17. *Democratic National Committee v. Wisconsin State Legislature,* Gorsuch concurring opinion, joined by Kavanaugh, https://www.supremecourt.gov/opinions/20pdf/20a66_new_m6io.pdf#page=2.

18. Kavanaugh concurring opinion, *Democratic National Committee v. Wisconsin State Legislature,* Kavanaugh concurring opinion, https://www.supremecourt.gov/opinions/20pdf/20a66_new_m6io.pdf#page=6

19. *Democratic National Committee v. Wisconsin State Legislature,* Kagan dissenting opinion, joined by Breyer and Sotomayor, https://www.supremecourt.gov/opinions/20pdf/20a66_new_m6io.pdf#page=24.

20. *Republican Party of Pennsylvania v. Kathy Boockvar, Secretary of Pennsylvania,* 592 U.S. ____ (2020), https://www.supremecourt.gov/opinions/20pdf/20-542(1)_3e04.pdf.

21. Pew Research Center, "Turnout Soared in 2020 as Nearly Two-Thirds of Eligible U.S. Voters Cast Ballots for President," January 28. 2021, https://www.pewresearch.org/fact-tank/2021/01/28/turnout-soared-in-2020-as-nearly-two-thirds-of-eligible-u-s-voters-cast-ballots-for-president. That was more than six in ten people of voting age, the Pew analysis showed. The increases in voting rates were most significant in places that offered widespread mail-in voting.

22. "Trump: Frankly, We Did Win This Election," YouTube video, posted by Bloomberg Politics, November 4, 2020, https://www.youtube.com/watch?v=OXiXDteb2X4.

23. Eugene Kiely, Lori Robertson, Robert Farley, and D'Angelo Gore, "Trump's Falsehood-Filled Speech on the Election," FactCheck.org, November 4, 2020, https://www.factcheck.org/2020/11/trumps-falsehood-filled-speech-on-the-election; ABC News (@ABC), November 4, 2020, 12:51 A.M., https://twitter.com/i/status/1323865415764873216.

24. "Transcript: Post Live Election Daily with Former White House Counsel Don McGahn, Maryland Governor Larry Hogan, and Biden Campaign Adviser Bob Bauer," interview with Robert Costa, *Washington Post,* November 4, 2020, https://www.washingtonpost.com/washington-post-live/2020/11/09/transcript-post-live-election-daily-with-former-white-house-counsel-don-mcgahn-maryland-governor-larry-hogan-biden-campaign-adviser-bob-bauer.

25. Ibid.

26. Author interview with Donald Verrilli, May 7, 2022.

27. Brian Naylor, "Read Trump's Jan. 6 Speech, A Key Part of Impeachment Trial," NPR, February 10, 2021, https://www.npr.org/2021/02/10/966396848/read-trumps-jan-6-speech-a-key-part-of-impeachment-trial; Libby Cathey, "'I Had to Do It': Trump Suggests He Got Virus as Act of Political Courage," ABC News, October 6, 2020, https://abcnews.go.com/Politics/trump-suggests-virus-act-political-courage/story?id=73452023.

28. J. Michael Luttig, "Opinion: The Republican Blueprint to Steal the 2024 Election," CNN, April 27, 2022, https://www.cnn.com/2022/04/27/opinions/gop-blueprint-to-steal-the-2024-election-luttig/index.html.

29. "Subverting Justice: How the Former President and His Allies Pressured DOJ to Overturn the 2020 Election," Committee on the Judiciary, United States Senate, March 31, 2021, https://www.judiciary.senate.gov/imo/media/doc/Interim%20Staff%20Report%20FINAL.pdf; Ryan Nobles and Paula Reid, "First on CNN: Giuliani Meets with January 6 Committee for More Than 9 Hours," CNN, May 20, 2022, https://www.cnn.com/2022/05/20/politics/rudy-giuliani-january-6-committee/index.html; "Former Chapman Professor John Eastman under Ethics Investigation by California State Bar," *Eyewitness News,* ABC 7, March 2, 2022, https://abc7.com/john-eastman-california-ethics/11614541; Kyle Cheney, "Eastman to Produce 10,000 Pages of Trump-Related Emails as Broader Legal Fight Looms," Politico, April 30, 2022, https://www.politico.com/news/2022/04/30/eastman-trump-related-emails-00029141; David Lee, "Texas Bar Files Disciplinary Action against Former Trump Attorney," Courthouse News

Service, May 8, 2022, https://www.courthousenews.com/texas-bar-files-disciplinary-action-against-former-trump-attorney; Michael S. Schmidt and Maggie Haberman, "Lawyer on Trump Election Call Quits Firm after Uproar," January 5, 2021, *New York Times,* https://www.nytimes.com/2021/01/05/us/politics/cleta-mitchell-foley-lardner-trump.html; Jaclyn Diaz, "Attorney on Call with Trump and Georgia Officials Resigns from Law Firm," NPR, January 6, 2021, https://www.npr.org/2021/01/06/953823383/attorney-on-call-with-trump-and-georgia-officials-resigns-from-law-firm; Tierney Sneed, "Inside the Effort to Disbar Attorneys Who Backed Bogus Election Lawsuits," CNN, March 10, 2022, https://www.cnn.com/2022/03/10/politics/ethics-complaints-attorney-misconduct-trump-election-reversal/index.html.

30.  Michael Crowley and Michael D. Shear, "Biden Calls Trump's Attack on Electoral Process 'Totally Irresponsible,'" *New York Times,* November 19, 2020, https://www.nytimes.com/2020/11/19/us/politics/biden-trump-electoral-process.html; "2020 Michigan Election Results," Office of Secretary of State Jocelyn Benson, November 3, 2020, updated November 23, 2020, https://mielections.us/election/results/2020GEN_CENR.html.

31.  *Donald J. Trump for President v. Secretary Commonwealth of Pennsylvania,* no. 20-337 (3rd Cir. 2020), https://www2.ca3.uscourts.gov/opinarch/203371np.pdf; *Pearson v. Kemp,* no. 20-14480 (11th Cir. 2020), https://media.ca11.uscourts.gov/opinions/unpub/files/202014480.pdf; *Feehan v. Wisconsin Elections Commission,* 506 F. Supp. 3d 640 (E.D. Wisc. 2020), https://www.wied.uscourts.gov/sites/wied/files/documents/opinions/20-CV-1771%20Feehan%20v.%20Wisconsin%20Elections%20Commission%2C%20et%20al%20%2883%29.pdf.

32.  White House, "Remarks by President Trump at the Operation Warp Speed Vaccine Summit," South Court Auditorium, Eisenhower Executive Office Building, December 8, 2020, https://trumpwhitehouse.archives.gov/briefings-statements/remarks-president-trump-operation-warp-speed-vaccine-summit; Robert Barnes and Elise Viebeck, "Supreme Court Denies Trump Allies' Bid to Overturn Pennsylvania Election Results," *Washington Post,* December 8, 2020, https://www.washingtonpost.com/politics/courts_law/supreme-court-trump-pennsylvania-election-results/2020/12/08/4d39e16c-397d-11eb-98c4-25dc9f4987e8_story.html.

33.  Donald Trump (@realdonaldtrump), December 11, 2020, 3:28:34 P.M. EST, https://www.thetrumparchive.com/?searchbox=%22If+the+Supreme+Court+shows+Great+Wisdom+and+Courage%22.

34.  *Texas v. Pennsylvania,* 592 U.S. ____ (2020), https://www.supremecourt.gov/orders/courtorders/121120zr_p860.pdf. Justices Alito and Thomas added separately that they believed the Court lacked the "discretion to deny the filing of a bill of complaint in a case that falls within our original jurisdiction." But they said that they would not have granted the relief sought.

35.  Richard L. Hasen, "Identifying and Minimizing the Risk of Election Subversion and Stolen Elections in the Contemporary United States," *Harvard Law Review,* April 20, 2022, https://harvardlawreview.org/2022/04/identifying-and-minimizing-the-risk-of-election-subversion-and-stolen-elections-in-the-contemporary-united-states.

36.  *Republican Party of Pennsylvania v. Degraffenreid,* 592 U.S. ____ (2021), https://www.supremecourt.gov/opinions/20pdf/20-542_2c83.pdf; *Moore v. Harper,* 595 U.S. ____ (2022), Alito dissented, joined by Thomas and Gorsuch; Kavanaugh wrote an opinion concurring in the majority's denial of the stay but expressing interest in taking up the state legislature issue; https://www.supremecourt.gov/opinions/21pdf/21a455_5if6.pdf#page=3; The justices have since scheduled oral arguments in the case of *Moore v. Harper,* no. 21-1271, for the 2022–2023 session.

## Chapter 11: The Supermajority

1. "President Biden 2021 Inaugural Ceremony," C-SPAN, January 20, 2021, https://www.c-span.org/video/?508135-3/president-biden-2021-inaugural-ceremony; Toluse Olorunnipa and Annie Linskey, "Joe Biden Is Sworn In as the 46th President, Pleads for Unity in Inaugural Address to a Divided Nation," *Washington Post*, January 20, 2021, https://www.washingtonpost.com/politics/joe-biden-sworn-in/2021/01/20/13465c90-5a7c-11eb-a976-bad6431e03e2_story.html; Amanda Gorman, *The Hill We Climb: An Inaugural Poem for the Country* (New York: Viking, 2021).

2. Edwin S. Kneedler to the Hon. Scott S. Harris, February 10, 2021, https://www.scotusblog.com/wp-content/uploads/2021/02/No.-19-840-US-Letter.pdf.

3. Joan Biskupic, "With Merrick Garland Pick, Biden Signals Stark Contrast with Trump," CNN, January 8, 2021, https://www.cnn.com/2021/01/08/politics/merrick-garland-biden-doj/index.html; Mark Sherman, "Trump Says He's the Nation's Top Cop, a Debatable Claim," Associated Press, February 19, 2020, https://apnews.com/article/politics-roger-stone-barack-obama-impeachments-donald-trump-7f48f53276aa0f4070dfb34e977c10d4.

4. Department of Justice biography of Elizabeth Prelogar, the forty-eighth solicitor general of the United States, https://www.justice.gov/osg/staff-profile/meet-solicitor-general.

5. Michael S. Rosenwald, "Re-Watching Joe Biden's Disastrous Anita Hill Hearing: A Sexual Harassment Inquisition," *Washington Post*, September 18, 2018, https://www.washingtonpost.com/news/retropolis/wp/2017/11/24/rewatching-joe-bidens-disastrous-anita-hill-hearing-a-sexual-harassment-inquistion; Joan Biskupic, "Joe Biden's Handling of Anita Hill Hearing Re-Emerges with Latest Controversy," CNN, April 6, 2019, https://www.cnn.com/2019/04/06/politics/anita-hill-joe-biden-senate-hearing/index.html; C-SPAN video of questioning: https://www.c-span.org/video/?c4369176/user-clip-biden-questions-hill.

6. *South Bay United Pentecostal Church v. Newsom*, 590 U.S. ____ (2020), https://www.supremecourt.gov/opinions/19pdf/19a1044_pok0.pdf; *Calvary Chapel v. Steve Sisolak*, 591 U.S. ____ (2020), https://www.supremecourt.gov/opinions/19pdf/19a1070_08l1.pdf#page=12#page=13.

7. *Roman Catholic Diocese of Brooklyn v. Andrew M. Cuomo*, 592 U.S. ____ (2020), https://www.supremecourt.gov/opinions/20pdf/20a87_4g15.pdf.

8. *Tandon v. Newsom*, 593 U.S. ____ (2021), https://www.supremecourt.gov/opinions/20pdf/20a151_4g15.pdf.

9. *Fulton v. Philadelphia*, 593 U.S. ____ (2021), https://www.supremecourt.gov/opinions/20pdf/19-123_g3bi.pdf.

10. *Fulton v. Philadelphia*.

11. Nicki Rossoll, "Donald Trump Calls Chief Justice John Roberts a 'Nightmare for Conservatives,'" ABC News, January 17, 2016, https://abcnews.go.com/Politics/donald-trump-calls-chief-justice-john-roberts-nightmare/story?id=36336627; Donald Trump (@realdonaldtrump), July 18, 2012, 9:25:10 A.M. EST, https://www.thetrumparchive.com/?searchbox=%22Congratulations+to+John+Roberts%22; Selena Simmons-Duffin, "Trump Is Trying Hard to Thwart Obamacare. How's That Going?," NPR, October 14, 2019, https://www.npr.org/sections/health-shots/2019/10/14/768731628/trump-is-trying-hard-to-thwart-obamacare-hows-that-going.

12. The Trump administration initially argued that only certain parts of the law, tied to the individual insurance requirement, should be struck down. Kaitlan Collins, Joan Biskupic, Evan Perez, and Tami Luhby, "Barr Urges Trump Administration to Back Off Call to Fully Strike Down Obamacare," CNN, May 5, 2020, https://www.cnn.com/2020/05/05/politics/william-barr-obamacare-supreme-court/index.html.

13. *California v. Texas*, 593 U.S. ____ (2021), https://www.supremecourt.gov/opinions/20pdf/19-840_6jfm.pdf.

14. *DNC v. Hobbs,* no. 18-15845 (9th Cir. 2020), http://cdn.ca9.uscourts.gov/datastore /opinions/2020/01/27/18-15845.pdf.

15. *Brnovich v. DNC,* 594 U.S. ____ (2021), https://www.supremecourt.gov/opinions /20pdf/19-1257_g204.pdf.

16. *Americans for Prosperity Foundation v. Bonta,* 594 U.S. ____ (2021), https://www.supreme court.gov/opinions/20pdf/19-251_p86b.pdf.

17. Ian Millhiser, "The Supreme Court Just Made *Citizens United* Even Worse," *Vox,* July 1, 2021, https://www.vox.com/2021/7/1/22559318/supreme-court-americans-for-prosperity-bonta-citizens-united-john-roberts-donor-disclosure.

18. Joan Biskupic, "Supreme Court Enters a New Era of Personal Accusation and Finger-Pointing," CNN, May 21, 2021, https://www.cnn.com/2021/05/21/politics/supreme-court-finger-pointing-kavanaugh-kagan-gorsuch/index.html; *Torres v. Madrid,* 592 U.S. ____ (2021), https://www.supremecourt.gov/opinions/20pdf/19-292_21p3.pdf; *Jones v. Mississippi,* 593 U.S. ____(2021), https://www.supremecourt.gov/opinions/20 pdf/18-1259_8njq.pdf; *Edwards v. Vannoy,* 593 U.S. ____ (2021), https://www.supreme court.gov/opinions/20pdf/19-5807_new2_jhek.pdf.

19. Erwin Chemerinsky, "Justice Breyer Should Learn from Justice Ginsburg's Mistake—and Retire Now," *Washington Post* perspective column, May 8, 2021, https://www.washing tonpost.com/outlook/2021/05/08/breyer-ginsburg-biden-trump; Danielle Kurtzleben, "Liberals Admire Justice Breyer. Now They Want Him to Retire," NPR, May 3, 2021, https://www.npr.org/2021/05/03/992411437/liberals-admire-justice-breyer-now-they-want-him-to-retire.

20. Joan Biskupic, "Stephen Breyer Says He Hasn't Decided His Retirement Plans and Is Happy as the Supreme Court's Top Liberal," CNN, July 15, 2021, https://www.cnn .com/2021/07/15/politics/stephen-breyer-retirement-plans/index.html.

21. *Biden v. Texas,* no. 21A21, August 24, 2021, https://www.supremecourt.gov/orders/court orders/082421zr_2d9g.pdf; Uriel J. García, "Revival of 'Remain in Mexico' Policy Could Have Deadly Consequences for Asylum Seekers, Advocates Warn," *Texas Tribune,* August 25, 2021, https://www.texastribune.org/2021/08/25/remain-in-mexico-supreme-court-ruling.

22. *Alabama Association of Realtors v. Department of Health and Human Services,* 594 U.S. ____ (2021), https://www.supremecourt.gov/opinions/20pdf/21a23_ap6c.pdf; Glenn Thrush, Michael D. Shear, and Alan Rappeport, "The Biden Administration Issues a New Eviction Moratorium as the Virus Surges," *New York Times,* August 3, 2021, https://www .nytimes.com/2021/08/03/us/politics/evictions-housing-moratorium-pelosi-yellen .html; "CDC Issues Eviction Moratorium Order in Areas of Substantial and High Transmission," press release, Centers for Disease Control and Prevention, August 3, 2021, https://www.cdc.gov/media/releases/2021/s0803-cdc-eviction-order.html.

23. Congressional Research Service, "Pandemic Relief: The Emergency Rental Assistance Program," report no. R46688, October 21, 2021, https://crsreports.congress.gov/product /pdf/R/R46688.

24. World Health Organization, "COVID-19 Weekly Epidemiological Update," August 31, 2021; Elizabeth Chuck and Corky Siemaszko, "Covid's Toll in the U.S. Reaches a Once Unfathomable Number: 1 Million Deaths," NBC News, May 4, 2022, https://www .nbcnews.com/news/us-news/covids-toll-us-reaches-1-million-deaths-unfathomable-number-rcna22105.

25. *National Federation of Independent Business v. Department of Labor, Occupational Safety and Health Administration,* no. 19-760, May 12, 2020, transcript, https://www.supremecourt .gov/oral_arguments/argument_transcripts/2021/21a244_kifl.pdf.

26. *National Federation of Independent Business v. Department of Labor, Occupational Safety and Health Administration,* 595 U. S. ____ (2022), https://www.supremecourt.gov/opinions /21pdf/21a244_hgci.pdf.

27. *Biden v. Missouri*, 595 U.S. ____ (2022), https://www.supremecourt.gov/opinions/21pdf/21a240_d18e.pdf.

28. Eugene Scalia, "What the Supreme Court's OSHA Ruling Means," *Wall Street Journal*, January 14, 2022, https://www.wsj.com/articles/what-the-supreme-courts-osha-ruling-means-vaccine-testing-mandate-covid-khan-biden-ftc-administrative-state-chevron-11642199704.

29. Richard Lempert, "The Vaccine Mandate Cases, Polarizations, and Jurisprudential Norms," *Brookings FIXGOV* (blog), January 15, 2022, https://www.brookings.edu/blog/fixgov/2022/01/15/the-vaccine-mandate-cases-polarization-and-jurisprudential-norms.

30. Antonin Scalia, "Judicial Deference to Administrative Interpretations of Law," *Duke Law Journal* 3 (June 1989): 511–21, based on the *Duke Law Journal* Administrative Law Lecture, delivered at Duke University School of Law, January 24, 1989, https://scholarship.law.duke.edu/cgi/viewcontent.cgi?article=3075&context=dlj; *Massachusetts v. Environmental Protection Agency*, 549 U.S. 497 (2007), https://www.supremecourt.gov/opinions/boundvolumes/549bv.pdf.

31. Stephen Breyer to President Biden, January 27, 2022, https://www.supremecourt.gov/publicinfo/press/Letter_to_President_January-27-2022.pdf.

## Chapter 12: "Zero. None."

1. The Supreme Court Bar memorial for Justice John Paul Stevens was also broadcast by C-SPAN on May 2, 2022, available online at https://www.c-span.org/video/?519759-1/supreme-court-bar-memorial-justice-john-paul-stevens.

2. "Abortion and the Supreme Court," editorial, *Wall Street Journal*, April 26, 2022, https://www.wsj.com/articles/abortion-and-the-supreme-court-dobbs-v-jackson-mississippi-john-roberts-11651009292.

3. "Justice John Paul Stevens Memorial," Special Session of the Supreme Court, May 2, 2022, https://www.supremecourt.gov/stevensmemorial/Associate_Justice_John_Paul_Stevens_Bar_Memorial_2022_a16c.pdf.

4. Josh Gerstein and Alexander Ward, "Supreme Court has Voted to Overturn Abortion Rights, Draft Opinion Shows," Politico, May 2, 2022, https://www.politico.com/news/2022/05/02/supreme-court-abortion-draft-opinion-00029473.

5. *Griswold v. Connecticut*, 381 U.S. 479 (1965); *Loving v. Virginia*, 388 U.S. 1 (1967); *Obergefell v. Hodges*, 576 U.S. 644 (2015).

6. *Roe v. Wade*, 410 U.S. 113 (1973); Joan Biskupic, "How the Supreme Court Crafted Its *Roe v. Wade* Decision and What It Means Today," https://www.cnn.com/2021/09/23/politics/roe-v-wade-history/index.html, based on background from the Harry A. Blackmun Archive (Library of Congress, https://www.loc.gov/rr/mss/blackmun/), Lewis F. Powell Archive (Washington and Lee University School of Law, https://law.wlu.edu/powell-archives/), and William J. Brennan Archive (Library of Congress, https://www.loc.gov/item/mm82052266/).

7. Illness forced Hugo Black and John Marshall Harlan to retire in September 1971, so the justices were down to seven when they first heard the case of *Roe v. Wade*. It was reargued in 1972 after Lewis Powell and William Rehnquist took their seats (Brennan observations in William J. Brennan Papers, Part II: Case Histories, 1958–1989, Manuscript Division, Library of Congress).

8. In the text of *Casey*, viability was set at twenty-three to twenty-four weeks.

9. Biskupic, "How the Supreme Court Crafted Its *Roe v. Wade* Decision and What It Means Today."

10. Joan Biskupic, *The Chief: The Life and Turbulent Times of Chief Justice John Roberts* (New York: Basic Books, 2019), 103–7.

11. Blackmun archive.

12. *June Medical Services v. Russo,* 591 U.S. ____ (2020), and *Whole Woman's Health v. Heller-stedt,* 579 U.S. ____ (2016).

13. Dobbs petition, https://www.supremecourt.gov/DocketPDF/19/19-1392/145658/20200615170733513_FINAL%20Petition.pdf; brief in opposition from Jackson Women's Health Organization, https://www.supremecourt.gov/DocketPDF/19/19-1392/150668/20200819155412230_39883%20pdf%20Scott.pdf; Emily Wagster Pettus and Mike Stobbe, "Doctor Named in Abortion Case Has Nothing to Do with Lawsuit," Associated Press, June 6, 2022, https://apnews.com/article/abortion-covid-us-supreme-court-health-c9d8c166a41f58acc88ca758f39ea7c4.

14. *Harris v. West Alabama Women's Center,* 588 U.S. ____ (2019) (Thomas concurring in denial of certiorari); Joan Biskupic, "Supreme Court Conservatives Want to Topple Abortion Rights—But Can't Seem to Agree on How," CNN, March 21, 2021, https://www.cnn.com/2021/03/19/politics/abortion-supreme-court-conservatives-thomas-roberts/index.html.

15. Docket for *Dobbs v. Jackson Women's Health Organization,* no. 19-1392, showing the multiple reschedulings of the justices' consideration of the Mississippi petition, https://www.supremecourt.gov/search.aspx?filename=/docket/docketfiles/html/public/19-1392.html.

16. *Roe v. Wade.*

17. Brief for petitioners in *Dobbs v. Jackson Women's Health Organization,* submitted July 22, 2021, https://www.supremecourt.gov/DocketPDF/19/19-1392/184703/20210722161332385_19-1392BriefForPetitioners.pdf.

18. See the earlier discussion of the S.B.8 law in the prologue of the present book.

19. *Whole Woman's Health v. Jackson,* 595 U.S. ____ (2021), Sotomayor opinion, https://www.supremecourt.gov/opinions/21pdf/21-463_3ebh.pdf#page=36.

20. *Dobbs v. Jackson Women's Health Organization,* no. 19-1392, December 1, 2021, transcript, https://www.supremecourt.gov/oral_arguments/argument_transcripts/2021/19-1392_4425.pdf.

21. "President Biden Names Twenty-Fourth Round of Judicial Nominees," White House statement, July 29, 2022, https://www.whitehouse.gov/briefing-room/statements-releases/2022/07/29/president-biden-names-twenty-fourth-round-of-judicial-nominees.

22. *Planned Parenthood of Southeastern Pennsylvania v. Casey,* 505 U.S. 833 (1992), https://www.law.cornell.edu/supremecourt/text/505/833.

23. Press release, Supreme Court of the United States, May 3, 2022, https://www.supremecourt.gov/publicinfo/press/pressreleases/pr_05-03-22.

24. Joan Biskupic, "Supreme Court Leak Investigation Heats Up as Clerks Are Asked for Phone Records in Unprecedented Move," CNN, June 1, 2022, https://www.cnn.com/2022/05/31/politics/supreme-court-roe-v-wade-leak-phone-records/index.html; Tierney Sneed, "Escalation of the Supreme Court's Leak Probe Puts Clerks in a 'No-Win' Situation," CNN, June 1, 2022, https://www.cnn.com/2022/06/01/politics/supreme-court-clerks-leak-investigation-phones-affidavit-abortion/index.html.

25. Joan Biskupic, "Clarence Thomas Calls Out John Roberts as Supreme Court Edges Closer to Overturning *Roe v. Wade,*" CNN, May 20, 2022, https://www.cnn.com/2022/05/20/politics/clarence-thomas-john-roberts-supreme-court-roe-wade/index.html.

26. *District of Columbia v. Heller,* 554 U.S. 570 (2008), https://www.supremecourt.gov/opinions/07pdf/07-290.pdf; *New York State Rifle & Pistol Association v. Bruen,* 597 U.S. ____ (2022), https://www.supremecourt.gov/opinions/21pdf/20-843_7j80.pdf; Joan Biskupic, "Clarence Thomas' Second Amendment Ruling Shows Power of Conservative Supermajority," CNN, June 23, 2022, https://www.cnn.com/2022/06/23/politics/supreme-court-guns-analysis-clarence-thomas/index.html.

27. *Rogers v. Grewal,* 590 U. S. ____ (2020), https://www.supremecourt.gov/opinions/19pdf/18-824_2cp3.pdf.

28. *New York State Rifle & Pistol Association v. Bruen.* Thomas is quoting from the 2008 case *District of Columbia v. Heller.*

29.  *Carson v. Makin*, 596 U.S. ____ (2022), https://www.supremecourt.gov/opinions
     /21pdf/20-1088_dbfi.pdf; Joan Biskupic, "How the Supreme Court Is Disman-
     tling the Separation of Church and State," CNN, June 27, 2022, https://www.cnn
     .com/2022/06/27/politics/supreme-court-church-state-kennedy-maine-analysis/index
     .html.
30.  *Kennedy v. Bremerton School District*, 597 U.S. ____ (2022), https://www.supremecourt
     .gov/opinions/21pdf/21-418_i425.pdf.
31.  "CPAC 2018—A Conversation with the Honorable Don McGahn," YouTube video,
     posted by CPAC, February 22, 2018, https://www.youtube.com/watch?v=WWbiUqq_
     Lqw (McGahn was interviewed by Dr. Larry P. Arnn, president of Hillsdale College);
     see also "User Clip: McGahn Quotes," C-SPAN, March 15, 2018, https://www.c-span
     .org/video/?c5004713/user-clip-mcgahn-quotes.
32.  McGahn's speech at Widener, February 25, 2020; *Chevron v. Natural Resources Defense
     Council*, 467 U.S. 837 (1984); *Natural Resources Defense Council v. Gorsuch*, 685 F.2d 718
     (D.C. Cir., 1982); Tamara Keith, "Wielding a Pen and a Phone, Obama Goes It Alone,"
     NPR, January 20, 2014, https://www.npr.org/2014/01/20/263766043/wielding-a-pen-
     and-a-phone-obama-goes-it-alone.
33.  *West Virginia v. Environmental Protection Agency*, 597 U.S. ____ (2022), https://www
     .supremecourt.gov/opinions/21pdf/20-1530_n758.pdf.
34.  *Dobbs v. Jackson Women's Health Organization*, 597 U.S. ____ (2022), https://www
     .supremecourt.gov/opinions/21pdf/19-1392_6j37.pdf; Joan Biskupic, "Chief Justice
     John Roberts Lost the Court and the Defining Case of His Generation," CNN, June 26,
     2022, https://www.cnn.com/2022/06/26/politics/john-roberts-chief-justice-roe-dobbs-
     analysis/index.html; Joan Biskupic, "Conservative Justices Seized the Moment and
     Delivered the Opinion They'd Long Promised," CNN, June 25, 2022, https://www.cnn
     .com/2022/06/24/politics/conservative-supreme-court-analysis-roe-dobbs/index.html.
35.  *Confirmation Hearing on the Nomination of John G. Roberts, Jr. to Be Chief Justice of the
     United States*, 109 Cong. 144ff. (2005) (statement of John Roberts), https://www.govinfo
     .gov/content/pkg/GPO-CHRG-ROBERTS/pdf/GPO-CHRG-ROBERTS.pdf     ("I
     do think that it is a jolt to the legal system when you overrule a precedent" and other
     references).
36.  Joan Biskupic, "The Inside Story of How John Roberts Failed to Save Abortion Rights,"
     CNN, July 26, 2022, https://www.cnn.com/2022/07/26/politics/supreme-court-john-
     roberts-abortion-dobbs/index.html.
37.  "The Court's Landmark Ruling Is Courageous and Correct," press release, Mitch Mc-
     Connell, June 24, 2022, https://www.republicanleader.senate.gov/newsroom/press-
     releases/the-supreme-courts-landmark-ruling-is-courageous-and-correct.
38.  *Egbert v. Boule*, 596 U.S. ____ (2022), https://www.supremecourt.gov/opinions
     /21pdf/21-147_g31h.pdf; Joan Biskupic, "The Force of the Court's Right Turn Has
     Shaken the Country," CNN, July 1, 2022, https://www.cnn.com/2022/07/01/politics
     /supreme-court-analysis-abortion-guns-climate-change/index.html.
39.  "Remarks by President Biden on His Nomination of Judge Ketanji Brown Jackson to
     Serve as Associate Justice of the U.S. Supreme Court," press release, White House, Febru-
     ary 25, 2022, https://www.whitehouse.gov/briefing-room/speeches-remarks/2022/02/25
     /remarks-by-president-biden-on-his-nomination-of-judge-ketanji-brown-jackson-to-
     serve-as-associate-justice-of-the-u-s-supreme-court.
40.  "The Nomination of Ketanji Brown Jackson to Be an Associate Justice of the Supreme
     Court of the United States," Committee on the Judiciary, United States Senate, March
     21–23, 2022, https://www.judiciary.senate.gov/meetings/the-nomination-of-ketanji-
     brown-jackson-to-be-an-associate-justice-of-the-supreme-court-of-the-united-states;
     see also "Jackson Confirmation Hearing, Day 1," C-SPAN, March 21, 2022, https://
     www.c-span.org/video/?518341-1/jackson-confirmation-hearing-day-1.

## Epilogue

1. Multiple public opinion polls showed approval of the Supreme Court at a record low, including those taken by Gallup and the Pew Research Center. Jeffrey M. Jones, "Supreme Court Trust, Job Approval at Historical Lows," Gallup, September 29, 2022, https://news.gallup.com/poll/402044/supreme-court-trust-job-approval-historical-lows.aspx; "Positive Views of Supreme Court Decline Sharply following Abortion Ruling," Pew Research Center, September 1, 2022, https://www.pewresearch.org/politics/2022/09/01/positive-views-of-supreme-court-decline-sharply-following-abortion-ruling. Roberts's remarks regarding the Court's legitimacy were made at a September 9, 2022, judicial conference in Colorado Springs, video of which is available at https://www.c-span.org/video/?522764-1/chief-justice-roberts-discusses-supreme-courts-legitimacy-public-opinion. For Alito's statement, see Jess Bravin, "*Kagan v. Roberts*: Justices Spar over Supreme Court's Legitimacy," *Wall Street Journal*, September 28, 2022, https://www.wsj.com/articles/kagan-v-roberts-justices-spar-over-supreme-courts-legitimacy-11664394642.

2. Joan Biskupic, "Analysis: Supreme Court Justices Respond to Public Criticism with Distance and Denial," CNN, September 13, 2022, https://www.cnn.com/2022/09/13/politics/supreme-court-public-criticism-distance-denial-roberts/index.html.

3. A video of Alito's full address from the July 21, 2022, Notre Dame Law School's Religious Liberty Initiative, is available at https://law.nd.edu/news-events/news/2022-religious-liberty-summit-rome-justice-samuel-alito-keynote. Jodi Kantor and Jo Becker, "Former Anti-Abortion Leader Alleges Another Supreme Court Breach," *New York Times*, November 19, 2022, https://www.nytimes.com/2022/11/19/us/supreme-court-leak-abortion-roe-wade.html; Josh Gerstein, "Justice Alito Denies Allegation of a Leak in 2014 Case About Access to Birth Control," Politico, November 20, 2022, https://www.politico.com/news/2022/11/20/justice-alito-birth-control-leak-allegations-2014-supreme-court-00069603.

4. Kagan addressed public confidence in the Supreme Court on July 21, 2022, at a judicial conference in Big Sky, Montana (see https://www.c-span.org/video/?521729-1/justice-elena-kagan-public-confidence-supreme-court).

5. David Leonhardt, "'A Crisis Coming': The Twin Threats to American Democracy," *New York Times*, September 17, 2022, https://www.nytimes.com/2022/09/17/us/american-democracy-threats.html.

6. The courtroom had been closed to the general public since March 2020. It reopened three days after the Jackson investiture, on October 3, 2022, as the justices allowed the public to return to arguments. Joan Biskupic, "Supreme Court Investiture Marks Another Historic First for Justice Ketanji Brown Jackson," CNN, September 29, 2022, https://www.cnn.com/2022/09/29/politics/supreme-court-jackson-investiture.

# INDEX